• • •
POLITICAL ECONOMY AND ILLEGAL DRUGS IN COLOMBIA

STUDIES ON THE IMPACT OF THE ILLEGAL DRUG TRADE
LaMond Tullis, Series Editor

• • •

A Project of the
United Nations Research Institute
for Social Development (UNRISD)
and the
United Nations University (UNU)

HV
5840
C7
T48
1995

POLITICAL ECONOMY AND ILLEGAL DRUGS IN COLOMBIA

Francisco E. Thoumi

LYNNE
RIENNER
PUBLISHERS

BOULDER
LONDON

AUDREY COHEN COLLEGE LIBRARY
75 Varick St. 12th Floor
New York, NY 10013

Published in the United States of America in 1995 by
Lynne Rienner Publishers, Inc.
1800 30th Street, Boulder, Colorado 80301

and in the United Kingdom by
Lynne Rienner Publishers, Inc.
3 Henrietta Street, Covent Garden, London WC2E 8LU

© 1995 by the United Nations University and the United Nations Research Institute for Social Development. All rights reserved by the publisher.

Library of Congress Cataloging-in-Publication Data
Thoumi, Francisco E.
    Political economy and illegal drugs in Colombia / Francisco E. Thoumi.
        p.   cm.—(Studies on the impact of the illegal drug trade ; v. 2)
    Includes bibliographical references and index.
    ISBN 1-55587-536-X (alk. paper)
       1. Drug traffic—Colombia. 2. Drug traffic—Government policy—Colombia. 3. Narcotics, Control of—Colombia. 4. Colombia—Economic conditions—1918–   I. Title. II. Series.
HV5840.C7T48   1994
363.4'5'09861—dc20   94-191659
                                                                     CIP

British Cataloguing in Publication Data
A Cataloguing in Publication record for this book
is available from the British Library.

Distributed in Japan and Southeast Asia by:
The United Nations University Press
The United Nations University
53-70, Jingumae 5-chome
Shibuya-ku, Tokyo 150
ISBN 92-808-0886-9

Printed and bound in the United States of America

        The paper used in this publication meets the requirements
    ∞ of the American National Standard for Permanence of
        Paper for Printed Library Materials Z39.48-1984.

5 4 3 2

*In memory of Luis Carlos Galán and Enrique Low-Murtra,
who tried to live true to their principles*

Contents

• • •

Foreword, LaMond Tullis	ix
Preface	xiii
Map of Population Concentration and Main Coca and Marijuana Growing Areas in Colombia	xvi
Introduction	1

Part 1 The Colombian Political Economy

1	The Conventional Economics Perspective	17
2	A Critical Institutionalist Perspective	67

Part 2 The Illegal Psychoactive Drugs Industry and Government Responses

3	Brief History and Overview of the Illegal Psychoactive Drugs Industry	123
4	The Illegal Psychoactive Drugs Entrepreneurs and Their Strategies	151
5	Why the Illegal Psychoactive Drugs Industry Grew in Colombia	167
6	The Size of the Illegal Drugs Industry	179
7	Colombian Policies Toward the Illegal Drugs Industry	203

Part 3 The Impact of the Illegal Drugs Industry and Government Policy Alternatives

8	Impact and Consequences of Production and Traffic	233
9	The Demand for Psychoactive Drugs and Drug Addiction	251
10	Drug Policy Alternatives for Colombia	275

Glossary	293
Bibliography	296
Index	310

About the Book and the Author	319
About the United Nations Research Institute for Social Development (UNRISD) and the United Nations University (UNU)	320

Foreword

• • •

LaMond Tullis

Francisco Thoumi has written an insightful, intriguing, even provocative treatise on Colombia's political economy and illicit drugs industry. He considers the two a culmination of a historical process that conventional "mainstream" and "left" economists have interpreted unsatisfactorily. Thoumi advances an alternative "institutionalist" perspective as a better interpretive model. The policy implications for illicit drugs are as astonishing as they are sobering.

Thoumi's analysis leads him to argue that for a quarter century or more Colombian political and economic institutions have progressively lost their legitimacy. The resulting caldron of violence, distrust, greed, and manipulation has all but invited the illegal drugs industry to step in and take advantage of a deteriorating situation.

Colombia's historical political economy, now overlaid with an illicit drugs industry, serves to delegitimize a capitalist, democratic economy and polity. Current drug-control efforts produce the unintended consequence of hastening the process through an increase in violence, militarization, and compromised government.

To reclaim legitimacy Colombia needs to implement a profound "national project of economic democratization." Doing so will require substantial political and economic reforms. However, because the delegitimation process is so advanced, the existence of Colombia's illicit drugs industry is a large obstacle to any such reforms: it promotes violence, concentrates income and wealth, feeds the underground economy, opposes some socially progressive reforms, and weakens the state. All these unfortunate consequences are exacerbated by a U.S. policy that focuses on supply suppression abroad as a means to control illicit-drug consumption at home.

Unfortunately, the elimination of the illegal industry itself as one way to enhance a national project depends on factors outside the control of the Colombian government—resting largely in international demand for illegal drugs or major consumer countries' domestic policies that promote clandestine profits through illegality. Because such outside factors are unlikely to change soon, the ability of Colombia's government to undertake a nation-building project after the fashion of democratic capitalism is not good.

Nevertheless, there are opportunities within Colombia which, if seized, could ameliorate the difficult national situation. In discussing them, Thoumi argues that the first task is to gain a clear understanding of the intermeshing of Colombia's political economy and the illegal drugs trade—their historical roots, the cultural ambience out of which both have developed, the cyclical reinforcement of a regime of control that is now totally counterproductive for Colombia's long-term well-being with respect to illicit drugs or anything else. On this understanding hinges the consequential impact of all illicit-drugs control initiatives.

Beyond dealing with matters of production, traffic, illicit-drugs control policies, and the socioeconomic and political impacts of all three, Thoumi's wide-ranging discussion treats a matter seldom discussed in political economy studies of the illicit-drugs traffic: the consumption of psychoactive drugs and drug addiction within principal producer countries. Contrary to expectations, Thoumi's findings—informed by an analysis of psychological and economic theories of drug consumption and addiction—show that alcohol and tobacco are the chief drug problems in Colombia, although the drugs under discussion here (principally coca derivatives, heroin, and marijuana) are making inroads. Among these, *bazuco* (coca paste mixed with tobacco and then smoked) is more frequently associated with multiple addictions. It is seen as a problem because of its link with violence, criminality, and difficulties in the workplace and home. But these drugs do not constitute the epidemiological problem in Colombia one would normally expect on the basis of availability, price, and social correlates. Drug-control policies for Colombia must therefore be considered in a different context than, say, for the United States.

Thoumi's excellent book is part of a multicountry study of the socioeconomic and political impact of production, trade, and use of illicit narcotic drugs. The project has been sponsored by the United Nations Research Institute for Social Development (UNRISD), the United Nations University (UNU), and Brigham Young University (BYU).

The project has been developed in two phases. The first, a review monograph and annotated bibliography entitled *Handbook of Research on the Illicit Drug Traffic: Socioeconomic and Political Consequences* (Westport, Conn.: Greenwood Press), was issued in 1991. The second phase is a series of country-specific books and monographs that both describe and analyze the interplay of economics, politics, society, and illicit drugs and drug-control policies through a careful analysis of causes and consequences of production, trade, consumption, and control.

Since the early 1980s the national and international traffic in and consumption of cannabis, opiate, and coca derivatives has exploded, perhaps now tapering off in the United States but vigorously expanding in Western and Eastern Europe and the republics of the former Soviet Union. Consumption has also rapidly increased in the principal so-called producer countries (e.g., Peru, Bolivia, Colombia, Mexico, Myanmar, and Afghanistan).

The socioeconomic and political costs of consumption and efforts to suppress it have mounted. Unfortunately, policy initiatives to reduce those costs have, in the worst cases, simply aggravated the problem, and in the best cases, they have apparently had only marginal impact.

Although the literature on illicit drugs is now rapidly expanding, most of it has focused on consumption and drug-control problems in major industrialized countries. Less attention has been paid to the impact of production, trade, and consumption of illicit drugs and international control policies in the developing countries. This is highly unfortunate, because illicit-drugs control initiatives have been mostly concentrated on supply-reduction efforts in developing countries. In the wake of a general failure of these supply-reduction strategies to control consumption anywhere (indeed, they may have served to expand it), a strong shift is now expected in international drug-control efforts.

The purpose of the country studies in this Studies on the Impact of the Illegal Drug Trade series is to expand the level of information and awareness about costs and consequences of the present policies and to consider the implications of proffered new solutions for developing areas. We desire to contribute to an enhanced quality of policy review discussions by bringing together a rich array of historical and contemporary information with careful analyses regarding specific countries. Francisco Thoumi's book makes a substantial contribution to this effort.

Aside from acknowledging the financial support of the UNRISD, the UNU, and BYU, we thankfully acknowledge the excellent support from Chelita Pate and her BYU staff of assistants in preparing the country study manuscripts. Lani Gurr, in particular, has rendered matchless service to this project. Susan Manning Sims, associate managing editor of publications at BYU's Kennedy Center for International and Area Studies, lent her substantial expertise to an editing of the entire manuscript.

LaMond Tullis

Preface

• • •

During the twentieth century Colombia has experienced exceptionally turbulent social, economic, and political changes. These have been characterized by relatively fast economic growth, high levels of violence, and, in the past twenty-five years, pervasive growth of an illegal psychoactive drugs industry. Colombian and foreign analysts have observed these changes from differing perspectives and ideologies. Most have provided unsatisfactory explanations of the deeply disturbing, puzzling, and challenging social phenomena now affecting Colombia.

In this book I attempt to develop an alternative interpretation of the social, economic, and political changes in Colombia. In so doing I move beyond my formal training as an economist. This is especially necessary because traditional economic interpretations of Colombia's history are inadequate. I hope that my effort helps to improve understanding of the Colombian drama and its development process.

At the outset I give three warnings to the reader. First, I have not written an academic volume; indeed, I am not an academic economist in the traditional sense. I am an applied economist with extensive experience in Latin American and Caribbean countries, both as an independent research consultant and as a staff member of the National Planning Department of Colombia, the World Bank, and the Inter-American Development Bank.

Second, the main goal of this volume is to explain a complex development process, which requires my moving across the formal disciplines in which professions and academic institutions are organized. However, I certainly do write from the perspective of an economist. In order to follow the arguments developed in this volume the reader should be literate in basic introductory economics. I have placed a short glossary before the bibliography to aid those unfamiliar with some economics concepts.

Third, although development and change in many countries may look the same on the surface, during my twenty years as an applied economist I have found that every country has a unique "story" to tell. Every country has its own institutions and history that condition its political economy and development policies. Beyond this uniqueness, however, lie the eyes and minds of the analysts. As every individual's interpretation varies, it is understandable that we should have not only unique experiences but unique views about these experiences. In this volume I develop my own interpretation of Colombia's processes of change and the growth of its illegal psychoactive drugs industry. I expect this interpretation to be controversial. Some parts of it may be eventually disproved. However, I am convinced that only by daring to put forward alternative interpretations and engaging in subsequent open debate can we improve our understanding of a deeply troubled society such as Colombia's.

Some readers may think that this is an awkward volume, that perhaps it should have been issued as two books—one on Colombian political economy and another on the Colombian illegal drug industry. I have opted to have only one volume precisely in order to show that the two subjects are intimately related and cannot be understood independently of each other.

The first part of the book deals with Colombia's economic development and its political economy. Here I attempt two things. The first is to analyze Colombia's post–World War II economic development in an effort to understand the deep social and economic changes the country has experienced and the reasons that economic policies were formulated and implemented. Following this, because the common explanations of this process appeared to me to be unsatisfactory, I have heuristically developed an explanation that differs from mainstream economics on the one hand and from traditional political left theorizing on the other. This alternative interpretation views political and economic variables as parts of an interactive whole. I have thus tried to establish links between political party development, the characteristics of the development process, the extremely high violence that characterizes Colombia, and other socioeconomic variables.

The second and third parts of the book deal with the illegal psychoactive drugs industry. In Part 2, I summarize what is known about the illegal drugs industry in Colombia—its history, structure, entrepreneurs, size, government policies—and develop a theory to explain why the marijuana industry burgeoned in Colombia in the early 1970s, to be followed by cocaine refining. I thus try to answer a simple but important question: why Colombia?

Part 3 deals with the impact of the illegal drugs industry on Colombia and the policy alternatives open to the Colombian government to relieve some of the nation's distress. The impact of the industry on the economy is analyzed, addiction theories are surveyed to understand Colombian addiction patterns, and an evaluation of supply and consumption control policies is set forth.

I extend sincere thanks to Dharam Ghai, director of UNRISD in Geneva, for inviting me to participate in the Institute's research program on illicit drugs. I owe the most to LaMond Tullis, of Brigham Young University, who directed the project and who encouraged me during the last two years. I also thank Albert Berry of the University of Toronto, Thomas Hutcheson of the World Bank, Rensselaer Lee III of Global Advisory Services, and an anonymous reviewer for keen and helpful comments on earlier drafts. As always in these cases, I heeded some suggestions but did not follow others.

In Colombia, several individuals helped me collect data and other information and debated many ideas for the book. In particular, I thank Manuel Ramírez, Juan G. Tokatlian, Ana María Avilés, Mauricio Reina, and Alejandro Vivas of the Universidad de Los Andes, Francisco Leal and Alejandro Reyes of the Universidad Nacional de Colombia, Guillermo Bonilla of the Departamento Nacional de Planeación, Carlos A. Carvajal, María Elsa Pulido, Alvaro Rodríguez, and María Cecilia Castro of the Unidad Coordinadora de Prevención Integral de la Alcaldía Mayor de Bogotá, D.C., and Juan Manuel García of Econometria Ltda.

F.E.T.

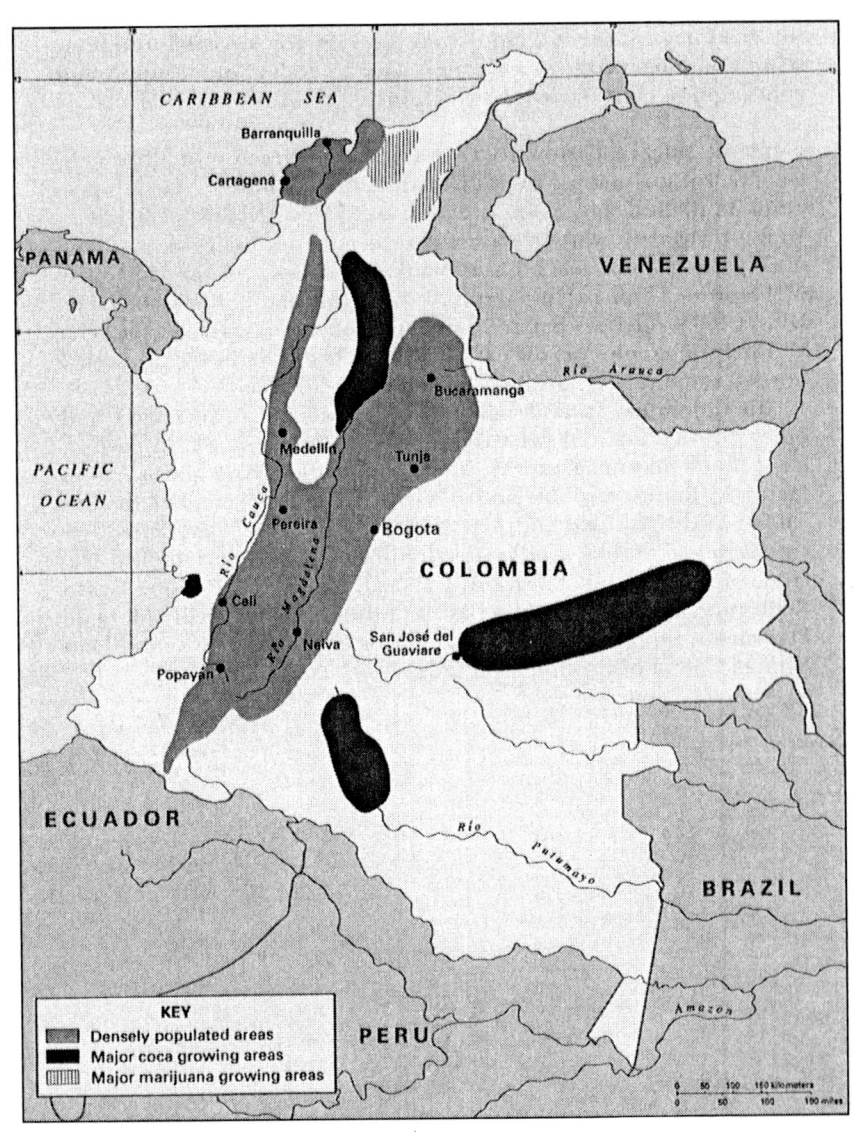

Population Concentration and Main Coca and Marijuana Growing Areas in Colombia

Introduction

• • •

Colombia's image in the early 1990s is of a country with a large, powerful illegal psychoactive drugs (PSAD) industry that is responsible for high levels of violence. While this is no doubt true, the description paints only a partial and imperfect picture of Colombia's economy and society. The role illegal drugs and violence have played in Colombia's recent economic and social development is complex and unclear. Taken alone, they cannot explain many important features of change in Colombia. Any attempt to explain why the illegal PSAD industry has flourished in the country, what short- and long-term effects it has had on the economy and on the country's social fabric, and how it has tried to become assimilated into Colombia's mainstream society, requires a deep understanding of Colombia's history and political economy. One must also understand relationships among the state, the legal private sector, the illegal PSAD industry, the non-PSAD underground economy, various political parties, and other social and political organizations.

Colombia's post–World War II social and economic development has been rather paradoxical. On one hand, during most of the period, Colombia has enjoyed a relatively satisfactory and stable income growth. Life expectancy, nutrition, health, and education levels have improved substantially. The growth of infrastructure has been impressive and the country has developed an integrated national market from a collection of small, fairly isolated, nearly self-sufficient regional economies. In addition, available data indicate that over the last twenty years income distribution has improved substantially—mainly due to a narrowing of the salary gap between unskilled and skilled workers (Londoño, 1990). Macroeconomic policy management has been conservative, allowing Colombia to escape many economic difficulties experienced by other Latin American countries. For example, during the 1970s Colombia borrowed cautiously on international markets, avoiding the debt crisis that affected the rest of Latin America.[1] As a result, the country did not experience drastic balance-of-payments and external-debt crises, a sharp increase in unemployment, or a decline in national income. Indeed, since World War II, Colombia's economic growth was actually more stable than that of the United States (García-García, 1991). The country's economic successes were accompanied by political ones, and Colombia has a comparatively outstanding record of elections and transfers of power between civilian governments.[2]

Despite Colombia's economic success, certain key variables have shown troubling signs. In particular, GDP growth rates declined sharply during the 1980s, to the point that now, achieving an annual GDP growth rate of 5.5 percent would be considered a great success, even though that was the average between 1960 and 1980. The government's concern with declining growth rates was the main justification for the Barco administration's program to open the economy (Departamento Nacional de Planeación, 1990), a program maintained by the Gaviria administration.

On the other side of the paradox, Colombia has persistently suffered a level of violence that is high by any standards. High even during peaceful times, the violence level has increased dramatically in the last decade. While actions of the army, police, guerrilla, and paramilitary groups have contributed to the increased violence, the proportion of violence not related to political activity has been much higher than in other countries. Common explanations for this unique problem include Colombians' propensity for attempting to solve conflicts violently, their frustrations with unequal income distribution, and their decreasing respect for prevailing power structures. Factors also include failed land and tax reforms, rising expectations, widespread corruption, inefficient government, a paralyzed judicial system, the rapid growth of criminal and non-criminal underground economies (especially involving marijuana, coca, and more recently poppy cultivation), and cocaine manufacturing and exporting. Regardless of whether each of these factors contributes to higher violence levels, they have, over time, weakened the government's ability to perform some of its most fundamental functions, such as providing justice and a conflict resolution system, police services, and personal security.

These factors have also contributed to a situation in which the majority of the population does not accept the current system as legitimate or worthy of respect. This continuing process of "delegitimation" expresses itself in a growing gap between the legal system (legality) and socially accepted behavior (morality).

A weak, ineffective state and persistent violence are features common to many other societies. However, in Colombia they have taken on peculiar characteristics that can only be explained in the context of the country's history and institutional evolution.

Social and economic developments since World War II have produced an environment conducive to the growth of the illegal PSAD industry in Colombia. Indeed, it is argued in this volume that through the country's process of regime delegitimation, coupled with factors outside the government's control, Colombia was destined to be a prime location to manufacture illegal PSADs for the U.S. market. In other words, the growth of Colombia's illegal PSAD industry was not accidental but rather related to the country's political economy.

Colombia's paradoxical development may then be summarized by stating that while the physical standard of living has improved, the country has actually become less livable. Colombians today enjoy better housing, health services, and education; they own cars, telephones, and have greater access to information about their country and the world; they are more broadly traveled and they have more material goods than in the past. But many fundamental aspects of the quality of life, such as physical security and property protection, have deteriorated sharply. At the same time the growth of the illegal PSAD industry is being stimulated by the economic milieu that has developed.

The literature on Colombia's politics and economics reflects this paradox, but it does not explain it. For instance, conventional analyses[3] emphasize economic growth in the past several decades, improvement in social indicators, the diversification and rapid urbanization of the economy, relatively low inflation rates (by high Latin American standards), the avoidance of an external debt crisis, and other encouraging aspects. In general, these studies portray a rapidly modernizing society and a well-managed economy, and provide the basis for relatively optimistic forecasts. More recent studies view the sharp decline of economic growth rates during the 1980s as Colombia's main economic problem and, in most cases, attribute this problem to what conventional analysts perceive as a closed economy.

Left-of-center and Marxist analyses, on the other hand, emphasize social problems: large housing deficits, high illiteracy, malnutrition, unemployment, increased violence, the evidence of frequent human rights violations, the peasants' struggle for land, and decline in GDP growth rates during the 1980s that virtually stagnated per capita income growth. However, such studies disregard data that show improvements in income distribution and social indicators. One common issue raised by left-of-center studies is the increased inequality in income distribution, which is substantiated with data about minimum wages, as well as the "pauperization of the middle class" due to the decline in salaries for white collar workers. For a long time such studies have forecasted gloom and doom, including the imminent uprising of the oppressed lower classes. These predictions have not only proven wrong, but have occasionally been fatal to those forecasters who, overwhelmed by their perception of social injustice and convinced of the accuracy of their analyses and the hopelessness of encouraging reform through ideas and studies, have resorted to political action.[4]

Both versions of Colombia's development process are partially valid. Interestingly, neither one acknowledges the existence of the other, such that the two bodies of literature have developed independently of each other, making virtually no reference to the conflicting argument. It appears that each group is satisfied with its own explanation and assumptions, disregarding alternative ones as unpleasant.

Mainstream economics literature provides an excellent discussion of how Colombia's stable and reasonably good macroeconomic policies produced a relatively satisfactory macroeconomic performance for a long period of time. However, this literature does not explain why the rate of GDP growth declined during the 1980s after at least 30 years of fairly sustained growth, nor does it attempt to explain why the level of violence increased or why the state has become increasingly unable to perform its most fundamental tasks. In such analyses the economic and the political aspects of the political economy are treated as if they were independent from one another.

Colombia's stable economic policy is no doubt one of the main reasons for its relatively successful growth performance, but it also allowed the political establishment to postpone needed institutional changes. Indeed, while economic stability and relatively satisfactory growth have allowed traditional power elites to buy time, they have not overcome the need for change or prevented the deterioration of the quality of life. Colombia's case clearly illustrates the fact that stable macroeconomic policy is a necessary but not sufficient condition for long-term economic growth. In a country such as Colombia, with traditional and inequitable social structures, stable macroeconomic policies have allowed elites to only tinker with social problems, avoiding drastic change and postponing long-term solutions. As a result, social conflicts may have been defused in the short term but have certainly exploded violently in the long term.

Left-of-center explanations are equally unsatisfactory. They are based on analyses of class struggle and conflict, which shed some light on social development in Colombia but also leave important parts of the picture unexplained. Colombians are characterized by a deep-rooted individualism, attributed by some to the isolation of many regions until the post–World War II period, as well as the isolation in which many peasants—the parents and grandparents of today's Colombians—worked (Torres, 1963: 68). This characteristic has hindered the development of a cohesive class identity (consciousness) and has left opposition movements fragmented and vulnerable to the establishment's mainly successful attempts to co-opt their leaders. No party or leader has been able to unify the opposition, except for short periods of time or in particular elections in which a candidate or a party succeeded in concentrating the protest vote. In fact, while social tensions persist and have perhaps increased, they have not produced a revolution or mass uprising that require a degree of class consciousness and cohesion.

These contradictory developments in Colombia's political economy coupled with the nature of the Colombian state were highly conducive to the growth of the illegal PSAD industry. Accordingly, the PSAD businessmen have moved to launder their capital by incorporating it into Colombia's economy, have sought political support and social legitimacy, and have forged coalitions with other groups. These activities have conditioned the various government responses to the illegal PSAD industry, as well as its ability to control it.

The illegal PSAD industry has grown quite large relative to the overall size of Colombia's economy, and it has had pervasive effects on society. The industry's illegal nature coupled with its substantial profits have exacerbated the problems of violence and have contributed substantially to the growth of the underground economy and corruption in society and state institutions. In many ways the illegal PSAD industry has acted as a catalyst that took advantage of and enhanced the weaknesses of the state, accelerating its decline as a provider of a framework in which society operates.

The illegal PSAD industry creates an additional fundamental conflict in Colombian society. In order to achieve lasting peace, Colombia needs a more open economic system with widespread opportunities, stable and transparent "game rules" that depersonalize important economic transactions, stronger private and public property rights, a government that is accountable and responsible to the citizenry, and, in general, greater movement toward democratic capitalism.

The illegal PSAD industry is an expression of primitive and raw capitalism that contradicts the spirit of change. This industry is an example of the predatory behavior at the root of the country's problems. What is more, the industry concentrates income, weakens the legitimacy of property rights, discourages growth in the economy's formal sector, makes it harder for the government to collect taxes, necessitates increased state expenditures, and legitimizes violence as the ultimate predatory weapon.

Colombia's governments have followed ambiguous policies toward the illegal PSAD industry. On one hand, they have been well aware of their limitations to act against the industry and have been tempted to welcome the influx of foreign exchange and capital generated by it. On the other hand, they have been reluctant and fearful to legitimize illegal PSAD capital and especially its entrepreneurs because of the violence, possible international retaliation, and disruptive impact on social and political structures such a move might cause.

This ambiguity has produced inconsistent policies that have tended to be reactive rather than proactive. The lack of consistent and proactive antidrug policies allowed the United States to heavily influence Colombia's official policy agenda, particularly in making the extradition of illegal PSAD businessmen the antidrug policy cornerstone. This fact implied the government's acknowledgment of its inability to cope with the illegal PSAD industry.

Colombia's governments have implicitly recognized their limitations and have insisted on separating the global "war on drugs," fought internationally, from Colombia's "war against narcoterrorism," fought domestically against the illegal PSAD industry. This approach concedes that Colombia cannot eliminate its domestic illegal PSAD traffic but that negotiations with illegal PSAD businessmen are possible if they can take place without violence.

Colombia's political system has historically been dominated by elites from two traditional parties (liberal and conservative) that have shared control of the state and provided economic stability. However, the exclusionary nature of the system nurtured the political dynamics that guaranteed long-term instability and turmoil (see Chapter 2). By the late 1980s it had become obvious to most Colombians that their institutions could not provide a workable framework for a modern society and that systemic changes were imperative. Recent Colombian presidents, beginning with Belisario Betancur, have been increasingly aware of the need to open the regime to change and have made efforts in that direction. However, the political establishment blocked many policies aimed at democratizing Colombian society during the Betancur (1982–1986) and Virgilio Barco (1986–1990) administrations.[5]

The PSAD industry helped to break this stalemate. Violence associated with elements of the PSAD industry began to increase sharply in 1986, leading to the assassination of three presidential candidates and other government officials and notables in 1989 and 1990. This forced the government into more aggressive action against the industry, and some of its leaders were pursued and killed. The worsening violence unified public opinion behind a call for reform. The result was a referendum that approved convening a constituent assembly to rewrite the 1886 constitution (which had been reformed several times in the past) and thereby open the political and economic systems.

Both Barco and the César Gaviria administrations supported the referendum approved in July 1991 and adopted programs designed to make the state more accountable to the people. Gaviria's reform program follows the lead of the Barco administration, in that President Gaviria was first Finance and then Interior Minister. First, it promotes the new constitution as its keystone to a "political opening," hoping to weaken the clientelistic characteristics of Colombian politics and provide channels of participation for small political groups. This is designed to break the power duopoly held by the two traditional parties. Second, the plan stresses increased regional autonomy through the decentralization of government decisions and the strengthening of local governments. Third, a "social opening" is to be implemented through increased social sector expenditures. Finally, an "economic opening" package relies on an international trade liberalization program, first implemented in February 1990 under the Barco administration, as the most important element. Together, these reform policies are meant to increase the degree of democracy in Colombia and to decrease economic privileges and rents.

Following the stated policy goal of eliminating narcoterrorism, the Gaviria government—after continuing the aggressive prosecution of PSAD businessmen associated with political violence—offered narcoterrorists the option of turning themselves in to serve time in Colombian jails, an approach that led to the jailing of the surviving Medellín cartel leaders. This policy essentially allows top illegal PSAD businessmen to enjoy and eventually legalize their capital after they serve their sentences, while it contributed to a sharp decline in PSAD-associated violence. However, the long-run impact of these developments on the illegal PSAD industry is uncertain, because it is unclear whether they will result in a smaller PSAD industry; many lower ranking PSAD businessmen are likely to continue and expand their business. Therefore, Gaviria's policy solves some of the conflicts between the state and large PSAD entrepreneurs, but it does not necessarily get Colombians out of the illegal drug business.

The recent institutional and political changes that the Colombian government has embarked upon are indeed the most sweeping ones experienced in the country in over a century. However, the government is forced to balance two contradictory goals: it has to open the political system and move toward a more democratic and egalitarian society, but it confronts a large raw capitalist sector that needs to legitimize its capital, aspires to political power, poses a threat of violence, and has proven its willingness to use it. The policy challenge posed by these contradictory forces is immense.

Part 1 of this book studies the Colombian political economy. Chapter 1 discusses the postwar Colombian development process from the vantage of conventional economics, drawing a generally positive picture: Colombia's economic growth has been relatively satisfactory; almost all social indicators have improved significantly; the government was able to design, implement, and maintain relatively stable policies that were adapted to changing economic conditions without great economic dislocation and trauma; the country followed a prudent, external debt policy and maintained a satisfactory balance-of-payments situation; and the government is currently engaged in what by Colombian standards is a radical policy reform designed to accelerate the rate of GDP growth above the rates of the 1980s. However, in spite of such progress, there are troubling economic signs: GDP growth slowed significantly during the 1980s, annual inflation has remained stubbornly pegged at about 25 percent per year and the more recent macroeconomic policies seem to be less effective than those of the past.

Chapter 2 presents a critical institutionalist interpretation of Colombia's development process. It surveys the history and high underlying level of violence, its rapid increase since the mid-1970s, its typology, and some of its possible causes. The chapter then focuses on the institutional crisis that confronts the country by arguing that the values and institutions that evolved from the colonial period produced an ethic of inequality and privilege that has pervaded Colombia's history. It analyzes the political elite's reaction to the *violencia* of the late 1940s and early 1950s, and the formation of the National Front that produced less violence but reinforced an exclusionary political system. And it outlines the growth of distributive coalitions and political clientelism that have led to the development of rent-seeking capitalism and a clientelist political system.[6] These developments promoted the growth of the underground economy and the decline of the state's capacity to regulate and guide economic activity, weakened social cohesion and national identity, and reinforced the traditional ethic of inequality. The chapter ends with a section on the role of the illegal PSAD industry and the government's policy agenda.

Part 2 studies the illegal PSAD industry and various policy responses. Chapter 3, which begins this part, provides a short survey of the history of the PSAD industry in the country; summarizes the development of the marijuana and cocaine industries; provides a picture of the industry's economic structure, emphasizing the conditioning effects of its illegality; and discusses the degree of competition at each stage of production and the possible cartelization of the industry, including the evolution of the so-called Medellín and Cali cartels.

Chapter 4 discusses the social origin and characteristics of the main actors in the industry, including their criminal backgrounds. It also looks at some of their behavior patterns, such as their willingness to use violence, their attempts to obtain political and social acceptance, and attempts to form coalitions with guerrilla and other groups. The illegal PSAD entrepreneurs' economic behavior and their involvement in Colombia's economy are also studied.

Chapter 5 attempts to explain why Colombia developed a competitive international advantage in the illegal PSAD industry. Industry profits are linked to risk taking, and the industry tends to locate in the lowest risk location. It is argued that the characteristics of the political regime, the economic system, the country's geography, and the large number of Colombian immigrants in the United States made Colombia the lowest risk location among the Andean, Central American, and Caribbean countries in which to manufacture cocaine, and promoted the development by Colombians of a sophisticated transportation and marketing system. Among all Andean and Caribbean basin countries, Colombia had the best package of illegal PSAD promoting factors.

Chapter 6 surveys and evaluates the various estimates of the size of the illegal PSAD industry in Colombia, including the amounts and value of illegal PSADs produced, and the capital absorbed into the domestic economy.

Chapter 7 studies governmental policies from the last 20 years toward the illegal PSAD industry. It argues that Colombia's governments have not had coherent, independent, long-term drug policies, and that drug issues have risen on the policy agenda mainly in response to threats from PSAD entrepreneurs against the establishment. During the 1980s the extradition of drug traffickers became the cornerstone of Colombia's drug policy, which led to increased violence and militarization of drug issues but did not significantly affect the volume of PSADs produced. These policies were conditioned by United States policies that stress interdiction, eradication at the source, and extradition, over demand-focused policies. The chapter also shows that Colombia's society and government have been ambivalent toward the illegal PSAD industry, because various Colombian administrations and private sector groups have welcomed income generated by its activities, but have tried to deny access to political and social participation to industry entrepreneurs.

Part Three studies the effects of drug traffic and of antidrug laws, and evaluates the policy alternatives open to Colombia's government. Chapter 8, which begins this part, looks at several social and economic impacts on Colombia of the growth of the illegal drugs industry. It argues that the main impact has been its role as a catalyst in the process of delegitimation of Colombia's regime. The industry has accentuated and accelerated a process of social, political, and economic change, and it has forced the political and economic powers to address the country's main social problems. This chapter also looks at the impact the PSAD industry has had on local and regional economies, on the balance of payments, on capital inflows and macroeconomic management, and on overall economic activity and growth. It also studies the domestic impact of money laundering and investment practices of the illegal PSAD businessmen, the capital flight financed by the industry, the industry's contribution to the increase in overall violent lawlessness and violence and consequent weakening of the state, and the development of paramilitary structures and the *sicario* (young assassins for hire) industry it has spawned.

Chapter 9 studies the impact of the PSAD industry on drug demand and addiction. The theories of demand for PSADs developed by conventional economists and psychologists are surveyed, and the chapter provides a short discussion of the domestic use of legal and illegal PSADs in Colombia and the country's resulting addiction problems. It also evaluates the possibility that Colombia may develop a cocaine-addiction epidemic.

Finally, Chapter 10 evaluates the policy alternatives available to Colombia's government. The failure of past and current policies and the need for policy change are emphasized. It is argued that the lack of solid knowledge regarding the nature and causes of addiction combined with the fears of the citizenry result in a policy mix based on moralistic and emotional grounds more than on a cool cost-benefit analysis of various policy alternatives. The policy implications of various addiction theories, and of the characteristics of the PSAD industry and Colombia's government, are studied. Further, past policies are evaluated in that light and policy alternatives for Colombia's government are explored. Policies toward PSAD production, marketing, and consumption can vary greatly, as they can have different degrees of tolerance, demand prevention, and so on. Relative costs and benefits for each policy mix vary significantly among countries and social groups involved. The past and current policy mix imposes a heavy burden on Colombia, but the government does not have the power to opt for policies that might lower the social costs paid by Colombia or that would eliminate the illegal PSAD industry. Colombia's government has few policy alternatives because the delegitimation it has experienced during the last few decades has weakened its ability to implement repressive policies that would eliminate the illegal drug trade. Neither legalization nor decriminalization is likewise an alternative.

Since it cannot succeed with repressive policies, the government is in a no-win situation as it tries to minimize domestic violence associated with the drug industry, neutralize the negative social and economic effects of the absorption of huge illegal resources, increase the level of grass roots democracy necessary to avoid social clashes, and appease foreign powers by appearing to wage a strong fight against the drug industry. In this situation, the best that domestic policies can do is buy some time, hoping that the drug problem will go away—a very unlikely prospect.

The predicament the government is in today is the result of past attempts to neutralize primary social problems without really solving them. The endgame that traditional elites have been forced to play is leading to their own demise. Or, as a chess analyst might say, the king is constantly in check and facing a possible check-mate because it could not keep the pawns' support.

On a more positive note, it is argued that there is a growing consensus in Colombia and the United States about the failure of drug-supply repression policies and, independent of whether PSADs are decriminalized, the need to change the policy emphasis toward prevention, education, research, and treatment on the demand side. This broadening consensus offers some hope of improving the international policy mix and lowering the high costs paid by Colombian society.

Before proceeding, it is important to say a word about the nature and quality of the data and other information used. The data on the formal sector of the Colombian economy tend to be reasonably good. However, as expected, the data on the illegal PSAD industry are quite sketchy, sometimes unreliable and contradictory, and the research and publications about the industry are frequently not very rigorous. A substantial proportion of the publications available are not academic in nature, but rather the product of U.S. and Colombian newspeople and journalists who have obtained a substantial amount of information while practicing their trade. These works are based on interviews with illegal PSAD industry entrepreneurs and peasants and on having worked with law enforcement authorities. Although these sources provide both quantitative and qualitative data, they are frequently difficult to interpret because their methodologies and definitions are not clear, and at least some of the authors seem not to have been aware of different concepts involved (for instance, the difference between revenues, value added, and profits). Therefore these sources of information must be viewed with great caution because of data and conceptual inconsistencies.

It should also be noted that official institutional sources containing illegal PSAD industry figures also tend to be biased and frequently contradictory. Methodologies used to obtain those data are often unclear or unspecified, and even sources that could be expected to provide the best data, such as those from the U.S. government, sometimes have had to change their estimates in view of new evidence that shows they have been off the mark.

In view of these characteristics of available information, it is necessary to use a good dose of skepticism in interpreting the data. An effort has been made to check information for consistency and to be cautious in deriving conclusions. Faced with these problems, I have tried to be as objective as possible; however, I am well aware that other researchers and readers might conclude otherwise.

Notes

1. See Revéiz and Pérez (1986) and García-García (1991) for analyses of the continuity and success of Colombian macroeconomic policies and the relative economic stability they have produced.

2. From 1900 to 1903 the country experienced a bloody civil war between the two traditional parties (liberal and conservative), but since 1903 it has been ruled by elected presidents, except for a short period (13 June 1953–10 May 1957) during which a military dictatorship held power and a shorter one (10 May 1957–7 August 1958) during which an interim military junta held power. However, it should be noted that when the military overthrew the civilian government in 1953, it did so to stop another bloody confrontation between the two traditional parties and had the support of most of the population.

3. Conventional analysis is perhaps best exemplified by the official economic reports of the Colombian government and the multilateral lending agencies, and shared by some private observers like Botero (1981), Segovia (1989), and Escobar (1990).

4. Father Camilo Torres in his "call to the Colombian people" just before joining the guerrillas with whom he died fighting the army in 1966, wrote "Now the people will no longer believe. The people do not believe in elections. The people know that the legal means have been exhausted and that no means remain but to arm. The people are desperate and resolved to

risk their lives so that the next generation of Colombians will not be enslaved. . . . I wish to tell the Colombian people that the moment has come" (Torres, 1969: 201–202). About 17 years later, Jaime Bateman, the leader of the M-19 guerrilla movement, argued that "The conditions in the country are ripe for the uprising. If it were not that way, one could not explain why the people are supporting us in larger numbers, why when they [the government] destroy our organization, as it has happened so many times, we rebound with gained strength" (Lara, 1986: 205, author's translation).

5. Martz (1992:34) summarizes the attempts of presidents Betancur and Barco and concludes that "in short, Barco's proposals for *apertura* [political opening] were effectively gutted as Liberal and Social Conservative [the new name of the old Conservative party] leaders joined to block all measures which might challenge their customary rule."

6. That is, a system in which the private sector's profits are highly dependent on obtaining preferential treatment and privileges granted by the government, and in which politicians depend on budget allocations and public jobs that are distributed to supporters in payment for their votes.

Part 1

THE COLOMBIAN POLITICAL ECONOMY

... 1 ...
The Conventional Economics Perspective

This chapter presents an overview of the conventional economics perspective of Colombia's economic development, policies followed by the government, and some of the economic conditions that developed during the last forty-five years. By "conventional economics perspective" I mean the approach used in mainstream economics that relies only on the study of economic variables and relations, largely excluding social and political variables. This overview is relevant because the conventional economics perspective is used in studies that present one of the sides of the Colombian "paradox" discussed in the introduction. It has also been the approach used by Colombia's government to formulate and implement policies, and by bilateral and multilateral agencies that have influenced those policies.

To explain the development and consequences of the illegal PSAD industry in Colombia, one must understand the country's processes of social and economic change. The conventional economics perspective provides a framework for a partial understanding of those processes. It helps our understanding of the main structural changes experienced by the society, the impact of external changes on the economy, government policies and responses to changing conditions, problems encountered in policy implementation, and so forth. However, this perspective leaves many unanswered questions. I address these in Chapter 2 in an institutionalist approach intended to complement the conventional one, thereby, in the specific case of Colombia, advancing an understanding of how the illegal PSAD industry could have taken such pervasive hold of the country and why heterodox measures will be required to turn the illegal PSAD matter around.

At the turn of the century, Colombia was one of the most backward countries on the continent, isolated from the rest of the world and internally divided into small self-sufficient regions that conducted little external trade. Ocampo (1984: 53) shows that in 1913 Colombia's per capita exports were only U.S. $34, above only those of Haiti ($31) and Honduras ($27) in Latin America, and just 10 percent of those of Cuba and Argentina. In 1920 the railroad mileage per capita was only 20 percent of the Latin American average, and higher only than the Haitian figure. Yet during the entire twentieth century, Colombia has undergone a strong process of internal economic integration that has led to the formation of a national market.

Development has especially been positive since World War II when evaluated through the lens of conventional economics. Economic growth during this period has in many ways been remarkable. Although Colombia experienced an early population explosion, per capita income grew steadily; then the country experienced a dramatic drop in population growth. The largely rural country became urbanized as economic growth remained stable and, while not spectacular, satisfactory. In addition, there were significant changes in the sectoral GDP composition and substantial improvements in many important social indicators. Economic policies varied through time, but changes were cautious and less drastic than those in most Latin American countries. These policies can be characterized as more pragmatic than ideological, and frequently taken in response, albeit with a lag, to changing external and internal political and economic conditions.

A number of things changed after World War II that led to Colombia's current economic structure. For example, rural violence led to land reform, while urban growth and the population explosion led to significant increases in spending for education and other social programs. Recurrent balance-of-payments difficulties led to replacing the fixed exchange rate with a creeping peg system, and several tax reforms were also attempted. In the early post–World War II period financial institutions were created to provide long-term capital to new industrial and agricultural sectors and, in the early 1970s, the financial system was restructured to allow for long-term housing financing. Beginning in 1967 nontraditional exports were promoted to decrease external sector dependency on international coffee prices. By the late 1970s, Colombia was spending heavily on infrastructure and mining so that, by the mid-1980s, exports of petroleum, coal, and ferronickel were significant. This economic evolution highlights a substantial degree of policy adaptation by Colombia's governments within a relatively stable and fairly conservative policy path.

Based on the evidence at hand, then, there is no doubt that Colombia has experienced dramatic changes in its productive structure during the last forty-five years, and that these were accomplished with the help of relatively continuous economic policies, a fact that sets Colombia apart from the rest of Latin America. Indeed, Colombia was the only country of the region that did not have a debt crisis, and the only one in which GDP did not decline in a single year during the 1980s. From the conventional vantage, the only major negative of Colombia's development has been its very unequal income distribution, but even in this respect things have been improving.

However, while most social and economic indicators showed a positive trend, there were signs of deep social and economic malaise as the country's level of violence and social unrest increased and GDP growth slowed during the 1980s to an average of only 3.2 percent. That rate was high relative to the rest of Latin America, but disappointing considering Colombia avoided the debt crisis. These factors moved the government to promote sweeping political reform highlighted by a new constitution that replaced the 1886 constitution. Political change was complemented by market liberalization measures, including opening the economy to international competition. The results of these significant policy changes and the departure from the gradualism characterized by past policy reforms are as yet unclear.

What follows in this chapter is a more detailed discussion of factors and decisions influencing postwar economic change. A review of demographic changes and improvements in social indicators and highlights of the main aspects of economic performance are followed by a survey of macroeconomic performance during several subperiods, including the policies followed, the motivations for policy changes, and policy results. This section studies the last twenty-five years in more detail than the earlier period. The chapter ends with concluding remarks.

Population Growth and Social Indicators Evolution

Colombia has experienced dramatic social and economic changes during the postwar period. As in most of Latin America at the end of World War II, population growth accelerated dramatically, peaking at about 3.2 percent per year by the 1960s.[1] This was due mainly to improvements in the coverage of drinking water and sewer services and the control of a few endemic tropical diseases, which lowered mortality rates while fertility rates remained high until about 1970 (see Rueda, 1990a). Census data show that in 1951 Colombia's population was 11.5 million, and by 1973 it had doubled to 22.9 million.

Beginning in the late 1960s the population growth rate began a remarkable drop so that the last intercensal (1973–1985) annual average growth rate was only 2 percent (Departamento Administrativo Nacional de Estadística [DANE], 1989: 64). Furthermore, DANE projects a continuous, but slower, decline in the growth rate to about 1.4 percent in the years 2005–2010.[2] Colombia's "demographic transition" occurred so quickly that the dire predictions in the 1960s of a long-term population boom leading to an overpopulation crisis proved false. Nonetheless, by 1990 the total population in Colombia was about 33 million, meaning it had tripled in forty years.

The population growth rate's sharp decline was partly in response to a quiet, effective population control policy initiated during the Lleras Restrepo administration (1966–1970).[3] By lowering birth rates then, the program effectively lowered labor force growth rates twenty years later, easing the pressure to generate new jobs. Other factors were also involved in changing demographic patterns. Life expectancy at birth was only about fifty years in the early 1950s, but it increased steadily to reach sixty-eight years in the late 1980s. The infant mortality rate in the early 1950s was very high (123.3 per thousand births), but declined continuously to 48.6 per thousand in the late 1980s.

The postwar population explosion was accompanied by significant rural-urban and rural-rural migrations and rapid urbanization. According to the 1938 census, 30.9 percent of the population lived in urban municipal centers.[4] By 1951 this had increased to 38.7 percent and continued to increase sharply so that by 1985, when the most recent census was taken, it had reached 67.2 percent. Therefore, around 1940 Colombia was mainly a rural society, but one that was urbanizing at an increasingly fast pace. Urban growth peaked in the 1950s and continued at a fast but slowing pace that consolidated the change from a predominantly rural to an urban economy by the mid-1980s. In addition, the relative importance of larger cities increased as they tended to grow faster than smaller ones.[5]

Colombia's migration patterns were complex. As shown by Urrutia (1990a), most migrants to large cities came from smaller urban centers, not from rural areas. Rural migrants tended to go to other rural areas or to small towns. Most large city immigrants had significantly higher education levels than the average resident of the area from which they came. Thus, rural migration to large cities tended to occur in stages, with peasants first migrating mainly to smaller towns, and a second generation of better-trained individuals migrating to larger urban areas. Most migrants to large cities were females, many of whom were attracted by household jobs that did not require many urban-specific skills. Several econometric studies have shown that the migration patterns can be explained very well by economic factors, particularly wage differentials (Nelson, Schultz, and Slighton, 1971, chap. 3; and Conroy, 1976). Thus, Urrutia concludes that most of the rural-urban migration was not caused by the rural violence that prevailed in the late 1940s and early 1950s, a point of contention in the literature discussed in Chapter 2.

Changes in population growth were accompanied by a significant change in the distribution of the economically active population. In 1960, 50.1 percent of the labor force was engaged in agriculture, 19.5 percent in industry, and 30.4 percent in services; by 1980 these figures were 34.3, 23.5, and 42.2 percent respectively. These shifts produced a different composition of economic output and, perhaps more importantly, altered the nature of many economic relations in the country. For example, traditional rural labor markets worked under pre-capitalist institutions inherited from the colonial past. These included sharecropping and other systems that tied peasants to the land and allowed in-kind payments of at least part of the wages and rents required from peasants for the use of landowners' plots. But migration from the *minifundia* and *latifundia* regions contributed to a significant modernization in rural labor relations and land tenancy systems.

Rapid urbanization and population growth presented very serious challenges to Colombia's government, as they put great pressure on public utilities and other services, and produced substantial changes in both the sectoral composition of GDP and the nature of social relations that had prevailed since colonial times. Governmental response to these challenges was, in many ways, quite successful as indicated by dramatic improvements of most of the quality of life indexes since 1950.

One striking example, as shown by Farné (1990), is that the quality of housing improved substantially. According to the 1951 census, 52.7 percent of the housing units had earth floors and 90.3 percent had walls made of "precarious" materials.[6] By the 1985 census these percentages had dropped to 17.1 and 24.4 respectively. Similarly, in 1951 only 28.8 percent of the units had running water, 25.8 percent had electricity, and 32.4 percent had sewage or septic tanks. By 1985 these figures had increased to 69.7, 78.2, and 77 percent respectively. In urban areas (municipal seats) these percentages were much higher: 89.8, 95, and 93.6 percent respectively. Overcrowding—defined as more than three residents per room, excluding kitchens and bathrooms—also declined sharply from 38.8 to 19.4 percent of all units, although the size of the average housing unit is likely to have decreased, particularly in large, high-density cities. Another positive housing aspect is the prevalence of owner-occupancy. In both 1951 and 1985, 67 percent of the total units and 74 percent of the units in nonmunicipal seats were owner-occupied. However, in urban areas (municipal seats) this percentage increased from 55 percent to 64.8 percent over the same period.

Farné (1990) also surveyed data on food security and, while the per capita calorie availability dropped somewhat between 1950 and 1970 (mainly because of fast population growth), it has recovered since then. Indeed, economic growth produced income increases at all levels, and the percentage of the population at risk of malnutrition declined sharply from 40.1 percent in 1972 to 20 percent in 1981. This decline has been most dramatic in rural areas, dropping from 72.3 to 20 percent! Another positive sign is evident in dietary changes made possible by the increased availability of more nutritious, less fatty foods.[7]

The coverage and level of education also improved substantially. After World War II, an ongoing debate continued about the roles of the Catholic Church and the state in shaping the education system because Colombia had a concordat with the Holy See that gave the Church an education monopoly in a substantial, albeit very sparsely populated, part of the country. The state eventually assumed responsibility for and control of the education system, which was highly inadequate at the time. In 1951, 44 percent of the population was illiterate. Selowsky (1969, 47) estimated that in 1955 only 57 percent of seven- to twelve-year-olds were enrolled in elementary schools and he targeted 90 percent as a goal. Under state control, elementary school enrollment increased beyond those expectations, reaching nearly 100 percent of the age cohort by 1970.[8] Increases in high school and college enrollments have been even larger. In 1960 high school enrollment was only 11.9 percent, while college enrollment was only 1.8 percent. By 1980 these rates had increased to 44 and 10.6 percent respectively. Some indicators of the quality of elementary education also show improvements as the number of students per teacher dropped from 38 in 1960 to 30 in 1980. Simultaneously, retention rates increased significantly, from 41.3 percent in urban areas and 3.2 percent in rural ones in the early 1960s to 62.4 and 18.3 percent respectively in 1980 (Rueda, 1990c: 134). These improvements lowered illiteracy rates to 27.1 percent in 1960 and 12.2 percent in 1980.

The changing role of the state in education is also reflected in the public sector's participation in intermediate and higher education. In the early 1950s most high school enrollment was in private schools (about 60 percent), while two-thirds of university enrollment was in public schools. Through time, the state increased its participation in secondary education to about 65 percent while it dropped its share of university enrollment to about 40 percent by the late 1980s (Rueda, 1990c: 129). The increase in tertiary education enrollment was accompanied by an explosion in the number of universities, which reached 156 in 1985. Most of these are private, but unfortunately are of low quality, and have poor physical facilities (Rueda, 1990c: 142).

Great access to tertiary education has contributed to improving other social indicators. For instance, the number of persons per medical doctor dropped from 2,603 in 1960 to 1,245 in 1984, and a similar drop occurred in the number of persons per medical auxiliary personnel.

Besides education, one of the most remarkable changes realized during the country's transformation was in the role of women in society. This is reflected in the sharp population growth rate decline discussed above, and in a corresponding increase in the rate of women's participation in the labor force from 27.8 percent in 1971 to 43.4 percent in 1985 (Rueda, 1990b: 104). However, the types of jobs held by women are significantly different from those held by men. A large but declining proportion of women are employed as household maids, and a significant number of others are employed in the informal economy.[9] Despite the fact that the education level of women has increased dramatically so that today it is similar to that of men, incorporating women into the labor market tends to be done through the informal sector. Indeed, female illiteracy is the same as that of men (12 percent) and about half of all university students are women (Rueda, 1990c). Yet salary differentials between men and women remain significant—even though they are shrinking under pressure from forces that have been reshaping income distribution (as discussed below). And despite their increased education and labor participation, women's political role and their participation in government employment are still not comparable to that of men. However, as noted by Rueda (1990b: 116), this is more likely the result of the traditional political system's resistance to any change than of gender specific discrimination.

Related to many of the factors discussed above is Colombia's income distribution. As in most developing countries, it has been very unequal; however, it has not remained static during the last fifty years. A recent comprehensive study dating back to the 1938 census (Londoño, 1990 and 1992) has shown an interesting pattern of change. Fifty years ago the structure of Colombia's economy differed substantially from the expected one for a country of its size and population. The education level of the labor force, education expenditures, and the industry sector's share in GDP were substantially below international standards, while agriculture's share of GDP was much higher. As industry began to grow faster than agriculture, skilled people demanded by new industries were scarce and their wages began to rise substantially. Compounded by a lag in investment in human capital (by way of education and training), this process led to a sharp increase in income inequality between workers of different skill levels.[10] Interestingly, the inequality of non-labor income remained relatively stable. Total income inequality peaked in the 1960s, after which education levels improved drastically and the relative income of agricultural workers improved somewhat—factors that led to a lower inequality in labor income. Accordingly, when inequality was on the rise, the global Gini coefficient increased about 10 points. But it fell a similar amount as the gap closed (see endnote 11). Such variations in the Gini coefficient are expected in the course of development, but in the case of Colombia they took place in a very short period: "It suggests that the Colombian history compressed in just 50 years what Great Britain took more than two centuries to develop" (Londoño, 1990: 23).

When one focuses on the income of the poorest workers, the picture is also positive. "The real income of the poorest workers did not fall in any sub-period observed. Based on a constant poverty line, the incidence of poverty has declined continuously during the fifty-year period. A head-count index shows that three-fourths of the population was poor in 1938, half in the mid-1960s, and one-fourth in the late 1980s."[11]

Other recent studies support the contention that income distribution in Colombia has improved in the last twenty years and that poverty has declined. Berry (1992) studies the performance of the agricultural sector during the recessionary 1980s and finds an apparent contradiction: while growth in the sector was slow, income levels improved and poverty in the *campesino* subsector declined sharply. That subsector produces most of the food crops available on the domestic market and generates most of the agricultural jobs. "The direct explanation of the slowdown in agricultural growth lies in a deceleration both of factor productivity and input quantum growth." In the years before 1980 there was a sharp "expansion of the large-scale crop sector, accompanied and supported by rapid technological change, modernization of the crop structure, and increasing capitalization." However, sometime in the 1970s growth in the modern capitalist agricultural subsector slowed, while the campesino subsector gained dynamism. Berry's explanation for the increased income and declining campesino poverty lies in the combined effect of several factors. The first involves a decline in land concentration due mainly "to the process of colonization and the division of large landholdings through inheritance" and a sharp decline in the frequency of tenancy. Second, as a result of integrated rural development programs implemented by the López Michelsen administration (1974–1978) that made credit and technical assistance available to small farmers, productivity increased substantially on small plots of land. Third, rural non-agricultural employment expanded and the labor market tightened. Interestingly, "the process of modernization of the rural labor market has manifested itself more in the evolving complementarity of farming income and wage income than in the outright proletarization of the campesinos." These combined factors not only compensated for the relative decline in prices for agricultural products, but allowed campesinos to increase their income levels.

Aguilar (1990) surveys the literature on income distribution in Colombia and also finds that income distribution inequality declined from the early 1960s due mainly to the growth in the type of public spending that had a redistributive effect. And yet Aguilar concludes that wage policies followed through this period, particularly those that set minimum wage levels, had uncertain effects on income distribution as they had both equalizing and unequalizing results. An interesting point brought up by Aguilar is that on average, propertied peasants have a lower income than non-propertied ones, a fact that he attributes to the lower mobility of small landowners that prevents them from taking advantage of employment opportunities in other areas.

Farné (1990) also finds a significant decline in poverty levels. Using a combined measure that includes minimum levels for three indexes (measuring housing deficiencies, and access to education and income), Farné defines as poor any family that fails to meet the minimum level in one of the three indexes, and as absolutely poor any family that does not meet two minimum levels. He finds that the poor declined from 70.5 percent of the country's population in 1973 to 45.6 percent in 1985, while the extreme poor declined from 44.9 to 22.8 percent.

GDP **Growth and Composition Changes**[12]

Colombia's annual GDP growth in the forty-five years after World War II was about 4.8 percent, a figure close to the average both for Latin

American and developing countries in general, but higher than that of the United States and of Colombia's other main trading partners.[13] Thus, growth performance can be considered satisfactory, but certainly not particularly high.

Likewise, income per capita growth in the 1950s was a rather low 1.6 percent, but it accelerated somewhat in the 1960s to 2.2 percent. In the 1970s, after the population growth rate began to decline, it reached a healthy 3.3 percent.[14] By 1980 income per capita was about 108 percent higher than in 1950, with most of the growth having occurred between 1968–1979 when it increased by 50 percent. As previously noted, during the 1980s economic growth declined significantly. But, since by 1980 population growth had slowed considerably, income per capita managed to post a modest 14.4 percent increase for the decade, a figure slightly lower than the one achieved in the 1950s when population growth was accelerating.

These figures indicate that Colombia's growth has been close to the average of developing countries, but it has been significantly different because it has been remarkably more stable. In fact, deviations in Colombia's GDP growth trend have been lower than those of the United States GDP (García-García, 1991).

Colombia's greater-than-average stability does not mean that GDP growth has not fluctuated. The early postwar period was one of rising international coffee prices and a time when coffee accounted for about 70 percent of Colombia's export earnings. Coffee prices especially increased after 1950, boomed in 1953, peaked in 1954 at a record high level, and remained at historically high levels until 1956.[15] Average GDP growth for 1950–1956 was 5.23 percent, although 1951 was a recessive year during which GDP grew at only 3.1 percent. During 1956 to 1967 coffee prices were low and the Colombian economy faced foreign exchange constraints that limited its growth; the overall GDP growth rate fell to 4.57 percent and during 1957 and 1958 Colombia experienced a recession, with GDP growth rates of only 2.2 and 2.5 percent respectively. Between 1967 and 1972 the economy rebounded to achieve an average 6.08 percent GDP growth.

The rebound was aided in early 1967 by what many consider the most important macroeconomic policy change of the period: a crawling peg replaced the fixed multiple exchange rate system that had prevailed until then. In addition, exchange controls were tightened, and export subsidies and other export promotion systems were established (see below). In the following years coffee prices improved, Colombia's chief trade partners enjoyed rapid income growth, and international prices of many of Colombia's primary products increased.

Exports expanded and their composition and markets became significantly more diverse, releasing Colombia from its foreign exchange constraint. Unfortunately, income growth decelerated after the 1973 oil crisis and in 1975 fell to only 2.3 percent in the midst of a world recession. Growth then rebounded from 1976 through 1980, with an average of about 5.4 percent, fueled by a new coffee price boom in 1975 through 1977. This period included a remarkably high growth rate of 8.5 percent in 1978, the highest on record. However, GDP growth has since been disappointing, averaging only 3.2 percent between 1981 and 1989, during which time it exceeded 3.7 percent only in 1986 (5.8 percent) and 1987 (5.4 percent).

Colombia's GDP composition has also differed from that of the "typical" less developed country of comparable size and income per capita. Indeed, in the 1940s agricultural output and total exports were relatively large compared to levels in countries with the same population and GDP (Londoño, 1990). This difference is attributed mainly to the country's geographic characteristics that made national integration of its regional markets difficult. Agriculture and livestock accounted for 37.8 percent of GDP in 1950, but that proportion declined to about 31 percent by the early 1960s and to 21.5 percent by the late 1980s (see Table 1.1). As agriculture declined, manufacturing was initially the engine of growth, increasing continuously from 14.8 percent of GDP in 1950 to a peak of 23.4 percent in 1974. However, since then manufacturing growth slowed, and the sector's share of GDP hovered between 22 and 23 percent until 1980. It fell somewhat during the 1980s, reaching 21.1 percent in 1988. This lack of dynamism in manufacturing has been a main source of concern about the performance of Colombia's economy since the mid-1970s, and it has frequently been blamed for the economic slowdown of the 1980s.

Since the mid-1970s, declines in agriculture and manufacturing have been picked up by services and mining. Mining had not really been important until the late 1980s. Historically, the most important mineral products had been gold and petroleum. Between 1950 and 1965 the mining sector's GDP share ranged between 3.4 and 3.9 percent. From then on, it declined in importance to the point that, in the latter 1960s and 1970s, it actually had several negative growth years. This decline was in large part due to the policy to keep gasoline and oil prices at very low levels throughout the 1960s and most of the 1970s, which discouraged exploration and investment in the sector.[16] When international oil prices quadrupled in 1973, Colombia increasingly became a net oil importer in spite of its long history as an oil exporter. By 1979 mining accounted only for 1.1 percent of GDP. But mining recovered and became a leading sector in the 1980s

Table 1.1 Sectoral Origin of Gross Domestic Product, 1950–1967 (percentages)

Years	Agriculture & Livestock	Fisheries & Hunting	Forestry	Mining	Manufacturing	Construction	Commerce	Transportation	Communications	Electricity, Gas & Water	Banking, Insurance & Real Estate	Net Housing Rents	Personal Services	Government Services
1950	37.8	0.1	0.3	3.5	14.8	2.7	15.6	5.1	0.4	0.5	1.8	5.2	7.6	4.6
1951	37.1	0.1	0.3	3.8	14.8	2.5	15.7	5.4	0.4	0.5	1.8	5.0	7.6	5.0
1952	37.3	0.1	0.3	3.6	14.9	2.5	15.5	5.8	0.4	0.5	2.0	4.9	7.4	4.9
1953	35.2	0.1	0.3	3.5	15.4	2.9	16.5	5.9	0.4	0.5	2.0	4.8	7.2	5.2
1954	33.8	0.1	0.3	3.4	15.7	3.6	17.3	6.1	0.4	0.6	2.2	4.7	7.0	4.8
1955	33.3	0.1	0.3	3.4	16.1	3.7	16.5	6.5	0.5	0.6	2.4	4.7	7.1	4.8
1956	33.1	0.1	0.3	3.5	16.7	3.7	15.7	6.4	0.5	0.6	2.6	4.8	7.3	4.8
1957	34.3	0.2	0.4	3.6	17.0	3.4	15.0	6.0	0.5	0.7	2.2	4.9	7.3	4.6
1958	34.6	0.2	0.4	3.6	17.4	3.2	14.7	5.5	0.5	0.7	2.0	5.1	7.4	4.8
1959	33.8	0.1	0.4	3.9	17.5	3.3	15.2	5.5	0.5	0.7	2.2	5.1	7.1	4.5
1960	32.5	0.2	0.3	3.8	17.9	3.0	15.4	5.8	0.6	0.8	2.5	5.2	7.2	4.7
1961	32.1	0.3	0.3	3.4	18.0	3.3	15.4	6.0	0.6	0.8	2.7	5.3	7.1	4.8
1962	31.5	0.3	0.3	3.2	18.3	3.3	15.4	6.0	0.7	0.9	3.0	5.4	6.9	4.8
1963	30.6	0.3	0.3	3.5	18.5	2.9	15.4	6.2	0.7	1.0	3.0	5.6	7.1	5.0
1964	30.5	0.3	0.3	3.6	18.5	2.7	15.6	6.1	0.7	1.0	3.2	5.7	6.9	4.9
1965	29.4	0.3	0.3	3.7	18.7	2.7	15.8	6.1	0.8	1.0	3.3	5.9	7.1	5.0
1966	28.9	0.3	0.3	3.4	18.9	3.0	16.1	6.2	0.8	1.0	3.3	6.0	7.0	4.9
1967	29.1	0.3	0.3	3.3	18.8	3.5	15.6	6.0	0.9	1.1	3.2	6.1	7.0	4.9

(continues)

Source: Banco de la Republica, Cuentas Nacionales, 1969.

Table 1.1 (continued) Sectoral Origin of Gross Domestic Product, 1968–1988 (percentages)

Years	Agriculture, Livestock, Fishing & Hunting	Mining	Manufacturing	Processed Coffee	Rest of Manufacturing	Electricity, Gas & Water	Construction	Commerce, Restaurants & Hotels	Transportation, Warehousing & Communications	Banking, Insurance & Services to Business	Housing Rents	Personal Services Except Restaurants	Household Services	Government Services
1968	26.8	2.6	21.3	3.9	17.4	0.7	3.7	12.2	7.3	5.6	8.4	3.7	0.9	6.8
1969	26.1	2.8	21.5	3.7	17.7	0.7	3.7	12.5	7.5	5.7	8.2	3.7	0.8	6.7
1970	25.5	2.7	21.5	3.3	18.2	0.7	3.5	12.5	7.8	6.4	8.0	3.7	0.8	6.9
1971	24.1	2.5	21.9	3.2	18.7	0.8	3.4	12.9	7.8	6.8	7.8	3.9	0.8	7.3
1972	24.1	2.5	22.5	3.0	19.5	0.8	3.3	12.9	7.9	6.5	7.4	3.9	0.8	7.4
1973	23.1	2.4	22.8	2.9	20.0	0.9	3.7	13.1	8.3	6.3	7.2	4.0	0.7	7.3
1974	23.0	1.7	23.4	2.8	20.6	0.9	3.8	13.2	8.5	6.5	7.1	4.1	0.7	7.1
1975	23.7	1.7	23.1	3.1	19.9	0.9	3.3	13.2	8.4	6.7	7.1	4.2	0.7	6.9
1976	23.4	1.6	23.0	2.5	20.5	0.9	3.5	13.2	8.5	6.6	7.0	4.3	0.7	7.2
1977	23.2	1.3	22.5	2.0	20.5	0.9	3.6	13.2	8.9	6.8	7.0	4.4	0.7	7.4
1978	23.3	1.2	22.9	3.0	20.0	0.9	3.2	13.1	9.2	6.9	6.9	4.4	0.7	7.3
1979	23.2	1.1	23.1	3.4	19.7	1.0	3.1	13.0	9.4	6.9	6.8	4.4	0.6	7.4
1980	22.8	1.3	22.5	3.4	19.2	1.0	3.4	12.8	9.4	7.3	6.8	4.3	0.6	7.8
1981	23.0	1.3	21.4	2.8	18.5	1.0	3.5	12.7	9.5	7.7	6.9	4.3	0.6	8.1
1982	22.3	1.3	20.9	2.8	19.1	1.0	3.6	12.7	9.9	7.9	7.0	4.4	0.6	8.2
1983	22.5	1.5	20.7	2.8	17.9	1.0	4.0	12.4	9.6	8.1	7.2	4.4	0.6	7.9
1984	22.2	1.7	21.3	3.0	18.3	1.0	4.2	12.3	9.6	7.2	7.2	4.3	0.6	8.3
1985	21.9	2.3	21.3	2.9	18.4	1.0	4.4	12.2	9.4	7.0	7.2	4.2	0.6	8.4
1986	21.5	3.6	21.3	3.1	18.2	1.0	4.3	11.9	9.0	7.0	7.1	4.1	0.6	8.5
1987	21.6	4.2	21.5	2.8	18.7	1.1	3.7	11.8	8.8	7.0	7.0	4.1	0.6	8.6
1988	21.4	4.2	21.1	2.3	18.8	1.0	3.9	11.9	8.7	7.3	7.0	4.1	0.6	8.9

Source: Departamento Administrativo Nacional de Estadística (DANE).

as real gasoline prices were raised, petroleum exploration was renewed, several large new fields were found and exploited, and exploitations of new large coal and ferronickel deposits were developed by large joint ventures between the government and foreign companies throughout the decade.

Although financial services, public utilities, and construction were the fastest growing sectors in the 1960s, manufacturing was the biggest contributor to overall growth. Public utilities enjoyed high growth rates in the first half of the 1970s, during which time personal services, transportation and communications, and manufacturing also had high growth rates. The second half of the 1970s witnessed fast growing financial, government services, and transportation sectors.

The government sector in Colombia is relatively small, at least in part because the government has never been very involved in the production of goods and services beyond public utilities. However, after structural changes were introduced during the Lleras Restrepo administration (1966–1970), government increased its role in the economy, and its annual growth from 1967 to 1988 exceeded that of GDP. This meant that during that period the relative size of the sector increased by about 25 percent.

During the 1980s, sectoral growth performance differed from that in the past. Large investments in mining made it the leading sector during the decade, followed by construction, public utilities, and government services. Simultaneously, the sectors in which private activity traditionally dominates—agriculture, commerce, finance, and manufacturing—fared badly. Noncoffee manufacturing experienced stagnation for four years (1980–1983), and the financial sector had a crisis that led to several major bankruptcies until it recovered in the late 1980s.

Based on the available data, then, it is clear that the economy's productive structure has changed a great deal in the post–World War II period. As shown in Table 1.1, the primary sectors of agriculture and mining have accounted for a declining share of GDP. Mining recovered in the 1980s, but agriculture continued its slow secular decline. In 1950, agriculture's share of GDP was 1.5 times higher than manufacturing's, but by 1974 their shares were similar. As noted above, manufacturing's share increased steadily from 1950 to 1974, but it has not been a leading sector since then. From 1975 on, the main growth sectors were urbancentric and related to services, including government and financial services, transportation, communications, and public utilities. The increases in their combined GDP share account for virtually all the decline in the primary sectors' shares through 1984. It must be noted, however, that during the 1980s the growth of the mining sector had an impact on the economy, first through the development of the mines and their transportation systems, and since 1985 because of increased production. Nevertheless, given the sector's small size, it may be argued that its growth has not greatly affected the economy's overall productive structure. On the other hand, the 3 percent increase in the sector's GDP share over a five year period (more than tripling the sector's share) is at least as large as any structural change that has taken place since 1950 in Colombia.

A particularly important structural change in Colombia's economy involves the substantial decline of GDP exported. As noted above, fifty years ago the GDP's export share was larger than expected, according to international comparisons with similar countries. Exports of goods and services in the late 1930s accounted for 24 percent of GDP, but that proportion declined continuously until the early 1980s when it reached 14 percent (Ocampo, 1991: 218).[17] Identifying the causes behind this decline is of great importance because the recent drastic policy changes have been predicated on the belief that the decline is an indication of an increasingly closed economy and a factor to which the decline in the growth rate during the 1980s is linked (see below).

Policies and Performance

Economic Stability, Economic Policy, and the Political System

During the last fifty years economic policies in Colombia have been mostly reactive, responding to changes in the global economy, to pressures from internal economic change, and to social clamor for increased equality in sharing the benefits of growth. Hence, the social and economic policies of this period can be characterized as adaptive. They were also applied gradually to avoid traumatic policy and power structure changes. Still, the changes enhanced the role of the state as it assumed new functions, increased the complexity of policy making, and added to the sophistication of economic policymakers. However, the main policy formulation centers, particularly the Central Bank and the National Planning Department, have been relatively removed from political concerns, and their cautious policy changes have been corrected or adapted when the results have not been satisfactory. Since the mid-1960s, highly trained technocrats in high policy making positions have had significant input in policy formulation, implementation, and change.

It must be remembered, though, that these skilled technocrats have served under various governments, each arriving in power with its own development platform or some ideas about long-term policies necessary to achieve economic development and/or social goals. However, meeting these goals depends largely on the policy leeway allowed by management of the foreign and fiscal sectors. And in Colombia's case there has been a clear dilemma between the long-term need for reform and the short-term need for stability. Very frequently governments have had to devote the bulk of their efforts to maintaining a minimum degree of stability, but are then accused of disregarding long-term goals and election campaign promises.

An example of this can be seen in Colombia's experience with inflation. Cautious policies have not prevented occasional spurts in the inflation rate and have not been able to reduce inflation once it has increased.[18] But they have succeeded in maintaining inflation plateaus, and in preventing long periods of acceleration and episodes of hyperinflation. The example of how economic policy has been affected by politics is provided by García-García (1991), who shows that historically, the inflation rate has been closely related to changes in the monetary base, which have depended more on government budget deficits than on changes in foreign exchange reserves. Colombia's budget deficits, despite relatively low levels (see Table 1.2) have therefore been the main long-term culprit in generating inflation because the government often increases money supply to meet budget shortfalls. During export booms, however, the primary contributor to a larger money supply has been foreign exchange reserve increases.

Since high inflation is associated with changes in the monetary base, it can be argued that inflation in Colombia has been mainly a monetary phenomenon. However, the budget composition and financing have been highly influenced by political institutions (Urrutia, 1991) so that inflation has implicitly had important institutional roots as well.[19]

These roots are evident in Colombia's power structure. Urrutia (1991), in a recent interesting work, argues that Colombia did not develop a populist system that has at various times been adopted by other Latin American countries (with disastrous results). Instead, a relatively sophisticated clientelistic system emerged because of a combination of factors. Colombia traditionally has had two strong political parties that never had a strong national organization. They have been a federation-like organization of local political bosses interested in maximizing narrow local and personal goals. After independence these parties played an important role as the strongest consolidating force in a country geographically divided into isolated regions. In the traditional clientelistic system that prevailed while Colombia was a mostly rural society, wealthy rural families extended favors and intermediated between the poor peasants and a weak government that provided very few services in exchange for the peasants' votes. As Colombia urbanized and government functions were extended and diversified, the system changed as individuals controlling shares of the government budget were able to build clientelistic political bases without having to own land or be rich. This allowed the development of a "political class quite distinct from the entrepreneurial class and from the labor unions. The business of this class is to get elected, and politics is the source of its income" (Urrutia 1991, 379). Urrutia points out that local bosses have two important concerns that have an impact on macroeconomic policies: they want to maximize their share of the government bounty, and they want to prevent high inflation rates that lower the purchasing power of most of their clients and destroy their political base.[20] Thus, the local clientelistic bosses support and have been satisfied with a system in which macroeconomic policies, designed and implemented by technocrats, provide long-term relative stability, but they fight for their shares of the budgetary and bureaucratic pie in Congress. One can therefore conclude that stability in Colombia's GDP growth rate and a reluctance to make drastic policy changes have resulted from the political system that developed in a clientelistic way rather than in a populist one.

Chief Economic Policies

While Colombia's political clientelism avoided populist excesses, polices still adapted to the needs of the times and changes in conventional economic interpretations of the development process.

In this section four subperiods are considered separately, each reflecting important changes in the domestic and external environments, as well as in policies followed by successive governments. The first period goes from the end of World War II to 1967. During this time the country experienced *la violencia,* made its first coherent attempts to cope with underdevelopment, and followed traditional import-substituting-industrialization (ISI) policies. The second period, from 1967 to 1974, was perhaps the Golden Age of Colombian development. Annual GDP growth averaged over 6 percent, the state became more modern and complex, and ISI policies were complemented

Table 1.2 Macroeconomic Indicators

Year	GDP Deflator % Change (1)	Wholesale Price Index Increase (1)	Consolidated Public Sector Deficit or Surplus as % of GDP (1)	Nontax Revenues from SEA as % of GDP (2)	Real Exchange Rate Index 1975=100 (1)	Real Exchange Instability Index (1)	Trade Balance (Millions U.S. $) (1)	Current Account Balance (Millions U.S. $) (1)	Current Account Balance as % of GDP (1)
1950			0.9		61		59	-14	-0.3
1951	10	8	-0.1		76		70	5	0.1
1952	2	-2	-1.4		79		89	29	0.7
1953	5	5	-1.1		74		84	15	0.4
1954	11	8	-0.2		69		35	-43	-0.8
1955	0	1	-1.2		68		-40	-125	-2.4
1956	8	7	-2.0		65		55	-12	-0.2
1957	17	26	-3.4		110		139	80	1.7
1958	13	16	-0.3		120		155	62	1.9
1959	7	10	0.0		109		125	61	1.6
1960	8	4	0.1		110		-1	-84	-2.1
1961	8	7	-1.7		94		-54	-142	-3.1
1962	7	2	-4.2		94		-61	-170	-3.4
1963	23	27	-1.9	0.0	98	8	-12	-137	-2.8
1964	16	17	-2.2	0.0	84	15	61	-131	-2.2
1965	7	8	-3.1	0.0	92	15	168	-13	-0.2
1966	12	18	-0.5	0.0	99	23	-105	-290	-5.3
1967	13	7	-2.1	0.0	100	5	94	-89	-1.5
1968	11	6	-0.7	-0.6	109	9	-6	-188	-3.2
1969	6	7	-2.0	-0.3	113	4	24	-213	-3.3
1970	12	7	-2.2	-0.3	111	3	-20	-291	-4.0
1971	11	12	-3.0	-0.1	110	2	-150	-456	-5.8
1972	13	18	-3.0	-0.2	102	5	116	-201	-2.3
1973	20	28	-2.8	0.0	103	4	260	-77	-0.7
1974	25	36	-3.1	0.3	101	5	-47	-405	-3.3
1975	23	25	-3.2	0.3	100	3	297	-127	-1.0
1976	23	23	-0.7	0.2	94	4	560	189	1.2
1977	29	27	-1.8	0.3	78	11	705	390	2.0
1978	17	18	-0.1	0.3	77	3	667	330	1.4
1979	24	28	-1.5	1.3	74	4	537	512	1.8
1980	28	24	-1.9	1.3	74	2	13	104	0.3
1981	23	24	-5.8	2.4	71	2	-1,333	-1,722	-4.7
1982	25	26	-8.7	2.7	68	5	-2,076	-2,885	-7.4
1983	20	22	-6.4	1.7	72	4	-1,371	-2,826	-7.3
1984	21	18	-7.4	0.1	78	11	-404	-2,088	-5.5
1985	26	25	-4.2	0.0	87	12	109	-1,586	-4.5
1986	28	22	-1.6	0.0	99	10	2,016	663	1.9
1987									
1988									
1989									

Notes: (A) Average of monthly data; (B) Debt service as a percentage of total exports.
Sources: (1) Jorge García-García, 1991; (2) Jorge García-García and Lea Guterman, 1988; (3) Santiago Herrera, 1990; (4) Sergio Clavijo, 1990.

Table 1.2 (continued) Macroeconomic Indicators

Year	Net International Reserves (Millions U.S. $) (1)	Profitability of Exporting Index (1)	Black Market Foreign Exchange Premium (%) (A) (3)	Total External Debt (1)	Debt Service Ratio (B) (1)	External Public Debt as % of GDP (1)	Gross Capital Formation as % of GDP (1)	Domestic Savings as % of GDP (1)	Total Factor 1950=100 (4)
1950	92	45					17	17	100.0
1951	141	55					15	15	96.7
1952	177	57					15	16	103.6
1953	187	60					15	16	107.4
1954	189	72					17	17	109.4
1955	102	61					18	16	109.5
1956	66	62					18	17	112.0
1957	210	78					20	20	112.7
1958	215	99					19	20	115.0
1959	264	85					19	20	120.7
1960	62	82					21	19	122.3
1961	-34	78					21	18	124.3
1962	-80	74					19	17	127.6
1963	-112	78					18	15	128.8
1964	-122	78					18	15	133.8
1965	-62	76					18	17	132.1
1966	-95	65					21	16	133.9
1967	-36	73		1,122	22	14.7	18	17	132.5
1968	35	75		1,263	23	16.6	21	18	135.7
1969	97	73		1,433	22	17.7	20	17	139.1
1970	152	89	12.0	1,776	21	18.3	20	16	142.4
1971	170	81	12.7	2,069	26	18.8	19	13	144.9
1972	345	86	6.2	2,510	24	19.9	18	16	151.0
1973	516	98	6.4	2,784	22	19.7	18	18	156.5
1974	430	103	5.4	3,258	24	17.9	21	19	163.1
1975	547	100	-1.5	3,572	17	18.9	17	17	165.9
1976	1,166	119	-1.4	3,746	15	16.7	18	19	169.4
1977	1,830	132	-5.6	3,832	12	14.3	19	22	169.9
1978	2,482	110	-6.8	4,060	13	12.5	18	20	176.1
1979	4,106	97	-9.0	5,303	17	12.4	18	20	176.1
1980	5,416	103	-6.2	6,457	14	12.5	19	20	178.0
1981	5,630	86	-4.7	8,514	22	15.5	21	17	175.3
1982	4,891	81	-0.7	10,269	29	17.5	20	15	169.0
1983	3,079	80	11.2	11,458	37	20.3	20	15	161.9
1984	1,796	86	13.9	12,350	36	23.1	19	16	161.2
1985	2,067	90	2.3	14,063	41	30.5	19	17	161.7
1986	3,478	115	-0.4	14,987	35	34.7	18	22	165.1
1987			0.4	15,651					165.8
1988			1.1						164.6
1989			1.1						164.9

by export-promoting ones that produced very satisfactory results. The third period, from 1975 to 1982, began with an international recession but continued with coffee, marijuana, and cocaine export booms. Capital markets were liberalized significantly, speculation in the economy increased, and government spending grew substantially as an externally financed massive infrastructure program was implemented. This process led to a recession, which although not as deep as that of the rest of Latin America and the Caribbean, thwarted growth. The fourth period began in 1982 and continues into the 1990s. It has been one of slow growth, domestic and external adjustment, reforms, and attempts to revive economic growth.

Traditional economic policies, 1945–1967. The first part of this period was characterized by la violencia, high international coffee prices, rapid manufacturing growth, and infrastructural development. The government had become keenly aware of the need for transportation and communications networks, as well as increased coverage of electricity, potable water, sewer, education, and health systems. At the same time, economic growth became a policy goal, and economic performance was relatively satisfactory as long as international coffee prices remained high. However, after a coffee boom that began in 1953, coffee prices began to fall in 1956, remaining low during the last ten years of the subperiod. Surprisingly, while the violence had measurable negative effects on growth, particularly in the coffee growing regions of western Colombia (Ocampo, 1991: 224), overall growth remained relatively high.

Fluctuations in international coffee prices have influenced Colombia's external policies since the early twentieth century. Beginning in the 1910s and until the late 1970s, coffee accounted for over 50 percent of Colombia's merchandise exports. This proportion increased during the first half of the century, and peaked at 78.7 percent between 1950 and 1954 (Ocampo, 1991: 220). Understandably, one of the chief policy problems was to cope with coffee price fluctuations. Colombia learned to do so over time and through several creative institutional developments. For example, the Coffee Growers Federation, formed in 1927, developed into a complex organization that at first administered certain relevant taxes, particularly those on the coffee fund established in 1940 to provide a mechanism to smooth out the price fluctuations. Although a private institution, the Federation played an important role in formulating and implementing economic policy.[21]

Coffee prices were not the only policy challenge in the early postwar period. Until March 1967, Colombia had a system of fixed and multiple exchange rates with exchange controls. Foreign exchange controls were established in September 1931 in response to a run on the peso during the Great Depression. These were enforced until 1991, with some exceptions granted for capital transactions during 1948 to 1967, when a freely fluctuating exchange rate applied to them (Ocampo, 1991: 233). The coffee price fluctuations, fixed exchange rates, and fiscal deficits financed by monetary expansion all resulted in periodic large devaluations (particularly when export earnings declined), in tariff increases, and in the development of a complex system of nontariff barriers to control demand for foreign exchange. The barriers included lists of prohibited imports and those requiring a license as well as the requirement to deposit, upon an import request, cash amounts proportional to import value in Colombia's Central Bank.

Traditional ISI policies had been pursued since the 1930s but the less difficult stages of ISI had been completed by the late 1960s. At that time continued pursuit of ISI on a national basis, to include increasingly sophisticated and capital intensive products, did not appear to be a potential motor for much growth. Indeed, during the mid-1960s attempts to extend the ISI process in the intermediate goods sector created several capital intensive and inefficient plants, particularly in the petrochemical industry (Berry and Thoumi, 1977).

Tariff protection for manufacturing, a standard feature of ISI, was complemented by credit policies. During the first twenty-five post–World War II years, Colombia's capital market was rather segmented, as conventional wisdom of the time legitimized capital market segmentation by the government in order to funnel credit to the "directly productive sectors," mainly industry. This sector benefited from long-term credit from external institutions and from the Banco de la República (the Central Bank). At this time there was great confidence in the government's ability to channel funds to specific sectors, and several funds and development finance corporations were created to do just that. However, because these institutions acted almost exclusively as channels that supplied long-term credit at nominal interest rates that were frequently below inflation, they did not contribute to increased savings.

Inflation was another policy challenge, one that has tarnished Colombia's overall macroeconomic management success. Table 1.2 shows the wholesale price index and the GDP deflator for 1950 to 1986, during which period the annual rate of inflation averaged 14 percent. However, the average inflation rate during 1950 to 1967 was relatively low at 11 percent. Unfortunately, it was highly variable, from as low as zero in 1955 to as high as 23 percent in 1963, reflecting the macroeconomic instability that characterized the period.

Certain social issues also demanded the attention of economic policymakers. For example, during la violencia most of the fighting took place in rural areas and was frequently related to the peasants' aspirations to obtain land—a factor that convinced the first National Front government, headed by Alberto Lleras Camargo (1958–1962),[22] of the need to implement an agrarian reform program. This need gained urgency after the triumph of the Cuban Revolution, and was supported externally by the Alliance for Progress. After a very heated internal debate and strong opposition, the Agrarian Reform Law was approved in December 1961. The law intended to redistribute land, either owned or purchased by the state, to peasant families, to provide them with technical assistance, and to build infrastructure (irrigation, marketing, etc.) specifically for the agrarian sector. The law also provided for compensation in cases of expropriation. Given the strong negative sentiment among some landowning groups and the shortage of resources, the actual land reform program focused more on opening up the agricultural frontier than on breaking up the old latifundia. It is thus not surprising that relatively few landless peasant families benefited from land reform, and that it covered only a small fraction of the country's arable land.[23]

Agrarian reform and other social issues led to an assumption that the state should have greater functions, which in turn produced a debate about national planning that resulted in the establishment of a National Planning Office and the formulation in 1960 of a comprehensive ten-year development plan that followed a traditional UN Economic Commission for Latin America and the Caribbean (ECLAC) format. One of the plan's main goals was to try to coordinate government spending on infrastructure. Although the government budget was assembled by Congress, fiscal policy was quite conservative and, as shown in Table 1.2, budget deficits were kept below 2 percent of GDP—except during years of external sector difficulties. Indeed, during 1950 through 1986 the combined public sector had only three years in which it did not run a deficit, and all three were during 1945–1967.

The primary macroeconomic policy management problems of this period were related to periodic devaluations and episodes of foreign sector crisis confronting Colombia. Several frustrating devaluation experiences, accompanied by major increases in staple goods prices and wages, included a November 1962 devaluation that was announced and extensively debated in Congress before it was implemented. This caused preemptive peso and salary increases that essentially nullified the devaluation's effects. After that and an ill-conceived liberalization scheme involving a fixed exchange rate in 1965 and 1966 that left the country's net external reserves in the red (Díaz-Alejandro, 1976: 190–206), Colombia was ready for a change. At the same time Colombia's social situation called for rapid growth, given the acceleration of population growth, rising expectations, and the wide income disparities among social groups. So, after Carlos Lleras Restrepo was inaugurated president in August 1966, Colombian authorities became convinced that a systemic change was in order.

Reform and rapid growth, 1967–1974. Carlos Lleras Restrepo, a well-known statesman interested and versed in economics, had extensive experience as minister and politician. He was inaugurated president in August 1966, following Guillermo L. Valencia (1962–1966), a traditional man of letters who had shown no special interest in economic matters. The Lleras administration soon became noted for the significant improvement it effected in the quality of economic management. The legacies of his government are notable. First and foremost was the switch to a crawling peg exchange rate, from the previous fixed peg that led to traumatic devaluations. This and other steps (see below) contributed to the subsequent boom of "minor exports" (i.e., exports other than coffee, bananas, sugar, or petroleum), which played an important role in moving Colombia onto a stable growth path. A second achievement was a major effort to increase public sector revenues. This allowed for a more vigorous investment policy and expanded expenditures on education and other social programs. Urban unemployment fell during the Lleras years, although it is not certain whether this resulted from more rapid economic growth. The government did not focus specifically on income redistribution as a policy goal, but its considerable emphasis on agricultural development, its push on agrarian reform, and its promotion of peasant associations to counter the political weight of traditional landowners could be analyzed in this light.[24] The beginnings of a discrete population policy may also be attributed to these years (McGreevey, 1980: 418). Third, Lleras's goals required the strengthening of such institutions as the Industrial Finance Institute (IFI) and the land reform institute (INCORA), as well as the creation of new ones such as PROEXPO, an export promotion fund. This institution-building process, supported by conventional wisdom and bilateral and multilateral aid and finance agencies, was useful in implementing the government's policies. However, this institutional proliferation has taken a toll in the long run as subsequent governments either found some of them inadequate relative to their goals or became stale bureaucracies that were ideal prey for the clientelistic ambitions of many politicians. Since more recent administrations have lacked either the will or the power to modify or eliminate some of the institutional deadwood, the institution building of the 1960s contributed to the fiscal rigidity that became particularly important in the 1980s.

As noted above, Colombia changed its foreign exchange system on 22 March 1967. Decree 444 established a crawling peg exchange rate, tightened foreign exchange controls, and put in place an export promotion system that included export subsidies and subsidized export credit. These measures were implemented after an acrimonious argument with the IMF, which opposed them, that was used by the government to demonstrate its independence from the multilateral lending agencies and to rally nationalistic feelings in support of the changes.

The crawling peg exchange rate helped maintain a more stable real exchange rate than in the past and encouraged exports, while also helping to end sizable devaluations. Other export promoting steps were taken, including the creation of PROEXPO, an institution designed to help find external markets and finance export industries, and the establishment of subsidies for minor exports, which had been growing for a decade or so, but from a very low base. Between 1967 and 1974 current dollar exports other than coffee and petroleum (which in any case ceased to be a net export in the early 1970s) rose by nearly sevenfold, or about 30 percent per year, from 28 percent of all exports (excluding petroleum) to a peak of 56 percent in 1974. Total current dollar exports rose by over threefold in this period, or 18 percent per year. The relative abundance of foreign exchange was such that when Colombia shifted from an oil exporter to a minor importer just as OPEC increased prices, the effects were not dramatic.

It should be noted that the 1967 policy shift did not eliminate protection for industries that had developed under ISI policies, but rather established a policy mix in which domestic market protection continued with some biases against exports weakened or compensated for.

Lleras realized he needed to strengthen the presidency to implement his reform agenda, so after cajoling Congress and even threatening to resign, he obtained constitutional and other reforms that allowed the executive to increase its control over economic policy. In particular, the Monetary Board's and the National Planning Department's powers were enhanced, and budget-making functions were transferred from Congress to the latter, which is an office in the executive branch. Lleras tried to make other changes, particularly regarding tax reform, but opposition in Congress prevented him from doing so.

During the Lleras administration inflation was kept low, the wholesale price index increased at 7 percent annually, and the consumer price index rose at a slightly higher pace. The government budget deficit was also kept at about 2 percent of GDP or lower.

During the administration's last two years the expansion of minor exports was already taking place and constraints related to the foreign sector were loosening, facts that allowed for a slow and selective decline in tariff and nontariff barriers. By the end of Lleras's term economic growth had resumed, state finances and the foreign sector were in good shape, inflation was under control, and it seemed a good foundation for long-term growth had been established.

Lleras was followed in 1970 by Misael Pastrana, a member of the Conservative party and the last National Front president. His margin of victory was very narrow. Gustavo Rojas Pinilla, the populist general who led the 1953 military coup, almost pulled off an upset in the midst of strong accusations of fraud.[25]

Pastrana's major policy innovation was a focus on urban housing as a motor of job creation and economic growth. The basic ideas behind these policies had been stated a few years back by Lauchlin Currie (1965 and 1966), who argued the only way to increase rural incomes was to raise rural labor productivity, which required decreasing the rural population, a goal that could be achieved only by generating enough urban employment to attract unskilled rural migrants. The labor-intensive urban housing program was a prime candidate for success in this framework. This strategy was unique inasmuch as it argued that rapid rural-urban migration was desirable at a time when conventional wisdom advocated measures to curtail that flow.[26]

The development strategy also made sense politically since most of the support for Rojas Pinilla had come from the largest cities, and the government feared an urban backlash. The new emphasis on urban housing and the political concerns about the urban electorate weakened agrarian reform efforts. After all, Colombia was now a mostly urban country.

The shift of resources toward construction required changes and innovations in the financing system. Thus, private savings and loan institutions were created and given the right to index deposits and loans. These institutions issued financial assets of "constant purchasing power" (UPAC) and were pioneers in establishing flexible and positive real interest rates. Incidentally, the UPAC system represented a move toward liberalizing capital markets, even though it was not created with that goal in mind (Jaramillo, 1982). The UPAC system allowed the construction sector to finally compete for funds with the privileged industrial sector, which impacted the latter negatively. The system also constituted an important increase in the degree of indexation in the economy that changes in the 1967 foreign exchange system encouraged, which complicated inflation control.

Since the Pastrana government did not come to power with this new development strategy in mind, and it took time and political maneuvering to establish a plan of action, these changes became effective only in 1972. The program generated heated policy debates about promoting rural-urban migration, the potential instability of a growth process relying on construction as a leading sector, and the impact of the financial changes on interest rates and the financing of other economic sectors.[27] The program also intensified regional rivalries as most UPAC loans were concentrated in Bogotá (Thoumi, 1983).

Not surprisingly, construction expanded for the last two years of Pastrana's term, as did minor exports. Pastrana's administration was aided by an international boom in primary product prices and high OECD growth, resulting in high and stable GDP growth during his presidency, averaging 6.5 percent for 1971–1974.

However, while income grew satisfactorily during the period, there were signs of trouble ahead. The consolidated public sector deficits that had exceeded 2.2 percent of GDP in only three years since 1950, increased to about 3 percent of GDP each year between 1970–1975, when current central government revenues declined and income and wealth taxes as a percentage of GDP slipped. An important factor in the growing deficit was decreased attention to, and efficiency in, tax collection.

As a corollary to the fiscal deficits, the inflation rate increased from 12 to 20 percent, a level that became seemingly permanent. Since 1973, except for 1978, the annual rate of inflation has always exceeded 20 percent. This acceleration of inflation, combined with the funds earned from the infant illegal drug industry, and strong restrictions on commercial bank operations, contributed to the creation of an "extra-bank" credit market. This market was by no means limited to traditional small-scale operations associated in all developing countries with the informal capital market (small moneylenders, etc.). Rather, large amounts of money passed through it, and both lenders and borrowers included large-scale operators (Berry and Thoumi, 1986: 149). One reason is that inflation led, as is normally the case, to some very negative real interest rates in the official banking sector before corrective steps were taken a few years later. Such rates were unattractive to lenders, and many borrowers who could not satisfy their credit needs in the official market were willing to pay high nominal rates corresponding to positive real rates during these rapid growth years.

Foreign sector booms and speculation, 1975–1982. The first post–National Front government, headed by Alfonso López Michelsen, inherited a booming economy and rising international reserves, but also an unacceptable inflation rate, from the Pastrana administration. It took office with a stated goal of tackling the chronic problem of unequal income distribution and associated severe poverty and malnutrition; its plan of action had been put together by a group of economists working as a team for several months.[28] Urban construction was de-emphasized, and the UPAC's real return was allowed to become somewhat negative. The first integrated rural development program to assist small farmers, as well as food and nutrition programs (PAN), were established. More generally, government spending on social services increased, particularly in rural areas and in providing minimum care and nutrition levels to rural and urban children.

In addition to increased spending, major tax reforms were undertaken in 1974 and 1975, following the general guidelines of reforms proposed in 1969 by Richard Musgrave in a report commissioned by Carlos Lleras (Musgrave and Gillis, 1971). Lleras liked the proposals, but had not succeeded in mustering enough political support for implementation. The reforms were designed to increase the overall income tax burden, to eliminate many loopholes, and to make the tax system more progressive.[29] Since income and net wealth tax evasion was widespread,[30] the main goal of tax reform was to increase income tax collections, and other goals were sacrificed to it. Income taxes increased and a minimum presumed tax as a percentage of total net wealth was established. The plan included an amnesty for those who had hidden assets to avoid taxes, and forgave the interest owed on unpaid income taxes. These measures contributed to immediate tax collection increases, but set a bad precedent for further tax amnesties under successive administrations.

Amnesties discouraged tax honesty as they not only eliminated the threat of penalties, but rewarded those who withheld income taxes and then paid them with depreciated currency. Furthermore, the reform did not account for inflation in calculating capital gains, nor did it take measures to prevent income tax bracket creep.[31] The reform also allowed asset revaluation of up to only 8 percent per annum, regardless of possibly higher inflation levels. Thus, these tax reforms carried an important implicit inflation tax and the seeds of future tax collection problems. Some of these characteristics were modified in further reforms in 1977, 1979, and 1983 that increased the inflation adjustment and eliminated the creeping tax bracket (Perry and Cárdenas, 1986: 41–42).

A second important policy measure was the liberalization of capital markets, effecting significant structural changes. This policy shift has been the subject of substantial debate in Colombia, and some authors (Kalmanovitz, 1988, chap. 8) have argued that it constituted a sell-out to the neoliberal ideology. However, as explained by Ortega (1982: 27–29), financial reform was a by-product of external sector success. In the early 1970s the only source of long-term credit was the Central Bank development credit lines. Institutional savings were very low, and financial institutions were not promoting savings. Up to this time, investment had therefore been financed with external credit without creating unduly inflationary pressures. However, as exports increased it was not possible to continue financing investment in this manner without either revaluing the peso or adding to inflation.[32] Another rationale behind liberalization was that the existing capital market produced an inefficient allocation of resources because interest rates for savers and portfolios of financial institutions were controlled.[33] Under the plan, interest rates on most financial assets were freed except for the imposition of a ceiling at about 5 percent above the "expected" inflation rate. Simultaneously, most of the existing portfolio constraints on bank lending were relaxed.

The policies of the López government met with varying degrees of success, some not accomplishing what they set out to do because of structural problems and/or because of external events.

The tax reform, hailed by international academics (Gillis and McLure, 1978), allowed the government to increase revenues in the short run, but its effectiveness declined sharply after 1976. With inflation remaining in the 20 to 30 percent range, the minimum income-to-wealth-ratio provision lost its bite because assets could not be revalued by more than 8 percent per year and cadastral assessments lagged, particularly in rural areas where the minimum income measure was more relevant. In addition, a couple of strikes by Ministry of Finance personnel led to bitter confrontations between their union and the government, which probably weakened tax collectors' morale and contributed to a growing inefficiency within the ministry (Berry and Thoumi, 1986; Perry and Cárdenas, 1986). Finally, higher income taxes induced taxpayers to search for legal and illegal ways to avoid taxes, a practice morally palatable at this time when the drug and other underground economic sectors began to boom. So, while tax reform succeeded in restoring the share of income and net-worth taxes in GDP, the importance of these direct taxes began to decline in 1976, and by 1981 they had reached a level of only 2.7 percent of GDP. Still, the fiscal deficit was kept modest under López because expenditures were held below what the government had planned on, and coffee taxes fortuitously rose.[34]

The capital market liberalization also belied government hopes, failing to produce a more productive allocation of resources. With inflation high, liberalization resulted in nominal interest rates of 30 percent and higher. At such levels investment in capital equipment is greatly discouraged, whether real interest rates are somewhat positive or somewhat negative, because cash flow becomes a substantial constraint. Furthermore, since capital market liberalization reduced restrictions on consumer credit, and since income was growing in the wake of foreign sector booms, credit redirected towards consumer durable goods and away from capital goods.[35] These changes fostered development in the financial sector as new institutions and services sprouted.

The foreign sector boom influenced key economic policies of the López government. While the original relaxing of Colombia's chronic balance of payments difficulties and shortage of imports achieved during the late 1960s and early 1970s was primarily the result of booming business in non-coffee exports—due to a combination of rising exports and improving terms of trade—the really large foreign exchange surpluses in the late 1970s were the result of unusually high coffee prices. Large revenues from marijuana and cocaine exports also boosted reserves. ECLAC's terms of trade estimates, which had declined from 100 in 1970 to 81.6 in 1975, reached 130.7 by 1980.

The influx of foreign exchange from both legal and illegal sources kept pressure on the government to appreciate the peso in real terms and to accumulate reserves, both of which exacerbated inflation. Indeed, foreign exchange reserve accumulation during 1976–1980 contributed significantly to the monetary base expansion (García-García, 1991: 21). Avoiding exchange rate appreciation was difficult since, beginning in December 1974, black market rates were below official ones. The black market discount reached between 5 and 10 percent during 1977 through 1980. The government did choose to limit peso revaluation, and in doing so accumulated large reserves. The main purpose of preventing a revaluation was to avoid lowering protection for the stagnating, internationally traded sectors (mainly manufacturing). Besides, the foreign sector boom was viewed as only temporary, making it convenient to accumulate reserves for a rainy day.[36]

Due to the large foreign exchange reserves, the government could not avoid slowing the devaluation pace, which eventually amounted to an exchange rate appreciation after allowance for the faster inflation in Colombia than in most of her trading partners. So by 1982, the real exchange rate index (Table 1.2) had reached a low point of 68 percent of the 1975 level.

The López policies, combined with increasing domestic demand, depressed non-traditional exports, and 1975 marked the end of rapid expansion for non-coffee exports. From 1974 to 1977 they simply maintained their level in nominal dollar terms, and given price increases, probably fell by 20 to 30 percent in real terms.

Beginning in 1975, international reserves increased to unprecedented levels. In 1974 reserves were at 20.5 percent of annual imports of goods and services, and by 1979 they had reached 104.2 percent in spite of an almost doubling of imports. In absolute terms the increase in reserves was spectacular: at the end of 1968 (a year of still serious foreign exchange constraint) they stood at U.S. $35 million, while by 1979 they had reached U.S. $4.106 billion and U.S. $5.63 billion by 1981.

The ready availability of foreign exchange during the mid-1970s and the government's concern with inflation contributed to Colombia's cautious external debt management, which resulted in a much lower debt burden than that of the other large Latin American countries. The Inter-American Development Bank (1984: 21) estimates Colombia's debt-service ratio was 20.9 percent of exports in 1975, compared to 26.6 percent for the whole of Latin America. Among the seven largest countries, only Venezuela had a lower ratio. By 1978, the debt-service ratio for Latin America had risen to 42.2 percent while Colombia's had fallen to 15.3 percent, the lowest among the large countries.

Critics have argued that a better set of policies could have been applied. Among several proposals, perhaps the most serious ones were to tax coffee exports more heavily to accumulate reserves at a lower peso cost, and to force exporters to hold part of their dollar receipts in accounts abroad.

The López policies obviously met with mixed results. In fairness, however, one must acknowledge that at the end of López's term inflation had subsided significantly, despite high inflation in the previous year that had been exacerbated by unusually bad agricultural crops. Further, average GDP growth between 1974 and 1978 was about 5 percent and the build-up of reserves cushioned the downturn of the 1980s. Probably the greatest disappointment for many observers was the administration's inability to achieve its social objectives, partly due to spending constraints resulting from the high priority assigned to inflation control, and partly to only minimal success of the tax reforms.

Julio César Turbay, a traditional politician with a very strong clientelistic base, was inaugurated president in August 1978. He advocated more market-oriented policies. In his inauguration speech he announced he was not going to have a development plan, since there had been twelve plans in the previous twenty-six years, and none had been satisfactorily implemented. What Turbay did not recognize at the time was that, even if development plans in Colombia are not fully implemented, they do have valuable functions. For example, they provide an overview of different government goals and policies and allow analyses of consistency and complementarity across sectoral development programs. Publicizing plan components limits discretionary policies that benefit special interest groups, a particularly valuable function in a rent-seeking society like Colombia. And a plan provides useful general guidelines for the private sector, giving it some idea of what to expect from the government (Berry and Thoumi, 1986).

Eventually, the Turbay government realized the advantages of having a plan, and proceeded to formulate the National Integration Plan (PIN) (Departamento Nacional de Planeación, 1980). Its major goals were to increase the degree of regional autonomy and political decentralization, to develop the energy and mining sectors, and to minimize inefficiencies in social sector expenditures. To achieve these goals the government undertook a massive public investment program to develop mining resources (coal and ferronickel) and to improve roads and communications systems, which were supposed to promote a greater level of regional economic decentralization.[37]

Perhaps the most serious flaw in Turbay's policies was that they allowed for a sharp deterioration in the government's financial structure, as well as the financial and industrial sectors, and weakened the effectiveness of monetary policy. This left the country vulnerable to changes in international conditions and made a financial crisis all but inevitable. That risk was exacerbated by a concurrent growth of the underground economy and illegal drug exports that contributed to a speculation wave affecting the financial sector.

Beginning in 1979, as the Turbay government implemented its massive public works investment plan, consolidated public sector deficits began to grow, reaching by 1981 an unprecedented level of 5.8 percent of GDP and then 8.7 percent in 1982. As explained by

Wiesner, the growing deficits were financed by extensive borrowing on international markets, the same borrowing used to finance the large public construction program.[38] In the four-year period that began in 1979, the total external debt increased at an average annual rate of 22 percent to reach U.S. $9.421 billion in 1982, a level that was 221.8 percent of that in 1978. This rapid increase in external debt was, ironically, accompanied by a comparably fast accumulation of reserves. The yearend figures for 1978 and 1981 show that during this period the increase in international reserves amounted to 85.5 percent of the increase in total external debt. Wiesner blames the unprecedented external debt and coincidental trade account surplus on the political system, which was an insurmountable barrier to fiscal responsibility. He notes that pork-barrel practices became widespread during this time and that political clientelism became more extensive.

Fiscal deterioration was also caused by increased tax evasion. Early in 1979 tax laws were changed to take into account the effects of inflation on asset and income values, and the government granted another amnesty that increased the tax base and contributed to higher tax collections that year (Perry and Cárdenas, 1986: 149).

The growing fiscal deficits also prompted the central bank to capture resources through large open market operations in 1979 in order to keep inflation in check, leading to high real interest rates.[39] These in turn crowded out private sector borrowers, and induced large drops in private investment in 1981 and 1982, while public sector investment grew massively.

Despite higher tax collections in 1979, direct taxation in the early 1980s declined. As this decline in importance emerged, so did a serious increase in the vulnerability of fiscal revenues to external sector trade and financial developments. Transfers to the central government from a "special exchange account" (SEA) grew particularly after 1978, and by 1981 they were similar in magnitude to funds collected from income and wealth taxes. The SEA—a peculiar financing instrument—was a government account at the Central Bank set up during the late 1960s mainly to subsidize imports of gasoline to keep its price low.[40] The account was funded by the tax on coffee exports, interest obtained from foreign exchange reserves invested abroad, net profits from gold sales and purchases, taxes on profit remittances by transnational corporations, and profits on foreign exchange purchases and sales. The SEA was drawn down by losses in any of these areas, as well as interest paid on some dollar-denominated bonds issued by the Central Bank. For example, during the late 1960s and early 1970s, purchases of foreign exchange were effected at higher prices than the subsidized sales so these operations produced a loss (see Table 1.2). Any overall surplus in this account could be transferred to the central government.

During the 1970s, problems with the SEA account began to develop. First, during the coffee boom, revenue from the coffee export tax increased greatly. Second, subsidized sales of foreign exchange declined in importance and, from 1974 on, purchases and sales of foreign exchange produced net profits. Third, as international reserves grew and international interest rates rose, interest income on the reserves increased. Such success tempted the government, which began to develop a risky financial dependency on an account so thoroughly linked to international markets. The situation was even more dangerous because included in the account were the essentially paper profits on purchases and sales of foreign exchange. According to the accounting procedures used, if the Central Bank sold foreign exchange it made a profit equal to the difference between the sales price and the average purchase price of the reserves in stock at the moment of the sale. Thus, as the peso was being devalued along the creeping peg, there were always "profits" on the sale of reserves.[41] In 1980, the profits on these foreign exchange transactions represented 61.7 percent of SEA transfers to the central government, and 11.5 percent of current central government revenues, a rate that increased to 15.2 percent in 1981. These paper profits were roughly the equivalent of printing money since, unlike taxation or the sale of government bonds, they involved no withdrawal of purchasing power from the non-public sector.[42] Their inclusion as a source of fiscal revenue was misleading in the first place and their rising share of reported revenues tended to disguise the government's failure to increase withdrawals from the income stream at a time when expenditures were rising rather sharply.

Simultaneously, coffee export taxes declined as the coffee boom passed, as did direct taxes (mainly income and wealth taxes), and the government's dependency on "profits" from the purchase and sale of reserves increased.

The capital market liberalization that began in earnest under the López government continued under Turbay. However, by this time some unexpected negative effects were already in evidence. The development of new types of institutions and activities, in the context of Colombia's concentration of wealth and power, were part of an evolution towards oligopolistic money markets rather than perfectly competitive ones. The government did not understand the dangers of liberalizing interest rates and other controls without taking complementary measures to secure a high level of competition among financial institutions.[43] The financial reform created financial investment alternatives to stocks, whose real price had to decline in order to provide higher competitive yields (Sarmiento, 1985). However, built-in protection measures for the financial system's stability were either ineffective or non-existent. As a result, powerful financial conglomerates developed and began to use resources obtained at high interest rates to purchase equity interests in firms whose shares had lost value, thus engaging simultaneously in financial and productive activities. These groups succeeded in manipulating stock prices to their own benefit, hurting small investors.[44]

Monetary authorities reacted to external sector booms and higher inflation rates with measures designed to constrain private sector credit, such as increasing financial institutions' required deposits. However, these institutions reacted by creating mechanisms that became known as "financial innovations," which allowed them to avoid the official measures.[45]

Financial liberalization and foreign sector booms in the 1970s were first taken advantage of by some private firms, but they eventually resulted in weaker financial positions for those financial institutions and conglomerates, some of which attempted to survive through Ponzi finance schemes by which they continued borrowing at high interest rates just to pay the interest on their debt. This situation could not be sustained and, by the middle of 1982, some of the financial institutions and conglomerates began to default, causing a grave financial crisis. This phenomenon had diverse causes. In some cases, mismanagement and fraud played a role,[46] but there were other factors resulting from the lack of proper regulation, such as liquidity problems caused by the fact that deposits in many institutions were short-term while their loans were long-term. In addition, the proliferation of many small high-cost financial institutions was promoted by market liberalization, as was the growth of financial groups that made extensive loans to their own industries, many of which were used for the pyramidal purchase of existing firms. Delays in passing legislation to cope with the changing conditions, the lack of organization, and the relaxing of controls over the financial system contributed to the problem.[47] It can be said, then, that rapid growth in the financial sector during a late-1970s speculation wave made it extremely vulnerable to inevitable change in the macroeconomic environment and therefore to crisis.

During the 1970s the industrial sector's financial structure also weakened, making it vulnerable to the same changes in the external economic environment. The debt-to-equity ratio of many firms increased substantially, investment in fixed capital declined, the maturity structure of the sector's debt became shorter, and as inflation increased so did nominal interest rates, increasing cash flow pressures on the firms. These changes had multiple causes: increased competition from other sectors for financial resources; tax law incentives for firms to pay interest, which were deducted as costs, instead of dividends, which essentially taxed dividends twice, first as profits and then as dividends; and the climbing inflation rates that increased the difficulty of obtaining long-term loans.[48]

Early in this period of change, export revenues grew rapidly. Including an estimate of drug revenues, total current dollar revenues in 1980 were more than ten times the 1967 level, and their import purchasing power was probably about three to four times greater.[49] However, exports peaked in 1980, and the world recession caused a sharp 18 percent drop in 1981 that continued through 1983 when their level in current dollars was about three-quarters that of 1980. At the same time, imports of goods and services rose an average of 9.1 percent per year between 1967 and 1980, not counting the effects of contraband financed by illegal exports, and continued to grow through 1982 and remained relatively high in 1983—at about 11.3 percent above the 1980 level. Reserves accumulated during the late 1970s were deliberately drawn down in 1982 as part of a policy to keep the level of imports up and to keep inflation down while the government deficit soared.

Another important economic development during the López and Turbay administrations was the rapid growth of the underground economy associated with the development of the illegal drug industry. Since the mid-1970s there has been significant evidence of export overinvoicing, import underinvoicing, and other forms of laundering illegal foreign exchange (Morawetz, 1981). As noted above, since December 1974 the black market exchange rate had remained under the official one, and the glut of foreign exchange in the black market led the Central Bank in 1975 to relax requirements to prove that real exports of services had occurred before purchasing the foreign exchange supposedly generated by them. This was the so-called "sinister window" (the name in Spanish is less sinister than in English) through which the Bank could buy illegal foreign exchange.[50] By the early 1980s some authors (Craig, 1981) estimated that illegal drug exports rivaled coffee in importance. Gómez (1985) used a common method to estimate the increase in the underground economy based on changes in the cash-to-M1 ratio, which is attributed to the more frequent use of cash in illegal transactions. This study estimates that in 1985 the underground economy accounted for 8.7 percent more of the GDP than in the 1974 to 1976 base period. The underground economy growth cannot all be attributed to the illegal drug industry; however, the underground economy growth acceleration did coincide with the development of that industry.

Crisis, adjustment, and the search for renewed growth, 1982–1992. The Betancur government was inaugurated in August 1982 in the midst of very complex economic problems: a financial sector on the verge of crisis, a growing fiscal deficit with public sector revenues extremely dependent on the special exchange account and on the health of a weakening external sector, and a high inflation rate. The external sector's problems worsened a few months later after massive devaluations in Venezuela and Ecuador, two very good markets for Colombian manufactures. Simultaneously, the manufacturing sector was in the deepest recession since the 1930s, urban unemployment was rising, and the illegal underground economy had grown so much that it had to be recognized as a policy issue. On the positive side, while international reserves were falling, they were still high enough to give the government some policy leeway.

The economic issues raised by Betancur during his election campaign did not, however, focus on the economic problems mentioned above, except for unemployment and the need to moralize the country's economic activities. In the last weeks of the campaign, Betancur promised two key programs to improve social justice: a housing-without-down-payment system and a correspondence university program. While these programs had great popular appeal, it is difficult to see how they could significantly improve social justice. Resource constraints imposed by the fiscal situation would prevent a massive housing construction program, particularly one without down payments. Meanwhile, with unemployment among college graduates already high, a correspondence university program would only increase the supply of labor with high income and status expectations, fueling frustration among college graduates. Assuming these proposals were essentially election ploys, there was little other evidence that the Betancur government was prepared to deal with Colombia's difficult set of short-run economic problems, although it did seem to have a clear enough idea of the long-term reforms it wanted to achieve. President Betancur was unfortunate to come to power when short-term economic management was pivotal, and when the potential for social reform was more limited than at any other time in the last twenty years.

Still, Bentancur addressed the short-term crisis in a plan called "Desarrollo con Equidad" ("Development with Equity"), which was presented by the government in February 1983.[51] It proposed policies to restructure the financial sector, to control inflation and inflationary expectations, to use housing construction to promote growth, to stimulate demand for domestic products, to increase private sector financing, and to reduce both the fiscal and current account deficits. Most of these short-term policy goals were set in response to the critical condition of the economy. The plan also revealed long-term programs designed to support sustained growth in areas involving agriculture, transportation, capital goods, mining, oil, and exports.

Among the first tasks of the new administration was coping with a growing fiscal deficit, an increasingly weak and overexpanded financial sector, and a wave of bankruptcies. The government attempted to deal with the fiscal crisis by legislating a tax reform under an economic emergency statute that allowed it to pass laws without going through Congress.[52] However, the Supreme Court declared most fiscal reform measures unconstitutional, arguing that several technicalities of the statute had not been met, which forced the government to follow the normal channels and seek congressional approval for the reforms. The reform package included a reduction in taxes on income and net profits and an amnesty on interest charged on overdue taxes. Taxpayers were allowed to include on their 1982 tax statements any assets previously omitted and to exclude false liabilities previously included, without these changes being subject to penalty. These measures produced the by now familiar result: an immediate tax collection increase followed by declines as taxpayers waited for the next amnesty.

To eliminate the importance of the special exchange account as a source of government funds and to restrict its impact on monetary expansion (Ocampo and Perry, 1983), the administration restricted the transfer to the central government of funds generated by profits on sales and purchases of foreign exchange and by the return on reserves. These steps were complemented by a tighter rein on government spending that curtailed some investment programs.

The Betancur administration was quick to realize that the best way to deal with many of the country's problems was to increase the level of political participation and the depth of Colombian democracy. The government initiated a dialogue with guerrilla organizations with the intent to make them part of the political process. That led to an amnesty and ceasefire agreement with the FARC (Colombian Revolutionary Armed Forces) in 1984. As part of the agreement, the government provided funds to help guerrillas rejoin the mainstream political society. Other important changes were made, preparing the way for the election of mayors, who until then had been appointed by governors, who in turn were appointed by the president. Fiscal measures complementing the political changes were implemented to strengthen local finances, such as increasing transfers from the central government and raising local governments' taxing capacity.

To deal with the financial crisis, the government took over several banks and finance companies and took legal action against the managers of financial conglomerates that had defaulted. These measures, unfortunately, meant the public assumed the costs of the bankruptcies, and they absorbed scarce government resources. The government sought to refinance and restore trust in the financial system and to avoid the closings of large industrial plants. It restricted loans to firms owned by financial groups, increased the equity requirements to collateralize loans, and eliminated some tax biases against equity financing. However, the development funds were not affected and continued lending at negative real interest rates. It can be said, then, that these policy changes were designed to control the financial crisis, and not necessarily to produce fundamental structural change in the financial sector.

To face the balance of payments (current account) deficit, the government restricted imports by strengthening the required licensing system for imports, raising tariffs, and providing guidelines meant to restrict government imports. Subsidies to promote exports were also generalized. The government was determined to avoid a major devaluation, which was recommended by several advisers, particularly after Venezuela devalued the exchange rate (by about 200 percent) that applied to most of its trade with Colombia. It appears the president was reluctant to set the precedent of abandoning the crawling peg system that had worked fairly well since 1967, fearing it would lower the credibility of government policies.

Unfortunately, limiting imports failed to prevent sharp reserve losses in 1983 and 1984. New negative factors influencing the economy included increased service payments on an external debt that had more than doubled in the previous four years, a drastic curtailment of short-term capital inflows, and in 1984, apparently strong capital flight. The financial crisis and government measures to deal with it effected lower interest rates on financial assets as people looked for security instead of high yields. This made investments abroad more attractive and contributed to capital flight, which was also encouraged by government refusals to undertake a major devaluation despite expectations for such, fueled by dwindling international reserves and external capital sources. The government instead promoted a slower rate of devaluation via the creeping peg, which encouraged capital flight by reaffirming the attractiveness of dollar investments and also pushed interest rates to levels that discouraged real investment in Colombia.

The government responded to the external sector crisis by increasing protection in an attempt to redirect domestic demand to domestically produced goods, while being very cautious about expanding total aggregate demand for fear of rekindling inflation. It even kept the cost of living adjustments for government employees during 1985 substantially below the inflation rate. The administration's reticence was strongly criticized within the country by economists who argued that, since the crisis was due to inadequate aggregate demand, the government should have aggressively expanded demand and should not have attempted to lower real wages as a means of achieving equilibrium in the external sector.[53]

Although spending cuts might have helped the government deal with the financial crisis, many of the infrastructure and mining development programs were costly to stop, and the government feared larger aggregate demand declines, so high deficits continued through 1983 and 1984.[54] By mid-1984 reserves had declined to approximately U.S. $1.5 billion (26.5 percent of the 1981 level), the external debt had indeed become a burden, and net factor service payments abroad (mostly interest) escalated from $200 million in 1981 to $1.2 billion. At this point, the government replaced its finance minister and began the adjustment in earnest. It further restricted imports, tightening nontariff barriers that had weakened in the 1970s, and accelerated devaluation of the peso so that in 1984 the real exchange rate was about 81.4 percent of its 1970 level, up from 72.2 percent in 1982. While this adjustment was milder than in the rest of Latin America, there is a great debate as to whether it could have been largely avoided had different policies been followed or had some policies been implemented more expeditiously.

In 1985, with international reserves now at relatively low levels, the Colombian government had to renegotiate its external debt with private banks and multilateral agencies. While the government did not sign a formal agreement with the IMF and reschedule payments, it accepted a "monitoring agreement" with the IMF in order to secure a net flow of funds from international bankers. Subsequent measures taken included an increase in government revenues achieved by an increase in the value-added tax base, a temporary 8 percent import tax surcharge, and a decrease in the real wages of government employees. These changes lowered the budget deficit to 4.2 percent of GDP in 1985.

The successful adjustment was aided by a sharp rise in international coffee prices in 1986, a year in which GDP growth again reached a satisfactory level (5.8 percent) and the budget deficit fell to a manageable 1.6 percent of GDP. The financial sector structure also improved as the government continued the financial reform process. Indeed, a recent study (Clavijo, 1992) argues that many of the stereotypes about capital markets in developing countries do not apply to Colombia today. The market is not repressed, real interest rates have been positive on average, financial deepening has taken place, and forced investments and reserve requirements have been declining. The main persistent problems are related to high market concentration resulting from high margins for financial intermediation, and to imperfect term transformation and low domestic savings and investment.

Unfortunately, the Betancur administration is likely to be remembered not by the relative success of its economic policies but by increased general violence levels, including open conflict between the illegal drug industry, guerrilla organizations, and the state. Among the important violent acts that took place at this time were the assassinations of a justice minister and many judges, and the dramatic takeover by M-19 guerrillas of the supreme court building, which resulted in the deaths of half of the justices and the burning of the building.

When the Barco administration took over in August 1986 the country's finances were relatively sound and the government could devote less energy to coping with macroeconomic problems and more to dealing with pressing social and political issues, especially the violence. Paramilitary groups largely financed by illegal drug money were already attacking political groups that sympathized with the guerrillas, and in urban areas "narcoterrorists" had increased pressure on the judicial and legal system. Nevertheless, the new administration continued attempts to assimilate the guerrillas into the political system. It revived agrarian reform, this time concentrating its efforts in areas in which there was rural guerrilla activity and pressure to change the land tenure system. The government also set a policy goal to eradicate "absolute poverty," concentrating government expenditures in social sectors without generating large budget deficits.

In 1987 economic growth continued at a satisfactory pace (5.4 percent) in spite of an almost 40 percent decline in international coffee prices. Urban unemployment, that had risen steadily from 7 percent in December 1981 to 14 percent in December 1986, declined to 10 percent at the end of 1987.

In 1986 the Barco administration implemented another tax reform that simplified many taxes and eliminated tax biases against equity financing. However, amnesty provisions of this reform were even more generous than those of the past, opening the door for the laundering of substantial amounts of illegally obtained funds.

Under Barco, coal and oil exports grew in response to earlier investments, and when the International Coffee Agreement collapsed in July 1989 and prices fell by about 50 percent, increased exports of those minerals more than compensated for coffee revenue shortfalls.

Growth slowed again in 1988 and has remained low since then. The government was faced with a low growth situation that could not be attributed to severe fiscal or foreign sector imbalances. As shown in Table 1.2, total factor productivity slowed during the 1970s and declined in the 1980s, pointing to the development of long-term growth problems that needed to be explained.

During Barco's term, increased violence, and particularly the assassinations of three presidential candidates and other notables in 1989 and 1990, catalyzed public opinion behind the need for deep systemic changes to solve what was increasingly seen as an institutional rather than a policy crisis. President Barco accordingly promoted a referendum that approved convening a constituent assembly charged with rewriting the 1886 constitution which had survived until the present (with several reforms). The new constitution, approved in July 1991, opened up the political system, and adopted programs designed to make the state more accountable and responsible to the citizenry. The reform program of the Gaviria administration, which took office in August 1990, follows the lead of the Barco administration. First it promotes the new constitution as its keystone to a "political opening." Second, the plan stresses increased regional autonomy through the decentralization of government decisions and the strengthening of local governments. Third, a "social opening" is to be implemented through increased social sector expenditures. Finally, an "economic opening" package relies on a trade liberalization program first implemented in February 1990 by the Barco administration as its most important element (Hommes 1992).

In the search for higher growth rates the Barco and Gaviria administrations fully accepted, perhaps for the first time, the conventional wisdom of mainstream economists, which attributed low growth rates to the lack of competition in domestic markets, the high degree of government regulations, and the low level of international trade that reflected the closed nature of Colombia's economy.[55] Early in 1990 the government began a comprehensive market liberalization program aimed at modernizing the economy, in what is likely to be the most radical policy change of the last fifty years (Departamento Nacional de Planeación 1990).

The international trade liberalization program lowered tariffs substantially and eliminated most nontariff trade barriers. New policies also included the elimination of the exchange control system to free foreign exchange transactions and international capital flows, the weakening of restrictions on direct foreign investment, drastic changes in the labor code to make labor markets more flexible,[56] and additional capital market liberalization measures.

The drastic policy changes begun during Barco's last year in office were followed by Gaviria in a remarkable example of policy continuity. The new administration was committed to controlling the fiscal deficit and lowering the inflation rate, as it was seen as one of the primary obstacles to successful reform. Thus, tight fiscal and monetary policies were implemented. In late 1991 yet another tax reform, granting amnesty to those who had illegally acquired assets and who had income abroad, was implemented to complement the elimination of the exchange control system.

The new administration has clearly gambled on the success of market liberalization policies to restore GDP growth rates to the 5 to 6 percent level. These policies have been accepted by most Colombians and questioned by few economists. However, they can be criticized on the grounds that they are based on the questionable assumption that the country's economy became increasingly closed to international competition, a process that led to increased resource allocation inefficiencies and a decline in the growth rate. While official data indicate that exports as a percentage of GDP declined secularly from the 1920s on, it is not clear that this was the case during the 1970s and 1980s when marijuana and cocaine exports grew dramatically. As shown in chapter six, foreign exchange revenues from these exports that entered Colombia's economy each year are likely to have been in the U.S. $1.5 to $2.5 billion range, indicating a substantially greater degree of international openness than official figures suggest. Similarly, since the domestic market was initially segmented by the lack of adequate domestic communication and transportation systems, when the appropriate infrastructure developed and the domestic market became increasingly integrated, the share of exports in GDP should have declined anyway.[57]

Criticism made by a small group of economists led by José Antonio Ocampo is that Colombia's economy enjoyed sustained growth for a relatively long period because of two main growth enhancing forces: the continuous development of transportation and communications infrastructure that integrated the domestic market and generated substantial economies of scale, and structural changes in the economy that encouraged new technologies. Ocampo argues that in the early 1970s, structural changes ended as the share of manufacturing in GDP stagnated, and technological absorption and adaptation slowed after the national market was already integrated and no new economies of scale were developing. According to this view, these factors caused stagnation in total factor productivity and slowed the rate of GDP growth.[58]

Chapter 2 develops an interpretation of Colombia's development complementary to Ocampo's. This interpretation argues that besides Ocampo's two growth constraining factors, there were other important ones that contributed to lower economic growth, including the growth of political clientelism and rent-seeking, and the growing inability of the state to perform some of its most fundamental functions. These conditions were exacerbated by the growth of the illegal PSAD industry that, as argued in chapter seven, has very likely had a negative impact on Colombian GDP growth. However, Ocampo's position is not supported by this author in one respect: structural change did not end in the early 1970s. While it is true that manufacturing's GDP share stopped growing, the productive structure continued to change and mining became the leading sector during the 1980s. Still, in agreement with Ocampo, while mining productivity was increasing, backward linkages for the sector were minor, and it did not generate as much additional economic activity as the manufacturing sector had previously done. In other words, not all structural change that introduces new high productivity technologies necessarily contributes to GDP growth.

It is unclear whether the official diagnosis of a low-growth crisis and the implemented policy prescription will restore the country's high growth rate. Indeed, during 1991 several troubling signs appeared in the economy. The international trade and capital liberalization programs resulted in a large influx of foreign exchange. Coming at a time when international interest rates, especially those in the United States, were declining sharply and Colombian rates remained high because of tight fiscal and monetary policies designed to lower the stubbornly high inflation rate, this influx prompted a de facto revaluation of the black market exchange rate despite the Central Bank's willingness to buy foreign exchange and a fast accumulation of reserves.

Conclusion

A conventional economics survey of the evolution of the main economic indicators and economic policies followed by Colombian governments in the last fifty years indicates there was significant improvement in the standard of living for most Colombians and, more recently, in the country's income distribution. Colombia grew satisfactorily until

1981, but then experienced a sharp decline in economic growth, even though its performance was better than in most of Latin America and the Caribbean. Government policies reveal a continuous accommodation, backed by highly technical criteria, to various external and internal forces, including the growing underground economy that has been the main cause behind a series of tax amnesties. Those amnesties increased short-term government revenues, but also legalized illegal income and capital. Successive governments followed cautious policy changes, avoided the big mistakes frequently made in other economies in the region, and succeeded in adjusting internal and external imbalances of the early 1980s and the financial crisis of the same period. However, government policies have been more suited to dealing with short-term macroeconomic adjustment problems than with needed structural change.

Beginning with Betancur, the government recognized the need not only to provide strong growth, but also to increase the degree of participatory democracy in the country, and implemented several measures designed to empower a larger proportion of citizens. At the end of the 1980s, as growth continued to be unsatisfactory, the government embarked on the most drastic policy changes since the Great Depression, believing that slow growth was due mainly to bad policies and not to structural economic factors.

Notes

1. Intercensal data show that during 1951 to 1964 the average rate of population growth was 3.2 percent. However, since this rate was accelerating, it was lower at the beginning of this period than at the end, and population growth rates should have peaked at higher levels. García-García (1991), based on work on census data done at the Corporación Centro Regional de Población, estimates that annual population growth rates peaked in 1959 to 1964 at 3.6 percent, a figure quite close to the biological maximum. However, ECLAC (1990: 3) estimates the peak of the population growth rate at 3 percent for 1960 to 1965.

2. The decline in the population growth rate has been due mainly to a sharp drop in fertility rates. However, the decline in the growth rate in the near future will not be fast because the number of childbearing women is still too large from the high growth rates of the 1960s. It is projected that when that generation passes the childbearing years, population growth will decline to about 1 percent per year between the years 2020 and 2025 (DANE, 1989: 66).

3. Colombia was the only Latin American country that signed the United Nations Declaration on Population on Human Rights Day, 10 December 1966 (McGreevey, 1980: 418).

4. "Cabeceras municipales" (Municipal seats).

5. In the intercensal period 1951 to 1964, Bogotá's metropolitan area population grew at an extremely high 7.7 percent per year, while that of the metropolitan areas of the next three largest cities, Medellín, Cali, and Barranquilla grew at 6.5 percent (see Thoumi, 1983: 156). While the relationship between city size and growth rate holds overall, there were some smaller cities that grew at even higher rates than the large ones (Conroy, 1976).

6. Just wood boards, compacted earth, or other temporary materials.

7. For instance, the use of lard has declined while that of white meats, vegetable oils, cereals, and some fruits has increased sharply (Farné, 1990: 56).

8. This is possible because older kids remain enrolled in lower school grades.

9. Rueda (1990b) finds that in Bogotá in 1985, 25 percent of the non-maids were in that condition.

10. As measured by the Gini coefficient and other dispersion measures. The global Gini coefficient increased from .45 in 1938 to .56 in 1964. Since then, it has fallen to .48 in 1988.

11. These estimates were based on the poverty line used by the World Bank (1990).

12. There are two National Accounts series in Colombia. The Banco de la República (BR) produced National Account data since 1950, but when the DANE was created, a conflict of functions arose between these two institutions that led to the transfer of the national accounts elaboration to DANE. The statistical appendix presents disaggregated sectoral composition and growth rate series of the national accounts based on the 1950 to 1967 BR data and on the 1965 to 1988 DANE data. The two series are not exactly comparable. First, the BR data are in constant 1958 prices, and the DANE data in constant 1975 prices. Second, the classifications used differ somewhat. In the old BR system, agriculture included some activities that were included as manufacturing in the new DANE system. Thus, the GDP shares of agriculture are somewhat higher, and of manufacturing somewhat lower, in the former series. Similar differences are found in other categories; perhaps the most important is in the government sector, which is about 40 percent larger in the new DANE series than in the old BR one. However, in spite of these differences, the rates of growth in the two series are quite similar in the overlapping years, so long-term growth trend analysis is not likely to be significantly affected by the series change.

13. Berry and Thoumi (1988: 63) estimate average annual GDP growth of 4.8 percent for the period 1945 to 1985, and García-García (1991) estimates an identical figure for 1950 to 1987. He also estimates the rates of growth of the country's main trading partners (3.2 percent) and the United States (2.6 percent).

14. The figures during the 1970s may have increasingly understated income growth due to their capturing only a part (probably a small one) of income generated in the illegal drug trade, and growth under-reporting in small scale industry, rental incomes, and perhaps other components of the total. In this event, growth of real income per capita may have been even faster than indicated above, say 4.5 percent per year.

15. Díaz-Alejandro (1976) is an excellent study of the economic policies and development of Colombia during this period.

16. Gasoline prices were set at such a low level that at times Colombia had the lowest gasoline prices in the world.

17. Notice that the growth of illegal drugs exports casts doubt on the validity of the official data that show a declining GDP export share through the 1970s.

18. Once a higher plateau is reached inflation feeds on itself and its own dynamics make it very difficult to bring it back down. As people learn to deal with inflation, more prices become indexed and the inflation feedback effect is greater.

19. This has been recognized quite openly by Calvo (1991) in his comments to Urrutia (1991).

20. The argument should not be that politicians as a class are against high inflation, since the country has in fact had a relatively high inflation rate for a long time, but rather that they are against unexpected increases in the inflation rate because these lower the purchasing power of the working class due to the lag in wage and salary adjustments.

21. Beginning in the 1930s, the Coffee Growers Federation built warehouses; negotiated international coffee agreements; financed production; marketed, processed, and transported the crop; marketed and subsidized agrochemicals needed in coffee production; developed assistance programs to promote technical innovation and diffusion; and established substantial equity positions in several banks and financial institutions and in the Grancolombian Merchant Fleet (Ocampo, 1991: 222).

22. The National Front system is explained in Chapter 2.

23. Fajardo (1986, 101–117) provides a concise summary of the process by which the land reform was approved and its achievements.

24. The Asociación de Usuarios Campesinos (ANUC) was created in 1968 with government support (Bagley, 1979).

25. As early election results were favoring Rojas Pinilla and the upset seemed imminent, President Lleras ordered the media to stop broadcasting election results. The next morning the official election results showed Misael Pastrana the winner on the strength of late-counted absentee votes from Colombians residing abroad.

26. This plan had originally been proposed in the early 1960s, but at that time the Lleras Camargo government opted for a traditional ECLAC-type plan which was used as a guideline during the Alliance for Progress years.

27. See, for example, Corporación para el Fomento de las Investigaciones Económicas, 1972.

28. Appropriately, the development plan of the López administration was entitled "Para Cerrar la Brecha," "To Close the Gap." See Departamento Nacional de Planeación, 1975.

29. They included some interesting innovative features such as a minimum permissible income to net wealth ratio of 8 percent in income tax reports, aimed at limiting income under-reporting, particularly among landowners.

30. Ibañez (1974), using income distribution data, simulated the income taxes that should have been collected and concluded that as much as two-thirds were evaded.

31. Tax bracket creeping refers to the increase over time in the tax rate corresponding to a given level of real income, as income and price inflation occurs in the context of a progressive tax system (higher tax rates for higher income).

32. When foreign exchange is abundant, external credit used to finance the domestic content of an investment project results in either increased foreign exchange reserves, which increase the monetary base, or increased foreign exchange supplies, which revalue the currency.

33. The liberalization of capital markets in less-developed countries had been advocated by McKinnon (1973) and Shaw (1973). McKinnon visited Colombia in 1973 and wrote a report which was influential in shaping the policies of the Pastrana and López governments.

34. For an alternative presentation of relevant fiscal information, see Richard M. Bird, 1984.

35. Sarmiento (1982, chapters 1 and 2), who was an active policymaker in this period, describes these as the main causes of the perceived failure of the capital market liberalization process.

36. Sarmiento (1982, 2) provides an excellent detailed discussion of the policies implemented at this time.

37. It is, however, highly questionable that better roads between larger and smaller cities contribute to decentralization; in lowering the costs of trips to the commercial, financial, and services centers they are more likely to have strong centralizing effects, as witnessed by the slow growth of cities like Girardot and Tunja after their highways to Bogotá were improved in the late 1950s and early 1960s.

38. Wiesner was head of the National Planning Department during the first two years of the Turbay government and in this position presided over the formulation of the Development Plan. In the second two years of the period he was the Minister of Finance and was instrumental in controlling the deficit. Wiesner has analyzed the budget deficit and in several papers and speeches has linked it to the external debt growth (Wiesner, 1982). Ironically, after presiding over the largest deficits in Colombia's post-war history, later on as a high IMF official he argued very strongly that the main cause of the Latin American external debt crisis had been the individual countries' inability to control their budget deficits (Wiesner, 1985).

39. It was politically easier to justify open market operations as an anti-inflationary policy than as a government financing mechanism, hence the apparently contradictory policies to expand and contract the money supply simultaneously.

40. A very detailed discussion of the functions and operation of this account is found in Jaramillo and Montenegro (1982).

41. Further, if on the same day an equal amount of foreign exchange was bought and sold at the same price, an accounting profit was recorded for the deal.

42. Typically internal inflation has occurred at least as rapidly as the rate of devaluation against foreign exchange, so the domestic purchasing power of the pesos used to buy a dollar has been at least equal to that of the pesos received when the dollar was resold.

43. Nor, it should be added, did most writers on these issues in the contemporary economic development literature, which showed a striking degree of naïveté about the ability of capital markets to operate efficiently without any government regulations. In the United States, after several financial crises in the nineteenth century, special institutional arrangements were developed to guarantee the safe operation of capital markets. These included the atomization of banking institutions, which were not allowed to expand beyond the city, county, or state level; the regulation of loans to bank

employees; the prohibition for financial institutions to have equity interests in other businesses, etc.

44. Sarmiento (1985) shows how the large conglomerates managed to concentrate profits in their hands and saddle the small investors with the losses. For instance, a firm partially owned, but controlled by a group, purchased from or sold goods and services to firms fully owned by the group at prices that transferred the profits from the firm to the groups' fully owned firms.

45. Acosta (1986), Jaramillo (1982), the Grupo de Estudios del Departamento de Investigaciones Económicas del Banco de la República (1982) and others have studied the ways in which the financial institutions bypassed government policies. For instance, the marginal 100 percent reserve on new deposits established in 1976 was bypassed by an illegal intermediation system arranged by the financial institutions in which the borrowers were allowed to get the funds directly from the financial institution's depositors. The financial institutions collected a commission and avoided the reserve requirements.

46. See for example Echavarría, (1983), and Jaramillo, Marín, and Arenas (1982).

47. Perhaps the best study of this process is Montenegro (1983). Other good analyses are Echavarría (1983) and Ortega (1982).

48. This process has been studied by several authors: Junguito (1979), Restrepo, Serna, and Rosas (1983), and Restrepo (1985).

49. Based on a comparison of the increase in these merchandise exports with the U.S. wholesale price index, the increase was 3.5 to 4 times. According to national accounts statistics, total exports (goods and services) rose by 120 percent and actual imports of goods and services were three times higher in the latter year. The ratio of exports to imports (current prices) in both years was about 1.05.

50. The "sinister window" purchases are attributed to several service exports and worker remittances. Therefore, in the official Balance of Payments there is not such a thing as a "sinister account," and questionable foreign exchange inflows are reflected in large changes in some accounts, mainly in services.

51. See Departamento Nacional de Planeación (1983). A detailed discussion of the plan and some of its implications is found in FEDESARROLLO (1983).

52. See a discussion of these measures in Ocampo and Perry (1983).

53. The main criticism came from the FEDESARROLLO group, that downplayed the dangers of inflation which they believed to be mainly a function of food prices which in turn reflected the abundance of traditional agricultural crops (see the editorials of *Coyuntura Económica* in all the 1984 issues).

54. A large share of the external borrowing begun during the Turbay administration went to finance the electricity sector. However, the demand for electricity slackened during the recession and the country found itself with useless excess capacity for which it was paying high capital costs.

55. This view had the support of multilateral lending agencies and the U.S. administration and was reinforced by World Bank studies (World Bank 1990b).

56. These changes involved the possibility to have an "integral salary" without fringe benefits for higher-paid employees, allowing firms to hire people for temporary periods of up to three years. It also included the

elimination of the legislated tenure after ten years of work that had led to the firing of qualified workers as they got close to that threshold, and other measures that made it easier to hire and fire workers.

57. It is well known that the share of international trade in GDP is inversely related to the size of the domestic market of a country. See, for example, Inter-American Development Bank (1982, part one).

58. Ocampo (1991 and 1992) presents concise and coherent English versions of this argument.

... 2 ...
A Critical Institutionalist Perspective

Despite the relatively rosy development picture presented in the previous chapter, Colombia's economic development has a dark side reflected in the country's deep and continuous socioeconomic problems. Indeed, Colombia has experienced a growing institutional crisis in which old political and legal frameworks have become increasingly unable to cope with social conflicts and economic change, and the political regime has suffered an erosion of its legitimacy.

The concept of legitimacy is frequently used in political science, but it is not used in economics. Unfortunately, political scientists have not built a consensus about the meaning of the term, and it is frequently used quite loosely in the literature.[1] In this work I use the term to denote the consistency between the regime, its institutions and policies, and the values that prevail in the society. Using the economist's jargon, every individual has a utility function that reflects his or her values and preferences. When there is a consistency between the regime and the values and preferences of most citizens, the regime is "legitimate."[2] According to this definition, legitimacy is a continuous variable; that is, no regime is perfectly legitimate unless everyone agrees with its institutions and laws, and no regime is totally illegitimate unless everyone disagrees with it. In this sense, every regime has a degree of legitimacy, and illegitimacy is only a way to refer to low levels of legitimacy. Following this definition, one can argue that legitimacy generates many positive externalities, and illegitimacy many negative ones. For example, when there is a high legitimacy level, civil society reinforces the legal system as social pressures make it costly not to comply with the law; trust and social cohesion are high, and many transaction costs are low as contracts are easy to enforce.

The growing erosion of the Colombian regime's legitimacy has caused a growing gap between the legal norms of social, political, and economic behavior, and socially accepted behavior; that is, a gap between de jure and de facto social norms.[3] This deep institutional crisis has symptomatically manifested itself in several ways such as an extremely high level of violence, the growth of a large informal economy, widespread rent-seeking and predatory economic behavior, and an increasingly weaker and more ineffective state.

In this chapter I attempt to develop a critical institutionalist interpretation of Colombia's development. I argue that institutional and ethical legacies of the past are important factors that condition the behavior of economic actors in Colombia, and that render both conventional economics, reflected in the so-called "Washington consensus," and left-of-center interpretations of the country's economic growth process quite unsatisfactory.

The standard left-of-center interpretations are based on class analysis, exploitation, and the contradictions of the capitalist system. There is no doubt that many of these approaches contain valid ideas. However, they are really inappropriate for Colombia. Consider, for example, class analysis. It implicitly assumes that within each class there is a sense of belonging, cohesion, or "class consciousness" that has never really existed in Colombia. Colombians are extremely individualistic; they show great distrust and a lack of solidarity towards, and social cohesion with, their fellow citizens. The modernization, urbanization, and industrialization processes that developed after 1945 broke up many traditional social and economic relationships, especially those prevailing in rural labor markets, but that did not result in the development of a class consciousness among large enough groups. Torres (1963) argues otherwise. He claims that one peasant reaction to la violencia was the development of class consciousness, and based on that conviction he predicted an imminent lower-class uprising. However, the extreme levels of violence did not result in a social revolution. Indeed, the fact that la violencia ended with an agreement among the two traditional multiclass party elites to share control of the government is the best proof that it was not the result of a class struggle (Wilde, 1978), and that class analysis sheds some light on, but is insufficient in explaining, Colombia's economic history.[4]

The economic structure that developed in the post–World War II period led to segmented markets, not to competitive ones, that help explain why class consciousness has not been strong among lower income groups. The most obvious form of market segmentation is the cleavage between formal and informal markets. However, formal markets are also segmented as a result of social mores, power, imperfect information, high transportation costs, and government policy. The behavioral response to market segmentation is not conducive to class-oriented actions, but to group- or sectoral-oriented ones, which are frequently multiclass. In these conditions, the political economy developed more along the lines of "sectoral clashes" than class struggle.[5] In other words, workers, capitalists, and managers in a particular sector of the economy find that they can all increase their income at the expense of the rest of society if they join together to lobby for policies that increase the rents of the sector. The natural labor market segmentation caused by the country's geography and poor communications, reinforced by labor legislation that provided a high degree of job security, also encouraged the workers to do so. This is why the industrial labor force is a labor elite.

In the case of the state's employees, they have become players in a clientelistic system in which their loyalty is to a particular party, dissident spin-off party, or local politician. As political parties became increasingly clientelistic, they lost their political meaning and their ideologies became blurred and unimportant (Leal, 1984), a development that did not foster class-conscious solidarity.

Right-of-center approaches to understanding Colombia are no better than those on the left. The conventional economic analysis employed by multilateral agencies and the United States government, and in vogue among many Colombian economists and policymakers, emphasizes the relative success of past, stable economic policies, but fails to explain the decline in quality of life in the midst of increased income or the substantial drop in growth rates during the 1980s.[6] Conventional interpretations attribute the GDP-growth-rate decline to difficult external conditions and to poor government policies that protect producing sectors against foreign competition and that attempt to control domestic markets. Accordingly, they recommend opening the economy to external competition, liberalizing domestic markets, especially capital and labor markets, and minimizing the government's intervention in the economy. However, these are at best only partial explanations for the decline in Colombia's growth—since protectionist policies were at their peak in the mid-1960s and have declined substantially since then. It is true that during 1982 to 1984 protectionist policies increased in Colombia, in response to the external sector problems discussed in the previous chapter, but these changes were short-lived. Contraband competition also increased during the 1970s and 1980s as the illegal drug booms cheapened black market foreign exchange. Thus, the economy during the 1980s was more exposed to external competition than when it was growing at a faster rate. Furthermore, the "easy" import-substitution stage had been exhausted by the late 1960s, and the lack of further import-substitution opportunities did not prevent the satisfactory growth performance of the 1970s.

It should also be noted that external conditions faced by Colombia during the 1980s were not significantly worse than those faced during the 1960s and 1970s. As noted above, Colombia was the only Latin American country that did not suffer an external debt crisis. While Colombia paid a "redline" price for being in the "bad Latin American neighborhood" and new international loans, particularly from private banks, were not easy to obtain, these financial obstacles were not insurmountable. Colombian exports suffered from the collapse of the important Venezuelan market in 1983, but it is hard to argue that these external conditions were worse than those confronted when coffee prices fell and international loans were less accessible in previous decades.

Another important weakness of the conventional analysis is that it blames poor economic performance on bad economic policies, but it does not explain why and how those policies came to be. After reading some of these analyses, one is left wondering if the flawed policies were drafted because decision makers were stupid or ignorant of economics. And after reading others one is left with a sense that somehow economics and politics are separate, that it is not the function of economists to understand policymaking, but just to prescribe the "optimum" economic solution to an economic problem, regardless of the political economy context.[7] However, such disregard does not prevent mainstream economists from making policy recommendations that have strong political implications.

It is worth emphasizing that both left-of-center and mainstream interpretations of Colombia's economic development presume a capitalist market system in which competition is fierce and prices are set in fairly anonymous ways. For instance, if labor markets were not segmented, competition would be very strong, one wage rate would prevail for similar work, and the only way for an individual worker to increase his or her wage would be to form a class alliance with other workers. If markets were not segmented, tariffs and other government trade policies would be the main obstacles to competition and efficiency, and opening the economy would increase competition and promote growth. However, both assumptions dismiss the role of economic and social institutions in shaping the way in which the market works. Particularly, they imply that Colombia has modern capitalist markets and institutions, even though these have not evolved sufficiently from their pre-capitalist state.

In recent years, frustration with development in Latin America has led some authors to provide alternative culture-based interpretations of the region's development failures. Harrison (1985) argues that values in Latin American societies are undemocratic, do not tolerate dissent, do not promote compromise, and encourage a world vision in which an individual's capacity to understand the world is limited. He argues that these recalcitrant values are the main reason that the region remains underdeveloped.

The interpretation of Colombia's growth process developed in this chapter acknowledges the importance of values, but in contrast, argues that the values of important groups have changed significantly, creating the current conflict between de jure and de facto social norms. Following the institutionalist tradition, I argue that value changes were driven by new technologies that were developed or assimilated into society. The term technology is used here in a broad "Veblenesque" sense: "Thus technology must be understood to include all human activities involving the use of tools" (Ayres, 1978: xv).[8] That is, as Colombians became familiar with new ways of doing things, as their knowledge of the world increased and they became aware of the existence of different societies, and so on, social change became inevitable, and the most that traditional institutions could do was to slow it down. However, the stronger the old institutions and mores, the greater the social turmoil and the intensity of conflict with new ones. Hence, violence was a result.

In this chapter, the evidence and evolution of the increasing level of violence is surveyed, as well as the few studies that have attempted to find relationships to explain it. This is done because, unfortunately, the high level of violence has become a trademark of Colombian society and it is the most glaring symptom of the crisis it experiences. Regarding the institutional crisis, I argue that, while there have been some changes in Colombian institutions, they have taken place at a slower pace than necessary to avoid the current crisis. Further, this chapter explains how the values and institutional legacy of the past have conditioned the way Colombia's market operates, and how they have hindered institutional change. It explains how institutions have resisted change, how many changes were undertaken to protect the status quo, how the clientelistic political system developed, and why there was a growing gap between the formal regime and the political and economic reality—a gap that produced an increasingly large underground economy, delegitimized the regime, and weakened the state. Conceptual differences between formal and informal economic activities are discussed. Evidence about the growth of underground economic activity and several important characteristics of Colombian policies that promoted that growth are identified. Finally in this chapter, I discuss the role of the illegal PSAD industry as a catalyst in Colombia's institutional crisis, the changes needed, and some possible effects of recent policy changes implemented in the attempt to democratize Colombian institutions.

The Insidious Violence

The Level of Violence

The most glaring symptom of Colombia's profound social problems and low quality of life is the high level of violence experienced in the post–World War II period. The infamous period of la violencia that, according to most analysts, began around the late 1940s, witnessed what has to be considered an undeclared civil war between the country's two traditional parties, the liberals and the conservatives. The conservative party was in power and used the force of the state, including the army and the police, to fight guerrilla groups supported by the liberal party. Some analysts argue that the roots of la violencia can be traced to an early violencia that began when the liberals won the 1930 presidential election after thirty years of conservative party hegemony. This power shift prompted a continual fight for the spoils of the state (Wilde, 1978). Some argue that la violencia lasted until General Gustavo Rojas Pinilla took power in a 1953 military coup that had vast popular support. Others argue that la violencia continued at a lower level until 1964, when there was a formal peace agreement with the main guerrilla organizations that had remained in arms after 1953.[9] Regardless of the dates set for the beginning and end of la violencia, the human toll was enormous and the deaths associated with it are estimated at between 200,000 and 300,000 of the country's 11.5 million people.[10] It should be noted that la violencia was not only characterized by a large number of casualties, but also by the extreme cruelty and inhumanity displayed by the warring parties.[11]

While violence waned after la violencia, it did not cease. Although data about many variables that reflect the level of violence in Colombian life are sparse, data on homicides and intentional deaths are staggering. Losada and Vélez (1988, 1989) surveyed homicide rates from 1955 to 1988, and estimate that at the beginning of the National Front in 1958 they peaked at 51.5 per 100,000 inhabitants. The homicide rate fell continuously during the 1960s and early 1970s, bottoming out between 1973 to 1975 at about 16.8 per 100,000. However, in the late 1970s, the homicide rate increased rapidly, reaching 62.8 per 100,000 in 1988. Losada and Vélez also show that, according to United Nations data on 70 countries, between 1955 and 1969 Colombia's homicide rate was among the top five, while during the 1970 to 1978 period, which can be considered a peaceful one, Colombia ranked between sixth and tenth. After 1978 the homicide rate returned to the top five, reaching third in 1988, behind only El Salvador and Zimbabwe.

It should also be noted that official data tend to underestimate the actual number of homicides because there is another death category, "deaths caused by injuries not known if intentional or accidental," in which some homicides are likely included (Thoumi, 1987). Still, this data bias does not necessarily raise Colombia's international ranking, as the homicide rate is also probably underestimated in other high-rate countries.

Of course, there are other Latin American countries that at times have had similarly high intentional violent deaths, but the extremely high levels have not persisted for such a long time as in Colombia, and in most cases the high rates coincided with periods of civil war or internationally recognized "dirty" wars, in which the state was a proactive force generating a large number of deaths, such as in Chile during the 1970s (Losada and Vélez, 1989).[12]

To help put the high Colombian violence in perspective, it is useful to look at homicides as a percentage of total deaths. According to DANE,[13] in the early 1970s homicides accounted for about 2.5 percent of total deaths in the country, a proportion that increased continuously to 5.4 percent in 1980 and to a remarkably high 8.1 percent in 1987. That is, in 1987 about one in twelve deaths was a homicide! Furthermore, during the last forty years homicides have been the main cause of death for males aged 15 to 44.

The level of violence varies substantially by gender and age group, and among population regions and cities. Losada and Vélez (1988) show that homicide victims are mainly males in the 25 to 44 year age bracket. The homicide rates are as high in rural areas as in cities, except Bogotá where the rate is significantly lower. Losada and Vélez (1988: 64–67) found that between 1979 and 1986 the following areas had the highest homicide rates:

1. the emerald producing zones of Boyacá and Cundinamarca;
2. the banana growing region of Urabá, with its history of labor conflicts, strong labor unions, guerrilla activity, and paramilitary self-defense groups;
3. the recently settled middle Magdalena River Valley, a region where property rights are still weak, where there is a long history of guerrilla activity, and where (more recently) illegal drug traffickers have bought large amounts of land and have financed paramilitary groups;

4. the fertile plains of north Antioquia, where illegal drug traffickers have invested heavily and where there have been guerrilla activity and paramilitary organizations;
5. the Indian reserves (*resguardos*) in the north of Cauca, where settlers, drug organizations, and guerrillas have tried to displace the economically depressed Indian populations;
6. some valleys in Cauca and Nariño, where coca is grown and where there is guerrilla activity;
7. parts of northwest Cundinamarca, where there are coca plantations and where drug traffickers have also purchased land;
8. southern Guajira, where marijuana was grown in the late 1970s, where new settlers are pressuring the Indian groups, and where contraband enters and exits Colombia in large quantities;
9. the north of Valle (the Cartago municipality) and the adjacent area of Risaralda, an old la violencia zone where coca is grown and drug traffickers have invested;
10. the basins of the Carare, Upía, and Cusiana rivers and the plains of Arauca and Casanare, and San José del Guaviare, all newly settled areas where coca and marijuana are grown, traffickers have invested, and where there is guerrilla and paramilitary activity.

Losada and Vélez (1988) also looked at the least violent municipalities and found that while it is possible to find a few in many areas of the country, they are basically concentrated in three groups: the coastal plains of Atlántico, Bolívar, and Córdoba, a region that historically and culturally belongs to the Caribbean; the southern highlands of Nariño, a region that has always had strong ties and cultural similarities with Ecuador; and the bedroom communities around Bogotá, and some mid-size cities like Bucaramanga, Cúcuta, Pereira, and Manizales.

The crimes that involve violence are obviously quite diverse and not limited to homicide. Kidnapping is another frequent violent crime that has affected Colombian society. Data on kidnappings substantially underestimate their frequency because, in many cases, the family or the employer of the victim does not report the crime to the police and negotiates his or her freedom directly with the kidnappers. In spite of such underreporting, the data on kidnappings are shocking. FEDESARROLLO and Instituto SER de Investigación (1990: 36–37) confirm that kidnappings have become a daily occurrence in Colombia, and that they increased substantially from 1988 on, reaching alarming proportions in early 1990. According to police data, the average number of monthly kidnappings from March 1988 to December 1989 was 59.1, a figure that skyrocketed to 158 in January 1990. These crimes have been committed by various types of organizations: guerrilla movements that use them to finance their activities, illegal drug organizations that want to pressure the government to change policies, and common criminals who have taken the opportunity created by political and drug-related kidnappings to turn that activity into a flourishing business.

The Types and Causes of Violence

Today, and after substantial research, there is no consensus as to the causes of la violencia, or of the continued high level of homicides and other violent actions. The causality relationships that determine the behavior of individuals who resort to the use of extreme force against others, or those who consume psychoactive drugs, are very complex and difficult to ascertain. These phenomena have multiple causes, and the interactions between the various possible causal variables are not clearly identifiable. While there is some consensus that the roots of la violencia were found in the quasi-religious sectarianism generated by party loyalties, in the peasants' fight to gain access to land, and in the political fight for the bounty resulting from control of the government, there is no agreement about the relative importance of these factors or their mutual interactions.

Independent of its causes, violence in Colombia has become widespread and diverse, and many types of violence can be identified in the country. In 1987 the Barco administration established a commission, composed of the best known academics who had studied violence in Colombia,[14] that was assigned the task of producing a thorough analysis of the high levels of violence and their causes. The commission's report (Comisión de Estudios sobre la Violencia, 1989: 19–21) identified ten important types:

1. violence generated by organized crime against politicians and journalists;
2. violence of organized crime against private individuals;
3. guerrilla violence against the state;
4. violence of armed groups against private individuals;
5. state-generated violence resulting from attempts to maintain law and order;
6. state violence against protest social movements;
7. state violence against ethnic minorities;
8. violence by unorganized private citizens;

9. violence by organized private citizens;
10. violence in the private life of citizens.

In general, the commission's report confirms that violence is pervasive in Colombian life; that it is present in the workplace, at home, and in public places; and that it constitutes a problem of utmost social importance.

Of particular concern to the commission was the growth of the assassination industry and the gangs of teenagers providing rent-an-assassin services (*sicarios*) to anyone willing to pay, as well as the growing impunity with which those committing violent acts could operate.

Persons or groups who exercise violence usually have social, economic, and political goals. The economic goal is simple: to appropriate the income or assets owned or protected by the violence victims. Political goals are diverse: some want to replace the political system, others want to gain access to and participate in the current system, and others want to maintain the current political status quo. The main social goal is to achieve higher status within peer groups or the larger community, a status that is considered unreachable through more conventional means.

The goals that various groups hope to achieve through the use of violence oppose each other and perpetuate violence. Political and economic goals are frequently related, as politically motivated violence requires financing that can best be obtained through violence, and because political power is used to obtain and maintain economic power.

The underlying reasons that violence is chosen to achieve these goals are many. The most frequent causes of violence cited in the literature are an undemocratic political system, high levels of poverty, and income inequality. The solutions posed by most analysts have to do with democratization to empower groups and individuals that have been marginal under the current system, and with the need to improve income and wealth distributions.

However, the relationship between poverty, inequality, and violence is quite complex, and while there is a consensus about the relevance of poverty and inequality as causes of violence in Colombia, it is not clear how those two factors have contributed to it. First, there are many very poor societies that do not experience the same level of violence as in Colombia. Second, as shown below, within Colombia there is *no* evident relationship between individual and regional poverty and violence. Third, in many cases significant change in violence levels occurs through time without change in poverty levels or inequality. Fourth, in other cases violence has increased as poverty has actually declined. Fifth, Colombia's income distribution inequality increased during the la violencia years, but declined during the 1970s and 1980s when violence was again increasing. This puzzling complexity indicates that, while it may be argued that poverty and other factors contribute to social violence, it is not clear what elements act as catalysts for violence to erupt. That is, poverty and inequality have been factors that help trigger violence when other conditions develop.

The paradoxical nature of Colombia's violence has made studying it difficult. A few studies attempt to characterize the most violent areas of the country and to develop a profile of the most violent individuals and regions. For example, Losada and Vélez (1988) tried to test the relationship between a weak state presence and homicide rates. They recognize it is difficult to accurately measure state presence in a region, but they developed indexes to gauge the quality of housing, health, education, and highways to reflect the level of basic-needs satisfaction in each municipality, and correlated those indexes with the homicide rate. Their results are very weak. The only statistically significant explanatory variables were school enrollment for children aged 5 through 9 and the percentage of houses with utility services. In all cases the correlation coefficients were quite low, explaining only about 10 percent of the variance. The results do suggest, however, that empowering citizens to influence conditions at the local level may lead to a decrease in the levels of violence.

The characteristics of the most violent regions listed above suggest that high levels of violence are related to uncertain property rights in newly settled areas, illegal mining and agriculture, and conflict generated by the drug traffickers' investments in areas where peasants and guerrilla groups have been fighting for land rights. The characteristics of the least violent regions suggest that cultural and institutional factors also influence violence levels, since regions that share cultural similarities with less-violent countries are the least violent in Colombia.

As surveyed by Losada (1991), there have been several studies addressing the problem of violence in Medellín, focusing on the nature and characteristics of the sicarios. The most rigorous study of this type to date is that of Torres de Galvis and Velásquez de Pavón (1990) based on extensive interviews with 112 young assassins (males aged 16 to 24) serving time in Medellín's jail, and 112 males of similar age residing in the same neighborhoods as the assassins. The results indicate that being an assassin is statistically significantly related to being unemployed, belonging to a gang, having a low education level, having been abandoned by one or both parents during childhood, and having a mother with a background of prostitution, alcoholism, and drug addiction (Losada, 1991: 165). While this study does not clarify the causal relationships between these variables,[15] it does identify some of the social problems positively related to the probability that a young Medellín slum resident will become an assassin-for-hire.

The Institutional Crisis

As discussed in Chapter 1, in the last fifty years Colombia has experienced a dramatic transformation that urbanized a rural society, changed labor relations and the role of women, consolidated a national market, increased communications and travel among the regions, dramatically raised the level of education, and familiarized many Colombians with other countries and cultures, and so on.

Similar changes took place in other Latin American countries. However, different institutions in each country reacted in somewhat different ways. For instance, the structure and strength of the Indian communities has shaped social evolution in Peru and Ecuador, and the lack of strong local communities has likely conditioned Colombia's. While there are strong similarities in the socioeconomic development of the Andean countries, there are also significant differences. After all, every society has its own history.

Some changes were similar to those previously experienced in industrialized nations. However, Colombia's change took place later and in a much shorter time than in Western developed countries. But while the forces of change placed greater pressure on traditional institutions and mores to adapt to new circumstances, those institutions have been more resistant to change than in Western developed countries. The strength of traditions cannot prevent change in the long run, but it can certainly slow it down. In Colombia, many changes in important political and economic institutions have taken place only when the cost of not changing has been perceived by power elites as extremely high—that is, when a crisis was imminent or had begun—and then many of those changes were implemented in a way to maintain as much of the status quo as possible.

In the last century both the physical tools used in society and the skills of the labor force changed drastically, as people became educated, information accumulated, and the use of machinery, books, systems, and other tools grew. Naturally, the traditional power structure supported by the old mores and institutions has had to change.

Accordingly, the recent history of Colombia is one of conflict between the old society and the newly forming one. To understand this conflict it is necessary to look at the legacy of the past and how it has affected the process of change, and at how slow institutional change resulted in a widening gap between accepted social behavior and the norms of the traditional society as reflected in the legal code and in expected traditional behavior patterns.

The Legacy of the Past, Inequality, and Paternalism

One of Colombia's fundamental problems is that the mores and institutions that provide the framework in which the economy operates are based on those developed during the Spanish colonial period. They have not evolved sufficiently and retain many pre-capitalist characteristics that are at the root of many of the country's social problems. In this section, a stylized description of some of the most important characteristics is presented.

The prevailing world view of the Spanish culture at the time of the conquest, which extended to Spain's colonies, resulted in a social structure that was closed, authoritarian, and hierarchical (Fals-Borda 1965). In the colonial era individuals generally had their place in society predetermined by birth and national origin. Wealth and status were ascribed by privilege in a system partly justified by the Catholic Church's concept of society (developed by Saint Thomas Aquinas), which contends life is just a trial that God puts people through to determine who goes to heaven or hell. The source of power did not lie with the people, but with the king, by the grace of God, who gave him the task and right to use it. Society was like the human body that had been created in God's likeness. People had been given different roles in the same way that the body had different organs that performed different functions. Every organ was important to the survival of the body and, similarly, every individual's role was important to society and had to be carried out with dignity, no matter how low it was in the social hierarchy. It was self-evident that all men were *not* created equal and, therefore, different individuals had different rights. A highly hierarchical and unequal society was natural, and it would be disturbing to go against God's will by rejecting the role that He had assigned each individual.

Society was not only hierarchical, but the degree of inequality was very great, with wealth, status, and rights differences between various social groups being very large. Thus, while a few individuals had most of the land and other assets, most people had very few rights, even suffering limits on the disposal of their own labor.

This concept of inequality was clearly accepted in economic relations. For over 400 years after the Spanish conquest there were only two factors of production that mattered: land (natural resources) and labor, as capital equipment was almost nonexistent and labor skills were primitive. The conquistadors found abundant land but scarce labor, particularly after the first fifty years of conquest, when illnesses brought by the Spaniards and the hard labor they imposed on the native population dramatically reduced the number of native workers.[16] Thus, an early economic problem the Spanish crown faced in exploiting its colonies was a labor shortage.[17] If the allocation of resources had been left to a market in which every participant had equal rights, the Indians would have been free to access abundant land, and native communities would have retained control over large tracts. Hence, Spanish immigrants would have been forced to work relatively small plots of land by themselves, prevented from attaining the high status they hoped for and thought they deserved when they went to America. They certainly benefited from the church's view of society and rights.

Labor shortages made it necessary for the Spaniards to develop a system that would guarantee control of the labor supply and allow them to exploit the land. To that end, several institutions were developed, including the *encomienda,* which entrusted the *encomendero* with a plot of land and a number of Indians attached to it. Further, in addition to various forms of tribute imposed on the Indians, the Spanish used the *mita* and *concierto,* taxes in the form of forced labor services imposed on Indian communities; that labor was assigned to the mines and haciendas of the region. These institutions were complemented with the introduction of slavery, used especially to exploit gold mines in the tropical jungle where the Indians did not easily survive. The encomienda did not grant the encomendero property rights to the land or its peasants, but was a privilege granted by the crown to exploit land and peasants for a period of time, most frequently a few lifetimes. Such uncertain property rights contributed to the system's demise and, during the late colonial period, it was replaced by a system of large haciendas in which peasants worked under pre-capitalist, paternalistic arrangements and were dependent on the *patrón.*[18]

The nineteenth century witnessed steady population growth and the inclusion of Colombia in the Western capitalist system, a gradual process that required substantial changes in its productive organization. This was also a period of growth for the hacienda system. Colombian economic historians have developed two interpretations of the period's economic evolution. Some see it as a slow evolution towards modernization and capitalism, as the hacienda had to respond to markets and price incentives—and other characteristics that did not apply to isolated, self-sufficient economies (Ocampo, 1984)—to survive. Others see it as a return to a feudal-like system, in a process that Kalmanovitz (1988) calls *enfeudamiento* due to the strengthening of the system that made peasants dependent on their landlords.[19] Supporters of the former view argue that these relationships were necessary for the hacienda to minimize the need for cash flow in an environment of very unstable markets and revenues. Those who support the latter view emphasize the inequality of power relationships within the haciendas and the dependence peasants had on the landlord.

These two interpretations of nineteenth-century hacienda development need not be exclusive of each other; that is, while the hacienda system did represent a move toward some capitalist markets, it also retained strong precapitalist characteristics, particularly those related to labor relations. Independent of which interpretation one accepts, the strengthening of the hacienda system promoted a paternalistic political system. And as long as economic transactions within the hacienda were among unequal individuals, one group would be denied some rights that the other had. Therefore, while it is true that population growth weakened the landlords' need to keep peasants tied to the land, promoted cash wage payments, and allowed the colonization of other regions (particularly the coffee-growing areas of Antioquia and the Old Caldas[20] departments), unequal labor relationships on the haciendas led to peasant dependency that allowed landlords to coerce them with nonmonetary methods (Kalmanovitz, 1988: 212).

Not surprising under such a system, local landlords became natural political leaders, and the lack of national party organizations (noted in Chapter 1) enhanced their autonomy and allowed them to use the political system to complement the economic dependency that existed on the haciendas. Peasants voted for anyone approved and supported by their landlords, and provided cannon fodder for their landlord's party in frequent civil wars during the nineteenth century. In exchange for these services, the landlord mediated between the peasants and the state, and protected them during economic recessions and other calamities. As argued below, this dependency relationship provides the basis for understanding the political characteristics of the clientelist system that developed during the last thirty years.

Regardless of how one views the hacienda system, it must be accepted that the system was an authoritarian and paternalistic one that, coupled with unequal income and wealth distributions, produced what Kalmanovitz (1989) calls an "ethic of inequality" that shaped institutions and values for society. Kalmanovitz argues forcefully that this ethic is one of the main reasons for Colombia's current social problems. Because Colombians have always lived in a society where inequality of wealth, income, rights, and opportunities has prevailed, many generations have grown to accept an unequal society as normal.[21]

Another factor related to the issue is the traditional Colombian characteristic of strong individualism. As noted in Chapter 1, Colombia was long one of the most isolated countries in Latin America. Not only were its exports and imports minimal compared to the rest of the region, but the sheer geographic obstacles to communication and internal trade isolated many regions of the country from each other until well into the twentieth century (Ocampo 1984). Camilo Torres (1963) argues that the noted individualism of Colombians is the result of isolated farmwork that many individuals had to perform. Their strong individualism leads to a deep distrust of the state, lack of loyalty to the nation as a whole, and strong loyalties to the family and other groups like the *roscas* (cliques) that are seen as necessary to survive in a hostile society.

Value Conflicts and Inequality

The combination of rapid social change and the ethic of inequality has produced a very hostile society. The old value system has lost its legitimacy but it has not been replaced by a new modern and egalitarian one. The current value system is a hybrid "in which people have not developed internalized control mechanisms against the excesses of individualism" (Kalmanovitz, 1989: 29, author's translation). On one hand, most Colombians have rejected their position in the old order and people do not accept their ascribed status when it is low. On the other hand, because of the ethic of inequality, people do not consider an egalitarian society realistic. These two conflicting forces result in a tendency for most Colombians to strive to climb the social ladder without accepting too many internal controls, engaging in widespread rent-seeking and predatory behavior.

As elaborated below, this behavior has been validated by the loss of legitimacy of existing income and wealth inequalities—and as a corollary, of property rights—and by a political system that has reinforced and accepted inequality in society. As discussed in the chapter appendix, the ethic of inequality and rising income expectations caused by the "demonstration effect" have led to a misperception of change in income distribution and to situations of high social conflict. However, these factors also allow the system to co-opt many opposition leaders. Activists frequently use a rhetoric of revolution and structural social change, but they are tempted by opportunities to climb the ladder of the steep social pyramid. In other words, most Colombians accept that if society has been and is always going to be unequal, one might as well try to be on top. This is why literature about the political system is full of references to the success of Colombian elites in co-opting most of those who have opposed them. The concept of revolution is left to a few idealists, who have failed to achieve substantial social change through armed struggle.

The loss of legitimacy of income, wealth inequality, and property rights. The traditional Catholic world vision legitimized inequality and provided the basis for a stable society. It began to be disturbed only when liberal ideas of the French revolution were propagated in Colombia. But traditional mores and institutions have been so strong that these new ideas still have not prevailed.[22] As argued by Galvis (1986), since independence there has been a continuous conflict between the Scholastic and Rationalist perceptions of the world. During the nineteenth century, the Rationalist influence was limited to a small educated elite, and it did not change the values of most Colombians. Thus when the Rationalist liberal tradition appeared to have won politically and the liberal Rionegro constitution was imposed in the midnineteenth century, it did not last. The 1886 constitution, scrapped only in 1991, reflected the strength of the traditional world view and the fact that Colombians accepted as normal a hierarchical society. Yet, during the twentieth century, as Colombia became a more educated and urban society and as old rural labor systems weakened, the conflict between world views intensified. But while the old ethic has lost ground, it has not disappeared. Instead, as the old legitimacy has been chipped away and new behavioral norms become socially accepted, there has been a growing gap between the country's laws and accepted social behavior.

It must be recognized that the gap between de jure and de facto norms is not new to Colombia and Latin America. Indeed, the well known old colonial dictum *"obedezco pero no cumplo"* ("I obey but I don't comply") and the lesser-known Colombian one *"la ley es para los de ruana"* ("the law applies only to those who wear the *ruana*") reflect precisely this gap. However, in the case of Colombia, the inequality was accepted, and those in position to break the law with impunity tended to be in the upper classes. The social changes that occurred in this century increased the ability of most Colombians, including many in the lower classes, to trespass legal norms, thus increasing the gap.

Inequality does not necessarily lead to social conflict when it is legitimized by broad social consensus. But one of the effects of the value conflict experienced in Colombia is that the social consensus about the legitimacy of unequal income and wealth distributions has been lost, so that they are perceived as arbitrary and unfair by most of the population.

During the colonial period, inequality was based on privilege. After independence, many factors that had an impact on income and wealth distributions were perceived as unfair or at best arbitrary. First, political power was used to arbitrarily transfer property rights for large tracts of the best land to benefit privileged groups. For example, the Catholic Church had gained control of substantial amounts of land through direct purchase and old grants from the crown. Further tracts were acquired from deceased faithful landlords, who left their land to the Church with instructions to use the income generated by the land to pay for masses, prayers for the soul of the deceased, or the construction of a *capellanía* for a priest (frequently a relative of the deceased). The Church could not sell the land, but it obtained a large income from rents, which it accumulated and used to become the largest, and frequently the only, significant lending institution in the country. The post-independence expropriation and immediate sale of Church property resulted in huge windfall gains for those who had any liquid capital to purchase those lands.[23]

Other public lands were also disposed of unfairly. For instance, Medina (1990) recounts the settlement of the Middle Magdalena Valley where land titles are based on auctions of government lands in the mid-1860s. However, since the area was then sparsely populated, isolated, and badly surveyed, the boundaries of the auctioned plots were unclear—a fact that allowed the new owners to expand their properties at the expense of public lands. A large tract had been reserved as public land to be used later by the departmental governments. However, neighboring private owners succeeded in chipping away at the public land through litigation in the courts,[24] so that the public land disappeared.

Second, government policies also resulted in large redistributions of income and wealth. For instance, in the nineteenth century some of the largest private fortunes were generated from the alcohol and tobacco monopolies (*estancos*) granted by the state, and frequent civil wars resulted in selective expropriatory taxation on political enemies.

Third, the export industry for primary goods was very unstable, creating large booms and busts. Investment in export industries was geared toward high short-term profits, and after the boom passed the affected regions had very little to show for it.[25] Ocampo (1984) calls this process production-speculation, that is, investment and production without a social past and future. In these cases, fortunes were made when international prices were high and quickly reinvested away from the sector that generated them. When fortunes were made, there was no relationship between production costs and the selling price, and the profits were clearly windfall gains associated with good luck. Conversely, the losses generated by the external price collapses were associated with bad luck.

Throughout Colombian history, most private wealth has not been accumulated in legitimizing ways such as by an innovative entrepreneur who increases productivity and is seen as generating social wealth, or that of the miser, which sacrifices consumption. Because of this, as social change resulted in a loss of acceptance for the traditional world view, privilege lost its legitimacy. This was not a sudden change, but an evolution that accelerated after World War II.

Similarly, as seen below, in most cases public property has not been administered for the social good, and it frequently became controlled by various groups who have exploited it to enhance their own economic position. Thus, public property has also lost its legitimacy in the sense that controlling and exploiting it for non-social goals became accepted behavior (Thoumi, 1990).

A corollary to the loss of legitimacy of traditional income and wealth distributions and of the regime has been the lost legitimacy of property rights. This applies to both private and public property, and legitimizes extreme predatory behavior so that today it is accepted for a person to take wealth from whomever has it, including the state, as long as it can be done (Kalmanovitz, 1989; Thoumi, 1990).[26] This behavior is so extreme that, as noted above, even kidnapping for ransom has become a thriving industry. Indeed, if wealth is perceived as illegitimate and the result of privilege, then kidnapping for ransom is just a way to transfer an arbitrary privilege. Another result of the process of regime delegitimation was the loss of the state's ability to protect property rights, a function that increasingly became privatized, as reflected by a booming private security business.

It must also be noted that recently there have been some important economic analyses regarding property rights. These studies have shown that in any society, "The rights that people have over their assets are not constant; they are a function of their own direct efforts of protection" of other people's capture attempts, and of government protection" (Barzel, 1989: 2). These studies follow the mainstream economics tradition and implicitly assume that individual preferences are constant and thus, they do not alter the propensity of individuals to devote resources to attempts to capture property rights. The argument developed here complements the economic analysis of property rights, but argues that changes in two key variables have weakened property rights in Colombia. On one hand, the government's ability to protect property rights declined significantly, and on the other, the individual propensity to challenge those rights rose as the rights of many individuals increasingly became seen as illegitimate.

Another characteristic of Colombia's economic system is that the accumulation of human capital and its remuneration has also been arbitrary. In a country where until recently illiteracy was quite high, the opportunities to accumulate human capital have been skewed in a way that has little to do with an individual's ability and drive. However, as shown in Chapter 1, during the last forty years the level of education in Colombia has increased dramatically, and many individuals look at education as a channel for upward mobility. Unfortunately, opportunities for equally trained individuals and the return to their human capital vary in a way that cannot be statistically explained without including personal connections and status as variables (Tenjo, 1990). That is, the return on the same type of human capital depends on what position an individual has in society. The fact that the relationship between human capital and salaries is perceived to be weak contributes to the conviction that the market operates unfairly, partially expropriating the human capital of those who do not have good social connections, since the return on their investment is significantly lower than that of those who are well connected.

The political system, clientelism, and other rent-seeking activities. The traditional political system was based on paternalistic relations that predominated in rural Colombia and reflected the normality and social acceptance of political inequality. The state was controlled by party elites who took this control for granted as part of their patrimony. The state's accountability and responsibility to the citizenry were extremely limited. Paternalism was a mediating instrument between peasants and the state, and common citizens did not have access to the state except through a patrón. However, the state's resources were limited, and it did not provide many services. In other words, the state meant less to peasants than did the local landlord.

As the state's role increased in the twentieth century and society modernized and urbanized, the state and regime continued to reflect the acceptance of inequality, as Colombia's political system has had a superficial democratic veneer and a deep undemocratic core.[27] Urbanization and industrialization diffused economic conflicts between the two traditional parties because the economic interests of elites in both parties soon substantially overlapped. Before, both parties were interested in the bureaucratic spoils of the state, but the conservative party had a strong rural base in the hacienda system and was closely identified with the Catholic Church, while the liberal party had a more urban support in the artisan and incipient manufacturing and services sectors and was identified more with secular society. Changes in the country's economic structure made it evident to the elites of both parties that they had a common future in the modern manufacturing, services, and agricultural sectors, and that their interests generally coincided. This helped diffuse their old ideological differences.

This coincidence of interests made it possible to end la violencia with a remarkable constitutional reform that ratified an agreement among party elites to share the spoils of the state in the form of the "National Front." This was a 16-year agreement to alternate the presidency between the two parties and to give an even share of all government jobs to each of them. Thus, one half of the ministers, senators, representatives, governors, mayors, and so on down the government bureaucracy had to be filled with members of each party. In cases of an uneven number of jobs, a military official would be appointed. The National Front agreement was equivalent to the legalization of a two-party cartel to control political power. Since the parties remained controlled by the elites, the National Front guaranteed that political power remained in the same old hands and excluded from effective political participation nontraditional parties and political extremists on both the left and the right.[28]

The National Front was relatively successful at lowering the level of violence caused by interparty conflicts. And in order to minimize political conflict, the old party structures had to co-opt new groups that expected a share of the power because of their new education, urbanization, and in some cases economic power. Thus, some newcomers were appointed or elected to government positions. The National Front ended in 1974, but it had been such a cozy arrangement for the political establishment that it was extended by a constitutional amendment requiring that the party in power give a fair share of power and bureaucracy to the opposite one.

The elites' sharing of economic interests allowed for the development of the economic policy consensus that produced the remarkable GDP growth stability and policy continuity discussed in

Chapter 1. However, the power monopoly implicit in the National Front arrangement carried the seeds of further violence as excluded groups found no formal channels to express disagreement with the establishment or to promote change. The National Front coincided with an increase in the government's role and budget, which institutionalized the two traditional parties' control over an increasing pie that promoted a clientelistic political system and an increase in rent-seeking behavior.

Political clientelism developed to fill the role that paternalism had in the old society. In both systems political relations are between citizens with unequal rights, and the weak must appeal to the powerful for access to the state, which is controlled by a group that uses it for its own benefit.

The need to co-opt certain segments of the population also encouraged development of a clientelistic system, as it put large portions of the state's budget and many state enterprises in the hands of political leaders. This system was quite successful, particularly at providing employment for the new middle class (Leal, 1989: 17), yet it slowly but surely weakened the state, causing it to become less autonomous and its services increasingly viewed as a bounty. In Colombia's clientelistic system, "state entities appear to be owned by the political bosses. This notion is prevalent in all social spheres, including that of the political bosses who publicly claim their right to use and manage the state entities" (Díaz-Uribe, 1986: 35, author's translation). In this system the state is a bounty to be distributed by political bosses in exchange for the support and vote of their clients. Therefore a vote is not a free expression of opinion, but a payment that citizens make to obtain services provided by the state—services that are denied to those known to be affiliated with the election's losers.

A side effect of the clientelist system is the de-politicization of the traditional parties, since citizens vote for a candidate on the basis of an expected pay-off (jobs and public services) and not on the basis of any political platform (Leal, 1984). Another impact of the system has been the weakening of public property rights and the loss of the social functions of state property. Citizens in a clientelist system cannot easily claim their legal rights before the state, since state institutions and enterprises are not run as public property and state policies are not formulated to satisfy broad social needs, or when they are so formulated their implementation does not follow the policies' spirit. In this system, state organizations become the property of a political group or boss. In the case of productive state enterprises such as utility companies, banks, commercial agencies, and others, the group or boss controls job appointments and other internal management polices. It is precisely because these enterprises are not public property, but rather a privatized bounty, that their labor unions can strongly oppose any formal privatization attempts even in the face of overwhelming evidence of waste, inefficiency, and mismanagement. In these cases formal privatization does not turn public property into private, but informally privatized property into formally private property.

The growing complexity and size of the state increased the incentives and payoffs of clientelistic and other rent-seeking behavior in Colombia. Economic policies, laws, and regulations with redistributive implications promoted the growth of rent-seeking organizations that succeeded in getting the government to formulate policies that clearly benefited narrowly defined economic interests. Since many of these policies are perceived by a large proportion of the population as benefiting small groups rather than society at large, breaking the rules and regulations imposed by the government is considered by most Colombians as a legitimate action, greatly contributing to weakening the state.

Government services as a share of GDP (see Table 1.1) have increased through time, but those data do not reflect the size of the public sector and the possible impact of clientelistic practices on Colombia's economy. Most of the public sector's GDP contribution is made of value-added activities not generated in government services, but in mining, manufacturing, banking, and other sectors. The nonfinancial consolidated public sector includes the central administration; 90 "decentralized" agencies that include 9 social security institutions; over 1,500 regional and local governments and agencies, including 170 local enterprises; and nearly 50 national nonfinancial public enterprises that include the National Coffee Fund; Colombian Coal (CARBOCOL); Colombian Petroleum Company (ECOPETROL); the electricity, telephone, and postal companies; IDEMA (the marketing enterprise for key agricultural products), and so forth.

The public sector has grown steadily during the last three decades, "partly as a result of the normal development process and partly due to a lapsed fiscal discipline. The 1982 international debt crisis and the economic adjustment program carried out during 1984–1986 have only slowed the growth of the public sector. Thus, by most measures, Colombia's public sector has continued to grow steadily over the last decade. The total expenditure (current and capital expenditures) of the nonfinancial consolidated public sector rose from 22.1 percent of GDP in 1981 to 23.8 percent of GDP by 1989. The public sector's contribution to GDP rose from 17.8 percent of GDP in 1981 to

21.5 percent of GDP by 1986, while the share of public sector wage in total wage bill of the economy also rose from 30.4 percent to 33.9 percent during the same period. Public investment has consistently contributed about half of the country's fixed capital formation" (World Bank, 1990c: 15).

The growth in the public sector, particularly in the number of public institutions, resulted in confusing and overlapping roles and "in a complex web of administrative relations within the state that progressively institutionalized disorder, and that helped consolidate the political system. The formal disorder within the state contributed to the politics required by the clientelistic use of public resources. The limits between legal and illegal use of public funds became blurred and the flourishing illegality became harder to detect" (Leal, 1989: 17, author's translation).

Not all government-generated rents were distributed through political clientelism. Political bosses and party machines have controlled parts of the budget and many state enterprises, and have exerted great pressure on Congress, but other economic policies that generate important rents have been isolated from these forces. Colombia's highly qualified technocracy was responsible for the country's economic performance, and the policy changes they made substantially altered the amount and distribution of individual rents.[29] Many of these rents originated in the ISI of the early post–World War II period. Government policy was designed to protect and promote certain industries, most of them private. Individual producers were granted de facto property rights over domestic markets that enabled them to impose the equivalent of excise taxes on consumers.

ISI and the large increase in the economy's size led to great economic diversification, a fragmentation of producer interests, and rapid growth of distributional coalitions created to protect the market rights of each industry. Business associations grew rapidly in number from 22 in 1950 to 51 (1960), 81 (1970), and 106 (1980) (Urrutia, 1983). This development followed the increase in conflict-of-interest situations among productive branches resulting from a more diversified and increasingly complex production structure. And distribution and coalition building have resulted in the creation of associations with ever narrower interests.

Producers' associations pressure mainly the president and the various ministries where relevant polices are made, and have relatively few contacts with Congress (Kalmanovitz, 1990). The importance of these distributional coalitions in shaping the Colombian economy has been a subject of debate. Bagley (1979) and Kalmanovitz (1990) give them great weight, while Urrutia (1983) is a great deal more skeptical about it. It is difficult to determine their actual success in modifying government policy, but their impact on the political economy could be considerable even if government policy is not significantly altered, for as the economy grows more complex, more of the associations' efforts are designed to neutralize each other. Independent of their actual success, the growth of distributional coalitions in a high-rent environment with an ethic of inequality reinforces the social perception that markets and prices can be manipulated by the powerful, and that wealth is obtained through these manipulations and not through fair market play.

Given the weight of the public sector in the GDP, the formal economy wage bill and capital formation, the growth in the number of distributional coalitions, and the increased scope and complexity of economic policies, it is clear that the social costs of rent-seeking activities are likely to be quite substantial. Further, since the size of the public sector and the number of distributional coalitions have increased continuously, the cost to the economy of rent-seeking activities related to government expenditures and economic policies has increased through time.

The crisis in the administration of justice. One of the main effects of Colombia's institutional crisis has been the collapse of its judicial system. As the regime and its laws lost legitimacy, it became increasingly difficult for the formal judicial system to solve civil conflicts and administer justice. This failure has led to a growing impunity that has promoted the "privatization" of essential public sector functions, and individuals have developed informal means to solve conflicts and administer justice, means that are frequently violent.

FEDESARROLLO and Instituto SER de Investigación's (1990: 17) pioneer study shows that the majority of criminal processes do not lead to a judgment because of case overload. Indeed, the percentage of cases judged was 46.1 percent in 1984, 24.1 percent in 1985, 25.2 percent in 1986, and 38 percent in 1987. Arbeláez (1990: 192–197) shows that during the 1980s the administration of justice did not receive a high priority in the government budget. The share of the central government budget ("Presupuesto General de la Nación") allocated to the judicial branch increased from about 2.5 percent in the early 1970s to about 3 percent in 1980 and 3.7 percent in 1983. However, it fell steadily after that to 2 percent in 1987.

The data about the justice system are incomplete, but the available data not only show an alarming level of impunity in Colombia, but also that the risks assumed by individuals who take the law into their own hands or undertake illegal activities are low. Indeed, the private "justice" system and its threat of violent retaliation might in some instances generate more risks to the criminals than the formal justice system.

The workings of the market system. Another key legacy of the inequality ethic and past institutional developments is that the nature of market competition in Colombia is significantly different from that considered standard by the economics texts. First of all, free markets are not necessarily competitive. Inequality and lack of solidarity produce an environment in which the distribution of power among market actors is skewed and frequently leads to concentration and exploitation. In Colombia many market transactions are not between anonymous participants, and social and political factors influence their outcome. Therefore, analyses that use "markets" as a category can sometimes be misleading if the relevant category is just a transaction, when the result varies depending on the participants. In other words, two markets with the same number of sellers and buyers that make the same number of transactions may differ substantially if the participants in one market have unequal social status, while those who participate in the other enjoy equal status.[30]

Second, the concentration of political power allows powerful market participants to alter or distort the "rules of the game." The government apparatus can be used to obtain high profits through such avenues as increased protection, subsidized credit, import privileges, and other economic policies, as well as by influencing the judicial, legislative, and police systems to increase landholdings or expel settlers. From the perspective of a market actor operating in this environment, the means to obtain a particular goal or to increase one's income and wealth are not limited to what economists include under the heading of "policy variables," but transcend into corruption and power abuse. Indeed, bribing a judge to obtain a favorable result or a public official to alter the route of a new highway could produce more profits or private wealth than lobbying for higher tariffs.

Third, contracts can easily be altered because the systems to enforce them are corrupt. Since the weak are at a disadvantage using the formal legal system, the ability to enforce contracts depends on the power of each individual. This clearly undermines property rights, because they depend on the power of the owner.

Fourth, many market transactions are seen as zero-sum games in which somebody gains at the expense of others. Consequently, there is continuous clamor for government intervention to regulate markets and protect the weak. Unfortunately, the government's autonomy from influential groups is necessary for this type of intervention to succeed. In Colombia, the state may have assumed the role of protector of the weak, but lost its autonomy and became hostage to clientelistic groups that use the distributional capacity of the state to their benefit. And yet, while the free market is clearly perceived as arbitrary, paternalistic government intervention is not objective either. In fact, attempts to regulate a market frequently result in greater arbitrariness and risk, as market rules can be altered at any moment.

Fifth, the nature of market competition is significantly different from that addressed in mainstream economics texts. Market segmentation is caused by social, natural, and economic policy factors. Some of the most important prices in the economy, such as those of labor, capital, and real estate (both rental and property transactions), are not set in markets in which atomistic agents enter with equal rights and information, but are often the result of transactions whose outcome depends on each individual's social, economic, and political position. Therefore, prices are not a clearing mechanism that incorporate complete information about costs and value, but are the result of negotiations in which the power of the different actors determines the result. Thus, many goods or services will *not* have "an established market price" equal for everybody, but a different price in each transaction.

This concept of the transacting and market mechanisms leads to several important conclusions. First, since some of the most important goods and services do not have a "market price," there is not necessarily a link between the cost of a product and its price, or its opportunity cost. For instance, wages, particularly those paid by the state, are not linked to productivity. Second, price discrimination is socially accepted and frequently institutionalized. For example, interest rates are different depending on the source and use of the capital.

Third, Colombian markets are biased against the production of good quality services, despite the abundance of low-priced labor inputs. The producers of goods can be physically separated from consumers, and they do not need to know each other. But with many services it is not possible to separate consumers and producers, and the social status of the participants in the transaction cannot be hidden. Thus, in some cases the superiority attitude of a service buyer obviates against viewing the supplier as an entrepreneur who is providing a service for a fee, and the servile attitude of the service seller (unable to ignore the social relationship to the purchaser) prevents him or her from finding pride and satisfaction in providing high quality service—an act that requires one to assume responsibilities and take independent initiatives. Therefore, quality services require a minimum degree of social equality and mutual respect between the transacting parties. It is thus easier for an affluent Colombian to obtain quality service from a local doctor trained abroad, who can be considered a social peer, than from a blue collar worker who may be seen as being socially inferior to the purchaser.

Fourth, important prices that are set as the result of a political transaction, and the lack of a direct relationship between cost and price or productivity and wage tend to create entitlements and price rigidities. Once a price, subsidy, or labor benefit is set, it is hard to change, and doing so requires new negotiations and power confrontations between the various actors.[31]

It is true that, as society urbanized and modernized, some of the power relations that affect markets became diluted. Nonetheless capital, labor, and other important markets remained highly influenced by power. And the state's growth in size and complexity during the post–World War II period made many new activities subject to power relations: getting a telephone line or an import license, being admitted to a public high school, getting the state to build a sewer pipe, obtaining a public job, and so on. Since these transactions still occur between unequal participants, rent-seeking and predatory behavior persists.

The Growth of the Informal Economy

The Legal and Illegal Economic Sectors

Before looking at the informal economy in Colombia it is important to clarify some concepts related to economic formality and informality. First we define legal income as that which is earned in compliance with prevailing laws of the state, which has jurisdiction over the actions and activity that generates the income; and illegal income as that which is not earned with such compliance. Legal and illegal activities may be used to produce the same goods and services; in most instances what determines legality is law compliance, not the type of product or service, or whether its consumption is moral.[32] Of course, what is a legal economic activity in one country could be illegal in another, and what is legal at one point in time might be illegal at another.[33]

While these definitions suggest that there is a sharp dividing line between legal and illegal incomes, there are different degrees of legality and illegality depending on the degree of compliance with the law. For example, in some cases the income-generating activity is illegal and all the income is illegal, but there are other cases in which the income-generating activity is legal, even though the producing unit breaks a few laws. While it may be argued that income generated in the latter case is as illegal as that of the former, there are significant differences in the difficulty of identifying it as illegal, in the government's ability to prosecute offending parties, and in the penalties that the legal system can impose. In reality, then, the differences between legal and illegal income do not result in a black and white division, but rather in a continuum on which gray prevails.

De Soto (1986), in the best known study of the informal sector of a Latin American country, provides a good example of these realities. He argues that in Peru there are "good" and "bad" laws that regulate and control economic activity. Thus, individuals who break "bad" laws in their economic endeavors generate "good" illegal income. Conversely, it is implied that economic activity that breaks "good" laws creates "bad" income. De Soto defines the informal economy as the part of the illegal one that results from legitimate economic activities which have to be done illegally because of "bad" government laws and regulations that are too costly or cumbersome, and that make legal activity nonviable for many low income entrepreneurs. There is no doubt that the informal economy so defined is very important throughout Latin America.

However, as shown in Argentina (Guissarri, 1989), there is no reason to expect that an entrepreneur who has broken a "bad" law, such as one that imposes a uselessly difficult set of requirements to get a permit, will not later break a "good" law that requires the payment to the government of sales or income taxes. Besides, legitimizing noncompliance with "bad" laws also promotes noncompliance with "good" laws.

Of course, in every country there is a proportion of GDP which is not generated in full compliance with the law. Some of it is created by transactions that only involve cash so as to leave no evidence and avoid taxes; some is income hidden by one party without the knowledge of the other, such as when a businessowner underreports retail sales. But although underground economic activities exist in all countries, their magnitude depends on the extent of government intervention to regulate and control the economy, the level and nature of various taxes, the government's ability to enforce its own laws, the magnitude of the penalties it imposes, and the willingness of citizens to comply with laws that inherently impose economic costs.

As argued by De Soto, the formality of legitimate activities (legality) and their informality have their own costs and benefits. These depend on the laws and regulations that prevail in the economy in which the activity is undertaken. A firm that operates within the formal system faces some costs not found in the informal sector such as sales, value-added, and income taxes; the costs implied by compliance with minimum wage laws and other labor legislation; and the costs of an accounting system that meets legal standards. It should be noted that in most countries, smaller firms tend to have fewer formality costs because some requirements are less stringent or do not apply to them. Among the benefits of the formal sector are easier access to formal capital markets, the ability to use the legal system for conflict resolution, the right to apply for import licenses or bid on government jobs, and to lobby legally for beneficial policies and laws.[34] In general, most costs of formality are benefits enjoyed (costs avoided) by informal firms, and vice versa.

There are also costs associated with illegality such as bribes paid to corrupt officials, the risks of jail sentences, fines, and even confiscation. These costs of informality may lead to significant resource misallocation and high social costs.[35]

In a society with significant parts of the economy above and underground, economic actors who break the law are not likely to be caught and punished, so profit-maximizing entrepreneurs may seek the benefits of both formality and informality. There are strong incentives for producers to operate in partial formality, as long as they can retain the advantages of the formal sector while accessing those of the informal sector. Of course, the larger the underground economy and the lower the probability of punishment, the stronger the incentives of partial formality. When the government's capacity to enforce laws is weak, formal and informal activities are complementary instead of substitutes, and firms will operate both formally and informally.[36] The only economic actors who would choose to operate fully within the law are either those who have strong moral values so they always respect the law, or those who are extremely risk-averse.[37]

Firms that operate simultaneously in the legal and illegal sectors can transfer resources from one sector to the other. They can "dirty" or "launder" income and capital, and can act as a bridge between the formal and informal sectors.

The complexity and continuous creation of laws and regulations are also sources of illegal economic activity when the government's enforcement capacity is weak. First, complexity provides a good excuse not to comply because the interpretation of the laws can always be questioned, and firms can argue they honestly misunderstood them. Second, keeping up-to-date with new laws and regulations is costly. Since the risks of noncompliance are low, businessowners may choose to disregard them, and plead ignorance in the unlikely event of getting caught breaking the law.

Similar to the differences between legal and illegal income, legal and illegal wealth can also be defined as having been accumulated with or without compliance with the laws of the relevant jurisdiction. Again, while the definition suggests a clear difference, in reality a continuum develops with a very wide gray area. For instance, there may be differences depending on whether the capital originates in an activity that is illegal per se, on whether the owner has knowledge of the capital's origin, on the proportion of the total capital illegally accumulated, and so on.

The Risks of Illegality and Consumer and Producer Behavior

The risks of having illegal income and capital depend on their grayness and size, the frequency of the illegal transactions, the effectiveness of concurrent legal activities as a protective shield, the way in which income is spent and wealth invested, the government's law enforcing efforts, and on the size of the country's illegal sector. In an economy where most citizens comply with the law, it is quite risky and costly not to comply, but in a society with few fully law-abiding individuals, it is costly to respect all the laws.[38]

The risks of having illegal income and assets detected depend on their size and the nature of the goods and services by which they are generated. Regarding size, every economic unit has a capacity to hide some income and assets without substantial risk.[39] The maximum amount that is safe to hide depends on the amount of resources devoted by the government to law enforcement and on the allocation of those resources. For example, given the high cost of a tax audit, the government has strong incentives to devote resources to investigate only taxpayers with high incomes and those who raise clear suspicions. Thus, small amounts of income can be hidden in most countries without risk, particularly when the income generating transaction uses cash and no receipt is issued. Also, in some cases larger amounts of illegal income and assets could be hidden without significant risks if they are not conspicuous.[40]

The consumption and investment patterns of those involved in illegal activities are influenced by the illegal nature of their income and assets. And the characteristics of certain goods and services make them particularly attractive for consumption or investment of illegal income and capital. Services and non-durable consumer goods are attractive because they do not leave easily detected evidence of their use; assets for which the price is hard to estimate are also attractive, because the resources used in their acquisition may be easily understated; assets located in areas where the government presence and sovereignty are weak are also attractive, as are those for which ownership does not require disclosure or may be concealed. Thus, goods with a high ratio of value to physical volume and weight, and those that keep their value through time, are likely to be in demand among those who want to hide income and assets.

In countries with a large underground economy, where the state has few resources to prosecute tax evaders and tax enforcers are easily bribed, the risk of penalty or jail sentence is extremely low even when the tax evader is caught. Indeed, income tax avoidance may even be a source of personal pride.[41]

The Underground Economy in Colombia and Government Policies

The growth of the underground economy was one of the main characteristics of Colombia's development process during the last twenty years. Data on the underground economy are sparse and incomplete and it is not possible to accurately estimate its size. However, government policies have frequently recognized its importance.

As noted in Chapter 1, Gómez (1985) uses a common method to estimate that in 1985 the underground economy accounted for 8.7 percent more of GDP than in the 1974 to 1976 base years. The magnitude of this estimate indicates that the underground economy was growing faster than the formal, and that it had become the leading economic sector during that period.

Another indication of the importance of the underground economy is the large amount of hidden income and assets that Colombians have, as reflected in successive tax amnesties that governments have implemented in the attempt to increase tax collections.[42] Again estimates of hidden income and capital cannot be accurate, but Ibañez (1974), in a study of possible implications of the 1974 tax reform, estimated that about one-third of the sales taxes had been avoided prior to the reform. And using estimates of the GDP and income distribution, Ibañez determined that the income reported in tax returns was only about one-third of the total reportable income.

Further evidence of the size of the underground economy is provided by the significant amount of export and import contraband. The National Federation of Retailers (Federación Nacional de Comerciantes—FENALCO) (1987) estimates that import contraband between 1980 and 1987, while fluctuating substantially from year to year, was valued as high as U.S. $1 billion per year, or about 22 percent of the 1988 registered merchandise imports (see Chapter 6).

The few estimates available confirm that the underground economy, as defined in the previous section, has been large and pervasive in Colombia, to the point that it can be stated there is virtually no Colombian resident who does not break a law associated with economic behavior. While some underground transactions are crudely illegal (like the bribes of judges and government bureaucrats), most of them are adapted to the laws, regulations, and government policies that are conducive to illegal behavior, particularly as the state's increasing weakness make laws less likely to be enforced.

As noted, there has been widespread underreporting of income and assets for tax purposes. For several decades until 1988, Colombia had a net worth tax which was justified theoretically as a progressive tax on rich capitalists, and pragmatically as a way to tax asset-rich individuals who hid their income and evaded income taxes, particularly large landowners who frequently claimed losses or very little income. Every income tax return was accompanied by a balance and a taxable net worth estimate. The weaknesses in tax collection and incentives for tax evasion were so great, and tax evaders so creative, that even a market for fictitious liabilities and costs appeared.[43] Evasion of this tax has been considered socially acceptable behavior, ratified by the various tax amnesties granted during the last two decades. Having helped to eliminate any possible social stigma attached to laundering capital, these tax amnesties have been pragmatically justified on the grounds that they increase the tax base. However, as shown in chapter one, they have done so only in the short run and have promoted tax evasion as taxpayers realize that every few years they may launder their income and assets if necessary.

The capital gains[44] tax, which contributed to asset undervaluation, was another tax to avoid. Because the annual inflation rate since the early 1970s has fluctuated in the 20 to 30 percent range, and asset revaluations have been allowed only at much lower rates, this has been a tax mostly on nominal gains. Thus, this has been a tax on inflation that taxpayers consider confiscatory; they have few moral constraints to evade it and do so whenever possible.

The undeveloped and segmented capital market also has had an impact on people's ability to hold illegal assets. As noted in chapter one, long-term financing has been difficult to obtain and subject to a wide variety of government regulations and controls, which were originally inspired by the attempt to funnel credit to priority sectors, but also influenced by organized groups that have lobbied successfully to gain privileged access to long-term financing. A particularly important distortion is clear in the scarcity of long-term financing for existing housing and other real estate assets, created by construction lobbies that obtained a virtual monopoly on formal capital market long-term financing, on the fallacious argument that financing existing housing does not create employment.

The combination of the lack of long-term financing, a net worth tax, and a capital gains tax that is primarily a tax on inflation, has made real estate an ideal sector to hide capital. Since most real estate transactions have been financed outside formal markets, their value has been greatly underreported for tax purposes, resulting in a situation in which virtually everyone who owns any real estate has had substantial hidden capital. And since almost all reported transaction prices are grossly undervalued, government auditors cannot use them to question a particular transaction's reported price. The lack of formal long-term financing also results in multiple nominal real estate asset prices at a particular point in time. That is, prices vary widely depending on the way the seller and buyer finance the transaction.

There are other socially accepted ways to hide capital or consume illegally sold goods and services, and contraband is one of the most obvious. Colombia's protectionist policies, being based on tariffs and nontariff trade barriers as well as other trade policies, promoted contraband as a socially acceptable economic activity. For example, in the mid 1950s the government decided to encourage the development of the 44 km^2 islands of San Andrés and Providencia, making them a free port from which Colombian tourists could bring back to the mainland a certain amount of tariff-free goods for personal use. This policy prompted the emergence of entrepreneurs who specialized in bringing to the mainland small amounts of contraband goods for sale. This business grew substantially and gained legitimacy to the point that what originally was a somewhat concealed trade became totally open; markets in which contraband is freely traded were established in most cities and goods can actually be ordered from many United States catalogs. Of course, not all contraband sold in these markets comes from San Andrés and Providencia, and indeed, it is likely that very little does. But they provided the beginning. Later developments like the creation of export assembly free zones in Colombia, and more importantly the Colón free zone in Panama, provided necessary storage and marketing facilities for imports awaiting licensing and nationalization, but also facilitated the movement of contraband into Colombia.

Business associations in the illegal contraband markets (known today as "San Andresitos," a name that recalls their origin) have used the political clout afforded by their numbers to obtain from local governments public services and police protection despite the flagrantly illegal nature of their business. Their political strength is such that politicians frequently seek their support, ignoring their illegal activities. These contraband markets are also good vehicles to bring in the proceeds of illegal exports. Prices for many goods sold in those markets are comparable to U.S. retail levels, suggesting that those who want to bring their illegal capital into Colombia via the contraband markets are willing to make only small profits or even lose a little in order to do so.

The legitimation of contraband in Colombia has also promoted the growth of other underground activities. Contraband competes with legal imports and therefore encourages legal importers to import illegally, either by underinvoicing or smuggling part of their imports.

Other government actions have also contributed to economic law-breaking. As noted in chapter one, from 1931 to 1991 Colombia had exchange controls that were tightened in 1967. These made it illegal for Colombian residents to hold foreign exchange or other financial assets in or outside the country. However, foreign exchange circulated rather openly, and the Central Bank relaxed at various times its foreign exchange purchase requirements, buying black market foreign exchange for many years through its so-called "sinister window." These purchases were justified pragmatically because the black market exchange rate was below the official one for substantial periods of time, and the purchases were seen as part of the exchange rate policy followed by the government. This practice facilitated asset laundering over time and contributed to the growing disrespect for the law, and while it has been temporarily abandoned at times, such as in 1984 after the assassination of Justice Minister Rodrigo Lara Bonilla, it has continued as pragmatism prevails in the long-run over moral constraints. It is clear that all administrations implicitly condoned the foreign exchange black market and the Central Bank actually monitored it, taking it into account to determine the official creeping peg devaluation rate.[45]

Additional examples of the widespread practice and acceptance of economic lawbreaking and of the importance to Colombia of its underground economy could be provided, but the basic points should be clear by now. First, the underground economy is large and, while there are no accurate measures of its size, it has clearly grown faster than the formal economy since the mid-1970s. Second, the state's ability to enforce its laws, and the respect and loyalty it commands are extremely weak, having declined through time. Third, most illegal economic activity in Colombia does not carry a social stigma, and in many cases has been institutionalized in a process in which the government itself has frequently participated, at least passively. Fourth, the country's laws, regulations, and institutions made some assets, especially real estate, a good vehicle for hiding capital. Fifth, many economic transactions in Colombia "dirty" money—that is, convert legally earned income and capital into illegal and hidden forms. Similarly, many activities also "launder" resources. In short, many of these actions are simply the accepted way to do business and government policies have contributed to such an environment.

It can thus be concluded that the delegitimation of the political regime has been accompanied by a similar process in the economic realm, further reflecting the weakening of the state. The gap between de jure and de facto economic norms has grown parallel to that of other social norms.

The Dynamics of the System, the Role of the Illegal PSAD Industry, and the Policy Agenda

It has been argued in this chapter that Colombia's crisis has developed gradually as the state's ability to enforce its laws has inexorably been chipped away. The increasing illegitimacy of the regime promoted the development of extreme predatory and rent-seeking behavior, and produced fundamentally flawed markets. This process took place through the interaction of several forces.

First, as the country became more urban and modern, and the old world view was rejected by a growing number of Colombians, more individuals realized that they could break laws with impunity. Deviant behavior became increasingly acceptable among different groups, increasing the probability of conflict among groups. A growing number of Colombians felt alienated from the traditional power structure, dropped any loyalty they had to broad national ideals, and accepted group conflict as the social norm. The diversity of accepted behaviors allows one to argue that most Colombians act as if they had their own "constitution" (set of rules) that gives them enhanced rights to the income and resources of other citizens and the state. In this environment the cost of doing business drastically increases, as many private resources must be devoted to protecting individual wealth and enforcing contracts.

Second, the growing illegitimacy of the regime led to the development of private conflict resolution systems and to the increased privatization of police and security services. Thus, people take the law into their own hands and very often resort to violence.

Third, predatory and rent-seeking economic behavior was also encouraged by the individuals' realization that they can obtain income and assets by changing, bending, or breaking the laws, rules, and regulations that influence economic activity, and that the state cannot protect property rights and enforce contracts.

Fourth, the state had always been a bounty for a few. But the increased role and size of the state, the National Front, and the clientelistic political system it promoted combined to allow more to compete for that bounty, which in turn increased the efforts and resources devoted to rent seeking.

The Colombian system produced reasonably good economic results for a long period of time (1950–1980), but the dynamics of the system were vicious. In order to maintain political and economic control, the establishment accepted and encouraged the gap between legality and reality, but could not keep that gap static or limit predatory and rent-seeking behavior. Once such behavior became tolerated, it snowballed and increasingly became the norm. Indeed, as argued elsewhere (Thoumi, 1987) the growing gap between legality and normality in Colombia has led to what can be described as a "dishonesty trap," that is, a situation in which it is legitimate to break many laws, in which the costs and risks of doing so are extremely low or zero and the benefits quite high. In order to escape from this trap, significant social change must take place. In other words, marginal policy changes used in the past to defuse social pressures no longer work. The time for politics as usual has passed.

Urrutia (1991: 376–377) sees development in Colombia in a more positive light. Explaining why it developed a clientelistic system instead of a populist one he writes: "In summary, the Colombian political system, very dependent on clientelistic practices, is not admired by national and foreign intellectuals, but it receives support from more than 80 percent of the voters in election after election. In the last two decades it has produced economic growth, an improved distribution of income, and fairly progressive government expenditures. Its very success is the main source of its weakness, since voters have systematically excluded minorities that want radical change from power, and this has driven such minorities to violence and guerrilla activity."

Urrutia does not claim the Colombian system was effective dealing with all situations, and it could no doubt be argued that Colombia's system was relatively good compared to others in Latin America. However, this explanation has two weaknesses. First, it implicitly attributes the decline in growth rates during the 1980s to external factors, a causal relationship rejected by arguments elaborated in this book (see Chapter 1). Second, in Colombia's clientelistic system, every voter faced a dilemma: in order to access the state one must play the clientelistic game or otherwise incur large costs, so most voters play the game. However, this does not prove that voters are satisfied with the system or happy to have it controlled by traditional elites.

Over time, the survival of clientelism required an increasing share of the GDP be devoted to satisfying ever larger clienteles, and the weakening of the State forced the private sector to devote more resources to obtaining rents and protecting property. Changes in the capital markets that took place in the mid-1970s and the growth of the illegal PSAD industry led to highly speculative investments, to a boom in the financial sector, and to the expectation of high short-term profits. But none of these changes were conducive to increases in productivity that would sustain economic growth. During the 1980s, investments in the mining sector contributed little to increasing productivity as they were capital intensive and did not have significant backward links to the rest of the economy; they also contributed to predatory behavior by enlarging the public sector. One can conclude, then, that the political and economic systems were stable in the short run but unstable in the long run, as increased rent-seeking behavior and other internal problems hindered growth, and as the government bounty had to keep increasing to keep more demanding voters satisfied.

The growth of rent-seeking and predatory behavior and the violence that pervades the country were greatly exacerbated by the growth of the illegal PSAD industry. Indeed, the industry's profits are fundamentally rents created by its illegal status. Besides, the industry's resources are large relative to the size of Colombia's economy (see Chapter 6) so that its illegal condition has contributed greatly to the expansion of the underground economy, encouraged money laundering activities, and hastened corruption in the government. However, as argued in Chapter 5, the de jure/de facto gap was one of the main factors that promoted the growth of the illegal PSAD industry in Colombia. This gap also opened up in other Andean countries; however, the process of regime delegitimation began earlier in Colombia, so that the country had a head start that made it a more attractive location for the illegal PSAD industry. In other words, characteristics of Colombia's political and economic systems made the country vulnerable to the development of the illegal PSAD industry, and were an important factor in the industry's location and development in Colombia. And by taking advantage of the social decomposition, the industry became a catalyst that rapidly accelerated it.

As discussed, total factor productivity growth in Colombia slowed in the mid-1970s and stagnated in the 1980s after peaking in 1980 (Table 1.2). Ocampo (1991) attributes this decline to the lack of an active industrial policy that put an end to the structural change that had been taking place. The interpretation developed here does not deny Ocampo's point; however, institutional deterioration was one of the main reasons that a proactive industrial policy became increasingly difficult to implement. An effective industrial policy requires a degree of government autonomy from pressure groups and an ability to make beneficiaries of that policy accountable to the government. These conditions existed perhaps to a degree during the Lleras Restrepo administration that ended in 1970, but gradually disappeared thereafter. Ocampo also disregards the catalytic impact of the illegal PSAD industry. These developments normalized predatory and rent-seeking activity, weakened property rights, induced speculative investments, and in general contributed to a decline in the rate of economic growth.

As noted in Chapter 1, a significant policy change began during the government of Belisario Betancur (1982–1986) to reform the political system and concluded with a new constitution approved in 1991. Simultaneously, slower growth rates led to a significant process of policy change that began in 1989. Inspired by conventional economic wisdom, it hopes to revive growth by liberalizing the economy. This position attributes low growth to poor policies—mainly high foreign trade barriers, price controls and subsidies, and interventions that distort capital and labor markets.

While the interpretation of Colombia's economic crisis provided here accepts that many government policies have to be changed, it differs from conventional economic analysis by giving causal priority to institutional inadequacies. In other words, slow growth is caused by institutional problems that run deeper than mistaken policies, and the return to a high-growth path requires not only policy but also important institutional changes.

Colombia's basic challenge is defined by the combined goal of building an economic system efficient in production, and one based on a broad social consensus about the fairness of the distribution of income and wealth. As Kalmanovitz (1989: 59) states, Colombia's tragedy is the existence of a capitalist system without its complementary ethics of individual responsibility, which has led to the development of a savage capitalism. Hence, for the system to be socially just, capitalism's efficiency must be complemented by socially perceived fairness. The link between authoritarian, paternalistic traditions and high income and wealth concentration requires reforms aimed at developing a "democratic capitalism" that is respected by its citizens, in which there is a sense of fairness in the way economic policy is formulated and implemented, and in which every citizen has something at stake.

This is a formidable challenge, and it is unlikely that any particular administration could succeed in meeting it during a four-year presidential period, or that several administrations will provide the necessary policy continuity. However, if the challenge is not met, one can expect further deterioration in Colombian society—that is, increased violence, economic stagnation, and a further decline in the quality of life.

The formulation of adequate policies needed to respond to the challenge is further complicated because institutions tend to evolve in ways not easily foreseen. One may argue that implementing the necessary reforms requires a political commitment to what could be called a "national project," which should have, among others, the following goals:

First, the creation of a market system in which the most important prices are set anonymously, that is, markets in which the social status of market participants is irrelevant—markets that both *are* not and do not *appear* to be manipulated by powerful groups. Of course, in order to have anonymous markets, it is necessary to spread out economic power.

Second, among the state's main functions should be the strengthening of the judicial branch to allow the state to regain its functions as law enforcer and arbitrator of civil conflicts. Its laws should minimize those conflicts and reflect economic realities.[46] They should be written in ways that make them easily interpreted, applied and enforced. Thus, important criteria in evaluating a law should be the state's ability to enforce it and to limit any loopholes, particularly those designed to benefit small groups. These criteria should take precedence over economic efficiency because a law or policy designed to achieve an economic optimum is likely to be more damaging than beneficial when it is unenforceable.

Third, government accountability and citizen participation should increase at all levels. This is not easy, as they require enough institutional change to force government bureaucracies to become accountable to the people and to weaken the stronghold that local politicians have on municipal power. Indeed, it ultimately requires the demise of the clientelist system that has developed during the last fifteen years (Leal, 1990).

Achieving these goals is obviously not easy. Policy recommendations to change institutions are always quite risky because it is not clear whether the government can implement them or even which institutional change must occur. Institutions tend to be society specific, and their evolution is not generalizable. This is the main reason that institutional analyses are long on diagnosis and short on policy recommendations. In spite of these risks, I dare make a few suggestions.

Government intervention should be focused on equalizing the economic opportunities of different groups in Colombia. It is necessary to develop a system in which income and wealth are associated with individual achievement and success in a fair game, and not with privilege or rent capture. The goal should be to provide a social safety net, and to promote equality of economic opportunities (not results). Therefore, government spending should first concentrate on sectors that equalize individual opportunities, particularly primary education, preventive medicine, and child care; and then in infrastructure to increase the degree of market integration and competition.

If one accepts that the state is not autonomous from the distributional coalitions that influence its policies, then a policy dilemma arises. One may argue that government should minimize its role as a promoter and protector of specific economic activities, and as a distributor of wealth, and that the state should act more as a referee to insure that the "rules of the game" are applied fairly and objectively to everybody. Accordingly, the state should not attempt to redistribute wealth, protect the weak, or act in a paternalistic way because its attempts to do so will fail. On the other hand, attempts to end government intervention may lead to the elimination of programs that benefit the politically weakest members of society, preserving those that benefit the strongest members. It is thus necessary to rethink and reformulate the state's role in Colombia so it becomes less vulnerable to manipulation by pressure groups and lobbies. A detailed policy prescription would require more probing into the political economy.

The difficulty in making specific policy recommendations may be illustrated by the following example. Recent comparisons between development patterns of Scandinavian and Latin American countries indicate that one of the main policy differences between the two groups of countries has been that in Scandinavia governments have increased the target groups' incomes without substantial interventions in the goods and factors markets (Blomström and Meller, 1991). Following this line of thought, one should argue that in order to satisfy basic needs, the government should not attempt to distribute income by altering the prices of the goods purchased and sold by the lower classes (which is intervening in the products and labor markets), but instead should transfer income directly to the target groups and let the market naturally allocate resources. However, the ability to transfer income in Scandinavia is likely related to a relatively high degree of social cohesion, which is lacking in Colombia.

Indeed, given the deep individualism in Colombian society, direct income transfers to the poor are most unlikely and it is necessary to disguise them as price and other subsidies.

The 1991 constitution clearly attempts to make the government more accountable to the citizenry. For one thing, it provides for the election of mayors, weakens regionally based clientelism by requiring representatives to Congress to be elected nationally, strengthens municipal finances, and provides for a significantly larger allocation of budget resources to the social sectors. Unfortunately, while it creates a large number of entitlements designed to guarantee the satisfaction of basic needs for all Colombians, it does not provide appropriate government financing to meet these expenditures. If Congress and the government take these entitlements seriously, there is a danger that Colombia will experience populist movements of the type common in Latin America, but that Colombia's clientelistic system has so far prevented.[47] There is also a danger that the new constitution will promote policies that "emphasize growth and income distribution and de-emphasize the risks of inflation and deficit finance, external constraints, and the reaction of the economic agents to nonmarket policies" (Dornbusch and Edwards, 1991: 9).

If one acknowledges the government's fundamental inability to implement many policies, then some policies of the Barco and Gaviria administrations are consistent with needed reforms, but prior institutional changes are required so the policies do not increase the concentration of wealth and power or market inequity. For example, capital markets should be made more competitive, but as restrictions are eliminated the power of large economic actors should be controlled to avoid greater wealth and rent concentration. The 1970s demonstrated that liberalizing capital markets in a system where most banks are owned by large economic groups that lend mainly to their own firms actually increased concentration and led to large bankruptcies. It is necessary to insure that small savers are paid positive real interest rates and that small entrepreneurs have access to capital. The long-term mortgage market should be made more competitive by increasing the financing available for existing housing. This would weaken the control the construction industry has over long-term real estate financing, make it easier to collect taxes on real estate transactions, and decrease incentives to hide capital (Thoumi, 1989). Of course, these changes would be greatly facilitated by a decline in the inflation rate that would weaken the pressures for indexation and eventually strengthen long-term capital markets.

Another example is the lowering of international trade barriers to decrease the bounty creation by the government and increase competition. The Gaviria government has made significant moves in this direction. Progress is also visible in new labor legislation that made the labor market more flexible, and in the moves to make the process of bidding on government contracts more transparent. A further step would be to make public the decision-making process for assigning government contracts so corruption within the government declines.

Unfortunately, the obstacles to establishing a capitalist democracy in Colombia are many. Perhaps the most important among them is the illegal PSAD industry, whose size, behavior, and illegality add a particularly complex dimension to any democratic capitalist reform needed by the regime to regain legitimacy. It is necessary to have a much smaller and weaker underground economy, an accomplishment unlikely to be achieved as long as the illegal PSAD industry continues to flourish. Further, even if the illegal drug flow is stemmed, Colombia cannot avoid confronting the fact that PSAD entrepreneurs are already extremely rich and—sooner or later—must be assimilated into the mainstream society.

However, such assimilation creates fundamental problems for the government. At a time of pressing need to build the basis for a democratic capitalism, the illegal PSAD industry generates forces in the opposite direction because of its income concentration and growing size, and the behavior of drug traffickers. The drug traffickers' investments in rural areas have increased the income and wealth concentration in those regions, and the nature of the industry's profits has contributed to the widespread rent-seeking and predatory behavior that pervades Colombia. Assimilating illegal PSAD capital legitimizes those behaviors.

Another problem regarding assimilation arises from the background and values of drug traffickers. Many have violent criminal backgrounds that would implicitly be condoned if they are brought into the mainstream (see Chapter 4), and many have shown highly paternalistic behavior patterns that conflict with the development of a capitalistic democracy. In addition, the actions of the illegal PSAD industry, such as its significant contribution to the development of paramilitary groups and to the violent repression of left-leaning political activists, have frequently been important obstacles to government attempts to open up the political system, a precondition to any democratizing effort (Leal, 1990; and Melo, 1990).

As elaborated in Chapter 10, the Colombian government has few policy choices in dealing with the illegal PSAD industry. Given the industry's illegality outside Colombia, the government cannot legalize or decriminalize it to eliminate the high profits it generates. However, the government cannot really try to eliminate the industry through repressive measures or confiscate assets accumulated by those involved in the business, because the state is too weak, the level of violence required is too high, and so much of the industry's capital is invested outside Colombia. Moreover, the large amount of "clean" hidden capital in Colombia cannot possibly be separated from the "dirty" capital that the government might like to confiscate (Thoumi, 1989).

Indeed, given the state's weakness and the structure of PSAD production and consumption, the industry would decline only in response to lower profits generated by declining demand. And it is unfortunately clear that to achieve lower global demand a very different policy approach is needed in both producer and consumer countries. There is a need to reallocate resources to drug addiction prevention, education, and treatment and to address social problems that contribute to demand. Alone, Colombia cannot do much to achieve these policy changes.

As long as profits in the illegal PSAD industry remain high, the industry will continue to prosper. Therefore, government actions that include destroying industry facilities or capturing and imprisoning drug traffickers will only increase the country's level of violence and industry profits, and at best will result in a temporary disruption of operations; new entrepreneurs will soon appear to continue the business. One policy alternative is to negotiate with illegal PSAD businessmen to avoid short-term violence. However, this cannot stop long-term trade and will subject the government to greater external pressures.

In order to combat illegal drug and income flows, Colombia needs the collaboration of governments of countries in which the PSAD are consumed and in which their profits are laundered. However, there are no signs that illegal PSAD profits will soon disappear from international markets, or that other countries will succeed in stopping the money laundering activities of their financial institutions, which have been accepted financial practice for a long time.[48]

While Colombia needs international cooperation to control demand, money laundering, the supply of chemical precursors, and so forth, there is the real danger that collaboration with foreign governments (particularly the United States) will result in an increased militarization of the drug policy. That would further increase violence, human rights violations, and power abuses in Colombia, particularly against left-of-center political groups.

In conclusion, the level of reform required in Colombia is nothing short of a drastic "national project" of economic democratization.

However, the existence of the illegal PSAD industry is a great obstacle to any such project because it promotes violence, concentrates income and wealth, feeds the underground economy, opposes some socially progressive reforms, and weakens the state. Unfortunately, the elimination of illegal PSAD profits depends on factors outside the control of the Colombian government. Since legalization and control of PSAD or a reduction in demand in principal consuming countries are unlikely to take place soon, the only hope to curtail those profits lies in a demand shift toward other PSAD produced and distributed by non-Colombians. Since this is also unlikely, as argued in Chapter 10, the ability of Colombia's government to undertake a democratic capitalism nation-building project is minimal, and will remain so as long as the illegal PSAD industry prospers.

Appendix 2.1
The Opposing Views of Income Distribution Changes

One of the most intriguing aspects of literature regarding Colombia's economic development is the diversity of various authors' perceptions about the evolution of income distribution inequality. As discussed in Chapter 1, econometric studies (Londoño, 1990 and 1992) show that income distribution became more unequal between the late 1930s and the mid-1960s, but has improved significantly since then. Fluctuations in income distribution were caused by changes in the inequality of labor remuneration, since the distribution of capital income and rents remained rather stable. In the first part of the period the real income of skilled workers and professionals increased substantially in response to the demand created by industrialization. However, as the education system caught up with demand and many more individuals received training, real incomes for professionals declined and overall income equality increased.

This process frustrated many educated individuals who perceived this change as a worsening in the income distribution. Studying this phenomenon, Orjuela (1990: 207–208) defines this process as the "pauperization of the middle class" and complains that one in ten professionals received a salary below the minimum wage level. He explains that "even though the cause for this deterioration is not very clear, the social mobility that facilitated the rise of the Colombian middle class was associated with educational mobility. This process seems to have stopped because of the lack in educational planning and of the economic system's inertia in generating new jobs" (author's translation). Orjuela goes on to argue that as the upward mobility channels closed in the formal economy, the illegal drug industry opened new channels that many frustrated educated people took advantage of, a position also sustained by Arango (1988: 145–148). Orjuela also argues that "in the late 1960s the salary of a single individual was sufficient to satisfy the needs of a middle-class family and it even allowed for some savings; by the end of the 1970s two individuals had to work to maintain that income level." Unfortunately, Orjuela does not supply data to support his statements.

As noted in Chapter 1, the growth of tertiary education since 1960 has been extraordinary, and college enrollment increased from 1.8 percent in 1960 to 10.8 percent in 1980. This huge increase in the supply of educated people had to lower their salaries substantially, and any expectation for the economy to generate enough jobs for them without lowering salaries was totally unrealistic. It is simply impossible to have an economic system that generates an increase in productivity sufficient to satisfy such expectations. In other words the upward mobility channel did not close, but simply became clogged by the rush of people trying to go through it.

A further conflict arises from the implied definition of middle-class income used by Orjuela, which is the one used in colloquial language in Colombia. To satisfy the middle-class expectations in a country with Colombia's income level, it would be necessary for "middle-class" people to have an income that would place them in the richest 5 percent of the population (if not higher), a feat impossible to accomplish without further impoverishing lower income groups. As argued elsewhere (Thoumi, 1981), the size of the GDP presents an insurmountable obstacle to satisfy the level of expectations among the middle class in countries such as Colombia, and the struggle to satisfy them would likely result in a large societal group that could not even satisfy them would likely result in a large societal group that could not even satisfy its basic needs. If a utopian government were to impose a perfectly egalitarian income distribution, or at least one that would guarantee every citizen a minimum income that would allow the satisfaction of basic human needs, the policies required to achieve these goals would require massive income transfers that would not be tolerated by the "middle class."

Critics of Colombia's development (like Orjuela) attribute the lack of high paying jobs to a "failed system." The point is, however, that while the system can be and is very unfair, those critics are victims of an "income illusion" because no system can satisfy these expectations. To do so requires a short-run GDP increase of a magnitude simply unattainable under any conditions, short of something like the oil boom experienced by a few very sparsely populated countries. A simple back-of-the-envelope example illustrates this point. Let's assume the "middle class" is made of only 10 percent of the population and that the minimum acceptable income is about U.S. $1,500 a month for a family of four. Given that the income per capita in 1988 in current dollars was U.S. $1,180 (World Bank, 1990a: 179), this implies that "middle-class" minimum satisfactory income would be equal to 38.1 percent of the country's GDP, a proportion that coincides with the income share of the top decile of the income distribution for 1988 (Londoño, 1990, table 27). Of course, since the income distribution of the highest decile is itself highly skewed, those enjoying an income equal to the average of the highest decile would be in the top half of the decile. Thus, the minimum income necessary to satisfy "middle class" needs is enjoyed at most by the richest 5 percent of the population. From this simple exercise one concludes that in order to satisfy the minimum income needs of the "middle class" the country's GDP should be significantly larger than it is, and those who think that it is feasible to do so have an "income illusion."

Of course, if there are individuals who believe that their lack of satisfactory income is due to the system's highly concentrated income, and not to the low GDP of the country, they are going to be very frustrated. If the number of such individuals is significant, and they are willing to take action—including breaking laws and being violent—then society is in for a rough time because no matter what policies are implemented, the goals of the frustrated group cannot be met. The simple fact is that if a country is poor and the middle class grows to any significant size, it must remain poor, i.e., its income cannot exceed the country's average by much.

A further complication would arise, as argued in this chapter, if the frustrated group shares the ethics of inequality that pervades Colombian society. If so, the college-educated group would find it extremely humiliating to have an income similar to that of a blue collar worker. This appendix concludes with the well-known Argentinean cartoonist Quino's rendition of these frustrations.

Reprinted from Quino, *A mí no me grite* (Buenos Aires: Siglo vientiuno Argentina editores S.A., 1973).

Caption translation:

—Only by working together will we be able to achieve a complete structural change.
—It is important that we build a new world, one without social barriers, without sectarianisms, one in which all are exactly the same. Do you understand?
—Yes.
—Yes, DOCTOR!

Notes

1. Examples of various uses of the term are found comparing Horowitz (1992), Rafuse (1991), Dewatripont and Roland (1992), Brotherson (1989), and Frank (1988).
2. This definition is consistent with the use by Leal (1989 and 1990) in the Colombian context, who implies that legitimacy is based on a broad political consensus among citizens.
3. Various aspects and implications of this gap have been researched by Herrán (1987) who refers to Colombia as a "society of lies."
4. The lack of class consciousness is not unique to Colombia and it is a characteristic of most Latin American and Caribbean countries.
5. Mamalakis (1969, 1971) argues that the political economy of other Latin American countries has followed a similar pattern of "sectoral clashes" rather than class conflict.
6. I call this the "conventional" view in lieu of a better name. It must be noted that applied mainstream economic analysis of the Colombian political economy does not necessarily lead to "conventional" conclusions, and that there are many conventionally trained economists that do not share the policy approaches recommended by multilateral financial institutions in what has been called "the Washington consensus."
7. As a colleague employed by a multilateral lending agency put it when questioned about the political viability of the conditionality required by a structural adjustment loan to a Latin American country: "My job is to design the policy conditionality; its implementation is the minister of finance's problem." Six months later the minister was unemployed.
8. The effect of technology on society shows that in the long run engineers and scientists have a greater impact than politicians and social scientists. For instance, the recent technological advances in information and communications systems have made it increasingly difficult to maintain authoritarian centralized regimes; widespread modern education undermines traditional religious regimes, and so on.
9. Since the Colombian parties have lacked strong central organizations, they have been more like associations of local political leaders. It was then very difficult for the party leaders to impose discipline on party affiliates across the country, and some guerrilla groups remained in arms in isolated areas of the country.
10. Figure provided by the 1951 census. Because of the high population growth rate, it is important to date the 11.5 million population figure.
11. For example, innocent civilians, children, women, as well as prisoners were frequently executed, and the methods used to kill them were designed to maximize their pain and humiliation. Some violent groups developed special ways to kill that were used as trademarks (Guzmán, Fals-Borda, and Umaña-Luna, 1962).
12. The exception is Mexico, which also has a high homicide rate, although it has not remained at the high Colombian levels.
13. See the yearly issues of *Colombia Estadística.*
14. This group of academics is known in Colombia as *"violentólogos,"* that is, "violence scientists."
15. For instance, unemployment can be an effect of the *sicariato* rather than a cause since the assassins make a lot more money than those devoted to other activities and thus, do not need to work in legitimate activities.

16. Kalmanovitz (1988: 28) surveys the data available and shows that in what is now Colombia, the native population of the densely populated conquered areas declined by about 80 percent in the first 50 years of the conquest.

17. This was a generalized problem across all the Spanish, French, and British colonies in Latin America and the Caribbean and led to profitable slave trade in the region and to inducements to promote the immigration of poor Europeans, convicts, etc. (See for example Williams, 1970, chap. 4.)

18. For instance, a substantial share of the labor remuneration was paid in kind (sharecropping and similar arrangements); since there were no capital markets, the only access to credit that the peasants had was from their landlords, a system that tied them and their families to the land.

19. It should be noted that the hacienda system was quite different from traditional European feudalism. As extensively discussed by Véliz (1980), the system that prevailed in Latin America during the colony and afterwards was never feudal. In the feudal European system the power of the king emanated from the acquiescence of the nobility who also had rights and power, thus making the king accountable. In Latin America there were no power checks and balances within the dispersed power cells; power was centralized in paternalistic and authoritarian individuals who were not accountable. Because of these factors, it is not accurate to refer to the economic institutions and markets that prevailed in Colombia as feudal, but perhaps more appropriately as paternalistic and pre-capitalist.

20. Which include the current Caldas, Risaralda, and Quindío departments.

21. This statement implicitly accepts that the experiences during the first years of a person's life are the main determinants of the person's values, and that for most persons, the ideologies and theories studied afterwards do not substantially modify their values.

22. Kalmanovitz (1989: 9–10) argues that the transition between the value system based on this old ethic to a modern one based on equality is the most important problem faced by Colombia.

23. Díaz-Díaz (1978–1979) studies the evolution and accumulation of Church property, the conflicts it generated, the expropriation by the liberal government in 1861, and its economic effects.

24. In which bribes and other "extra market" elements were likely to have played a role.

25. This is a common occurrence when production responds to short-lived external-sector booms that create "Dutch disease" effects. (See Glossary for an explanation of this concept.)

26. Kalmanovitz (1989: 29) puts it this way: "The absence of an individual ethic of personal responsibility, supported by reason, led to a formal morality which is superficial, exhibitionist, and concerned with appearances, under which there is another dishonest one that strives to take from everyone, particularly the state, anything that the individual can get for himself" (author's translation).

27. Political scientists and economists have referred to Colombia's twentieth century political system in different ways that reflect that fact: "oligarchical democracy" (Wilde, 1978), "consociational" (Dix, 1980; Hartlyn, 1985, 1988); "elitist" (Berry, 1971). These references always imply a deeply unequal society, in which the state is controlled by a group that benefits from it.

28. The old party elites' control of the regime can be illustrated by the 1974 election, the first one after the formal "National Front" agreement

expired, in which the three main presidential candidates were two sons and a daughter of former heads of state.

29. For instance, they could alter import tariffs and quotas, the exchange rate, interest rates and sectorally assigned development credit, some utility rates, some tax rates, and other price and quantity variables.

30. The capital markets and their evolution discussed in Chapter 1 illustrate this point as the attempts to liberalize the market led to concentration, fraud, and large bankruptcies.

31. This is why the left-of-center literature refers to many prices and subsidies as "conquests in the class struggle."

32. There are many examples of legal activities that are immoral according to the ethics of many of the members of a society: alcohol consumption, working during religious holidays, abortion, using legal technicalities to free confessed criminals, money laundering allowed by banking secrecy laws, and so on.

33. This is so much so that some countries have made a business of having laws different from those of other countries to "complement" them, providing as an export service industry the possibility to safely break those other countries' economic laws. The Caribbean tax havens clearly fall in this category (Maingot, 1988).

34. The informal sector can also lobby, although in most cases in indirect and more convoluted ways as its illegality puts it at a disadvantage. In Colombia some illegal businessmen, like contraband retailers, have lobbied openly and successfully.

35. De Soto (1986) argues that in Peru, these risks have led to underinvestment in housing built on untitled lots, and in machinery and equipment in illegal factories.

36. For example, when tariffs are high, a legal importer with access to local capital markets and other benefits of formality will have a strong incentive to import some goods legally and some illegally, and his capacity to import illegally is enhanced by his ability to import legally since the risks of smuggling products into the country decrease when similar products are imported legally.

37. There are many examples of individuals and businesses that choose partial legality. It is well-known that many respectable companies in Latin America, including transnational corporations, have several sets of accounting books which are used for tax, credit, and other purposes. The legal set of accounts normally underreports profits, investments, and other activities, resulting in partial formality. However, partial formality is not limited to large firms and underdeveloped countries. For instance, in the United States many law-abiding families do not report income earned by some of their members who babysit or do neighborhood yardwork. While this example might seem trivial because the amounts involved are not large, it illustrates the point that even in societies where the law is generally respected, many laws that affect its members' income and wealth are not fully respected even by reputable citizens.

38. Theoretical models of value formation and economic behavior show that the costs and risks of full law compliance (honesty) to a particular individual depend on the average level of compliance (honesty) in the society (Sah, 1986). Therefore, the larger the illegal sector the lower the costs and risks of noncompliance.

39. This is so even in countries reputed to have law-abiding citizens. For instance, in the United States the probability that a household with a U.S. $30,000 annual total income that fails to include in its income tax return $100 babysitting income will face a tax evasion suit or fine is zero.

40. Looking again at the United States, a family that has a low key consumption behavior may own a middle-class house and two cars without raising questions about the origin of the wealth used to acquire them.

41. This type of pride has been reported in Argentina (Guissarri, 1989).

42. Interestingly, as noted by Kalmanovitz (1989: 62–63) the Colombian supreme court has judged that tax evasion is not a criminal offense.

43. For example, poor non-taxpayers would, for a fee, sign documents stating that rich taxpayers owed them money; also, firms would offer free holiday meals to the homeless and other poor, who were required to supply their *cédula* (national identification card) number and sign a blank receipt for services rendered to these firms, which would use the receipts to inflate their accounting costs and lower their income taxes.

44. This was part of a broader "irregular" income tax that also covered inheritances, lottery winnings, and other such income.

45. The Central Bank officially denied for a long time that it monitored the black market for foreign exchange. However, in an article by a Central Bank economist published in the June 1990 issue of the Bank's economic journal (Herrera, 1990), the author supplies a monthly series for the black market exchange rate from January 1970 to December 1989.

46. For example, inflation generates substantial and arbitrary transfers of wealth. Thus, the laws, regulations and policies should either lower inflation substantially, or allow asset revaluation for tax purposes, indexation of contracts, and so on. A legal system that accepts the concept of constant purchasing power so that it would make easier to implement policy measures conducive to limit the transfers of wealth and income induced by inflation.

47. It would be extremely ironic that at a time when the rest of Latin America has moved away from populism, Colombia might be in danger of developing a populist system after over 40 years of very stable economic performance.

48. On the one hand profits will continue to be high as long as demand remains strong and PSAD are not legalized, and on the other, the financial institutions of several developed countries have a lot at stake in the laundering business which has been encouraged, or at least tolerated, by them as a way to absorb the flight capital that came out of less developed and socialist countries in past decades. Also, the international financial markets do not have good ways to differentiate "legitimate" from "illegitimate" flight capital. See Naylor (1987), for a good study of flight-capital laundering in the world capital markets.

Part 2

THE ILLEGAL PSYCHOACTIVE DRUGS INDUSTRY AND GOVERNMENT RESPONSES

... 3 ...
Brief History and Overview of the Illegal Psychoactive Drugs Industry

The tropics have provided the world with most of the natural PSAD, which have a long history of production and consumption in Colombia and the other Andean countries. At the time of the Spanish conquest, all native cultures used PSAD. However, their use was not the source of social problems, as the people used them for ceremonial and medical purposes under controlled circumstances. In a word, PSAD had been domesticated. The native tribes used PSAD to get in touch with spirits, as part of rites of passage and other ceremonies, and to cure illnesses.[1] In Colombia the natives used coca, tobacco, *chicha* (a fermented corn beverage), and several other drugs, some of which are hallucinogenic (Bula, 1988).

The first reaction of the Spanish conquistadors and the Catholic Church when confronted with widespread PSAD use was to oppose it. Indeed, in 1567 a religious council in Lima declared coca a "talisman of the devil" (Arango and Child, 1987: 21). However, the widespread practice of coca chewing among natives, and the realization that its use calmed hunger and allowed the user to work longer hours without food or rest, prevailed over the church's moral arguments and the scruples of some Spaniards so that, under pressure from the colonies, the crown agreed to allow its use. From then to the midnineteenth century, there were regions of Colombia in which peasant wages were paid partly in coca leaves. *Chicha* was also used ceremonially among the natives. But the conquest broke down societal controls, and drunkenness among the Indians became a problem, exacerbated by the Spaniards' introduction of *aguardiente* ("firewater"), a sugar cane–based distilled drink with high alcohol content to which anise is added for flavor in a fashion similar to the strong grape-based Middle Eastern drinks.

PSAD consumption was an important source of government revenue during the colonial period. The colonial government established official monopolies for the sale of tobacco and alcoholic beverages, particularly aguardiente, that were used to generate substantial revenues. Some of the most important popular uprisings that led to independence originated as protests to the high taxes imposed by the government on the consumption of tobacco and aguardiente.[2]

Coca use, however, was, in the nineteenth and twentieth centuries, not as widespread in Colombia as in other Andean countries. Its production and chewing was extensive only in a relatively small region of southern Colombia that had been under strong Inca influence before the conquest, mainly the departments of Cauca and Huila. Until the mid-1940s chicha consumption was considered the cause of the most important addiction problem in Colombia. Heavy chicha drinking was widespread, particularly among the lower classes. Chicha was produced with primitive technology and, in some cases, under unsanitary conditions. By the late 1930s several activist groups spearheaded by Dr. Jorge Bejarano, who became the Public Health Minister in 1946, became concerned with the health effects of both chicha and coca consumption. In 1938 the sale of coca leaves was limited to medically prescribed doses filled only in pharmacies, and in 1941 all new plantings of coca were prohibited (Rubio, 1988). In 1947 there was a lengthy public debate about the social costs of chicha and coca consumption, and about the role coca chewing had played in landlord exploitation of the Indians. This led to a decree signed by President Ospina in March 1947 that prohibited the possession, growth, distribution, and sale of coca and marijuana, ordered the destruction of existing plantings, and established jail and fines for those who violated the decree. These prescribed sentences also applied to possession, production, and trafficking of other illegal drugs like morphine and heroin (Rubio, 1988: 39). This decree generated a political backlash mainly from the Cauca *hacendados* who, advised by the young Representative Víctor Mosquera Chaux,[3] obtained a one-year delay in the application of the decree. However, by the time the stay expired, Dr. Bejarano had resigned from his post and the decree was not reissued and was never enforced (Rubio, 1988: 39–40).

The debate about chicha production and consumption continued. Arango and Child (1987: 67–69) argue that chicha outlets played an important social function as centers for community activities, both in the cities and the haciendas where wives of the *mayordomos* (hacienda overseers) had a chicha monopoly for the hacienda market. They also argue that chicha entrepreneurs had humble origins, a reason why they were opposed by the traditional elite that had strong interests in the aguardiente and rum industries, both state monopolies, and in the private beer industry that had been growing since about 1880. Furthermore, after the violent spontaneous popular uprising of 9 April 1948 in response to the assassination of populist leader Jorge E. Gaitán, there were many rumors about rioters having been drunk with chicha. The government either believed these rumors or used them as a pretext to outlaw the production and consumption of chicha in June 1948. This measure led to a heated debate about the real motives behind it. Many argued the policy goal was to protect the interests of the modern alcohol industry instead of the health of the masses.

Marijuana and cocaine have been produced in Colombia throughout the twentieth century along with smaller quantities of other illegal drugs. However, as long as legal and illegal PSAD consumption remained limited to peasants, socially marginal groups, and a small number of upper class eccentrics, writers, and actors, their production and consumption were not major public policy issues (Camacho Guizado, 1988). That would help explain why the ban on coca and marijuana production was never reissued in 1948. Yet by the mid-1970s marijuana cultivation appeared in significant quantities and generated an illegal export boom. Simultaneously, its consumption began to spread among young middle- and upper-class consumers. Only then did production, trafficking, and consumption of illegal PSAD become an important policy issue.

It was a problem that developed over several years rather than one that appeared overnight. The existence of illegal PSAD manufacturing before the late 1960s is confirmed by the following incident. In the late 1950s a group of Colombian smugglers had established a laboratory in Medellín, which by the standards of the time was reported as large. They refined cocaine, heroin, and morphine which were exported to Havana, where the American mafia managed the distribution. The laboratory was discovered and destroyed by the Colombian secret service in cooperation with the FBI.[4]

The Growth of the Marijuana Industry and Its Export Boom

Marijuana has a long history of small cultivation volume in Colombia. Evidently it was introduced by the Spaniards during the colonial period to produce hemp. Then in the early twentieth century it was brought again to Barranquilla and Buenaventura, the two chief

Colombian ports, by East Asian and Caribbean sailors (Camacho Guizado, 1988: 45). It appears that its use spread in the ports and in some of the sugar producing areas in the Valle del Cauca. Arango and Child (1987: 85) point out that during the Ospina/Pérez administration (1946–1950), marijuana was also imported from India under the auspices of the government, which had intended to use it as a source of hemp. These authors also argue that by the late 1950s marijuana use was widespread, but the evidence provided is not quantitative. Still, it is agreed that its use was not perceived at the time as a significant social problem.

Marijuana production appears to have grown somewhat during the 1960s in response to increases in domestic demand, particularly among an elite group that had visited or been educated in the United States. Several authors (Arango and Child, 1987; Camacho Guizado, 1988) argue that the U.S. Peace Corps contributed substantially to popularizing the use of marijuana and some varieties of mushrooms in Colombia during this period.[5] However, their production and trafficking did not become significant until the early 1970s.

In the late 1960s a substantial share of the American market was being supplied with Mexican marijuana until a large part of the crop was eradicated through a joint United States—Mexican program that used paraquat, the now infamous herbicide. This eradication program created a supply shortage, and a corresponding shift in demand away from Mexican marijuana as American consumers became worried it might be tainted (Tokatlian, 1990: 300). The origin of Colombia's marijuana boom can be traced to the subsequent search for a new source to supply the United States market.

Ruiz Hernández (1979) based a detailed study of the marijuana industry during the 1970s on extensive fieldwork. He found evidence that American traffickers went to the Sierra Nevada de Santa Marta and the nearby Serranía de Perijá, which borders Venezuela, and supplied peasants with seeds, financing, and technical assistance to begin the production of marijuana.[6] This zone produced most of the marijuana exported to the United States. At one point that region's marijuana, known as Santa Marta Gold, became highly reputed in the United States market. Colombians seized the opportunity offered by the new market, and rapidly replaced the Americans organizing production to become marijuana exporters, but Americans retained marketing control; Colombians produced and exported the product and Americans imported and marketed it in the United States.

The Sierra Nevada de Santa Marta is an isolated mountain knot on the northwest Colombian coast, geologically independent from the Andes, that until recently remained inhabited almost exclusively by a few Indian tribes. Most of the Sierra is made up of ecological and Indian reserves and national parklands, although it has experienced some settlement activity. There is evidence that for the most part the Indians have kept themselves out of the marijuana business.[7] By the late 1970s marijuana cultivation had spread outside the Sierra Nevada region. Ruiz Hernández (1979) estimates that about 40 percent of the marijuana crop was then produced in other regions, mainly in areas of recent settlement in the Eastern Prairies (*Llanos*).[8]

Marijuana presents smuggling difficulties because of its relatively high volume per unit of weight and value. These characteristics fostered the smugglers' search for other products that were easier to export and that could use the marketing channels established by marijuana exports. Hence, the attempts to diversify product lines led to export of methaqualone jointly with marijuana shipments. Methaqualone was either imported in large quantities from Europe for contraband re-export, or produced at least partly by the legitimate Colombian pharmaceutical industry using imported compounds (Ruiz Hernández, 1979: 180; Reuter, 1992a).

One important question that could be raised by surveying the literature is whether the marijuana boom followed the course of most primary product export booms and was short-lived. Indeed, Molano (1987) argues that in the Guaviare region it was short-lived and its collapse caused an economic bust in that growing region. Fabio Giraldo Isaza (1990) shows that marijuana fueled a construction boom in Barranquilla that collapsed after 1983. There are domestic and external factors to indicate that marijuana had a production cycle and that Colombia lost at least part of its international advantage in producing it.

Focusing on domestic factors, immediately after the 1978 election of Julio C. Turbay, he was implicated along with Defense Minister Abrahám Varón Valencia and Labor Minister Oscar Montoya of having links to drug traffickers by a U.S. General Accounting Office study leaked to the well-known television program "60 Minutes" (Craig, 1981: 252). These accusations were corroborated by widespread rumors within the United States government (Tokatlian, 1990: 294). By the time President Turbay took office in August 1978, he was clearly under pressure to deal harshly with the marijuana industry. After looking at several alternatives, and confronting President Carter who pressured the Colombian government to spray paraquat, he began a manual eradication and interdiction campaign (with heavy military involvement) that avoided the use of defoliants and herbicides. The campaign was considered quite successful, as attested to by the United States ambassador to Colombia (Asencio, 1979: 11–12), since many planes, boats, and processing facilities were seized and substantial acreage was eradicated.

There were also external reasons for Colombia's marijuana boom to subside, such as the new and substantially stronger *sin semilla* ("seedless") variety that had appeared in the United States where cultivation was increasing (Gómez, 1988: 95). In other words, there seems to have been a strong import-substitution process taking place in the main market. However, its actual impact remains somewhat murky. Reuter (1992a) argues that potent sin semilla marijuana is not a good substitute for the milder Colombian variety, and that marijuana consumption in the United States actually declined after the Colombian eradication campaign. That is, consumers did not replace Colombian marijuana, but simply lowered consumption levels.

As discussed in Chapter 6, the data on marijuana and other illegal PSAD are extremely weak and inconsistent. The most frequently used data sources are the annual reports of the National Narcotics Intelligence Consumers Commission (NNICC) and the U.S. Department of State, which in the case of marijuana do not provide estimates for the period before 1982. Independent studies such as those conducted by Ruiz Hernández (1979) and Junguito and Caballero (1982) estimate the marijuana cultivation area in the late 1970s at about 30,000 hectares, a figure that grossly exceeds the 1982 NNICC estimate of 8,250 hectares. In spite of these data incongruities, available data show that the marijuana industry was not wiped out by the 1978–1979 campaign, but recovered, and that from 1982 to 1984 it actually grew significantly.

In 1983 and early 1984 Colombia witnessed a confrontation between some traffickers such as Pablo Escobar, who had gotten himself elected as a substitute congressman, and Justice Minister Rodrigo Lara Bonilla, who argued that the illegal drug industry's influence was corrupting congress (Gugliotta and Leen, 1990). The drug industry retaliated, claiming the minister had received campaign contributions from a trafficker. Lara Bonilla, an honest man with strong antidrug values, denied any knowledge of the donor's connection to the illegal PSAD industry, and claimed to have been set up by the illegal drug groups. After an acrid public debate, Pablo Escobar was forced out of congress. On 30 April 1984 Rodrigo Lara Bonilla was assassinated, apparently in retaliation for his antidrug stand. This event convinced President Belisario Betancur to fight the illegal PSAD industry more directly.

Betancur implemented several measures (see Chapter 7), including the use of controversial herbicide aerial spraying on marijuana plantations in the Sierra Nevada. This action generated strong reaction from Indian groups who have always inhabited the Sierra and who do not grow marijuana, and from the region's political establishment. The spraying was "successful," but while it weakened the industry, it did not eliminate it. The available data indicate a 20 percent drop in the cultivated area in 1985, followed by sharp increases in 1986 and 1987, when the cultivated area was estimated at over 30 percent above the 1984 figure (U.S. Department of State 1990). Tokatlian (1990, 324–326) argues that the spraying simply induced the industry to shift locations, mainly to the Cauca region, where yields per hectare proved to be over three times higher than in the Sierra Nevada. Department of State reports (1990, 1991) indicate that the eradication campaign continued with support from the U.S. government and that a substantial part of the crop was wiped out: "In 1986, Turbo Thrush agricultural spray aircraft of the State Department Bureau of International Narcotics Matters (INM) were used to eradicate cannabis cultivation in a campaign which has virtually eliminated the crop. Aerial reconnaissance in 1990 found only limited amounts of cannabis cultivation, most of which was immediately eliminated. North coast traffickers, however, still transship marijuana, believed to be cultivated mostly on the Venezuelan side of the Serranía de Perijá" (U.S. Department of State, 1991: 95). However, it is worth pointing out (see Chapter 6) that aerial reconnaissance systems, while sophisticated, have not been very accurate in the past and these data may prove wrong.

Even accepting the Department of State's data, it is obvious the 1987 eradication campaign, which destroyed an estimated 8,000 hectares out of a total 13,085 planted, did not dissuade marijuana growers from planting 9,200 new hectares in 1988, of which 5,012 were eradicated. Only by 1989 did the cultivated area fall substantially to 2,400 hectares. A key question raised by these data is whether the success of an aerial eradication campaign depends on the government's ability and willingness to sustain it year-in and year-out. Given location shifts and the marijuana industry's proven capacity to rebound, it is likely that a credible continuous threat is necessary to keep the industry in check as long as opportunity costs and markets are favorable.

Another important question as yet unanswered, is to what extent the decline in marijuana cultivation has been due to the eradication campaign and to what extent it has been the result of a decline in its relative profitability. Marijuana is the least profitable and hardest to transport of the illegal PSAD, and it is also the drug for which technological change has shifted the productive advantage in favor of the

United States. Furthermore, while the area under marijuana cultivation has dropped, that has not been the case for coca, which according to State Department data has remained stable. In addition, there is clear and growing evidence that opium poppy, perhaps the most profitable illegal crop, has been growing in Colombia in recent years as evidenced by 1,156 hectares of poppy having been manually eradicated in 1991 (U.S. Department of State, 1992: 107). Thus, the effectiveness and impact of the marijuana eradication campaign remains questionable.

The Growth of the Coca and Cocaine Industry

As noted, by 1970 Colombia had a long but limited tradition in coca production. The beginning of greater involvement in cocaine dates from about the mid-1970s, although marijuana was then still perceived as the main illegal PSAD export.[9] According to Gugliotta and Leen (1990: 23–26), in 1970 cocaine was a "cottage industry" based in Chile, but when Pinochet took power the government set out to destroy it. Some Chilean traffickers moved north, but Colombians virtually eliminated or forced them out of business within a couple of years. A group of Colombians had already been involved in cocaine traffic in small quantities, but these were soon replaced by a new group of young, more ambitious, brazen smugglers. The development of Colombia's cocaine industry followed a very different path from that of marijuana. These differences can best be understood after the cocaine production characteristics are laid out.

The processes of coca growing and cocaine manufacturing are well-known and have been discussed frequently in recent literature.[10] Coca can grow in a large area covering parts of Bolivia, Peru, Brazil, Colombia, and Ecuador and it can likely grow in parts of Venezuela, Guyana, and other countries. Coca growing requires simple field clearing (slash and burn), seedbed preparation, seedling transplanting, and field maintenance. Harvesting is manual, after which the leaves are dried in the sun. There are over 200 coca plant varieties that grow in tropical South America, although only a few are used commercially (Morales, 1989: 51). The cocaine content of the leaves varies substantially; the Bolivian and Peruvian varieties, and one of the several used in Colombia, produce higher yields than the rest. The cocaine content declines with time from the moment the leaves are harvested to when they are processed. Increased farmer mastery of the growing process has improved yields substantially in recent years.[11]

The manufacturing process is simple. To produce coca paste the coca leaves are mixed with sodium bicarbonate to release the alkaloid in them. This process normally takes place in a simple container, frequently a pool made of wood sticks and a plastic sheet. Sulfuric acid and kerosene or benzene dissolved in water are added. After about twelve hours the mixture is passed through a press or filtered, and then it is air dried to produce coca paste, an easily transportable product. The only equipment needed besides chemicals are filters and toilet paper, and a maceration pit or plastic sheeting. This process requires so little equipment that many of these "laboratories" are portable, and are moved frequently to avoid detection (Morales, 1989).

Cocaine base is obtained from coca paste through a somewhat more complex process that uses garbage cans, electric generators, filters to remove impurities, and drying equipment. The chemicals used are ammonia, potassium permanganate, and sulfuric acid. A recent innovation that increases the conversion factor from cocaine base to cocaine requires the use of hydroxide in the production of cocaine base. Bazuco, a drug commonly used in Colombia, is tobacco mixed with cocaine base; this frequently has many impurities that make it particularly dangerous as a cause of brain damage.[12]

Because cocaine manufacturing from cocaine base is more complex, it is done frequently in urban centers. It requires a building, electric generators (when public electric service is not available or reliable), filters, drying equipment (heat lamps, fans, microwave ovens), a hydraulic or manual press, hydrochloric acid, ether, acetone, chemical recycling facilities, packaging materials, washing machines, and garbage cans. This process requires some "cooking" and can be dangerous because of the ether's flammability. The quality of the final product depends on the overall proportions of leaves to chemicals used, on the quality of the chemicals, on the cocaine content of the leaves (which depends on the variety of coca leaves used and the time elapsed since they were cut), and on the skills and experience of the "cook" (chemist) who judges these variables. However, the process is simple enough so that any good chemist should only need basic instructions and some trial and error to produce good quality cocaine.[13]

The preceding description makes it easy to relate coca and cocaine production with the productive resources available in Colombia. As shown, these are relatively simple agricultural and chemical processes that are in many ways ideally suited to a less-developed country; they are not capital intensive, they do not have large economies of scale, they use abundant domestic raw materials, the labor skills required are not that great or scarce, the chemical products needed are relatively common, and most of them have many sources and other uses. Ether and acetone are the only precursor chemicals not produced in significant quantities in Colombia, and must be imported. Acetone has various other uses in Colombia, but ether has very few. Ether also has relatively few world producers, perhaps a dozen multinational corporations. Until 1984, most of the legally imported ether ended up in the hands of cocaine refiners (Gugliotta and Leen, 1990: 201–202). Coca growing location is affected by climatic factors, and coca paste must be produced near the source because of the high volume of coca leaves. However, cocaine base and cocaine manufacturing do not have to be tied to a particular location.

The cocaine industry that grew in Colombia toward the mid-1970s began as a manufacturing and marketing enterprise that imported the coca paste or base from Bolivia and Peru; some chemical precursor products were imported from the United States and Europe, while others were obtained locally. Success promoted the establishment of domestic coca–growing as an import-substituting agricultural development. During the 1980s the industry became more vertically integrated in Colombia as coca–growing increased substantially, although domestic coca production replaced imports only partially and Colombia remained the most important processing center for Bolivian and Peruvian coca paste. The U.S. Department of State (1990: 123) estimates that in 1989 approximately 566 metric tons of cocaine were refined or distributed through Colombian organizations. This amounts to 73 percent of the total 776 tons of worldwide cocaine production estimated for that year.

The increase in coca cultivation can be traced to the mid-1970s, but rapid growth did not appear until the early 1980s. Sarmiento (1990: 69–70), using data from the United States General Accounting Office and the NNICC, estimates that by 1980 Colombia produced 3.7 percent of the world coca leaf crop, a share that increased to 11 percent by 1987. The latest estimate of the U.S. Department of State (1991) puts the cultivated coca area in Colombia at 40,100 hectares in 1990, or 18.8 percent of the cultivated area in the Andean countries, producing about 13.7 percent of the coca leaf volume.

The growing cocaine industry also gave rise to the illegal traffic and production of chemical precursors. The Colombian government has made attempts to control imports of ether and acetone since it became obvious that the amount imported greatly exceeded what legal industries could reasonably have used. However, since the precursors are quite common and, except for ether, have a wide range of uses in Colombia, it has been difficult for authorities to restrict their overall availability. Because smuggling channels can work both ways, cocaine exporters have also engaged in importing contraband, not only of chemical precursors but, perhaps more importantly, of arms. It should be noted, though, that authorities have been able to use chemical contraband imports to trace the location of cocaine refining centers.[14]

Colombians' participation in the industry did not stop at the manufacturing level, as they became quite involved in cocaine marketing, particularly in the United States.[15] Cocaine is a much more attractive product to smuggle and sell than marijuana because of its higher price per unit of weight and volume. These greater incentives induced Colombian businessmen to develop a complex transportation, manufacturing, and distribution network. Thus, Colombians not only participate in coca paste and base smuggling into Colombia, and cocaine manufacturing and smuggling into the United States,[16] but they also participate at certain levels in its distribution. This arrangement is aided by the large number of Colombian immigrants residing in the United States.[17]

The Structure of the Illegal PSAD Industry

General Characteristics

The illegal PSAD industry in general, and the cocaine branch in particular, appear to have the typical structure of many agriculture-based industries. The main raw material is produced by a large number of farmers and the market is competitive. At each stage in the manufacturing process there is a decline in the number of participants, and there is a trend towards oligopolization as the product becomes more elaborate. At the wholesale level for the final product there are fewer sellers. Yet as the product advances in the distribution channels, the markets become more competitive so that at the retail level there are many sellers.

In spite of the similarity between this structure and that of legal agricultural products, there are crucial differences that arise from the illegality of production, distribution, and consumption of the industries in question. Illegality greatly affects the market structure and the behavior and strategies of producers, sellers, and consumers. Illegality encourages a risk-minimizing behavior at each stage of production and marketing that is reflected in the nature of the entrepreneurs, the locations chosen, the relationships between participants, and the high level of violence associated with the industry. The industry's illegality also results in great market segmentation and difficulty in transmitting market information, high transaction costs, great rents and profits, and the frequent use of violent methods. Because of these factors, illegality generates barriers to entry that could limit competition, at least in some stages of production. The actual level of market competition is hard to determine since the number of independent actors and the degree of coordination among them is unknown. It must be emphasized that the most important features of these markets are determined by their illegality and not by the number of competitors, which itself is highly influenced by illegality. For instance, if the cocaine market were legal, it is likely that Colombian and other cocaine producers would form an export association resembling what coffee growers have successfully developed. That would decrease competition.

Illegality turns violence into a resource whose use, real or potential, has several purposes. First, violence is part of the conflict resolution system when business deals go sour and it is a threat to enforce deals. Second, it can be used as a threat against competing persons or groups to prevent them from infringing on one's market or from reporting the business to authorities. Third, it protects the unlaundered, illegally obtained property that is hard to protect legally and may be a target of those willing to steal. Fourth, it can be used against authorities to force policy changes, or simply to eliminate those law enforcing agents who oppose the industry.

Illegality produces forms of market competition normally not encountered in legal markets. As argued by Krauthausen and Sarmiento (1991: 25), "illegal firms tend to combine economic, political, and military resources in a very different way from firms that operate in legal markets" (author's translation). One of the main differences between legal and illegal markets is that in the latter, violence plays an important role, and so, the firms use "military resources."

Another difference from a legal market is that the value added in the illegal PSAD industries is not proportional to factor costs in the legal market. In Colombia's illegal PSAD industry this is particularly notable in the coca and cocaine branches. The value of cocaine increases rapidly in a way proportionally related to the risks and the degree of monopoly at each stage of production and marketing, not to factor opportunity costs (Reuter, 1985).

In these industries, most of the value added can be attributed to risk taking; that is, it is a remuneration for risk, and so profit maximizing strategies seek to minimize actual risk. Of course, value-added profits can also be attributed to a degree of monopolization in the industry, even though the small number of firms in some stages of the production and distribution process more nearly reflects product illegality.

The importance of illegality in determining added value is clearly illustrated by Sarmiento (1990b: 19), who estimates that if the cocaine market were free and legal, the retail price of cocaine in the United States would be determined by factor costs, and could be one twenty-fifth of the 1990 street price.

Since the high value-added price in the industry is mostly due to its illegal nature and the risks involved in its production and trade, peasants in Bolivia and Peru (where a proportion of the coca crop is legal and where producing peasants are actually organized in legal unions) get a very small share of the final sale price because their risk is not particularly high. Most of the price increase takes place in marketing and distribution in the United States and other industrialized consuming countries where risks are higher (Reuter, 1985).[18]

When the prices of coca leaves, coca paste, cocaine base, and wholesale cocaine in Colombia and the United States are compared, various sources report Colombian wholesale prices somewhere between 10 and 20 percent of the United States price. This difference is a reflection of the high risk involved in smuggling and transporting the cocaine in the United States. Obviously, from the Colombian PSAD entrepreneur's point of view, the lion's share of profits is to be made at this stage of the business. Therefore, the incentives for Colombian entrepreneurs to organize themselves to control transportation and smuggling have been enormous, and have induced them to join forces and form the so-called "cartels" (like exporter cooperatives or syndicates) to minimize the risks of operation. High profit levels also contribute to violence among those engaged in this stage of the process.

Illegality also leads to market segmentation. The importance of this in illegal PSAD industries has been stressed by Reuter (1985, 88), who shows that prices of illegal PSAD vary substantially at any point in time—even within the same country or region—as they depend on the access of each buyer and seller to distribution and marketing networks. A producer or dealer connected with a good marketing network commands significantly higher prices than one that is unconnected. Attempts to lower the degree of market segmentation create a dilemma. They improve the transmission of information, making the markets more transparent, and thereby lower the probability of selling at a low price or buying at a high price. Yet they simultaneously increase the risk of detection and seizure by the authorities, and/or raise the cost of bribes.

Illegality makes the transmission of market information difficult in several ways. First, information about similar transactions is hard to obtain because they are shrouded in secrecy. Second, the information that members of trafficking networks can obtain about the workings of the industry tends to be limited to the minimum necessary for them to operate. For example, a buyer of one kilogram of cocaine in the United States does not have information about the importer and the refiner. Third, information about the purity and quality of the product, particularly at the retail level, is quite imperfect. This is a frequent cause of overdosing.

Transaction costs also increase significantly because of illegality. Since contracts are not written, it is important to make sure all parties understand what is expected of each one of them to avoid confrontation and violence. Thus, a great deal of effort is devoted to choosing business partners and to preparing each actual transaction. The need for secrecy and the risks involved in each transaction also increase packaging, transportation, and other transaction costs.[19]

Illegality plays a role in a slow supply response to demand increases. Since illegality slows and sometimes prevents the transmission of market information, and promotes market segmentation, it hinders the supply response. Besides, in higher risk stages, such as transportation and smuggling into the United States, the industry must continuously look for new ways to introduce the product into the country. At times, the need to use new channels could create a bottleneck for the industry, restricting its ability to respond to demand. Because of these difficulties, the industry is demand-driven. For instance, as shown in Chapter 6, during the 1980s cocaine's U.S. wholesale prices declined about 75 percent, while cocaine output increased several fold. At the beginning of the decade, profits were enormous and in excess of what they should have been if the market had been in long-term equilibrium, given the risks involved in the business. However, the supply adjustment was slow over a period of several years, during which prices declined as output increased to satisfy demand.

Because of the complex characteristics of the industry, "The transactions and relations in the illegal market always take place under two opposite poles: trust and violence" (Krauthausen and Sarmiento 1991, 197, author's translation). The participants in the industry have to trust their partners to be able to do business, but have to be ready and willing to use violence to enforce their agreements.

While Colombia produces several kinds of illegal PSAD, the following discussion of the industry structure will be devoted exclusively to the marijuana, coca, and cocaine branches.

The Marijuana Industry

Both marijuana- and coca-growing take place on relatively small plots, very frequently on untitled lands in newly settled regions where property rights are weak and/or questionable. Such lands are advantageous because, if an illegal planting is discovered by the authorities, it is difficult to identify and prosecute the land owner; but they are also disadvantageous because they are subject to violence, as the plantings and their revenues are not protected by a legal system.

Ruiz Hernández (1979) found that the average marijuana plot size in the Sierra Nevada de Santa Marta was only about three hectares; he also found very few plantings of over fifteen hectares, which he classifies as big. The small plantation size was part of the risk minimization strategy followed by processors and exporters. Small plantings are harder to locate, and the risks inherent to the growing process are then assumed by a lower income individual with little to lose and who might even get the sympathy of authorities if caught. When the land is titled, the owner often finds a partner to act as a sharecropper and with whom he splits the profits. The partner provides an alibi for the owner to deny any knowledge of the illegal nature of the crop. In the case of marijuana, it was not planted twice consecutively on the same plot, and was frequently mixed with other crops like corn to lower the risk of detection. Growers tended to maximize the use of family labor, but when family labor was not sufficient for larger plantings, they tended to make arrangements to share profits with workers rather than to pay a wage. That way, every worker became a partner with a stake in preventing the planting's detection. In addition, groups of about five small growers tended to be formed to increase the supply of family labor available to each, and to improve their bargaining power in negotiating with the buyers.

The marijuana market was highly segmented and its participants tried to keep it that way. Ruiz Hernández (1979: 165–169) found that peasants sold their product to a processor, who cleaned and packed the marijuana and sold it to an exporter. Marijuana buyers tried to purchase only from a few peasants or groups of peasants. Each exporter used secret landing strips and ports to facilitate transportation, and each did business with only one importer in the United States. The landing strip and port owners were often the exporters and the wholesalers who readied the merchandise for export.

The importance of risk as a value-added generator is illustrated by the marijuana industry's system of payments. According to Ruiz Hernández (1979), the price received by the Colombian exporter depended on whether any international transportation risks were assumed. The exporter received a proportion of the arranged price at the time of delivery, and the rest only if the shipment was "crowned," that is, if it arrived successfully at its destination. The price paid to the exporter was inversely related to the proportion received at the time of delivery.

An interesting result of the property rights weakness of the cultivated land, the market segmentation, and the business illegality is the high dependence of the industry on the informal capital market. Since the Colombian capital market is very segmented, as in many developing countries, Ruiz Hernández (1979) found that peasant marijuana growers frequently had difficulty financing their crops despite high internal rates of return for their operation.

Ruiz Hernández (1979: 140) also found that many small marijuana producers with a long history of being peasants wanted to continue being peasants, so they frequently retired from the business after a couple of successful crops—having accumulated enough capital to obtain a satisfactory standard of living by producing legal crops.

The Coca and Cocaine Industry

The coca and cocaine industry's structure is dictated in part by its illegality. However, it differs from the marijuana industry in several important ways, including overall higher profits, cocaine's higher value per unit of weight and volume, and the fact that cocaine requires manufacturing.

Focusing first on coca growing, it is found that most of the Colombian coca crop comes from areas of recent settlement in the Eastern Prairies and the Amazon basin, particularly in the Guaviare and Caguán regions. As with marijuana, most of the coca is produced by small settlers (Molano, 1987; Mora, 1989). The use of family labor in coca growing is extensive, and small farmers have also organized themselves to improve their bargaining power with coca leaf buyers.

Both the Caguán and Guaviare regions have attracted many migrants in the last 40 years.[20] The first migrants were peasants displaced by la violencia. Some had been associated with guerrilla movements and had fighting experience, while others were simply escaping the violence in their home regions. The newly settled regions did not have developed infrastructure, and were very isolated from the rest of the country. The isolation and lack of transportation infrastructure were, and in many places still are, so great that there was no economically viable way to take the produce to market because transportation costs exceeded market prices. Indeed, settlers went there because of strong expulsion factors in home regions, rather than because of the pull factors of the settlement areas. So it is not surprising that the economy in these regions before the illegal—crops boom was one of self-sufficiency that kept peasants at subsistence levels. This production structure also made the peasantry vulnerable to bad crops. Molano (1987) and Jaramillo (1989) found that any time there was a bad crop, peasants tended to sell their land rights when they had title, or their rights to land improvements they had made that are recognized by Colombian law, and move farther into the jungle to make a new settlement. This process led through time to an increase in the degree of land ownership concentration, something that most settlers and their community organizations wanted to prevent since many of them came from latifundia (landed estate) regions where they had not had access to land ownership. Under these circumstances, the illegal drug crops offered a unique opportunity to increase the peasant standard of living and preserve land rights.

Coca began to grow in these two regions somewhere in the mid- to late-1970s, and experienced a boom until 1981 when coca prices collapsed. The boom attracted a new migration wave with very different characteristics from prior ones. The new migrants were not in search of land to settle, but of quick profits. Their origin was more urban, some had common criminal experience different from the guerrilla activities, and some had higher education. Some migrants were chemists who came to work in the laboratories, and others were from the educated young urban unemployed in search of fortune.[21]

Some new immigrants came from the emerald mining region and transplanted the productive and violence organizations they had previously developed to exploit government-owned mines (Krauthausen and Sarmiento, 1991: 143–144; and Molano, 1987: 64). Corruption and violence prevention in the emerald mines has been one of the persistent problems faced by the government in that region. An illegal system known as *planteo* developed in the emerald region to exploit the mines: an emerald trader (*plantero*) supplied a number of miners with primitive mining equipment, arms for their own protection, and some cash advances for their subsistence and that of their families. The miners, in return, were bound to sell any emeralds they could mine to the trader. Each miner and his family faced the threat of death if the agreement was broken, but received protection against other miners from the plantero who organized armed protection groups in which the miners participated. This system—based on dependency relationships—produced strong loyalties, close-knit organizations, and high levels of violence in the region. Violence was primarily used to settle conflicts between the planteros and in their fight for control of mining areas.

The plantero system was well-suited to the illegal coca industry, and therefore easily transplanted. It is thus not strange that many second-wave immigrants had prior experience in the illegal emerald industry and became coca and cocaine entrepreneurs. As it worked with coca, a trader frequently provided seeds and technical advice to small farmers who produced the coca for the trader, thereby establishing a mutual dependency relationship that promoted loyalty and secrecy.

Due to the isolation of the coca growing regions, the state has not had a strong presence there. The power vacuum has consequently been filled by guerrilla and community organizations such as the Community Action Committees (Juntas de Acción Comunal). Cubides (1989), referring to the Caguán, argues that peasants *want* a stronger state presence to provide conflict resolution systems, public services, and infrastructure. However, he explains that "the continuous successful operation of the guerrillas for a fairly long time is a military and political fact that sets well defined limits (to the state) in the region, and that is helped by the (region's) geographical characteristics" (Cubides 1989, 231, author's translation). This is one reason that coca growing continues to flourish.

In the Caguán region, part of the Amazon River Basin and jungle, coca is grown and processed into coca paste, and most of it is then sent to other locations for transformation into cocaine base and cocaine. Hence, in the cocaine industry the Caguán region has played a similar role to that played by many growing areas in Bolivia and Peru. The Guaviare is part of the Eastern Prairies, and there most coca is also grown by family-sized agricultural units, but some large cocaine producers have purchased land and established cattle ranches that house refining laboratories. Thus, a larger proportion of the locally grown coca is processed in the Guaviare than in the Caguán.

Looking now at the cocaine industry, one finds the expected illegal industry risk-avoiding characteristics. However, the economic and social stakes in cocaine are much higher than those in marijuana, and the behavior and strategies followed by cocaine entrepreneurs have been exacerbated by the size of incomes generated by the industry relative to the size of Colombia's economy.

One effect of the high stakes in the cocaine industry, therefore, has been the generation of a high level of violence. The risk of violence results from the confrontation between illegal PSAD entrepreneurs and the authorities, and from the fact that many business conflicts involve large sums of money which encourages the use of violence in conflict resolution. Conflicts within the industry have many sources: misunderstandings that naturally develop in an industry without written records, deals gone sour, the reporting of a partner or competitor to the authorities in order to protect one's business or increase prices, and so on. Participants in this industry always see their business partners as potential informants to legal authorities.

As an alternative to the use of violence, some wealthy cocaine entrepreneurs have attempted to build a political base to gain legitimacy, a task aided by the clientelistic nature of Colombia's political system. For example, Pablo Escobar underwrote the development of a local welfare system in Envigado, his home town, and also built a housing development in a slum and gave away 1,000 houses to low-income residents. He used this base to run for congress and was elected as an alternate deputy. Until the Colombian constitution was replaced in mid-1991, there were two people elected to each seat: a representative and an alternate, who was free to attend sessions and actively participate when the representative did not attend. This system was used frequently to bring into congress individuals who coat-tailed behind well-known personalities, who were not interested in being active in congress, but who could be elected because of their popularity or name recognition, that is, a substitute for a member of congress who frequently did not show up to congressional sessions. Carlos E. Lehder tried to gain political support for his activities in Armenia, his hometown, where he founded a nationalistic political movement with some Nazi overtones, the Movimiento Latino Nacional Party, and where he established *Quindío Libre*, a regional newspaper.

The size of the business has also encouraged entrepreneurs to influence policy by bribing and intimidating politicians and law enforcement authorities, and to finance virtual private armies to protect their investments and attack industry enemies, real or imagined. This extensive influence has increased the level of corruption in the rest of society.

The cocaine industry's organization is clearly established to minimize risk.[22] Every participant has few contacts with other participants. Any coca buyer or paste or base manufacturer tries to minimize the number of sellers being dealt with, and normally sells the product to only one or two buyers. The structure is designed to limit the information about the overall business that individuals could provide to authorities if caught.

In general, business participants know only about their role and about persons in the layer below them with whom they deal, but know very little about the layer immediately above them and do not have a good picture of the overall industry. The use of relatives and close friends as partners is also widespread as a way to minimize risk.[23]

The locations of coca refining laboratories also reflect the risk-avoiding needs of the industry. In the rural sector they are located on haciendas owned by the illegal PSAD entrepreneurs, but usually titled in somebody else's name. There, the industry has landing strips and provides its own security. In urban areas the laboratories are disguised under the umbrella of other business, mainly in areas where the illegal PSAD industry has built some political support. In general, the footloose nature of the cocaine refining production process makes it easy to select laboratory locations to minimize risks, and they have therefore been found spread throughout the country.[24]

As noted, the largest proportion of overall profits for Colombian residents comes from transporting and smuggling cocaine to the United States. This is the part of the industry that clearly has economies of scale, and in which coordinated efforts by several manufacturers can reduce risk. For instance, every exporter knows there is a probability that a single shipment will be seized. However, every business unit can lower its risks if it joins other exporters and sends several shipments in which all partners have a share. This way, everybody makes profits even if some of their cocaine is seized. Higher profits at this stage cause the industry to devote more resources to it than to other stages of the business.

Because of the attempts by various illegal PSAD entrepreneurs to collaborate in performing these functions, it is claimed they have formed a cartel, and it is common to refer to the cocaine exporting organizations as being cartelized. However, the meaning of "cartel" is not always clear in such references. For instance, the press and official government sources in Colombia and the United States continually make references to the Medellín, Cali, and other cities' cartels, which is quite confusing (at least to an economist), since that implies the existence of two or more cartels in the same market, which refutes the existence of a cartel. No doubt it is politically useful for many groups to call cocaine export organizations cartels, a word that recalls unpleasant memories of OPEC and of raw market exploitation, and that conveys the image of a conspiracy against consumers. Independent of public relations and the political implications of calling an organization a "cartel," it is important when studying the structure of the cocaine industry to determine if it really corresponds to that of a cartel, since the impact of many policies towards the industry depends on whether there really is a cartel.

The evidence speaks against such a system. First, the illegality of the cocaine industry makes it difficult to form a workable cartel. The risk minimizing strategies that must be followed to succeed as an illegal operation encourage a loose structure, in which it is not possible to plan production levels and to give orders to be carried out through several layers of production and distribution. Further, the institutional organization of the industry is rather precarious, and precludes the development of anything resembling a bureaucracy, especially one that survives after its leaders are replaced (Krauthausen and Sarmiento, 1991: 36). Finally, relations between peasants who produce coca, those who gather coca leaves, those who manufacture coca paste, those who transport it, those who refine it into cocaine base and cocaine, those who export it, and those who distribute it in the main markets tend to be very fluid; the structure of the industry adapts itself to changes in the business environment brought about by activities of law enforcement agencies and other factors. Hence, while there is no doubt that desires to preserve and increase industry profits encourage attempts to collude and create a suppliers' market agreement, or cartel, strong forces are also pushing in the opposite direction.

When cocaine exports began from Colombia in the mid-1970s, it was transported by human "mules," individuals who for a fee would smuggle small amounts (perhaps 1 kg) in their luggage or bodies. This system was cumbersome and slow. As the demand for cocaine began to grow, the need for a system that allowed exporters to smuggle larger quantities became clear. Carlos Lehder's main contribution to the business was the establishment of such a service in 1978. He acquired Norman's Cay, a small Bahamian island with a good landing strip that became an important transshipment point from which he began sending a flotilla of small cocaine-laden planes to the U.S. mainland (Gugliotta and Leen, 1990: chap. 5).

Large cocaine producers in Colombia began to make use of Lehder's island, and thereby forged personal relationships that led to opening other U.S. cocaine routes, and to sharing their concerns about growing transportation needs. Gugliotta and Leen (1990, chap. 8) trace the origins of what became known as the "Medellín cartel" to a meeting of some of these larger producers in 1981 at one of the farms owned by the Ochoa family, several of whose members are leaders in the cocaine industry.

Castillo (1987, chap. 4) traces the formation of the so-called cocaine export cartel to 1982, when the Ochoa family head summoned a group of traffickers to a meeting in Medellín to discuss how to respond to the M-19's abduction of his sister, Martha Nieves Ochoa, on

21 November 1981. MacDonald (1988 and 1989) argues that most of those summoned were part of the Medellín cartel, implying there was already at least one syndicate. The number of participants in this meeting is unknown. Castillo claims a waiter in attendance reported it was a small group of fewer than twenty, while MacDonald claims there were 200 leading capos, and Gugliotta and Leen (1990: 150) put the number at 223 present.

Regardless of when the first attempts to coordinate activities among various exporting groups took place, the Medellín meeting was very important because the Muerte a Secuestradores (MAS) was created there. MAS is a paramilitary group created to prevent kidnappings and to attack those who had dared seek the potential returns of kidnapping illegal PSAD businessmen and their relatives. At the Medellín meeting each participant agreed not to pay any ransom and to supply either cash, arms, or manpower to MAS for their mutual protection. Soon after the meeting, a number of M-19 members were kidnapped and assassinated by MAS, and Martha Nieves Ochoa was freed after some M-19 members had contacted MAS and an apparent truce was established.[25]

Castillo (1987: 111–115) argues the meeting was also used to debate alternative strategies that illegal PSAD entrepreneurs could follow in response to the recently approved extradition treaty between Colombia and the United States. The participants scheduled a new meeting at a hacienda equipped with appropriate security.

In the second meeting the group tried to reach an agreement to regulate and coordinate cocaine exports to increase profits. Castillo (1987) reports the main issue discussed was the transportation system used to bring cocaine into the United States. The major leaders established a transportation insurance mechanism that could be used by smaller participants who joined in large cocaine shipments. Risks could be lowered by putting together large amounts of cocaine and exporting them along different routes to the United States. That way, the risk a single businessman had of losing a whole shipment was eliminated, and since the profits are so high, even if the group were to lose one or more shipments, they would all make satisfactory profits. Besides, the large entrepreneurs who had organized smuggling routes realized they could collect substantial fees by simply shipping cocaine to the United States for smaller dealers and insuring it. This is why cocaine shipments that are seized by the United States are frequently reported to be packaged in small bundles, each with a different color or other marking, which identifies its owner. Smaller cocaine producers frequently piggyback their small shipments on the large ones of the main traffickers (Krauthausen and

Sarmiento, 1991: 31; Gugliotta and Leen, 1990). Although the system appears to be well-organized, many of these relations are short-lived, and those who participate in one shipment or transaction do not have to participate in others.

The need to develop new smuggling routes is ever present and there is a constant shifting of routes to lower risks. Most cocaine is believed to come in small- and medium-size planes from Colombia, but there are many other ways in which cocaine is smuggled into the United States. For instance, Colombians fly it to an intermediate spot in Central America, Mexico, or the Caribbean, from where it is re-exported either by plane, sea, or land to the United States. Cocaine is also shipped by sea from Colombia and sometimes it is smuggled first into Canada, from where it is easily transported to the United States. Cocaine has been found mixed with other shipments (flowers, hollowed wood planks, and so on), or chemically incorporated into another export product, from which it can then be chemically recovered. Larger export groups can more easily afford different ways to smuggle cocaine into large consumer markets, which lowers their risks. Thus, one of the main functions of the cocaine export syndicates is to "research and develop" new transportation routes; the continuous need for new routes promotes cooperation among syndicate members.

A byproduct of organizing joint export ventures is that by lowering overall risk, the possibility for others to participate as financiers opened up. These are people who put up some capital to buy cocaine in Colombia to send to the main markets. Since the total amounts of cocaine are large, they are sent in various shipments, and the chances of small investors losing their money are drastically lowered. This system, equivalent to selling shares in several shipments, is known as "*la apuntada*" (Krauthausen and Sarmiento, 1991: 74; Arango and Child, 1987: 130–131). The apuntada has been used by illegal PSAD businessmen to involve individuals with an apparently clean record, and to increase the social and political support for the industry.

Another of the issues reportedly discussed in the second meeting was the distribution of the U.S. markets. Castillo (1987: 115) claims the New York market was assigned to the Cali group that was already controlling it, while Florida, which had been a distribution center for much of the United States, was given to the Medellín group. Curiously, Castillo argues, California was not assigned and was left up for grabs to whomever could control most of it. Castillo says it ended up in the hands of the Cali group.

Most of the available literature discusses the Medellín "cartel" or its members. Although it is acknowledged there is a Cali "cartel" and that several other exporting and smuggling organizations exist, there is much less known about them. However, there is ample evidence of frequent violent clashes between the various groups, particularly between the Cali and Medellín. Thus, despite attempts to form a unified front, the institutions of the industry breed violence. For instance, Castillo (1991: 19–25) explains how attempts by Pablo Escobar to increase control over cocaine exports by the Medellín group led to a violent confrontation with the Cali group, after the latter reported to authorities the route that Jorge Luis Ochoa was to have followed to attend a meeting in which a new marketing agreement was to be discussed. This tip led to Ochoa's capture on 20 November 1987. Gugliotta and Leen (1990: 566) attribute a marked increase in violence among New York cocaine dealers in the late 1980s to an attempt by the Medellín cartel to wrestle that market from the Cali cartel.

There are several other pieces of evidence that support the cocaine industry's description more as a loose association of producers and exporters rather than a single cartel. To begin with, the Colombian groups have very little control over production volumes. Even if they were to control coca production in Colombia, which does not seem to be the case, most of the industry's raw material is produced in Bolivia and Peru by independent groups that sell to the Colombians and others. It is remarkable that, while still referring to the industry's structure as a "cartel," the U.S. Department of State (1991: 95) claims that some 150 to 200 Colombian organizations engage in cocaine trafficking, and that those have relations mainly with the Cali and Medellín groups. One can only wonder how this number of market participants can be coordinated in an illegal underground!

Second, a similar situation is found at the retail end of the market. Cocaine is distributed by many small groups and gangs that fight for market share or "turf" among themselves, without any control by Colombian exporters. It is thus not surprising that, as shown in chapter six, prices of coca and cocaine during the 1980s tended to decline sharply, as output increased substantially. Third, the death or capture and incarceration in Colombia and other countries of several industry leaders—like Carlos Lehder, Pablo Escobar, the Ochoa brothers, and Gonzalo Rodríguez-Gacha—has not produced any significant disruption of the cocaine markets. Fourth, the high degree of violence and internal "wars" that have prevailed among the Cali, Medellín, and other groups attest to the difficulty that any group has in exercising strict control over the industry in general and their organizations in particular.

Summarizing, it appears that the illegal PSAD businesses attempted to form an organization to influence the market, but the end result resembles several export cooperatives or syndicates more than a formal cartel. The most pressing reasons that the *narcotraficantes* tried to organize themselves involved desires to counter the government's extradition policy and the threat of further kidnappings, two elements not directly related to cocaine pricing, market share fights, and other traditional goals of economic cartels.[26]

The Knowledge Gaps

A survey of the marijuana and cocaine industry literature in Colombia finds important knowledge gaps, such as how many people are involved and at what stage. The supply side descriptions of the market always argue that the Cali and Medellín "cartels" supply a large proportion of the United States market, perhaps 60 to 80 percent. A proportion of the coca grown in Bolivia and Peru is processed there, and some of the cocaine produced in those countries also finds its way into the United States. There are also frequent references to small Colombian cocaine producers that use the transportation services provided by larger ones or their own less sophisticated systems. It should be emphasized that, even at low United States prices, the incentives for small smugglers are very high.[27] Thus one can conclude that besides the Medellín and Cali "cartels," there are a significant number of cocaine exporters although one cannot know how many or what their market share is.

The literature has many other gaps as well. It suggests that during the early 1980s Colombians imported coca paste from Bolivia and Peru. But after the Colombian government's strong anti-narcoterrorism campaign in 1989, Bolivian and Peruvian groups developed processing capabilities and alternative distribution channels, so that most current Colombian imports are cocaine base. Yet it is not known what percentage of coca processed in Peru and Bolivia is actually refined in Colombia, and the knowledge about the relationship between Colombian, Bolivian, and Peruvian drug groups is at best fuzzy. For instance, it is accepted that most Peruvian cocaine base is bought by Colombians in the Upper Huallaga Valley and exported to Colombia. However, the share of that production step that is actually in Colombian hands is not known. Similarly, cocaine transportation and smuggling from Colombia to the United States is accepted to be mostly under Colombian control, although there are many non-Colombians involved: pilots, government officials, and law enforcement agents who have to be bribed in Central America, Mexico, and the Caribbean; and Mexicans, Jamaicans, and others who smuggle cocaine into the United States by various means (over land, sea, air, through Canada, and so on). There is no accurate information about the cost of bribes and other services paid by Colombians to bring their product into the United States, the stability of their relationship with non-Colombians, or the latter group's share of Colombian exports.

Another issue that clouds the picture is the growing importance of the European, Japanese, and other cocaine markets such as Brazil and Argentina. The linkages between these and the American market are not known. Therefore, the degree of market competition, the actual Colombian market share, and profits cannot be truly assessed.

Colombian involvement in cocaine distribution in the United States is acknowledged as important. Arango (1988: 24–25) explains that Medellín cocaine exporters sent trusted individuals to the United States to organize their distribution channels. These individuals became known as *traqueteros*, worked mainly with Colombians, and returned to Medellín with high status. Gugliotta and Leen (1989: chap. 1) provide extensive coverage of the battle for cocaine distribution control in Miami in the late 1970s and argue that Colombians gained control of the market. However, a wide knowledge gap exists concerning the depth of Colombian involvement in cocaine distribution beyond the wholesale level, their profits, and their relationship with Colombia.

Notes

1. The great variety of PSAD and their widespread use has prompted Arango and Child (1987, 53–54) to state: "The strongest impression received by whomever enters the Amazonia is living with a rich mosaic of psychoactive drugs. . . . Each drug has its ritual, its own social time to be consumed and its consumption is either authorized or prohibited for each person in the community. These circumstances protect the community from the negative effects of their consumption, and there is never drug abuse" (author's translation).

2. See for example the excellent history of the aguardiente industry and taxation in the eighteenth century by Mora de Tovar (1988).

3. Ironically, after a brilliant political career that included lengthy periods as senator and a stint as First Designate to the Presidency (Colombia did not have a vice-president), and as ambassador to the United States in the late 1980s and 1990, Dr. Mosquera Chaux took a very strong pro-criminalization PSAD position.

4. Arango and Child (1987: 119–120) interviewed one of the old Colombian smugglers who spent two years in a jail in Cuba before being deported after the Cuban revolution. According to their version, he claimed that the laboratory produced about five pounds of heroin a year, and it operated only a few months a year to minimize risks.

5. Arango and Child (1987: 147–148), who have a strong nationalistic vein and are prone to believe in international conspiracies by evil institutions, claim that the Peace Corps was used by the Pentagon to spread the use of marijuana and mushrooms among Colombian youth to prevent the spread of the revolutionary ideas fostered at that time by the Cuban revolution. This unproven assertion is important because it may sound credible to many Colombians, since it is true that in the 1960s many Peace Corps volunteers and other progressive Colombians who had lived in the United States experimented with PSAD use.

6. For instance, Ruiz Hernández claims to have seen copies of a pamphlet in Spanish that explained how to produce marijuana, and that peasants said were distributed by Americans.

7. Ruiz Hernández (1979: 118) argues that a few Indians tried growing marijuana, but were cheated by non-Indian buyers with whom they were not culturally prepared to deal. Further, Indian leaders saw the cultivation of marijuana as a catalyst in a de-culturation process they wanted to avoid, and prohibited marijuana cultivation by Indians.

8. See also Molano (1987).

9. For example, in March 1979 the National Association of Financial Institutions (ANIF) organized a symposium on illegal PSAD that dealt exclusively with marijuana (ANIF 1979).

10. See Morales (1989) for a detailed description.

11. The U.S. Department of State (1990) attributes some of its own previous underestimations of cocaine output during the 1980s to unaccounted increased coca yields as growers developed improved plant varieties and growing techniques, and increased the use of fertilizers and herbicides.

12. Arango and Child (1987: 143) argue that bazuco was introduced to the Colombian markets in 1981 when the cocaine base produced in eastern Colombia did not find an international market due to a fall in international cocaine prices. They claim that the Eastern Prairies base was of lower quality because of the use of impure chemicals, a fact difficult to explain.

13. Curiously, Arango and Child (1987: 125–126) argue that the technology to produce cocaine was introduced in Colombia during the mid-1960s by the Peace Corps. They claim that the Peace Corps members who enjoyed marijuana when they arrived in the early 1960s discovered coca chewing, and in their search for bigger, better and higher "trips," introduced the cocaine refining technology in Colombia. However, as noted above, they also argue that in the late 1950s a laboratory that refined cocaine, heroin, and morphine had been destroyed in Medellín. While it might be that some young Americans could have been instrumental in expanding cocaine production in the 1960s, there is no doubt that Colombia had then a large number of chemists able to produce cocaine without foreign technical assistance, and some who had experience doing so.

14. In one well-known case in 1984, a radio device that sent signals to a satellite was installed by the DEA in a couple of double-bottomed drums full of ether that were to be sold to a suspected supplier of the Medellín "cartel." The path of the drums was traced through satellite to locate the "tranquilandia" refining center, which, when destroyed, yielded what at the time was the largest amount of cocaine ever seized in one operation (Gugliotta and Leen, 1989: chap. 12).

15. As explained below, these vertical linkages differ from commonly integrated industries because it does not imply control concentration.

16. One of the main transportation entrepreneurs was Carlos Lehder who developed a sophisticated cocaine transshipment base in Norman's Cay, his private island in the Bahamas. Lehder used small airplanes and fast boats to smuggle large amounts of cocaine to the United States (MacDonald, 1988: 107–111).

17. Independent Colombians control a portion of the wholesale business. Cocaine is sold four or five times before reaching the retail level. Colombians are involved in those stages, but once cocaine is at the retail level, it is in the hands of countless independent sellers who rarely have any connection to Colombian traffickers.

18. The references of large price increases at each distribution stage refer to the U.S. market, which has been the most important for Colombian cocaine. Wholesale prices in Europe are reported to be about two to three times higher than in the United States; however, it is likely that the percentage markup between wholesale and retail in Europe is not as steep as in the United States.

19. For example, cocaine has been found incorporated into plastic products, in hollowed hardwood planks, and other products imported to the United States. Similarly, speed boats and small airplanes used to smuggle cocaine are frequently abandoned.

20. The development of the Guaviare has been studied in detail by Molano (1987), and that of the Caguán by Cubides (1989), Jaramillo (1989), and Mora (1989).

21. The growth in coca production also had disruptive social effects in the growing regions of Peru and Bolivia due to the differences between the new migrants and the old settlers (Morales, 1989; Flores and Blanes, 1984).

22. See the detailed work of Krauthausen and Sarmiento (1991).

23. Krauthausen and Sarmiento (1991: 38–44) provide several examples.

24. Notice that in spite of the higher technology required in the paste-to-cocaine labs, they are still makeshift as manufacturing processes go.

25. There are, however, conflicting versions about whether the Ochoa group paid a large ransom for the release of Ms. Ochoa. Castillo (1987: 114) is inclined to believe that a ransom payment was highly unlikely, while Gugliotta and Leen (1989: 154) are inclined to believe rumors that the M-19 settled for U.S. $535,000.

26. However, because current literature and journalistic sources refer to the Medellín and Cali groups as "cartels," I will continue to apply the same term even though, as discussed, the groups do not represent a cartel.

27. For instance, even in late 1991 the wholesale cocaine price difference between a kilo of cocaine in the United States and Colombia was somewhere between U.S. $12,000 and U.S. $15,000, a figure that is between 10 and 12 times Colombia's annual income per capita. Besides, since in Colombia the price is about U.S. $2,000, the profit margins for small-time smugglers remain extremely high.

... 4 ...
The Illegal Psychoactive Drugs Entrepreneurs and Their Strategies

This chapter attempts to determine who the illegal PSAD entrepreneurs are, what their goals are, how they behave toward the rest of society, and how they have attempted to incorporate themselves into mainstream Colombia. The PSAD entrepreneurs' behavior is important because it affects the impact that the industry has on Colombia's society and economy, on the ability of the government to formulate and implement policies, and on the effects of those policies.

The information about the background, personality, values, goals, and behavior of the illegal PSAD entrepreneurs is sketchy and sometimes contradictory. There are many short references to their characteristics, as well as a few biographical works available on some of the most prominent illegal PSAD entrepreneurs written by journalists who have come in contact with the business. However, these accounts are partial because they cover only a few years or some aspects of the lives of the entrepreneurs. There are also reports from official sources that provide some data. In spite of their weaknesses, these works shed interesting insights on the narcotraficantes, on the way they have tried to incorporate themselves and their capital into mainstream society, and on their relations with the political establishment, guerrillas, and other social groups.

It should be noted at the outset that there is great diversity among those who work in the illegal PSAD industry. There is no unique profile of those in the business, and obviously the characteristics discussed below do not apply to all of them. What is important is that the characteristics mentioned appear to apply to a larger proportion of the individuals involved in the industry than of the population at large.

Perception of the Law and the Establishment

Perhaps the most generalized characteristic of the actors in the illegal PSAD industry is their lack of respect for the country's legal system and formal institutions. As noted in chapter two, this characteristic has become increasingly widespread in Colombia. However, the industry's actors appear to be more advanced than most Colombians in their disrespect and in believing in the illegitimacy of the country's institutions. They have fewer moral constraints to their actions and are willing to use any means to achieve their particular goals. Of course there are other groups that do not participate in the illegal PSAD industry, but share their beliefs and attitudes toward the establishment.

The lack of legitimacy of political institutions makes it easy for those in the PSAD industry to believe in the legitimacy of their economic activities, their income, and their accumulated capital. Several authors and biographers support this position.

Krauthausen and Sarmiento (1991: 141–142) are prompted to claim that "deep inside, the narcotraficantes tend to be convinced that to break the law is per se, not reproachable" (author's translation). Rincón (c1990: 68), in his short biography of Rodríguez-Gacha, writes: "He slowly built his own moral framework that did not recognize the guidelines provided by the judicial system that existed within the institutional framework of the society in which he lived" (author's translation). Further, Rodríguez-Gacha did not appear to have had any doubt about the legitimacy of the capital he had accumulated, and he was willing to use any means, no matter how violent, to protect it (Rincón, c1990: 73–74).

In an anonymous (1989) small book written by an illegal PSAD entrepreneur as an open letter to the Colombian people,[1] there is a section entitled "I don't feel like a criminal," in which the author argues that he pays taxes, attends mass, is a good father, and in general is a good person. He also claims that his friends, some of whom are priests, military men, and politicians, do not think of him as a criminal and that society in general does not condemn his activity. He claims that in Colombia almost everybody would like to be in the illegal PSAD business, but most people simply don't have to opportunity to join it or don't know how to. Statements like this can be construed as grandstanding by illegal PSAD entrepreneurs who need to legitimize their own behavior, but they are consistent with, and supported by, the increase in overall corruption in Colombian society discussed in chapter two, and with the growing difficulty to separate "clean" from "dirty" capital and income in the country.

Another example of attitudes within the industry is that many see law enforcers as enemies who are not morally superior to them but who represent other powers, such as the traditional elite or international imperialism that oppose illegal drug traffic. The illegal PSAD businessmen simply do not see themselves as morally flawed and reject moralistic arguments against them or their activities.

Criminal Background

One common characteristic of many well-known illegal PSAD entrepreneurs is a prior criminal background. Given the widespread disregard for the law in Colombia, this is certainly to be expected. Some of them had experience as common criminals, while others had engaged in white-collar crimes, and several had used violence and intimidation when committing crimes before participating in the illegal PSAD business.

Some examples illustrate this point. Gonzalo Rodríguez-Gacha, known as "El Mejicano," had extensive experience in the illegal emerald business in which he had achieved a prominent position but had also made quite a few enemies.[2] Castillo (1991, 13) claims that in 1973 his organization killed several members of competing groups of emerald traffickers. The conflicts that had arisen in the emerald business followed him years after he had become successful with illegal PSAD and, in the late 1980s, erupted in a bloody gang war between Rodríguez-Gacha's men and those of his former friend and associate Gilberto Molina, known as the "Emerald King." This conflict may have led to the death of both gang leaders. On 27 February 1989 Rodríguez-Gacha's men ambushed a party attended by Gilberto Molina, killing him and a number of his men (Rincón, c1990).

There are two versions of what happened next. The gang war continued in jail, where Rodríguez-Gacha's son was detained on illegal gun possession charges and where several inmates were killed. Rincón (c1990) argues that the government found it difficult to protect Rodríguez-Gacha's son in jail because of an ongoing emerald gang war. Besides, this pressured Rodríguez-Gacha to use all the legal resources at his disposal to obtain his son's freedom. It was then highly convenient to free the son and place him under surveillance with the expectation that he would eventually lead them to his father. However, when these actions succeeded, authorities followed the son to his father; a battle ensued in which both died. Castillo (1991: 276) argues that the cartel heads decided to sacrifice some of their middle-level men to appease the security forces and the government, and turned in some. One of these, who was quickly extradited, decided to gain some clemency by acting as an informant and provided information about a cocaine shipment to be sent soon to the United States. When the security forces tried to intercept the boat that was about to leave Colombia's coast, they ran into Rodríguez-Gacha and the shoot-out followed.[3]

As a young man in the United States, Carlos E. Lehder also had a criminal record. In Lehder's biography, Orozco (1987: 21) refers to him as "a vagabond car thief in New York, marijuana retailer and vicious consumer of the herb" (author's translation). Lehder, who migrated as a young man to the United States, had sometimes shipped stolen cars to South America. He was arrested in Mineola, New York, driving a stolen car, and in 1973 was charged in Detroit for interstate transportation of stolen vehicles. In spring 1974 he was arrested again on several marijuana trafficking charges, and sentenced to four years in prison (Castillo, 1987: 94; Gugliotta and Leen, 1990: 34–36).[4]

Verónica Rivera, who became known as the "queen of cocaine," began her career as a businesswoman in a "San Andresito," selling smuggled household appliances. After becoming a successful cocaine exporter, she maintained her links with the import contraband business (Krauthausen and Sarmiento, 1991: 143).

Pablo Escobar also had a youth police record: "Escobar began his criminal career in adolescence, stealing headstones from local graveyards, shaving off the inscriptions, and reselling the blank slabs to bereaved relatives at bargain prices" (Gugliotta and Leen, 1990: 27).

Arango (1988: 106) interviewed twenty middle- and high-level illegal PSAD entrepreneurs in Medellín during late 1987 and early 1988 for what became the only study based on actual interviews with industry actors. One of the twenty cited contraband as his prior main activity, and three others cited other criminal activities. Since the question asked inquired only about the previous main activity, it is likely that other interviewees also had engaged in illegal activities but did not answer accordingly when they had another profession, or when they had another activity that they used as a front to cover illegal actions.

Castillo (1987) and Gugliotta and Leen (1990) provide many other examples of persons who had participated in illegal activities and had used violence before getting involved in the illegal PSAD business.[5]

Other Values and Mores of the *Narcotraficantes*

The results of Arango's (1988) survey of members of the Medellín group show an interesting profile of the illegal PSAD entrepreneurs.

One common characteristic is their belief in fate and providence, and practice of frequently praying very piously for the success of their individual business deals,[6] a fact that confirms their belief in the legitimacy of their activities.

The use of PSAD by the industry's entrepreneurs, including their own products, is common. According to Arango, 70 percent of the illegal PSAD entrepreneurs interviewed used PSAD. The survey indicated that the preferred drug of 35 percent of those interviewed was alcohol, of 20 percent cocaine, of 10 percent marijuana, and of 5 percent bazuco. There are no data about multi-drug users, which many of them are likely to be. The Arango interviews show much greater illegal drug use among his informants than in the population as a whole (see Chapter 9), and indicate that the consumption of PSAD can be a problem within the industry. Indeed, Gugliotta and Leen (1990) argue that many of those who had participated in the business in the United States were users, and that almost all the witnesses who testified against Carlos Lehder in his trial, and who had been involved in the business, had experienced substantial addiction problems. Gugliotta and Leen (1990: 68) also claim that cocaine use was widespread in Norman's Cay, that Lehder himself was a user there, and they even show a photograph in which Carlos Lehder is apparently sniffing cocaine. These authors also claim that Lehder's frequent consumption of cocaine led to his being isolated by other members of the Medellín cartel.[7] It is likely that many industry entrepreneurs are not illegal drug users, especially those in high positions. However, a significant proportion appear to use drugs, particularly those involved in marketing and distribution, which creates problems for the industry since it increases instability and the level of violence. These factors prevent orderly business relations.

The drug traffickers interviewed by Arango all associated with the Medellín cartel and were all over thirty years of age, although only 15 percent were over fifty. Their average education level was relatively low: 55 percent had only an elementary education, although some (10 percent) had a college education. While there have been notorious female traffickers, such as Verónica Rivera, most industry entrepreneurs are strong *machistas*—75 percent said they had mistresses and 60 percent claimed to have more than one.[8] Most liked to show off their wealth; they had large luxurious houses, wore abundant jewelry, and so on. Most (80 percent) expected to educate their children abroad, 90 percent hoped that their children could work in legal activities, and only 10 percent hoped for them to continue their father's business. They expressed a strong preference to legalize their capital, but a significant number (25 percent) acknowledged that they would continue in the illegal drug business even if they were allowed to invest their capital legally.

Assimilation in Colombian Society

One of the main objectives of illegal PSAD entrepreneurs is to be assimilated into mainstream Colombian society in order to protect and legitimize their property, legalize at least part of their wealth, obtain an economic status and social recognition comparable to other rich Colombians, actively participate in the political process, and access public office.[9] To achieve their goals, they have established relationships with political and economic institutions, government policy making and law enforcement organizations, and other societal groups, such as the guerrillas and paramilitary organizations. These relations have forged a "clandestine network" of members of the government, politicians, lawyers, chemists, bankers, military personnel, and others (Krauthausen and Sarmiento, 1991: chap. 3). During the 1980s the most important specific common goal of all illegal PSAD groups was to eliminate the extradition treaty with the United States, which posed a threat to the main illegal PSAD entrepreneurs. This goal was achieved when the new 1991 constitution banned extradition of Colombian nationals.

The growing delegitimation of the regime, the weakening state, and the deep social crisis have diluted the social stigma associated with the illegal drug trade and facilitated illegal PSAD industry attempts to establish links with the social power structure, a process that has been helped by the income and wealth generated by the industry. The integration of illegal traffickers into the Colombian economy has been subtle, but pervasive; as Krauthausen and Sarmiento (1991: 17) state, the industry has "penetrated the last crevices of society, politics, the economy, and even cultural and sports activities" (author's translation). There are several detailed journalistic reports of this process (Gugliotta and Leen, 1990; Castillo, 1987 and 1991), but, not surprisingly, they have been difficult to verify and quantify. This section attempts to summarize the verifiable integration of illegal PSAD entrepreneurs in Colombian society. No doubt the picture drawn here is an incomplete one of their total social participation.

Various cocaine groups have given different weights to their assimilation goals, and have used different means to achieve them. Some have emphasized the legalization of their assets, while others have tried to obtain political power and social recognition; some have opted for confrontation and widespread use of force against the establishment, while others have followed a more low-key approach, using their wealth to gain the favor of politicians, clerics, military leaders, and other relevant members of the establishment.

It appears that all illegal PSAD groups have established some close relationships with, and gained influence over, the political establishment. This has been accomplished by financing political campaigns and politicians, trying to get members of the Colombian elite to participate in the business, and forging coalitions with groups with whom the illegal industry entrepreneurs have some goals in common.[10]

The Medellín group has been confrontational with the Establishment, has freely resorted to the use of violence, and has been accused of most of the assassinations of high government officials and judges attributed to the drug industry. The government has identified the Medellín group as the main source of "narcoterrorism," and has linked it to the assassination of Minister of Justice Rodrigo Lara-Bonilla, newspaper editor Guillermo Cano, presidential candidate Luis Carlos Galán, and others. Thus, the government activities have been concentrated against this group.

The members of the Cali and other groups have taken a low-key approach in their attempts to integrate themselves with mainstream society. This is perhaps in part because some already belong to it, and because they found they could develop the necessary social and political contacts to be accepted without having to publicly "come out of the closet."

As discussed in more detail in Chapter 7, the establishment has not tolerated and has reacted against the open political activities of these societal intruders, although at least parts of it have been receptive to the industry's low profile assimilation approach (Orjuela, 1990). Such a reaction is expected given Colombia's clientelistic system, in which political power is based on one's access to the government budget, because any new political organizations with independent funding would be extremely threatening to established political machines.

Political Integration

Most members of the Medellín group come from social groups with few connections to the old Colombian elites, and they have been intent on obtaining social recognition. Arango (1988) attributes at least part of the group's violent behavior to the refusal of that city's elite to accept them as peers.[11] This group has tried to obtain direct political power by creating political parties, developing a clientelistic base, and running for office. Several of the major illegal PSAD entrepreneurs affiliated with the Medellín group have followed the paternalistic tradition of Colombia's political system. They have attempted to create populist political movements, and have played the role of traditional patrons by dispensing benefits to their clientele.

Writing about Rodríguez-Gacha, Rincón (c1990: 102) affirms that among the various adjectives used by people to refer to him, he liked "Patroncito" best. Castillo (1991: 21) also tells us that the illegal drug business leaders prefer to be called godfathers because that allows them to call their employees godchildren. Pablo Escobar, Carlos Lehder, and other colleagues have used their capital to assist the poor and needy and finance community festivities, actions that have allowed them to play a paternalistic role in their regions (Orozco, 1987: 103–106; Krauthausen and Sarmiento, 1991: 103–107). Since the structure of the illegal industry is based on personal trust and dependency relationships, it shares an affinity with the clientelistic and paternalistic political systems of Colombia. Relations within the industry are then easily transferred to the political realm and the rest of society.

As noted above, Carlos Lehder financed a new political party that had a nationalist, neo-Nazi and populist rhetoric, and a platform with two primary goals: the elimination of the extradition treaty with the United States, and the legalization of personal doses of marijuana (Orozco, 1987). Pablo Escobar founded a local civic movement (*Civismo en Marcha*) in the Medellín area, and as noted in Chapter 3, used his wealth to build a local power base; he got himself elected as a representative to Congress, from which position he enjoyed immunity, and opposed government officials and politicians who were against the illegal drug trade or who supported the extradition treaty with the United States.

Both Carlos Lehder and Pablo Escobar became highly visible figures. Lehder was frequently unpredictable and reckless, openly expressing his opinions against the extradition treaty, calling treaty supporters traitors, and arguing that illegal drugs were an anti-imperialist weapon to be used against the United States. This behavior came back to haunt him when tapes of interviews he had given to the Colombian press were presented as evidence against him in his trial in the United States.

The illegal PSAD industry has also sought political influence by building its "clandestine network" as part of a more low-key approach that takes politically powerful individuals as partners or simply buys them out. There is evidence that members of the political and military establishments have developed links with the illegal PSAD industry. For instance, as shown by Orjuela (1990: 232–233), there are several examples of former Colombian senators, representatives, diplomats, and other government officials found guilty of drug trafficking and money laundering by United States courts; and Castillo's (1987) journalistic best-seller provides innumerable examples that attest to the pervasive influence of the industry on Colombian politics and society.[12]

The "Narco-Guerrilla" Connection and the Formation of Paramilitary Organizations

The relationship between the illegal PSAD industry and guerrilla organizations has been one of its most publicized and politically explosive links with other socially powerful organizations. The illegal PSAD industry and the guerrillas have been strange bedfellows. At times the government has been their common enemy, but they have fundamentally opposite goals. The industry represents a crude, unrestrained form of capitalism, while guerrilla organizations have their origins in the fight against the unfair, crude capitalism that has prevailed in Colombia. The conflict between the long-term goals of these two social groups is irreconcilable.

Nevertheless, the illegal PSAD industry and the guerrillas found common ground in the early 1980s, as guerrillas were then a ready source of protection for the industry's manufacturing and shipment operations in parts of the sparsely populated eastern half of the country that the guerrillas controlled. In the 1984 capture and destruction of the Tranquilandia manufacturing complex in the Amazon jungle there was evidence that guerrillas had provided such protection, a fact that led U.S. Ambassador Lewis Tambs to formulate a theory about a "narco-guerrilla" drug conspiracy. This theory was also supported by Carlos Lehder's rantings against American imperialism, by some evidence of links between the Sandinistas and the illegal PSAD industry (Gugliotta and Leen, 1990, chap. 16), and by the M-19 guerrilla takeover of the Supreme Court building on 6 November 1985 (in which files of cases against illegal PSAD entrepreneurs were destroyed). The "narco-guerrilla connection" provided a possibility for the United States to kill two birds with one stone, since it could link its antidrug policies with anticommunist policies in the region.

However, alliances between the illegal PSAD industry and the guerrillas have proved temporary and fraught with conflict. In some guerrilla-controlled areas, coca growing started being promoted by the illegal PSAD industry which weakened guerrilla organizations because it shifted peasant loyalty. As illegal PSAD businessmen invested in other guerrilla-controlled areas, such as the Middle Magdalena Valley, the guerrillas tried to impose on them the "taxation" methods they used on traditional landowners; in some cases, they went so far as to kidnap the industry's entrepreneurs and their relatives to extract ransom payments. These tactics prompted a strong reaction, the formation of paramilitary groups within a legal framework that provided for the establishment of self-defense groups. These groups not only protect industry investments, but have used violence against anyone who has sympathized with social reform.[13] The illegal PSAD industry has therefore replaced the guerrillas with their own protection branch.

The drug industry has also established links with gangs of young assassins-for-hire (sicarios) who dispose of the industry's enemies, settle accounts with business partners, or eliminate competitors. Salazar's (1990) work, based on in-depth interviews with sicarios, shows that some of them were first trained by the M-19 guerrilla organization. However, these young persons found the Marxist rhetoric rather irrelevant to their life experiences and preferred to use their newly acquired skills in the capitalist marketplace.

In conclusion, while there have been connections between guerrillas and the illegal PSAD industry, these relationships have been fundamentally unstable because the long-term goals of the two groups are diametrically opposed. Indeed, these relationships are similar to those the illegal PSAD industry has forged with other social groups—that is, when convenient, the industry has formed alliances with or bribed military personnel, judges, politicians, financiers, and others. However, those relationships do not constitute the existence of "narco-congress" or "narco-judiciary" conspiracies.

Economic Integration

The economic integration of illegal PSAD entrepreneurs is hard to determine because of the difficulty in identifying all the drug-related income and capital. An attempt to measure the industry's economic impact on the country can be found in Chapter 8.

The economic activities of the different drug groups have varied significantly. The Medellín group has shown a preference for urban and rural real estate investments, and has purchased large tracts of land in rural areas of the country.[14] The size of these investments has been so large relative to the size of the pertinent local economies that they have extraordinary economic and political impacts, and have been highly disruptive of the local communities.[15] The Cali and other smaller groups have invested more in urban enterprises and, utilizing the widespread social tolerance for contraband imports, have apparently been the main source of what is sold in the "San Andresitos," found in almost every Colombian city. Yet, while it is clear that contraband imports have been used to bring illegal capital into the country, once there it is not known how it is invested or consumed. A similar problem is presented by other ways of importing illegal funds, such as import underinvoicing, export overinvoicing, fraudulent service exports and so on; the import channel may be detected, but the final use of the funds is unidentifiable.

The economic assimilation of the illegal PSAD industry has also been influenced by economic institutions and government policies. During the 1970s and 1980s it was facilitated by periodic tax amnesties and holidays that the various governments implemented to increase the tax base, and by the frequent loosening of the requirements regarding the sale to the Central Bank foreign exchange earnings attributed to service exports. As noted in Chapter 2, the growth of the underground economy has made it difficult to separate "clean" and "dirty" illegal capital and income, to the point that any policy aimed at bringing above ground illegal "clean" capital opens the door for "dirty" capital legalization.

As also discussed in Chapter 2, the combination of the lack of long-term financing, a net worth tax, and a capital gains tax that was primarily a tax on inflation made real estate an ideal sector to hide capital. By extension, real estate became a prime vehicle for money laundering and a favorite investment of illegal PSAD entrepreneurs.

Illegal drug monies have been invested in other activities, of course, but given the widespread lack of respect for laws that apply to economic transactions, there is no way to determine how this has been done. For example, as noted in chapter two, most firms in Colombia operate simultaneously in the formal and informal economies. Formal sector entrepreneurs who have financed illegal PSAD shipments through the system of the *apuntada* would be able to reinvest drug profits in their formal activities without being detected. Another example is provided by small-time Colombian drug dealers in the United States who have accumulated capital, that by industry standards are small, but that by Colombian standards are significant. Some of these dealers have invested their money in legitimate Colombian businesses without being detected.[16]

It may then be concluded that while some assets such as real estate have been good money-laundering channels, and import contraband and other systems have been used to bring "dirty" funds to the country, it is not possible to determine either the size of these funds or their final portfolio. However, given the magnitude of these inflows, it is likely that PSAD industry-generated funds have found their way into many, if not most, economic activities in the country.

The drug money inflows are also used for consumption purposes. There are many reports of conspicuous consumption and expenditures by illegal PSAD entrepreneurs, some of which can be verified. However, some of these expenditures are made on goods that satisfy both investment and consumption needs and that facilitate money laundering. Art objects and fancy antique cars have been popular consumption/investment goods.[17] Consumption patterns have also included gold flatware and gold-plated bathroom hardware (Castillo, 1991: 81).

One of the most visible illegal PSAD entrepreneur investments is in the professional soccer league, a strategy that has multiple purposes. Politically, it can provide some support for the industry because its great resources have been used to produce the best Colombian soccer in the history of the country,[18] perhaps following the old Roman prescription to provide bread and circus to the masses. The investment in soccer teams has also provided money-laundering channels since altering gate receipts can be used to launder dirty pesos, and at least part of the soccer stars' salaries can be paid in under-the-table dollars.

Conclusions

The illegal PSAD entrepreneurs are diverse in their social origins, connections with the Colombian power structure, goals, and ways of operation. They share with most Colombians a lack of respect for the law. Many of the industry's leaders have had prior encounters with the law and, before joining the illegal PSAD business, had been prone to appeal to violence or had been used to dealing outside the legal framework.

Illegal PSAD use within the industry seems to be significantly higher than among the population at large. That fact is likely to increase the difficulties inherent to an illegal operation, since illegal PSAD drug use can result in paranoia and other psychological conditions not conducive to smooth business operations.

The industry's assimilation into Colombian society has been complex, diverse, and conditioned by the illegal nature of the business, by Colombia's institutions, and by the weakness of the state. The industry's attempts to create an independent political base have so far failed, although entrepreneurs have gained political influence by following a low-key approach that does not attempt to openly disrupt the political establishment. The industry's resources allow it to compromise legal, political, and law enforcement organizations, and to form alliances with parts of the establishment as well as with some guerrilla organizations. The fundamental differences between the industry's goals and those of guerrilla groups, as well as the large investments by industry entrepreneurs in guerrilla-influenced areas, have led to the industry's development of paramilitary groups that have clashed with the guerrillas and social and economic reform sympathizers in those regions.

The great diversity in social background and goals within the illegal PSAD industry, the personal characteristics of its entrepreneurs, and the loose structure of the industry raise many questions about the success of industry-wide negotiation with the government. It might be possible for a government to negotiate successfully with those entrepreneurs who want to legitimize their capital and who do not have political aspirations, but it would be impossible to do so with those who want direct political power, to continue their business, or who simply look at the government as an enemy they want to oppose. In this atmosphere, negotiations can only be a short-term strategy to deal with the violence caused by the illegal PSAD industry, but will not provide a long-term solution to the "drug problem."

The size of the illegal PSAD industry's resources, the widespread illegality of many economic activities, and the large underground economy in Colombia have provided good channels for the industry to launder its capital. However, while the industry's economic influence is evident in some regions and sectors due to large real estate investments, it is not possible to ascertain to what degree illegal PSAD industry-generated capital has been invested in the economy or its various sectors, although real estate has been a favorite sector for industry investments. However, it is highly probable that industry-generated capital has found its way, at least indirectly, into many economic activities.

Notes

1. Written in late 1989 presumably by Pablo Escobar, whose cartoon-drawn face appears in the page before the introduction, perhaps in response to the government offensive against the illegal drug industry after the assassination of Luis Carlos Galán on 18 August 1989.

2. See the short biography of "El Mejicano" written by Fabio Rincón (c1990) shortly after Rodríguez Gacha died in battle with the authorities in December 1989.

3. This event was a very important victory for the Barco administration since Rodríguez-Gacha was the first leader of the illegal drug industry

captured or killed after the government declared an all-out war on the industry in reaction to the assassination of Luis Carlos Galán.

4. He served his sentence in Danbury, Connecticut, in the same prison where G. Gordon Liddy, of Watergate fame, was serving his.

5. One should point out, of course, that these works are basically of a journalistic nature, and that some of the statements made in them may be mistaken. However, the examples provided by Castillo and by Gugliotta and Leen are so abundant that even if some of them are inaccurate or false, they still comprise strong evidence for the existence of a significant relationship between the illegal PSAD entrepreneurs and prior illegal activities.

6. The Virgin venerated in the church of Sabaneta, a town near Medellín, became very popular among the illegal PSAD businessmen, many of whom prayed there regularly every Tuesday. This practice became well known because of the traffic jams and the large crowds at the shrine on that day of the week (Arango, 1988: 37–41).

7. However, Orozco (1987) mentions in several places that Lehder was not a cocaine, alcohol, or tobacco user, but that he was greatly addicted to marijuana.

8. Arango (1988: 35–36) very curiously argues that this machismo has had a rather positive indirect effect on the Medellín region income distribution: because it has generated a demand for females as entertainment for the illegal PSAD entrepreneurs which "has been without doubt, one of the most effective channels to redistribute income and to raise the social condition of wide sectors of Antioqueño society" (author's translation).

9. "Their vicious tactics notwithstanding, Colombia's drug lords do not seek to overthrow the state, but rather to reach an accommodation with it. In the final analysis, they want to consolidate their economic position and win social acceptance while insulating themselves from legal prosecution" Bagley (1989–1990: 158).

10. For example, joining rural landowners in the support of self-defense armed groups in response to the extortion and kidnapping business of guerrilla groups.

11. However, it must be pointed out that a significant number of the members of the Medellín group, including some of its leaders such as Rodríguez Gacha and Lehder, were neither born nor raised in Medellín.

12. This is indeed not an academic work, and possibly a proportion of the links that Castillo mentions are false. However, the number of cases described by Castillo are so many that even if many of them are spurious, the links of the illegal PSAD industry with the establishment are still pervasive. I must note that in two instances in which I know the individuals mentioned by Castillo, his assessment was correct. A few personal interviews with Colombian notables corroborated the overall accuracy of Castillo's book.

13. Of particular importance have been the paramilitary organizations that the Medellín group has supported in the Middle Magdalena Valley.

14. Arango (1987: 126) reports that for 45 percent of the illegal PSAD entrepreneurs surveyed, urban and rural real estate was their first investment choice, for 20 percent it was cattle raising, and for 10 percent construction. None of the entrepreneurs considered manufacturing as his first investment choice.

15. Perhaps the most socially disruptive drug industry investments have been made in the Middle Magdalena Valley.

16. This statement is based on the author's contacts with some of the individuals engaged in these activities in the United States.

17. For example, when the Medellín building where Pablo Escobar had a main residence was heavily damaged by a bomb in January 1988, the authorities found a collection of original Van Gogh, Botero, and Grau paintings, eight antique Rolls Royce cars and other expensive vehicles (Castillo, 1991: 81). It must be noted that Botero and Grau are two of the best Colombian painters, and that since the mid-1950s, when car imports where very tightly restricted in response to a sharp balance of payments crisis, until the mid-1970s, car ownership in Colombia had an investment component as the real depreciation of many cars was slow; at times, cars actually appreciated in real terms (faster than inflation).

18. Colombian soccer had a golden age in the 1950s when Colombian professional teams brought many players from Argentina during one of the economic crises of that country; however, as the coffee boom that Colombia experienced in the early 1950s subsided, so did the quality of its professional soccer teams as the imported players moved to greener pastures. From then on, Colombian soccer was mediocre until the late 1970s when the soccer league's funding improved. Since then, Colombian professional soccer clubs have frequently made the final rounds of the South American Cup for league champions and have won it on one occasion. The violence that pervades the illegal PSAD industry also touched the professional soccer league in late 1988. Near the end of the professional championship competition, a referee was killed after a game between teams from Medellín and Cali over a controversy in reference to a penalty kick. This assassination led to the suspension of the national championship competition for the rest of the season.

... 5 ...
Why the Illegal Psychoactive Drugs Industry Grew in Colombia

The growth of the illegal PSAD industry in Colombia raises several questions. Why is it that Colombians got involved in the illegal drug trade? Why are the main cocaine exports to the United States and a significant share of cocaine marketing in that country controlled by Colombians? And why have the main cocaine manufacturing centers been located in Colombia and not in other countries? The answers to these questions are neither obvious nor trivial, since after all, PSAD can be and are produced in many locations. And in the case of cocaine, Colombia's main illegal PSAD, the country is not the main producer of coca, and its domestic market for cocaine and derivatives like bazuco is too small to support a large industry.

The literature on the illegal drug industry in Colombia includes several attempts to answer these questions. Since the importance of cocaine overshadows that of the rest of the industry, most of the literature on illegal PSAD in Colombia is focused on this drug. Some prominent Colombian politicians have argued that the country's advantage in producing cocaine is simply due to its location, halfway between the main producing regions and the largest market.[1] The view that the geographical location is an important determinant of Colombian involvement in the cocaine industry is shared by other authors. MacDonald (1988: 28) states, "first and foremost, the South American country benefits from its geopolitical location. It is strategically located between the coca producing nations of Peru and Bolivia and the routes through the Caribbean and Central America that lead to the lucrative North American and European markets." However, MacDonald (1988) does not think that location is the only reason that Colombia developed the industry, as he also cites three other important elements: the vast forest that makes it easy to conceal laboratories and landing strips, the entrepreneurial skills of Colombians that allowed them to develop a sophisticated refining and marketing system, and the willingness of part of the Colombian community in the United States to function as a distribution network. MacDonald (1988: 29) also argues that these factors interact as a package and that "other nations have some of these factors, but not all, the most important being the lack of geopolitical location. Only Mexico in Latin America may come close." The geographical advantage of Colombia is also highlighted by Whynes (1992): "The geographical location of Colombia as a point of infiltration by air and sea into the USA was, and remains, ideal."

Other analysts have advanced various arguments to explain why Colombia developed an international advantage in the cocaine industry. Arango and Child (1987) and Arango (1988) argue that the cocaine industry grew as a result of a set of factors that induced Antioqueño entrepreneurs to get involved in the cocaine business,[2] including higher unemployment in Medellín resulting from a decline of the textile industry that had grown from the 1940s to the early 1970s, but that since the mid-1970s could not compete with an increased level of contraband; the long tradition of contraband in Antioquia; Antioqueño values that measured an individual's social worth by his or her wealth regardless of its origin; and, finally, the fortuitous fact that many North Americans confused Colombia with Bolivia and made frequent inquiries to Colombian smugglers in Panama about cocaine sources, inducing the Colombians to look for ways to supply cocaine.[3]

Dombois (1990) has argued that the negligible presence of the state in many areas and widespread bureaucratic corruption, due at least partly to a clientelist political system, and the existence of an active guerrilla movement created a very auspicious environment for the industry's growth. In an earlier work, Craig (1981) argues that the Colombian environment was particularly conducive to the growth of the illegal drug industry because of the prevalence and social acceptance of contraband, the large growth of the underground economy during the 1970s, and the willingness of Colombian illegal drug dealers to use violence.[4] Craig (1981: 246) sums up his assessment of the Colombian environment and entrepreneurial abilities this way: "They (the Colombians) are, indeed, master smugglers. Yet even the greatest of talents requires a proper arena in which to perform. In this regard, Colombia constitutes a virtual amphitheater." More recently, Sarmiento (1990b: 33) argues that Colombians developed a comparative advantage in illegal drugs by mastering the appropriate technology to successfully break antinarcotics laws and thwart enforcement efforts of the producing and consuming countries' governments. According to Sarmiento, the main technological elements are "transportation, commercialization, the capacity to bribe and intimidate, and above all, to mobilize the [economic] surplus" (author's translation). This last point is important because drug profits give illegal PSAD traffickers the ability to buy or provide sufficient protection to operate successfully.

The explanatory power of these analyses vary substantially. In general, all of them pose plausible reasons why Colombians became involved in the illegal drug trade, but they do not systematically explain why Colombia and not other countries developed an international advantage in the illegal drug industry.[5]

Focusing on these proposed reasons for the growth of the cocaine industry in Colombia, one finds first that given the huge difference between production costs and U.S. wholesale prices, and cocaine's high value per unit of volume and weight, neither physical distance between the supply sources and the product markets nor transportation costs plays a role in determining manufacturing location. The geopolitical argument does not explain why cocaine refining has taken place mainly in Colombia, since the relative simplicity of the process would allow it to be located near the raw material sources, and it does not explain why Colombians control the marketing and transportation of coca paste and cocaine. Besides, Colombia is not mainly a cocaine transshipment center, as some Central American and Caribbean countries have been, in which case geopolitical location is important. Distance is important in the marijuana industry because it is bulky to transport, making Colombia a good location, but not ideal since many Caribbean, Central American, and Mexican locations provide better access to the U.S. market.

Other suggested causal factors such as the growth of unemployment, state corruption, and a contraband tradition may indeed be important, but they are also present in countries such as Peru with a long history of coca production and consumption, and they do not necessarily indicate that Colombia is the country where production should be located. Furthermore, the causality relations posed by some authors might be contradictory. For instance, it can be argued that the decline of Medellín's manufacturing sector could have been at least partially due to currency revaluation and other "Dutch disease" effects of the lucrative illegal drug exports. The difficulty of the textile industry attributed to the increase in unfair contraband competition may also be the result of the growth of illegal exports that generated the foreign exchange to bring in the contraband. The ethnocentric explanation based on Antioqueño values might be relevant, but it leaves unexplained why other large drug "cartels" developed outside Antioquia and why some of the main leaders of the Medellín "cartel" are not Antioqueños. The explanation about the confusion between Bolivia and Colombia might be ingenious, but it is simply not plausible that people in the smuggling business would confuse Bolivia with Colombia since the nature of the business itself requires a minimum knowledge of geography.[6] The higher than average unemployment level in Medellín as a cause of narco-industry development is not convincing either, since there are many cities in Andean countries that have had higher unemployment levels than Medellín's, particularly during the early 1980s, but they did not produce illegal drug entrepreneurs. Besides, as discussed in Chapter 1, internal migration has been important in Colombia during the last forty years. Medellín had a larger protected manufacturing base than other Colombian cities and its workers had higher than average incomes. Medellín also had the best municipal public utilities in the country, providing better services than those of other large cities. These factors made Medellín a particularly strong magnet for migrants that resulted in a higher equilibrium unemployment level.[7] High unemployment in Medellín and the Antioqueño cultural idiosyncracies may be factors in the growth of the sicario industry, which is concentrated there, but they don't explain the trafficking side of the business.

Sarmiento's (1990b) argument that Colombians developed the appropriate "technology" is appealing from an economist's point of view. However, as he points out, the elements of this "technology" are corruption, intimidation, and the ability of drug dealers to use their income for those purposes. This ability is treated as a "factor of production." This approach is unsatisfactory on theoretical and policy grounds. At a theoretical level, there are two issues. First, to validate his "comparative advantage" explanation, Sarmiento must show that the ability to mobilize the economic surplus was greater in Colombia than in other countries, and this is not done. Indeed, the ability to mobilize the economic surplus to protect the industry is not necessarily greater in Colombia than in other countries. For instance, that ability could have been greater in Panama, where there was no need to convert foreign exchange and where the secrecy of the financial system was much greater, having been developed to help individuals break other countries' laws. Second, the production function of a firm is traditionally defined as the physical relationship between inputs and outputs—a relationship independent of the market structure and institutional framework in which the firm operates.

However, Sarmiento's approach makes the production function dependent on these elements that he treats as factors of production. From a policy point of view, treating the institutional environment as a factor of production of the firm allows the analyst to sweep under the rug the main institutional deficiencies and weaknesses that lie behind the growth of the illegal drugs industry, instead of confronting them. In other words, widespread corruption, intimidation, and other such elements are the result of a decaying institutional environment, a fact that is not dealt with when they are considered "factors of production" that, as such, have a positive productivity and whose increase should conceivably be promoted (i.e., if violence is a "factor of production," then it would be socially beneficial to increase it).

Value-Added Characteristics of Illegal PSAD and Colombia's International Advantage

As argued above, the high value-added price in the PSAD industry is due mainly to its illegal nature and the risks involved in its production and trade. Since most of the illegal PSAD manufacturing processes are footloose, including the cocaine industry after coca paste is made, these industries tend to locate themselves in the lowest risk locations. Thus, to explain Colombia's advantage one should focus on the factors that lower the industry's risks in Colombia. The main point is precisely that for a long time Colombia has had a set of conditions that minimized the illegal PSAD industry's risks, attracted the cocaine refining industry, allowed Colombians to control coca leaf marketing in Bolivia and Peru, and promoted their involvement in the United States cocaine market. Low risk therefore allowed Colombia to develop an international competitive advantage in those aspects of the industry. In other words, Colombia offered the "best incentive package" to the illegal PSAD industry.

When one looks at the production function of other illegal drugs produced in Colombia, one finds similar characteristics: the production of marijuana is makeshift in the sense that it can grow naturally almost everywhere, and that there are hydroponic high-yield varieties available; and methaqualone can be manufactured in many chemical laboratories that produce other legal drugs if the right chemical compounds are available. Neither of these products require large capital investments, their production technologies are available in most countries, and their production costs are not significantly affected by the scale of production. Therefore, their illegal production will also tend to be located in the lowest-risk location.

The Basis of the Colombian Advantage

The first important factor behind the country's advantage in the illegal PSAD industry has been the process of delegitimation of the regime. As discussed in Chapter 2, during the last forty-five years many outward signs of growing regime delegitimation and a weakening of the state have appeared. As Colombia's economy grew more complex, the state assumed an increasing number of functions that it could perform less and less effectively. Many laws were increasingly disregarded, government bureaucracies became more inefficient and increasingly unaccountable and unresponsive to citizens, private and public sector corruption increased, and the state grew unable to exert effective control over large areas of the country. A widening gap developed between the *de jure* and *de facto* socially acceptable behavior, and the underground economy greatly expanded.

The increasing delegitimation of the regime and the weakening of the state has been common in other Latin American and Caribbean countries, and their states have also grown weaker and increasingly incapable of enforcing their own laws and controlling their territories. However, comparing Colombia to such countries, particularly the Andean ones with a tradition of coca cultivation and use, one finds two important differences: in Colombia the delegitimation process began several decades earlier, and it has been accompanied by an extremely high level of violence, much higher than that present in any other Andean country.

In Colombia the crisis of the regime and the weakening of the state were evident by the late 1940s when la violencia started, while similar crises materialized in Peru and Bolivia from the mid-1960s on. Thus, Colombia had a head start that allowed underground entrepreneurs to gain significant experience before establishing the illegal drug industry.

The higher level of violence in Colombia has also had effects relevant to PSAD industry development. First, la violencia led to the loss of government control over large areas of the country to several guerrilla organizations. Other Andean governments also had a limited presence in many parts of their countries, but it was clear in Colombia that the government could not control some parts of the country even if it wanted and tried to.

Second, high levels of violence implicitly lowered the value of human life and made Colombians more prone to use violence to solve their conflicts, a useful trait in a high profit, high risk business in which conflict cannot be resolved through legal channels. Colombian drug dealers have been prone to use violence to wipe out their competitors.[8] Indeed, Colombians have used violence as an effective "barrier to entry" to the cocaine industry.

Other factors that helped Colombia develop its productive and trade advantage are also related to the regime's delegitimation. Colombia has a long tradition of contraband, with some peculiarly Colombian characteristics. Import contraband has taken place throughout Colombia's and other Latin American and Caribbean countries' history. However, Colombia has been one of the few countries which also had an export contraband tradition. Contraband exports of manufactured products and livestock to Venezuela and Ecuador have been persistent through time. Coffee contraband exports have frequently taken place to bypass International Coffee Agreement quotas. More importantly, for a long time Colombian emeralds have been smuggled out of the country. Workers in government mines steal the gems and sell them to smugglers and smugglers have also developed illegal wildcat mining organizations. Emeralds export smuggling provided the initial know-how to sell on international black markets and launder foreign exchange, and (as discussed in Chapter 3) it developed a close-knit organization in which loyalty played an important role—a structure that was transplanted to the coca and cocaine industry. Thus, many emerald smugglers became involved in illegal PSAD exports.

As discussed in Chapter 2, the contraband of many consumer goods was institutionalized in the mid-1950s, and promoted the development of a flourishing business that gained legitimacy and destroyed the social stigma attached to that activity. This trade contributed to establishing links between Colombian and foreign smugglers, and allowed Colombians to gain experience and develop further know-how in money laundering and other shady international capital transactions.

Colombia has been the only Andean country that had exchange controls and nontariff restrictions since 1931 to the middle of 1991. The exchange control and import licensing systems were tightened in 1967 and, coupled with high import tariffs, provided powerful incentives for the development of an active foreign exchange black market, which originally was mainly supplied by emerald exports, worker remittances from Venezuela and the United States, tourism, and legal export and import misinvoicing. The foreign exchange obtained in this market was used mostly to finance capital flight, tourism, and contraband imports. The active foreign exchange black market provided additional money laundering know-how and channels for drug profits and capital to be brought into the country.

There are other factors unrelated to the loss of regime legitimacy and the weakening of the state that also contributed to the development of the illegal PSAD industry in Colombia. The geography and size of Colombia played a role, but not because of Colombia's location halfway between the traditional coca growing regions and the United States. Rather, Colombia's geography kept many regions isolated and fairly self-sufficient, and generally lacking a state presence. Such factors contributed to the government's lack of control over them, and made them good locations for production facilities of the illegal PSAD industry. In addition, Colombia's relatively large size made it more attractive to illegal PSAD entrepreneurs than smaller Central American and Caribbean countries because detection is more difficult and because, in order to have an illegal PSAD operation in a small country, it is necessary to bribe its high authorities, while in Colombia it has only been necessary to bribe local authorities in isolated regions, a cheaper and less risky action.[9] Third, the relatively short distance to the U.S. market was technologically important because there were small planes with the range to fly to the United States without stopovers.

Another factor is Colombia's brand of capitalism that has always operated with the expectation of high short-term profits. Ocampo (1984: 61) has argued that the successive nineteenth century booms, as well as obstacles to internal transportation that produced segmented markets with large price differences, generated an entrepreneurial class based on "production-speculation." Entrpreneurs invested little in long-term capital equipment, focused on commerce, and expected quick turnover and high short-term profits. The modernization and structural economic change that took place after World War II encouraged changes in this behavior by promoting the development of more stable economic activities and depersonalized markets. Yet, while some entrepreneurs invested with longer horizons in mind, many continued their rent-seeking traditional behavior. However, during the early and mid-1970s two important changes reinforced the old "production-speculation" mentality: the capital market liberalization begun during the Pastrana administration (1970–1974) and strengthened by the López government (1974–1978), and the coffee boom of 1975–1978 (see Chapters 1 and 2). Capital market liberalization led to a wave of financial speculation, high short-term returns, and a series of large bankruptcies in the early 1980s, while the coffee boom provided high windfall gains and the expectation of high profits.

A last but no less important factor has been the large Colombian legal and illegal migration to the United States. This emigrant group, with weak loyalty to the host country, provided excellent distribution channels for illegal exports.[10] Here again, the large emigration from Colombia preceded by a couple of decades of similar emigrations from the other Andean countries, contributing to the Colombian international advantage.

To conclude, the conjunction of these factors allowed Colombians to create the country's international competitive advantage in cocaine manufacturing and distribution. The earlier start of the delegitimation process and the traditionally high level of violence in Colombian society made Colombians prone to eliminate competitors and, thus, control coca leaf purchases in Bolivia and Peru and distribution channels in the United States. The existence of large areas of the country where the government did not have a presence, and which had been proven to be outside of its control, provided safe havens for the establishment of coca labs, landing strips, and so on. The existence of organized guerrillas intent on further weakening the state also contributed to safety for the cocaine manufacturing industry.[11] Indeed, in the late 1970s and early 1980s guerrilla organizations sold protection to the cocaine entrepreneurs. The "production-speculation" capitalist tradition also contributed to the growth of the industry, as did the export smuggling experience of the Colombians. To complete the picture, the large Colombian contingent in the United States lowered illegal export risks. As MacDonald (1988) indicates, no other South American or Caribbean country had such a "package" of characteristics conducive to the development of the illegal PSAD industry, but the relevant characteristics are more complex than what MacDonald argues, and they are relevant because they all lower the risks in manufacturing and marketing of illegal PSADs in general, and cocaine in particular.

As a final note, one may speculate whether the Colombian international comparative advantage is a lasting one. Among the Andean countries Colombia has had the best "package" of illegal PSAD industry facilitating factors. However, recent developments in other countries, particularly Peru, and a possible social backlash in Colombia may erode the country's advantage.

In Peru, the "Shining Path" has controlled large areas of the country where coca is produced, and the underground economy growth has been remarkable. Since late 1989 the Colombian government has been able to increase pressure on the illegal drug industry and it appears there has been some manufacturing displacement out of Colombia. Similarly, other Peruvian and Bolivian organizations have increased their cocaine market share in the United States.

Would these developments lead to a loss of the Colombian competitive advantage in cocaine? It is difficult to give a definitive answer to this question because there is no way to determine the weights of the various characteristics that comprise the facilitator factors package. However, one may argue that some factors are more important than others. For instance, the violence that Colombians are prone to use is probably a key package factor, and one in which Colombia is likely to maintain an advantage, while it is likely for Colombia to lose the advantage generated by money laundering know-how. If this is so, the delegitimation of the region's regimes, the increasing number of Peruvian, Ecuadoran, and other immigrants in the United States, and other factors are likely to weaken but not eliminate the Colombian advantage.

It is important to differentiate between the advantage for the illegal PSAD industry to be located in Colombia, and the advantage that Colombians have in the industry. The pressure of Colombia's government on the industry, like that generated during the "war" declared after Luis Carlos Galán's assassination in August 1989, may increase the risks of operating in Colombia and will displace some productive facilities from Colombia. However, while this might increase the participation of Bolivians and Peruvians, there is no reason to expect that many Colombians already part of the production and marketing networks will not remain in the industry. Thus, the most likely result of regime delegitimation in the rest of the Andean region that parallels the one experienced in Colombia for a longer period, and of increased supply repression efforts by the Colombian government, would be a decline of the Colombian cocaine market share and a partial displacement of productive facilities from Colombia, but that would not end Colombian involvement in the industry.

Notes

1. For instance, the Colombian ambassador to the United States has argued that "because of its location in the northwest corner of South America, Colombia has been chosen by the narco-trafficking gangs as one of the main crossroads from where cocaine is brought to the United States" (Mosquera Chaux, 1989: 3).

2. Medellín is the capital of the Antioquia Department, which has the reputation of producing the most entrepreneurial Colombians, and which in the first half of the twentieth century became the cradle of Colombian industrialization. There is a well-known body of literature that has studied why the Antioqueños have developed those entrepreneurial skills (see for example López-Toro, 1970; and Twinam, 1980).

3. The belief that North Americans confuse the two countries was reinforced by President Reagan who made this mistake during his visit to Colombia in the early 1980s. While this cause may seem trivial to most researchers, it has been seriously advanced by Arango and Child (1987: 128) and Arango

(1988), two influential Colombian journalists and academics, one of whom was the head of the economics department at the Universidad de Antioquia. For this reason it should be mentioned, if only to dismiss it. Their statement was based on an interview with a former smuggler who during the late 1960s was supposed to have acted as a link between the smugglers in the Colón Free Zone in Panama with the Antioqueños.

4. For example, Craig (1981: 248) cites a DEA agent whom he interviewed: "I've worked in narcotics for many years in several countries, but never have I seen anything like the Colombian trafficker. He is really one mean bastard."

5. I hesitate to call this a "comparative advantage" since comparative advantage theories explain the advantage in terms of the relative endowment of factors of production: natural resources, raw and skilled labor, capital, and technology. And as I argue, the Colombian advantage was not developed based on relative productive factor proportions, but on institutional factors such as corruption, lack of state legitimacy, and its inability to control large regions of the country.

6. Even if a few American buyers had confused the two countries, their confusion would have made for a good joke, and would have been easily clarified. A simpler, more likely hypothesis is that since the Colombian smugglers were supplying the Colón Free Zone from the south, they were either asked if they could bring in other products from that general direction, or they themselves searched for those products.

7. Actually, Medellín's case is a very nice illustration of the Todaro (1969) migration and unemployment model: a region with better paying jobs and higher average standard of living attracts more migrants than other regions until higher unemployment discourages further migration. Thus the higher unemployment level in Medellín is expected because of its better paying jobs and infrastructure. In this case higher unemployment acts as a migration control mechanism.

8. For instance, Bagley (1988b: 75) argues that in a gang war fought in 1978 and 1979 in South Florida the Colombians "systematically eliminated" the Cuban-Americans and others involved in the cocaine business.

9. Local authorities are poorer and they are not as frequently in the limelight as national authorities. National authorities also have a lot more resources at their disposal, and may have more contacts with international and foreign law enforcement agents. It is worth noting that in Colombia until recently most high national authorities have remained untainted by the illegal PSAD while in the smaller Central American and Caribbean countries some of them have been active participants in the industry.

10. Reuter (1985) has argued that this is an important factor to explain Colombia's cocaine exports to the United States and the relative lack of Colombian penetration of the European markets in which the Brazilians have an edge given by their emigrant number. A similar point is made by Krauthausen and Sarmiento (1991: chap. 3). Arango (1988: 25) argues that Colombians who returned to Medellín after organizing the marketing and distribution in the United States have enjoyed very high status and have become respected and influential.

11. Reyes (1990), Molano (1987), Jaime Jaramillo (1989), Mora (1989), and Cubides (1989) study various aspects of the relationship between the drug industry and guerrilla organizations.

... 6 ...
The Size of the Illegal Drugs Industry

Determining the size of the illegal PSAD industry is vital to understanding its impact on Colombia's economy, but that is a difficult task.[1] The most obvious problem is presented by the data. Most available data are weak and obtained indirectly, and various data sources have used different and, at times, unclear methodologies. Not surprisingly, the resulting estimates must be interpreted and used with great caution, and authors who have tried to measure the industry's size warn readers about the "science-fiction" nature and weakness of their estimates (Caballero, 1988; Reuter, 1984; Nadelmann, 1986; etc.).[2] Nevertheless, size must be addressed if the industry is to be understood.

Before embarking on any rigorous attempt to measure the size of the industry, it is necessary to clarify certain concepts. For instance, should value added in the industry be measured? Employment estimated? What about the revenue of Colombian residents or citizens generated by the industry? Or should one consider the total foreign exchange generated by the industry that comes into the country?

As noted above, Colombia produces several illegal drugs, but most studies that have attempted to measure the size of the industry have focused on cocaine, the most important branch. There are also a few estimates of the size of marijuana production and revenues, but there are no estimates for the rest of the illegal PSAD industry. The estimates available focus also on the international side of the business, and do not provide figures for domestic revenues. Thus, the available estimates of the size of the illegal drug industry in Colombia tend to *underestimate* the size of the industry since they do not include methaqualone, opium and heroin, and the domestic revenues generated by bazuco and other illegal drug sales.

Estimation Issues in the Marijuana and Cocaine Branches

To estimate the size and generated revenues of the cocaine and marijuana industries, and the amount of foreign exchange brought into the country by them, several steps have to be followed. First, it is necessary to determine the amount of raw materials available to the industry by estimating how much coca and marijuana are produced. Second, the amount of the illegal PSAD that can be produced from the raw material should be calculated. Third, revenues must be estimated for each stage of production and distribution. Fourth, revenue estimates should be divided among the nationals of the countries involved so as to determine Colombia's share. And fifth, the proportions of these revenues consumed and invested in each country have to be estimated.

Most estimates of the industry's size begin with National Narcotics Intelligence Consumers Committee (NNICC)[3] estimates, based on data collected by several agencies—such as the U.S. Central Intelligence Agency (CIA), whose satellite pictures are used to estimate the area cultivated with coca, marijuana, and other illicit crops. As Nadelmann (1986) points out, these estimates are likely to be inaccurate because of technical difficulties in determining the nature of a particular plantation, and because marijuana and coca plants are frequently grown with other crops that hide them. Some authors like Gómez (1985) claim that NNICC estimates are the most accurate available, but others (Reuter, 1984) argue they are not only inaccurate, but they are biased to protect the particular interests of the agencies represented in the NNICC.[4] Independent researchers who have done extensive fieldwork in Bolivia and Peru have consistently produced significantly higher estimates of the cocaine production potential of those countries than the ones produced by U.S. government agencies. For example, Morales (1989: 92) estimates that the illicit cocaine production potential in Peru in 1984 was "400 tons of high-quality [uncut] cocaine hydrochloride," a figure close to three times larger than the estimation of the total cocaine output in all producer countries based on NNICC data (Nadelmann, 1986).

After figures on the cultivated area are obtained, productivity estimates are used to determine how much marijuana and coca leaves are produced. Among the factors that affect these estimates are the differences in growing systems, fertilizers and herbicides used, and geographical regions. In some areas marijuana and coca are single crops while in others they are mixed with other crops in different ways. The amount of fertilizers used has varied substantially through time, and output per hectare varies between countries and regions. Once the size of the marijuana crop is determined, it is relatively easy to proceed from there. But in the case of coca this is just the beginning, because conversion factors are needed to determine how much coca is needed to produce a unit of coca paste, how much paste produces a unit of cocaine base, and how much base is needed per unit of cocaine. As noted in Chapter 3, these conversion factors vary with the quality of the leaves, chemicals used, and the ability of the chemists (or "cooks"). Conversion factors also vary through time because of improved cultivation methods, the development of higher yield plant varieties, and yield-increasing chemical innovations. This succession of statistical estimations results in large increases in the variance of each step, rendering rather questionable conclusions.

Determining marijuana prices and those at each stage of the cocaine manufacturing process presents another difficult problem. As one should expect, there are no official price series, although the Drug Enforcement Agency (DEA) has annual price estimates. These are adjusted from time to time, but the adjustments change not only the estimate for the last year, but frequently for several years, significantly changing the old time series. As discussed in Chapter 3, illegality produces segmented markets in which it is difficult to estimate prices. To arrive at an average price in these markets, it is necessary to know the prices in and the relative size of each market segment. Thus, it is not surprising to find large price differences and apparently contradictory data: the Colombian press simultaneously reported wholesale 1981 cocaine prices in Bogotá of U.S. $4,000 and U.S. $15,000 per kg, and of U.S. $40,000 to U.S. $55,000 per kg in New York (Junguito and Caballero, 1982: 291); wholesale cocaine prices in Europe are reported to be two to three times higher than in the United States (Caballero, 1988; Gómez, 1990). These price variations add uncertainty to the estimates and increase the variance associated with any estimate of total illegal PSAD revenue.

Prices of chemicals used in the refining process and costs of transportation at each stage are also needed to estimate profits and the value added in the industry. Information provided by captured pilots, as well as listed chemical export prices in the United States and Europe, provide some benchmarks, but these sources are not very reliable because different pilots may be paid different amounts and chemical export prices do not necessarily reflect the actual costs to cocaine manufacturers.

Revenue estimates for the Colombian drug trafficking business also depend on the amount of coca leaves that are used for legal and illegal domestic consumption in Bolivia and Peru, the amount processed by entrepreneurs of other nationalities, the amount wasted at each stage of production, the amounts seized by the authorities, and the share of these seizures that find their way back into the market. Some estimates are relatively good, others are unreliable, and still others are simply impossible to make. For instance, historical consumption levels can be used to make relatively good estimates of coca leaves used in chewing, coca teas, and legal medicinal products in Bolivia and Peru, but any estimation of bazuco consumption in Colombia is subject to greater uncertainty, and estimates of seized cocaine that finds its way back to the market are impossible to calculate. So are the costs of Central American, Mexican, American, and other facilitators and intermediaries. Revenue adjustments due to some of these factors are expected to vary in magnitude. Some are likely to be small relative to total industry revenues and are not likely to add much to overall estimate variance (although they could be important relative to the size of industry profits spent in cocaine producing countries[5]), but others might be relatively large.

The next step consists of assigning total revenues to the various production and distribution stages, estimating payments at each stage of production and of the value added in Bolivia, Peru, Colombia, the United States, and Europe. These estimates are useful to determine the contributions of the illegal drugs industry to gross national product, but they do not show the impact the industry has on each country. For example, it is likely that a portion of the profits generated by cocaine processing and exporting from Colombia is invested abroad, while some of the value added by Colombian marketing in the United States is invested in Colombia. Similarly, some of the value added by transportation and smuggling cocaine to the United States does not accrue to Colombians, but to American pilots; bribed Central American, Caribbean, Mexican, and U.S. facilitators and government personnel; and some of the non-Colombian business members.

To determine the actual and potential influence of the illegal PSAD industry, one would also want to obtain estimates of the income accruing to Colombians, of the amount they invest and spend in Colombia, of the size and composition of the assets that illegal PSAD entrepreneurs have accumulated both in and outside Colombia, and the asset distribution and concentration among those involved in the business. But any attempt to make these estimations has conceptual and methodological problems.

Colombian value-added estimates in the cocaine and marijuana business tend to underestimate the amount that Colombians make because, for one thing, the value added generated in Colombia is only part of the total, since Colombians also make money transporting coca paste from Bolivia and Peru and distributing cocaine and marijuana in the United States. In other words, part of the value-added profits generated outside Colombia belongs to Colombians. Indeed, most Colombian profits are generated by the transportation and smuggling side of the business and by Colombian involvement in production and distribution outside Colombia. However, the degree of their involvement is unknown, which weakens any estimation. A further complication arises because some Colombians involved in cocaine marketing in the United States are either permanent U.S. residents, or have become U.S. citizens. Technically, none of this income is Colombian, but from the point of view of its real or potential impact on the Colombian economy, a portion of that income is identical to the income generated in the transportation and smuggling facets of the illegal PSAD business.[6] Further, as mentioned above, there are no estimates about methaqualone and other illegal PSAD that Colombia is reported to have produced and exported, or imported and re-exported. Recent reports of poppy cultivation and opium and heroin production in Colombia add another underestimation factor to the puzzle. Finally, there is no information about the involvement of Colombians in marketing cocaine in Europe, although it is accepted that this involvement is not likely to be large.[7]

There are, of course, other factors that tend to create opposite biases and tend to overestimate the size of the industry's income. First, value added in transporting the final products to the United States includes bribes, landing fees, and fees for other services paid to non-Colombian facilitators; and second, a portion of the profits generated in the cocaine export process from Colombia to the United States goes to non-Colombians who are involved in the business. For instance, Colombians may export to Jamaica, from where cocaine is known to be re-exported by Jamaicans to New York.

Capital Inflow Estimate Issues

After obtaining an estimate of the amount made every year by Colombians involved in the illegal PSAD industry, one should determine how much is actually brought back and absorbed by the Colombian economy. Illegal foreign exchange is brought into Colombia and absorbed through several channels, including underinvoicing imports and overinvoicing and faking exports of goods; faking service exports (mainly tourism and labor remittances); and the financing of domestic capital flight, profit remittances by transnational corporations, contraband, tourism, education, health, and other services purchased by Colombians abroad.

Some black market foreign exchange inflows can be detected in the official balance of payments; others cannot. Using balance of payments data, it is possible to estimate "normal" pre-drug-era levels of tourism flows and labor income and compare those with the ones actually recorded. A similar procedure can be used with some service imports. Estimations of under and overinvoicing of merchandise trade, although difficult, may be made. However, domestic capital flight, contraband, illegal profit remittances by transnational corporations, tourism, and medical and educational expenditures abroad are very difficult to estimate and most of them are not reflected in the official balance of payments. Attempts to link official balance of payments data to the illegal PSAD industry face another problem because this industry is not the only source of illegal foreign exchange flows and contraband. Even if there were good estimates of fake services trade, contraband, and so on, it could not be argued that all the foreign exchange used by these imports is generated by the illegal PSAD industry, as there are other black market foreign exchange sources like coffee contraband exports and expatriate worker remittances.

Estimates of illegal flows of capital and goods based on official balance of payments data are useful to understand how these flows affect important macroeconomic variables such as the monetary base and international reserves, and to study how the government reacts to changes in those variables.[8] However, they cannot be used as a measure of the actual illegal PSAD income and capital that have been brought back to the country or of their impact on the Colombian economy.

Estimating the capital accumulated by Colombian illegal PSAD entrepreneurs presents further problems. To begin with one would need estimates for the *relevant* group of businessmen, which is made up of those whose income and capital have a direct impact on the country today or that could have an impact in the future. This group includes illegal PSAD business owners with income from Colombian value-added activities, and also Colombians who obtain illegal income abroad and who are likely to bring their capital back to Colombia. One would need to estimate the composition and value of the assets this group has in Colombia and abroad, and the return they get from their investments. As mentioned, a particular estimation problem is presented by Colombians involved in cocaine marketing in the United States who are either residents or citizens of that country. It is worth noting that, even though the United States has historically received a large number of immigrants, the emigration of foreign-born residents has also been substantial. Warren and Marks (1980) estimate that between 1908 and 1957 foreign-born emigration equaled 31 percent of the immigration total, a percentage that declined to 18 percent in the 1960s. Few immigrants would have stronger return migration incentives than Colombians who have made a few million dollars in cocaine distribution. For, in the United States they would be, at best, well-to-do foreigners who are only partially assimilated into mainstream society, and who will always have a risk of being identified with the illegal PSAD industry. If they return to Colombia they could be at the top of the income and wealth distribution and become influential social members, particularly in small and medium-size cities.

A further problem arises because the accumulated capital that was generated in the illegal PSAD industry might not be owned by individuals who are easily identified with the industry. For instance, some of this capital might be in the hands of current or former government officials who received bribes, or bank officers, lawyers, and others who helped launder illegal profits, as well as illegal PSAD entrepreneurs who retired from the business undetected, among others.

The Available Estimates

As noted above, all available estimates begin by determining the total output of marijuana and cocaine. Table 6.1 summarizes the main estimates of the size of the cocaine industry discussed in this section. The pioneering work of Junguito and Caballero (1982), based on data supplied by the U.S. embassy in Bogotá, estimates that in 1978 Colombia exported about fourteen tons of cocaine to the United States. Their estimates of marijuana output have a large range because estimates of the cultivated area at the time ranged from 30,000 to 70,000 hectares. Using alternative wholesale U.S. price assumptions, they estimate that total cocaine exports did not exceed U.S. $154 million while marijuana's ranged between U.S. $435 million and U.S. $756 million; however, these authors believe that the real marijuana exports were closer to U.S. $500 million than to their higher estimate.

Gómez (1988 and 1990) uses NNICC and U.S. Department of State estimates of the cultivated and eradicated marijuana area for the 1977–1988 period. These data show a substantially smaller cultivated area than Junguito and Caballero (1982): between 8,000 and 10,000 hectares from 1977 through 1985, increasing to 13,085 in 1987 and falling again to 9,200 in 1988. These data also show very successful

Table 6.1 Estimates of the Size of the Cocaine Industry in Colombia

Year	Cocaine Export Volume (tons)							Export Price per Ton (thousands of dollars)				Cocaine Export Value (billions of dollars)			
	Junguito and Caballero (1982)	Kalmanovitz (1990)		Sarmiento (1990)		Gómez (1988) (1990)	Caballero (1988)		Kalmanovitz (1990)	Sarmiento (1990)	Gómez (1988) (1990)	Junguito and Caballero (1982)	Kalmanovitz (1990)	Sarmiento (1990)		Gómez (1988)	Gómez (1990)
		to United States	to Europe	min.	max.		to United States	to Europe						min.	max.		
1976		20							70				1.1				
1977		30							70				1.7				
1978	14	35							70			0.2	2				
1979		40							70				2.1				
1980		50							60				2.4				
1981		70		23	67.5	50			60	60	52		3.4	1.4	4.1	1.8	2.6
1982		80		44.7	72.1	90			60	60	52		4.3	2.7	4.3	3.3	4.7
1983		100		48.1	90.7	99.4			50	50	27		4	2.4	4.5	1.9	2.7
1984		120		16.3	57.3	73.9			45	45	26		4.3	0.7	2.6	1.4	1.9
1985		130		45	104.6	61			40	40	30		4.2	1.8	4.2	1.4	1.8
1986		160		43.5	121.3	84			30	33.5	22		3.8	1.5	4.1		1.8
1987		200	30	54	140.7	90.9			25	26	15		5.2	1.4	3.7		1.4
1988		230	40	52.3	147.5	75.1	270	40	18	22.5	15		4.9	1.2	3.3		1.2
1989		200	50						22				5.5				

annual eradication rates of 40, 75, 78, 69, and 56 percent from 1984 through 1988, respectively. Marijuana export value estimates are about U.S. $250 million in the late 1970s, decline to about U.S. $170 million in the early 1980s, and drop sharply in 1985 and 1986 to a minimum of U.S. $27.9 million, rebounding to U.S. $88.9 million in 1988.

To estimate cocaine exports and revenue, Gómez (1988 and 1990) estimates coca cultivation and yields in Colombia, conversion factors related to coca paste, coca paste imports from Bolivia and Peru, conversion factors related to making cocaine base and from it to cocaine, and United States wholesale prices. According to these estimates, Colombia exported between 24 and 31 tons in 1979, and 50, 90, 99.4, 73.9, 61, 84, 90.9, and 75.1 tons from 1981 to 1988. During these years the estimated U.S. wholesale prices per kilogram are, in thousands of U.S. dollars, 52, 52, 27, 26, 30, 22, 15, and 15 respectively. These two data series are unfortunately inconsistent with what is expected about the demand for cocaine. If one assumes that the demand function does not change from year to year (or that changes are small), one may argue that the price-quantity data show points on the same demand curve. Using these data to estimate the arc-elasticity of demand, one finds that the demand curve was perfectly elastic in 1981–1982 and in 1987–1988, while it had near zero negative price elasticities (as expected) in 1982–1983 (-0.16), 1984–1985 (-0.19), and 1986–1987 (-0.20), a negative elasticity close to one (-1.03) in 1985–1986, and a large *positive* elasticity (7.80) in 1983–1984—indicating an upward sloping demand curve. These inconsistent results may be due to demand changes, but they are very difficult to explain, particularly when cocaine exports are shown to increase 90 percent in a year while the wholesale price remains constant!

Gómez (1988 and 1990) also estimates the net revenues of Colombian illegal PSAD businessmen. He estimates their total input and transportation costs and assumes that Colombians sell the product at the U.S. wholesale price. The weaknesses of these estimates surface again when the 1988 and 1990 essays are compared. The former covers the 1981–1985 period and the latter 1981–1988. The earlier estimates for 1981–1985 in U.S. dollars are $1.8, $3.3, $1.9, $1.4, and $1.4 billion, while the second ones are $2.6, $4.7, $2.7, $1.9, and $1.8 billion. The estimates for the three most recent years are $1.8, $1.4, and $1.2 billion. These estimates show a net revenue decline because the United States wholesale price declined sharply from 1982 on.

Kalmanovitz (1990) estimated cocaine and marijuana income for 1976–1989, based on data from the U.S. General Accounting Office

(1988), which vary from the data used by Gómez. His estimates show much higher cocaine exports from 1984 to 1989 than those estimated by Gómez: 120, 130, 160, 230, 270, and 250 tons respectively. This series is very confusing; it does not show the decline in 1984 exports that Kalmanovitz (1990: 20) himself attributes to that year's destruction of the large "Tranquilandia" cocaine refining complex. His United States wholesale price series shows extremely high prices of $70,000/kg for 1976–1979, $60,000/kg for the next three years, $50,000/kg in 1983, and $45,000, $40,000, $30,000, $25,000, $18,000, and $22,000/kg in the following years, all in U.S dollars. He also assumes that beginning in 1987 Colombians began to export to Europe (30, 40, and 50 tons in successive years) where the wholesale price was much higher (U.S. $50,000/kg). Kalmanovitz's estimates assume that Colombian drug traffickers control 80 percent of the exports from Colombia, and that cocaine losses and input and production costs represent about 15 percent of revenues. He also assumes there is no participation of Colombians in cocaine distribution in the United States. Thus he concludes that Colombian profits are 65 percent of the total revenue generated by exports from Colombia.[9] However, the table in which his estimates are presented (Kalmanovitz, 1990: 19) shows that the income attributed to Colombians is 80 percent of the total instead of 65 percent. His marijuana income estimates are fairly close to those of Gómez. The estimates of the total Colombian illegal PSAD industry income are about $2.5 billion in the late 1970s, about $4.3 billion from 1982 through 1985, somewhat lower in 1986, and over $5 billion annually from then on, all in U.S. dollars.

Sarmiento (1990a and 1990b) uses data from the NNICC to estimate the minimum total cocaine output, and uses higher estimates of the coca grown in Bolivia and Peru to determine an upper output range. Unfortunately, he does not cite the source of these higher figures. He assumes that between 40 and 50 percent of the coca base produced in Bolivia and Peru is exported to Colombia. The wholesale price series used is equal to the high one used by Kalmanovitz until 1985, and slightly higher for the last three years. Sarmiento's estimates of the cocaine export value have a wide range. The low estimates, in U.S. dollars, range from a minimum of $0.7 billion in 1984 to a high of $2.7 billion in 1982, and are in the $1.2 to $1.8 billion range for 1985–1988. The high estimates reach a maximum of $4.5 billion in 1983, a minimum of $2.6 billion in 1984, and range between $3.3 and $4.2 billion in the next four years. Both series reflect a minimum in 1984, when the large "Tranquilandia" refining complex was destroyed.

Other authors have been less ambitious than Gómez, Sarmiento, and Kalmanovitz and have produced rough estimates for only one year. Nadelmann (1986) points out many of the pitfalls of trying to estimate cocaine output and income, and provides what he considers to be ballpark estimates based on United States government data. Nadelmann does not separate by country the value added by the cocaine industry, but rather presents estimates at different stages of production. These rather stylized estimations for 1984 and 1985 assume a United States wholesale price of $30,000/kg, and total cocaine output of 150 tons—of which 65 tons are exported to the United States. The balance is assumed to be consumed in the producing countries or exported somewhere else. The value-added breakdown obtained is $400 million for peasants who grow coca, $133 million for coca paste processors, $360 million for coca paste transportation, $360 million for coca base producers, $150 million for cocaine refiners, and $1.37 billion for those who export cocaine from Colombia and sell at wholesale in the United States. Thus, 56.8 percent of the total income generated by the cocaine business, to the point where cocaine is sold in the United States to wholesalers, accrues to those who transport it and smuggle it into the United States. These estimates do not include the cocaine that is exported somewhere else.

Lee's (1988) study is even less ambitious and uses only what can be considered extremely rough estimates. He argues that in the early 1980s, "South American cocaine traffickers earned between U.S. $5 and $6 billion annually from international sales in the United States market. Perhaps $1.5 to $2 billion flowed back to the cocaine-producing countries" (Lee, 1988: p. 89).

Caballero (1988) makes other ballpark estimates of net revenues for Colombian narco-businessmen in 1988. However, he uses coca output data from *Fortune International*, which show total 1988 cocaine exports of 270 tons to the United States and 40 tons to Europe. Using U.S. and European wholesale prices of U.S. $19,000/kg and $50,000/kg, data on seizures, domestic coca consumption, etc., he estimates that the net income of Colombian cocaine processors and exporters was $4.1 billion.

Urrutia (1990b), Gómez (1985), and Sarmiento (1990a) estimate the amount of illegal foreign exchange that shows up as income in the service account of the official balance of payments. Gómez uses a regression in which the explanatory variables are the black market exchange rate differential, the real exchange rate level, dummy variables to reflect periods of tighter enforcement of foreign exchange laws by the government, and the Venezuelan GDP (a variable that takes into account the fact that contraband to Venezuela and remittances from Colombians working in that country supply foreign exchange sold to the Central Bank or in the black market). Only the black market exchange rate differential and the Venezuelan GDP level were statistically significant, and the black market exchange rate differential has a substantial elasticity (1.6) with respect to the amount of black market dollars that show up on the income side of the balance of payments. The estimates obtained are quite low, somewhere around U.S. $200 million per year in the late 1970s and early 1980s, and decline sharply and actually become negative in 1983 and 1984 when black market exchange rates were above official ones, becoming slightly positive in 1985 and 1986. Urrutia follows a simpler approach. By looking at the time series for tourism and labor income he concludes that genuine tourism and worker remittances should contribute about $400 and $150 million a year respectively. Based on these figures, he estimates that in 1987 there were about $250 million unexplained on the income side of the balance of payments. In the early 1980s the unexplained amounts were higher (about $500 million) and also became negative in 1983–1984. Both estimates, all in U.S. dollars, show that the unexplained amounts fluctuate pro-cyclically, and they declined sharply when Colombia's international reserves also fell sharply in 1983–1984.

The balance of payments account that has raised the most questions about causes for its fluctuations is the transfers from Colombian expatriate workers. Colombia has had net emigration for at least forty years, and today there are large Colombian communities abroad, mainly in Venezuela and the United States. The emigration to Venezuela declined sharply and at times was reversed after 1982, when that country's development ground to a halt and its GDP declined. Sarmiento points out that workers' remittances were only about $20 million a year in the mid-1970s, and that they increased dramatically to $610 million in 1987, and argues that most of this increase is due to drug money. Indeed, a more careful look at expatriate remittances shows a remarkable pattern. Balance of payments data show that in 1970 Colombian expatriate workers transferred $6 million. This figure increased steadily to $18 million by 1975, and jumped to $42 million in 1976, when the marijuana boom materialized. In 1981 this figure reached $99 million, but declined during the next three years to $71, $63, and $73 million respectively, all in U.S. dollars. This was the period of highest international cocaine prices, and coincided with Venezuela's external debt crisis, the United States recession, and difficulties in the Colombian economy. This was also a time when the black market exchange rate exceeded the official one in Colombia.

After 1984 Colombian expatriate workers appear to have been a lot more "generous" with their Colombian brethren, and their transfers skyrocketed to $105 million in 1985, and $393, $616, $448, $459, and $488 million for the period that ended in 1990. These figures are simply too high to be attributed to changes in the numbers of emigrants and their behavior. However, Urrutia (1990b) argues that they are not inconsistent with what average expatriates send to other countries, and thus, most of these transfers are legitimate. Nevertheless, if the high levels of the late 1980s are consistent with the numbers of Colombians abroad, one is left to explain why these remittances were so low before. Considering the extreme changes in the series, one has to agree with Sarmiento (1990a and 1990b) and accept that most of the expatriate transfers are not legitimate and are likely to be financed by drug-earned foreign exchange.

Gómez (1990), Kalmanovitz (1990), and Sarmiento (1990a) attempt to shed some light on other uses of illegal PSAD dollars, particularly contraband and capital flight financing. Gómez estimates that between 1981 and 1988 the illegal PSAD businessmen made about $14.2 billion. According to the Bank of International Settlements (BIS), the financial assets that Colombians accumulated outside the country between 1978 and 1988 was U.S. $4.2 billion. This figure is based on official balance of payments data, and as noted by Gómez, it does not include illegal drug monies.[10] Therefore, $18.4 billion were available to finance contraband, capital flight, and other black market uses of foreign exchange. Gómez indicates that FENALCO estimates contraband at about $1.1 billion a year, or $8.8 billion from 1981 to 1988. Subtracting from the BIS data the invested international reserves of the country, he obtains an estimate of $2.8 billion as observed capital flight. Subtracting from $18.4 billion the contraband and capital flight estimates, a balance of $6.8 billion (or $850 million per year) is obtained. This is an estimate of the amount available for increasing cash foreign exchange balances in Colombia and to finance unobserved capital flight, the amount Colombian PSAD businessmen and other Colombians have invested abroad, tourism, and other underestimated variables on the expenditure side of the balance of payments, etc. If the validity of this estimate is accepted, then it must be concluded that most of the Colombian illegal drug profits have been plowed back into the Colombian economy.

It should be noted that estimates on the size of contraband are quite weak and that the contraband value seems to have changed over time.[11] FENALCO (1987) estimates differ substantially from those mentioned by Gómez. These estimates are based on data gathered through opinion surveys of businesspersons affected by contraband and are thus subject to great uncertainty. However, they indicate that contraband amounts have varied substantially from year to year, in response to changes in the gap between the black market and official exchange rates, and to the fluctuations in economic activity. The estimated annual values were high—between $600 million and $1 billion in 1980—but declined sharply to about zero in 1983 when the black market rate substantially exceeded the official one for the first time in nine years, and when the Colombian economy was in recession. Since then contraband values increased and in 1987 were comparable to those of 1980.

In contrast to other variables, import and export misinvoicing have been estimated in studies that do not deal with the illegal drug industry directly. Meisel (1988) compares data on trade with Colombia provided by the country's main trading partners with that of Colombia to check for discrepancies. He assumes that transportation and insurance costs averaged 6.5 percent of the export value. This study found that the level of misinvoicing was not too significant. Between 1976 and 1985 minor exports misinvoicing was estimated to range between 10 percent underinvoicing and 8 percent overinvoicing, depending on the official/black market exchange rate differential and the amount of export subsidies. Another interesting finding of this study was that the sectoral differences of misinvoicing were rather significant: in some sectors there was persistent underinvoicing of exports or imports, while in others there was overinvoicing. It should also be noted that some data discrepancies were explained, at least partially, by export quotas, contraband to Venezuela and Ecuador, and accounting methods.[12]

Kalmanovitz argues that import underinvoicing has been more frequent than what Meisel estimates. He assumes that underinvoicing was not important in 1974 to 1976 and the existance of a constant import-value-to-weight ratio. He notes that this ratio declined substantially since its 1974 to 1976 base years, and attributes this decline to a statistical mirage due to increased underinvoicing, discounting the influence of changes in the composition of trade. Using this method he estimates rising import underinvoicing to about $1 billion by 1979 and $2.2 billion by 1983. From then on this estimate fluctuates between $1.4 and $1.9 billion a year. Kalmanovitz also argues that some of the "non-refundable" imports are financed with black market funds.[13] Further, in 1977 the Central Bank bought gold worth only $10 million, and in subsequent years these purchases increased sharply, averaging about $400 million since 1985. These are supposed to be purchases of domestically produced gold only. Kalmanovitz indicates that during the Betancur administration (1982–1986) the domestic gold price was substantially above the international price to promote production, making gold smuggling financed with illegal drug dollars very profitable.

Kalmanovitz also argues that a different type of contraband, referred to as "witches' mail," grew substantially during the 1980s. This is contraband mostly of spare parts and small pieces of equipment.[14] It is reported that many Colombian businessmen and entrepreneurs save on inventory costs by having an agent in Miami or Panama who quickly supplies equipment and needed parts that are smuggled into Colombia. Kalmanovitz makes back-of-the-envelope estimates for the "witches' mail," adds estimates of gold, regular contraband, and rough estimates for capital flight and tourism financing, and concludes that the amount of black market foreign exchange (mostly illegal PSAD currencies) that actually comes into the country is over U.S. $4.5 billion a year, a figure dramatically higher than Gómez's estimate. However, this estimate also implies that most of the income made by Colombian illegal PSAD entrepreneurs finds its way into the Colombian economy, and that the amount they have accumulated abroad is relatively small.

Meisel (1990) presents a rebuttal to Kalmanovitz, pointing out that the latter's measure is very sensitive to changes in the composition of traded goods. In 1974, Colombian fuel imports were only 0.2 percent of the total, but increased very rapidly to an average of 7 percent between 1976 and 1985, and even reached 17.5 percent in 1979 (Meisel, 1990: 102). Since fuels are low-value-per-unit-of-weight products, this change exaggerates Kalmanovitz's import underinvoicing measure. A similar problem arises with any weight-based estimate of export overinvoicing since Colombia's export composition also changed after 1985 to include a significant amount of fuels. In this second article, Meisel uses a higher transportation and insurance figure of 10 percent of the traded value.[15] Based on this work, Meisel argues that the amount of import underinvoicing has been small, and that it did not significantly contribute to a *de facto* opening of the Colombian economy during the mid- to late 1980s.

Gunter's (1991) capital flight work also estimates trade misinvoicing. This work differs from the preceding ones in that its main goal is to determine capital flight out of Colombia, not into Colombia. He uses the same data used by Meisel, but argues that the difference attributable to insurance and freight should be 11 percent, higher than the one used by Meisel (1988 and 1990). Gunter finds a sectoral misinvoicing pattern similar to Meisel's (1988), but his estimates are somewhat higher due to the higher insurance and freight costs. He also finds significant variations through time in response to changes in the black market/official exchange rate differentials and devaluation expectations. His main conclusions were that "during the 1977–1987 period, imports from Colombia reported by the industrial countries (adjusted for CIF [cost, insurance, and freight]) exceeded Colombian exports by an average of 8.3 percent. This result is consistent with under-invoicing of exports in order to facilitate capital flight" (p. 129). However, "during the 1977–1987 sample period, adjusted exports from other countries to Colombia exceeded imports reported by the Colombian government by an average of 8.3 percent. In other words, instead of over-invoicing of imports that might facilitate capital flight, Colombian residents under-invoiced imports" (p. 130) to facilitate capital inflows. The values estimated by Gunter show that on balance, misinvoicing was used to bring an average of U.S. $141 million per year into the country, with a maximum of $465 million, and in three years a negative capital inflow (capital flight) that reached as high as $269 million. This apparently conflicting pattern is actually consistent with sound economic behavior. People underinvoice imports to avoid tariffs and value-added taxes, and in the case of quotas and licenses, to import more scarce products; and they underinvoice exports to avoid income and value-added taxes, while they overinvoice exports when they can get enough export subsidies to compensate for the higher taxes.

Sarmiento (1990a and 1990b) also estimates import underinvoicing financed with black market dollars. The value of the average ton of imports has increased much less than the implicit price index for imports used in the national accounts. He uses this difference to estimate the underinvoicing of imports, which has reached, according to this estimation, almost 30 percent of declared imports. Using these figures, Sarmiento argues that the amount of illegal foreign exchange inflows that can be estimated using official balance of payments data, and which are expected to come mostly from drug sources, has ranged between U.S. $900 million and $1.3 billion per year. Further, Sarmiento looks at monthly worker remittances and finds substantial variations, as well as major drops every time the government has pressured the drug industry in the wake of the assassination of important political figures. He also finds relatively high correlations between worker remittances and both minor exports and other service exports, suggesting that some of these are simply fictitious exports used to launder illegal monies. A look at other balance of payments accounts series confirms this pattern. For instance, the amounts of foreign exchange used to buy education services abroad are also correlated with worker remittances, and with the black market/official exchange rate differentials. When the black market peso is strong, there are few expenditures in education abroad, and vice-versa. Because of these correlations, the above figures represent a lower limit for the amount of illegal foreign exchange coming into the country that is captured in official balance of payments data.

Comments on the Estimates

To begin, it must be emphasized that all authors estimating the size of the illegal PSAD industry in Colombia are aware of many of their limitations and their high degree of uncertainty, and warn the reader about their inaccuracy and weakness.

The Junguito and Caballero, Gómez, Kalmanovitz, and Sarmiento estimates focus on the value added in Colombia, and thus, their estimates have a downward bias because they exclude the amount that Colombians make in coca paste transportation out of Peru and Bolivia and in cocaine marketing in the United States. However, these estimates also have an upward bias as they do not take into account some of the costs of doing business in the Caribbean, Mexico, and Central America, and they assume that all smugglers are Colombian. It is likely, however, that the overall bias is downward since the Colombian income generated in the U.S. marketing may be large relative to the total Colombian value added. These estimates, as well as Nadelmann's, produce values of the total drug income of Colombians generated outside the United States that fluctuate between U.S. $2 and $4 billion a year. These figures depend on the accuracy of the estimates of coca and marijuana production, particularly the former. Events in the last few years suggest that these figures have been grossly underestimated, at least after 1984. For example, Gómez (1990) estimates that in 1988 Colombia exported 75.1 tons of cocaine, while Caballero (1988) provides the highest estimate of 310 tons of cocaine produced that year. However, thirty tons of cocaine were seized in the United States in one week in the fall of 1989 without reported subsequent higher cocaine prices at street level. This prompted the State Department to increase its estimates and, in its next annual report on narcotics control published in March 1990 (Department of State, 1990), it reported that the coca crop was sufficient to produce 776 tons of cocaine.[16] The likelihood may then be argued that during the late 1980s the illegal PSAD business produced significantly higher revenues than the estimated ones.

Kalmanovitz's study has a downward bias because it excludes the profits obtained by Colombians transporting coca paste to Colombia from Peru and Bolivia, as well as the profits of Colombians who are residents or citizens of the United States. However, it also has an upward bias because his price estimates for earlier years (1976–1980) are much higher than the ones given by all other sources, and his estimates of Colombian profits do not subtract the 15 percent of export revenue he attributes to production costs and waste. The values of Kalmanovitz's physical output series are significantly higher than those used by other researchers (particularly the last years), and so are his estimates of industry revenues. However, his estimates appear to contain biases tending to both under- and overestimate total profits.

As mentioned, Colombians naturalized or residing in the United States present another significant problem to estimating the actual and potential impact of the illegal PSAD business on Colombia. Reuter (1988) estimates 1988 U.S. retail prices of $250,000 per kg, which had declined from about $600,000 per kg in the early 1980s. Therefore, the U.S. cocaine retail price is tenfold or more the wholesale price received by Colombian exporters. Thus, assuming that Colombians are involved mostly in the first marketing layers, and that they handle only half of the cocaine imported, they should be making an amount at least comparable in magnitude to what Colombian producers and exporters make. Of course, these are just speculative estimates, but they do provide strong indication that the amount of capital originating in the illegal PSAD industry that is owned by Colombians residing in and outside the country, but who could consider investing it in Colombia, is substantially higher than the estimates based only on the value added in Colombia.

There are other reasons why the illegal PSAD income of Colombians is underestimated. As noted, Colombian drug traffickers are reported to produce and export other PSAD besides cocaine and marijuana, such as methaqualone and more recently, opium and heroin;[17] besides, they also sell cocaine and bazuco in the domestic market. Colombians are also involved in the transportation of cocaine base and coca paste from Bolivia and Peru to the laboratories owned by Colombian cocaine refiners and in the smuggling of the chemicals used in the manufacturing process. Therefore, part of the cost of the cocaine inputs is also income for the Colombians involved in the illegal PSAD industry. The income generated by any of these activities is not included in the estimates discussed above.

Colombians have been involved in illegal PSAD production and trafficking for at least twenty years. Therefore, they have accumulated income earning assets in and out of Colombia that were generated by the illegal industry. Gómez's (1990) estimates indicate that total illegal PSAD income has been about U.S $14.2 billion, but he does not estimate what they have accumulated. Kalmanovitz (1990) argues that the illegal PSAD businessmen's wealth is significantly higher than that. Since according to his estimates the industry's profits have been in the U.S. $4 to $5 billion range a year since 1980, he argues that if they have saved and invested $2 billion during ten years (capitalized at 10 percent), they should by now have 30 percent of the total wealth Colombians have in and out of the country. However, he does not indicate how the total wealth is estimated or how large it is. In any case, the amount that participants in the illegal industry have accumulated is likely to be very large relative to the size of Colombia's economy, and will continue to have a large impact on it for many years. A simple exercise illustrates this point. Assuming that the industry's participants accumulated only U.S. $1 billion a year from 1975 to 1979 and $2 billion from 1980 to 1989, and that their investments yielded only 7 percent a year, by 1989 they would have earned $39 billion. If one assumes a larger asset accumulation of $3 billion from 1980 to 1983 and $4 billion from 1984 to 1990, their net worth today would exceed $66 billion. Of course, these figures are just back of the envelope estimates, but they illustrate the fact that the illegal PSAD entrepreneurs are likely to have a "very large" amount of capital that would yield an annual income as great or greater than the estimated illegal PSAD profits!

The possibility that figures of such magnitude are real is very threatening to Colombia's power structure, as they suggest the illegal PSAD businesses would have huge combined drug and capital incomes relative to the size of the country's economy. For instance, between 1976 and 1986 gross private fixed investment ranged from U.S. $1.6 to $3.7 billion and averaged $2.8 billion,[18] figures that clearly indicate that the illegal businessmen had the capacity to invest in Colombia an amount as large as what official data attribute to the country's whole private sector. These figures also indicate that Colombian policymakers must take into account a possibly large "illegal PSAD capital external overhang," made up of the amounts that could be brought into the country in the future. It should be pointed out that these are estimates of "tainted" capital and income, and not just of those of the drug barons—since there has been some "spreading of the wealth" to lawyers, chemists, politicians, pilots, guards, and so on.

Balance of payments data show that the amount of unexplained foreign exchange received by the Central Bank has not been as large as many would expect, since unexplained tourism and labor income in most years has not exceeded U.S. $500 million. The estimates of trade misinvoicing vary significantly, and indicate a dual flow of capital; that is, misinvoicing is used both to bring capital into and to take it out of the country. A characteristic of these estimates is that those based on comparing Colombian trade data with that of its trading partners produce a lower estimate of misinvoicing than estimates based on alternative measures. Since it is likely that some misinvoicing occurs both in the exporting country and in Colombia, it may be argued that official data comparisons produce estimates that are biased downwards.[19] Therefore, the real misinvoicing is likely to be higher than that estimated by Gunter and Meisel, and may approach the higher levels estimated by Sarmiento.

Incoming contraband figures are obviously hard to estimate and are subject to great uncertainty, but as noted above, FENALCO estimates annual volumes between almost nothing and U.S. $1 billion for the 1980–1987 period. These estimates of illegal inflows exclude the financing of private capital flight, and of tourism, education, and medical services abroad. It is likely that as political instability, violence, and insecurity increased in recent years, "clean" capital flight has increased, being at least partially financed by illegal capital inflows. Therefore, "dirty" capital has replaced "clean" capital. The magnitude of this phenomenon is difficult to estimate, and Kalmanovitz uses U.S. $500 million a year in his study, but he does not explain how he arrived at that figure. However, as seen in Chapter 8, Gunter (1991) estimates capital flight out of Colombia at about $1.2 billion a year, confirming the importance of this phenomenon. Similarly, black market foreign exchange is used to finance tourism and other expenditures abroad such as education and health services. These values are not included in the above mentioned estimates, but may be important. For example, balance of payments data show that the expenditures for trips taken by Colombian residents in 1988 amounted to U.S. $601.6 million, while 541,530 people left the country by air (DANE, 1989). Assuming that 75 percent of the departing passengers are Colombian residents, these figures indicate an expenditure of $1,480 per person. This includes international air fares and assumes that Colombians who left the country by land did not spend anything abroad. Thus, one can conclude that official estimates are low and tourism imports are underestimated (Kalmanovitz again uses an estimate of U.S. $500 million a year, but again does not explain how it was made). Therefore, the amount of the illegal PSAD capital that has entered the Colombian economy could be substantially larger than that estimated on the income side of the balance of payments plus contraband. However, not all illegal capital inflows originate with drugs; they could be generated by export underinvoicing, returning emigrants, and so forth.

Independent of the accuracy of the estimates, the illegal drug income is so large relative to the magnitude of some important economic variables in Colombia that the illegal PSAD capital can easily alter the status quo of the society. For instance, as mentioned, illegal PSAD entrepreneurs have purchased large tracts of land in the middle Magdalena Valley, in the eastern plains, and in parts of Antioquia and Córdoba. These have been low-land-price areas, particularly when guerrillas have been active. According to World Bank experts interviewed, prices in those areas have ranged from about U.S. $500 to $2,000 per hectare. That is, accepting the Nadelmann (1986) figures, the profits from a small planeload of cocaine that smuggled 250 kilos into the United States in 1985, after paying $150,000 to the pilot and ditching the $100,000 plane, were enough to purchase between 1,200 and 4,800 hectares. In other words, the size of illegal profits is so large relative to the value of many Colombian assets that, even if one accepts the lower estimates of drug income, their impact on the Colombian economy can be extraordinary.

While estimates of the overall size of the illegally generated income and wealth indicate they are of great importance relative to the size of the Colombian economy, it is not possible to determine who has made the money and who owns the capital. The most obvious beneficiaries of the illegal PSAD industry have been the entrepreneurs engaged in transporting and smuggling drugs to the United States. However, there are many individuals who could have financed some shipments, others who received bribes, politicians whose campaigns have been financed with illicit monies, those who helped launder profits, and others who are not identified directly as part of the illegal industry and who have profited from it. Therefore, the estimates only indicate that the amount of income and capital that has been tainted by illicit drug activity is quite high; but neither the distribution of that capital today or the proportion that has been legitimized in the Colombian economy is known.

Conclusions

Several authors have tackled the difficult task of estimating the size of the Colombian illegal PSAD industry's income. They have concentrated their efforts in the measurement of the volume of illegal drug exports, the revenues generated, and the level of profits accruing to the illegal drug businessmen. Although subject to great uncertainty, these estimates suggest that Colombian industry profits have fluctuated between U.S. $2 and $5 billion per year. These estimates are based only on Colombian value added and are likely to underestimate the actual profits of Colombians involved in the illegal drug business in the United States, Bolivia, and Peru. Further, recent cocaine seizures have prompted the U.S. government to greatly increase its estimates of cocaine production, suggesting that the illegal industry's profits have been substantially higher than once thought.[20]

There have also been estimates of drug money inflows based on official balance of payments data. These are useful to analyze the impact of the industry on macroeconomic variables and policies as the government reacts to changes in the official balance of payments, but they greatly underestimate the illegal drug capital inflows into Colombia which, given the limitations of the available information, cannot be accurately estimated. Estimates have been as high a U.S. $4 billion and as low as $500 million per year. However, these inflows could have easily been at least $2 billion per year, an extremely high amount relative to the size of private sector investment in the country.

The full impact of the drug industry's wealth on Colombian society has not fully been felt and could be dramatic, and drug traffickers could easily become the dominant economic group in the country. Furthermore, a portion of the illegally generated capital is today owned by individuals not easily identified with the illegal PSAD industry, so the true impact on the Colombian economy transcends that caused by those who can be identified as current or past drug traffickers.

The illegal foreign exchange funds have also financed a significant amount of capital flight from the country. Thus, the "dirty" capital inflows have not only been large relative to the size of the economy, but they have substituted for "clean" capital that has flowed elsewhere, increasing the relative importance of the "dirty" capital to the economy.

Notes

1. Some of the material presented in this chapter is taken from Thoumi (1992).

2. Sometimes data have been used so loosely that contradictory figures appear even in consecutive pages of the same article. For instance, Van Wert (1988) states on page 3 that Americans spend over $50 billion annually on illicit drugs, while on page 4 he argues that the United States drug market is estimated to exceed $100 billion annually. At other times, the figures cited are simply implausible and quite confusing, not to mention nonsensical. For example, MacDonald (1988: 45) accepts Freemantle's (1986: 211) "estimate" and cites: "Drugs provide Colombia's biggest source of foreign income, nearly 36 percent of its gross national product."

3. This is an intergovernmental committee in which several agencies are represented. The committee produces estimates of the size of the illegal PSAD revenues, the number of drug addicts, etc.

SIZE OF THE DRUGS INDUSTRY • • • 201

4. For instance, some agencies tend to favor small figures and others large ones, depending on the impact that those figures have in their budget requests, or on the evaluation of their past actions.

5. That is, some of the illegal PSAD industry profits spent in Colombia come from domestic bazuco and cocaine revenues, and the domestically made profits could be an important share of the illegal PSAD businessmen's funds consumed and invested in Colombia. However, there is no way to derive an order of magnitude of these revenues and profits.

6. Notice that these problems are similar to those that arise trying to measure the impact on various countries of legitimate transnational corporations that use transfer pricing in their transactions and have several sets of accounting books.

7. Reuter (1985: 89) argues that Colombians are involved in the distribution of cocaine in the United States because their large numbers in the United States made it very easy to develop trusted marketing relationships. Since there are few Colombians living in Europe, one would not expect Colombians to be greatly involved in cocaine marketing there. Reuter (1985: 89) also argues that most of the cocaine exported from South America to Europe goes through Brazil because there are substantial numbers of Brazilians living there. Krauthausen and Sarmiento (1991) also stress the importance of nationality ties in forming a business in which trust and violence play such important roles.

8. Urrutia (1990b) provides interesting insights about the way in which Colombian government policies have been affected by the illegal capital inflow that shows up in the official balance of payments.

9. This estimate is somewhat confusing since Colombians' profits should equal those generated by the 80 percent of the cocaine exported by Colombians plus profits on the balance sold f.o.b. Colombia.

10. This figure substantially underestimates the amount that Colombian residents have invested abroad. The BIS estimate is not based on data reported by private banks about the nationality of their depositors, or by governments about the nationality of real estate and other asset owners, but it is actually based on, and consistent with, International Monetary Fund balance of payments and World Bank external debt data. Therefore, this estimate does not necessarily reflect the real capital accumulated by Colombians outside the country. The BIS is very much aware of the estimate's limitations, and warns the user about the fact that it underestimates the amount of private assets abroad and refers to it only as a measure of official "flight capital" (BIS, 1989: 136).

11. An interview with a former FENALCO economist indicated that contraband was one of the main concerns of the Federation during the 1980s, and it was frequently studied by them. However, they had great difficulty estimating contraband, the methods used were not always well defined, and the series of contraband volume estimated on different occasions varied substantially.

12. For instance, the formula used to establish the foreign exchange amounts that coffee exporters were required to sell to the Central Bank prior to October 1987 frequently determined a higher value than that of the actual sale.

13. Under Colombia's exchange controls system that remained in effect until 1991, "non-refundable" imports were those made with foreign exchange not supplied by the Central Bank. For instance, foreign investors could import machinery and equipment for their project, returning emigrants and diplomats could bring in household equipment and a car, etc.

14. FENALCO (1987) supports this claim.

15. Curiously, Meisel (1990) does not make any reference to Meisel (1988), and does not provide any explanation for the change in methodology.

16. In April 1990 during a workshop at the Institute of the Americas and the Center for Iberian and Latin American Studies of the University of California at San Diego, Mr. José Guillermo Justiniano, a former agriculture minister of Bolivia and Mr. Guy Gugliotta, coauthor of *Kings of Cocaine*, argued that the new State Department figure still greatly underestimated cocaine output capacity that could have been at the time as large as 1,500 tons a year!

17. The U.S. Department of State (1992: 28) estimates that the Colombian poppy crop that was not eradicated was enough to produce 27 metric tons of opium.

18. These data come from the Interamerican Development Bank data bank, and are based on the official national accounts of Colombia.

19. For example, casual empiricism in Miami indicates that many U.S. exporters are willing to underinvoice their exports to Colombia, so that their export bills would match the Colombian import bills. This type of underinvoicing is not captured by trade data comparisons. A short visit to the large warehousing area west of Miami's international airport would support this assertion.

20. Indeed, the U.S. Department of State (1992: 29) acknowledges: "after analyzing field studies conducted in Peru and Bolivia, in 1991 we concluded that we were underestimating the *potential* yield of the coca crop in Bolivia and particularly in Peru" (emphasis in the original).

... 7 ...
Colombian Policies Toward the Illegal Drugs Industry

Policy Ambivalence and Inconsistency

Since the illegal PSAD industry began to grow in Colombia in the early 1970s, successive Colombian governments have followed ambivalent, inconsistent, and conflicting policies towards it. These characteristics apply to policies that prevailed at particular points in time and through time, and reflect the nature of Colombian politics and policy making. During this period the government's social and economic policies have had to respond to complex and conflicting forces, and have had multiple goals that frequently work at cross purposes. Furthermore, most policies have been drafted in response to immediate political, social, and economic pressures, the result of neither social consensus, nor an ideology or social model toward which society should have advanced. Consequently, redistributive reforms were limited in scope and application, as discussed in Chapters 1 and 2. La violencia and rapid urbanization before the 1970s led to several important policy experiments aimed at redistributing wealth and income such as land reform, integrated rural development programs, and expanded social sector expenditures. Other policies, such as the shift towards export promotion and capital market liberalization, tried to make the economy more competitive and modern. All along, inflation and budget financing were of paramount importance to the government, and tax reforms were approved. Policy challenges arose from the growing significance of regional interests and the evolving clientelistic system. And in spite of the country's success with breaking the foreign exchange constraint in the early 1970s, there was continuous need to monitor the balance of payments and to set policies accordingly.

All governments had to cope with the lingering malaise caused by the continued existence of various guerrilla movements and with frequent political expressions by disgruntled groups that were not part of the political establishment. For example, after the 1970 presidential election surprise in which the anti-establishment candidate Gustavo Rojas Pinilla appeared to have won, the elected Pastrana administration had to appease the loser's supporters, an action that used up valuable political resources and added another important policy goal to the government's agenda.

There are several reasons that the control of the illegal PSAD industry was not on the policy agenda in the mid-1970s when the industry's growth became apparent. First, the policy agenda was already quite crowded and the growth of the illegal PSAD industry was an added pressure on the already strained policy formulation capacity of the government, that policymakers preferred not to confront directly.

Second, the government's implicit recognition of its inability to implement and sustain many policies was also an incentive to shy away from formally bringing illegal drug issues to the forefront of the policy agenda. Third, the government realized that, in order to have an independent drug policy, Colombia would have had to establish a policy dialogue with the United States, something that could have led at the time to some undesired confrontations.

Fourth, in a country accustomed to exchange controls since 1931 that recognized foreign exchange scarcity as one of the most, if not the most, important continuous economic growth constraint, it was very difficult to muster enough support against an industry that was generating large amounts of foreign exchange. The socially negative macroeconomic effects resulting from the accumulation of reserves that took place in the late 1970s were just too complex to be understood and accepted not only by the "man on the street," but by many politicians and policymakers who were glad to see the country enjoying an export boom. Other negative social effects were disregarded or underestimated (Sarmiento, 1990a and 1990b). Fifth, in the early 1970s the only popularly known PSAD to be exported was marijuana, a drug that at the time was considered rather harmless.

Sixth, as noted in Chapter 2, the growth of the underground economy and general tolerance of economic law breaking meant that most respected well-to-do Colombians avoided taxes, had illegal foreign dollar accounts or hidden capital, bought contraband, and so on. Since a large portion of private wealth has always been associated with privilege, good luck, corruption, and the capture of rents, these made it very difficult to separate "clean" and "dirty" income and wealth, and have weakened property rights. In this environment, the income and wealth generated by the illegal PSAD industry are not necessarily less legitimate or more immoral than others. Drug traffickers were even seen as supporters of the system, albeit not of the establishment, since they were great capitalists and rabid anti-communists.

Seventh, in the early and mid-1970s Colombians tended to see the drug consumption issue as an "American problem" that had its roots in the Vietnam War and the rebellion of American youth against the establishment. The drug problem, if there was one, had to be dealt with on its demand side. Eighth, the U.S. foreign policies have always been perceived as unprincipled and applying double moral standards. In a pluralistic society like the United States, foreign policy toward a particular country is strongly influenced by the strength of domestic interest groups that have something at stake in that country. Thus, the foreign policies of the United States toward one country are frequently inconsistent with its policies toward another country, and general foreign policy principles are applied discriminately to various countries—projecting a double or multiple moral standard.[1] In addition, many U.S. policies, such as allowing the sale of arms to guerrillas, are viewed as unprincipled. From the Colombian point of view, if the United States behaves in this manner, why should Colombians care about the American drug problem? This feeling clearly reinforced the perception that the drug problem was a consumption (not production) problem, and it had to be solved in consumer countries.

Just as the drug issue was not high on the policy agenda, the illegal PSAD entrepreneurs and their profits evoked rather ambivalent feelings in Colombian society. It was true that drug traffickers were an odd group of exotic entrepreneurs and social climbers, that perhaps included dangerous individuals the establishment did not want to socially assimilate. However, many members of the establishment were quite willing to use the foreign exchange generated by the industry, to participate in money laundering, and to benefit from selling their overpriced assets (mainly real estate) to the newly identified "emerging" class. Their large resources allowed the drug entrepreneurs to get political support mostly at local and regional levels, but also within Congress and other government branches.

As noted, the ambivalence and inconsistency of Colombian policies toward the illegal PSAD industry have masked the weakness of Colombia's government and the delegitimation of the regime, both of which limit the government's capacity to implement strong antidrug policies even if there were the will at the highest level to do so. Because of this, it has been easier to define the illegal drug problem as being one of demand, than to admit the government was unable to control the illegal PSAD industry on Colombian territory.

A symmetric position was taken in the United States, where the increase in illegal drug consumption was viewed as an imported problem to be solved by controlling external supply. This attitude reflects the U.S. inability to come to grips with the main causes of PSAD demand. It is politically more convenient for the United States to define the problem as one created by supply than to explain why PSAD consumption has increased, and what social changes have contributed to that increase, because that would require the government to confront the social and economic implications of those changes. In reality, the U.S. political system has also experienced delegitimation, particularly in the relatively uncontrolled inner city ghettos, where the illegal drug trade is visibly rampant. Indeed, one may argue that parts of some of these ghettos are to the United States what the guerrilla-controlled areas are to Colombia.

The result of these circumstances was that in the mid-1970s Colombia had anti-illegal PSAD legislation, but had no active policy towards the illegal PSAD industry: policy instruments were not directed toward production or trafficking and illegal drugs issues were low on the government's policy agenda. By the time some policymakers perceived that the illegal PSAD industry was getting out of hand, and that strong policies were necessary to neutralize its negative effects, the industry was already a formidable foe.

Not surprisingly, drug policies have been piecemeal, and actions against the illegal PSAD industry have occurred in spurts—mostly in reaction to specific situations and to pressure from the United States. In one sense, Colombia's reaction toward the growth of the PSAD industry was no different from its approach to other problems, in that it muddled through from year to year without seeking long-term solutions. Government policies had short-term goals designed to cope with the industry and external pressures. These mostly reactive policies became decisive only when the illegal drug industry's actions made it a threat to the regime or when U.S. pressure increased.

At the same time, a large part of the government acted as if in denial, to minimize the economic impact of the illegal drug industry. For example, economic analyses of government agencies disregarded for a long time the industry's effects. In these studies, policies that were taken in response to the industry's actions or that were influenced by it, were justified on other grounds, implicitly minimizing the economic importance of the industry or denying its existence.[2]

Colombia's systemic inability to identify and acknowledge the illegal drug industry as a social and economic problem that had to be dealt with came with very high costs to the country. First, there was no attempt to form a broad social consensus about how to deal with the industry, to formulate a coherent policy, or to search for alternatives to policies implied by existing legislation or postulated by the United States. Of course, the much greater power of the United States relative to Colombia made it difficult to establish a policy dialogue between the two countries.

During the mid-1970s President Alfonso López-Michelsen emphasized PSAD demand as the cause of the drug trafficking problem (Orjuela, 1990: 217), but the lack of an independent debate and Colombian policy naturally resulted in its adoption by default of the U.S. supply control policy strategy. This inherently precluded the Colombian government from formulating serious policy alternatives that might lower the costs borne by Colombia. For example, the extradition of high-ranking drug entrepreneurs became the cornerstone of the antidrug policy package, despite its total lack of effectiveness on cocaine production and trafficking. Further, as time went by the supply control strategy became increasingly militarized, contributing to increases in Colombia's already high level of violence. These policies produced very high costs to Colombian society, costs that are significantly higher than those of possible policy alternatives (see Chapter 10).

Second, since the illegal drug industry was not part of the policy agenda, the issue surfaced only when there were specific actions that required a response. By the late 1970s it had become apparent that the underground economy had grown significantly, and a group of new entrepreneurs with large amounts of capital, apparently accumulated in the marijuana industry, were investing in several sectors of the economy. The economic implications of these developments created some concern within the establishment and the economic effects of the marijuana industry became a policy issue. By 1980 it was clear that some illegal PSAD entrepreneurs wanted to gain political power, so their actions and political influence became a political issue. Spurts of violence against the judicial system also brought the industry to the top of the policy agenda. In all these cases, government policies were reactive to new conditions, did not lead to a coherent and continuous policy toward the industry, and lost intensity when the industry's threat to economic stability or the political system subsided, and other more pressing policy goals appeared on the policy agenda.

Policies Toward the Illegal Drugs Industry

In the latter half of the 1970s the Central Bank began to see a large increase in the foreign exchange supply and began to accumulate unprecedented amounts of foreign exchange reserves (see Chapter

1). At the same time it was apparent that a hitherto unknown group of Colombians associated with the marijuana industry controlled a sizeable amount of resources. This group began to be referred to in the press and colloquially as the "emerging class." Conspicuous consumption and major investments by these "emerging" Colombians sparked the attention of the established business class and government. It was also recognized that the growth of the underground economy had mainly been fueled by these funds. However, the growth of the marijuana industry coincided with, and followed, a coffee boom in 1975 and 1976, which made it difficult to determine the size of the illegal PSAD funds that were coming into the economy. Indeed, many mainstream studies have attributed the increase in reserves to the coffee boom, including those purchased through the "sinister window," since it was widely accepted that official coffee exports were underinvoiced.

Recognizing the importance of the illegal PSAD industry was a slow process that first focused on marijuana's role in the underground economy. Significant growth in that sector prompted concerns about its assimilation into the mainstream economy. At the time Colombians associated the illegal PSAD industry with the marijuana produced in Colombia; the involvement of Colombians with cocaine was not apparent. Marijuana consumption was seen as rather harmless and tolerated in the United States, since several states had decriminalized it. It was these factors that led President Alfonso López-Michelsen to argue the illegal drug problem was demand-generated. The government then tried to follow a pragmatic path, and the Central Bank opened its "sinister window" to deal with the foreign exchange supply growth. These actions led to frictions between Colombia and the United States (Tokatlian, 1990: 293–294).

The marijuana industry was seen in Colombia as complicating macroeconomic management and distorting the use of resources, but it was not seen as creating a crisis that required drastic measures.[3] Primarily, the problems were the need to compensate the Central Bank's reserve accumulation with lower government spending to avoid higher inflation, and the misallocation of resources due to the illegal funds not being invested in highly productive branches. As Tokatlian (1988: 139) puts it: "clearly in the 1970s the Colombian system did not see itself seriously threatened by (1) the political-institutional reach of the marijuana business; (2) its negative effect on national security; nor (3) the financial consequences of its production and trade. Thus, Colombia did not accentuate, unilaterally, repressive measures in its attempts to control and eradicate this traffic."

The growth of the marijuana industry did lead, however, to an interesting national debate about the assimilation of the industry's accumulated capital and its possible legalization. This debate was promoted by the ANIF. Its president, Ernesto Samper Pizano, was seen as an advocate of marijuana production and trade legalization and organized a widely publicized symposium (ANIF, 1979). Samper's actual proposal was relatively mild, consisting of establishing a bilateral commission with the United States to explore legalization possibilities (Tokatlian, 1990). Samper acted on the belief that there was a growing realization that policies to limit production and output were not yielding satisfactory results, and that there was a growing acceptance to marijuana legalization or decriminalization in the United States (Tokatlian, 1990: 304). However, there were those who argued that marijuana legalization would most benefit the financial sector, so that is why ANIF was supporting it (Orjuela, 1990: 216).

The symposium produced a heated debate in which most of the media and the government were against legalization. For example, *El Tiempo*, the largest and most influential newspaper, Belisario Bentancur and Julio César Turbay, the two main presidential candidates, and the López-Michelsen administration were all opposed (Tokatlian, 1990). Some reactions to the legalization proposal were especially virulent, and there were those who clamored for Samper's excommunication from the Catholic Church (Orjuela, 1990: 217; Tokatlian, 1990: 306).

A year after the symposium, Samper reiterated his legalization thesis, and the small industries association (ACOPI), with the support of other producer associations, proposed the legalization of capital generated by the illegal drug traffic, thereby transforming the marijuana legalization debate into a tax amnesty issue (Tokatlian, 1990: 305–306). Other private sector organizations such as the Colombian Farmers Society (SAC) and the Finance Corporation of Valle also proposed a tax amnesty for "hot" capital. The private sector argued that this capital did not contribute to the tax base, and also saw in it a solution to an ongoing shortage of working capital (Orjuela, 1990: 219). Among the main private sector associations, only FENALCO, which was the main victim of contraband financed with illegal monies, raised a "moral" objection to the amnesty (Orjuela, 1990: 219).

The debate lost intensity, partly because marijuana prices fell and partly because the foreign exchange acquired through the "sinister window" also declined (Orjuela, 1990: 216). By then the new Turbay administration acted under the "conviction that legalization was impossible, unnecessary, and immoral. However, the 'sinister window' remained open" (Tokatlian, 1990: 307, author's translation). It should be noted that, while the United States opposed marijuana legalization, its pressure was not as decisive as the many internal forces that also opposed such a measure.

The August 1978 administration change was a major factor in changing the Colombian government's drug policy attitude. As noted in Chapter 3, President Julio C. Turbay's international image had been tarnished after being implicated in the TV program "60 Minutes" of having connections with the drug industry. And there were other external and domestic pressures on the new administration. In the United States there were widespread rumors that the marijuana industry had infiltrated the highest government levels, the administration had begun "Operation Stopgap" in which spy planes were used to locate and intercept marijuana boats, and President Jimmy Carter himself increased pressure on the Colombian government to become more active. Domestically, Turbay realized that the size of the marijuana industry was too corruptive, and that it could threaten his control over the government (Tokatlian, 1990). Turbay, the quintessential politician, had strong support in Congress that gave him autonomy, and he had a need to prove to the international community that he was above reproach. He then proceeded to shape a multifaceted and more aggressive antidrug policy.

One measure the U.S. government was trying to force the Colombian government to take was to spray the marijuana growing region with defoliants, particularly paraquat, that had been used successfully in Mexico. However, this policy alternative generated great national and international opposition because of its likely negative ecological effects. Turbay tried to deal with this issue by appointing a scientific commission to study the possible effects of using several types of defoliants; its negative report made the defoliant alternative even more politically costly.

The high political and ecological costs of chemical eradication made a military alternative relatively less expensive, so at the end of 1978 the Turbay administration began "Operation Fulminant" that engaged 10,000 army personnel in manual marijuana eradication in the Guajira and Sierra Nevada de Santa Marta. This operation was short-lived because the military supported it only reluctantly; the consensus was that it shifted resources away from antiguerrilla activities, and the military was wary of the corruption dangers of involvement in antidrug activities and of the negative reaction of peasants against the army.

An important step taken by the Turbay administration was enacting the National Security Statute, which enhanced government and military powers to arrest and take action against both the drug industry and guerrilla organizations. One particularly important feature of this statute was that it permitted the establishment of self-defense groups, a provision that was later used by the drug industry to develop their paramilitary forces to oppose the guerrillas and the political left.

The most important antidrug policy of this administration, although one that has been ineffective and very costly to Colombia, was the treaty it signed with the United States to extradite Colombian drug traffickers. As clearly shown by Tokatlian's (1990) excellent work, the Colombian presidency has a great deal of autonomy in international matters, at least in part because of a weak external relations ministry and a fragmented external policy-making mechanism. The president took advantage of his autonomy to negotiate the extradition treaty with the United States in a rather secretive fashion. The treaty was signed quietly in Washington by Virgilio Barco, then ambassador to the United States, and U.S. Secretary of State Cyrus Vance.

President Turbay had to use all his political skills to get Congress to approve the treaty in November 1980. The U.S. Congress approved it in March 1981, and it became valid in April 1982, five months before the end of Turbay's presidential term. However, in order not to increase social conflict during the presidential campaign then in progress, the United States did not request any extraditions, and Turbay did not have to extradite anyone. The extradition treaty was then left for the next president to enforce.

The extradition treaty's implications were deep and broad:

> It implied an almost total lack of confidence in Colombian law enforcement; assumed that it would decisively contribute to reducing drug trafficking and consumption; it gave the United States government the opportunity to use an enormous discretionality to determine which citizens and for which crimes the extradition could be requested; it suggested that only the United States laws were correct and effective to judge those linked with the narcotics business; it established a unilateral measuring parameter to verify the Colombian authorities' commitment to fight drugs; it increased the law enforcement logic's priority to deal with drug issues; it *de facto* internationalized all aspects—external and "domestic"—of the narcotics problem, reducing the "domestic" margin of action of the Colombian government in these matters; it implied the acceptance of the United States "prescription" to fight narcotics; and questioned the extent of Colombia's national sovereignty in the "war against drugs," favoring a rationality which de facto implied the notion of limited sovereignty in dealing with these matters (Tokatlian, 1990: 309; author's translation).

The extradition treaty became the cornerstone of the Colombian antidrug policy and its elimination the main goal of the Colombian PSAD entrepreneurs. Unfortunately, the treaty was approved without any serious debate about its effectiveness to cut either supply or demand, or of the potentially serious impact on Colombian society. It is hard to know whether policymakers had the conviction that extraditing the industry's leaders would seriously affect its supply, although they appealed to it with increasing zeal any time the industry threatened the establishment, which suggests that they believed in its benefits. However, the study of the industry's characteristics points to a very loose and constantly changing structure and extremely high profits, which indicate that the capture and extradition of its leaders would at best only have a temporary impact on supply. That is, one could expect extradition to produce many pyrrhic victories but no solution to the drug demand or supply problems.

Soon after Belisario Betancur was inaugurated on 8 August 1982, the United States made its first formal extradition request. President Betancur's strong feelings about Colombian sovereignty made him oppose the extradition treaty. At the time, the treaty's validity was in doubt because during the ratification process several legal technicalities had not been observed. The attorney general expressed his opinion that the treaty was unconstitutional, but on 26 October the Supreme Court supported the treaty's constitutionality. The newspaper *El Espectador* and Virgilio Barco provided strong public expressions of support for the treaty. President Betancur procrastinated about a month before deciding on the United States request, and finally did not sign the extradition papers. The United States then requested a second extradition that was also turned down (Tokatlian, 1990: 315–316). The Colombian government argued through its justice minister that the country had to act independently and that some of the treaty's articles had to be revised. When in November 1983 the U.S. Congress approved the Hawkins-Gilman amendment establishing an annual certification requirement for countries to access aid funds, this measure was perceived in Colombia as pressuring the government to enforce the extradition treaty. However, it may also be argued that this measure was just part of the "war on drugs" that President Reagan had declared in early 1982, which linked drug trafficking to U.S. national security.

At the time, President Betancur had two main priorities: to promote a peace process that would allow for the political incorporation of the guerrilla groups, and to deal with economic problems inherited from the Turbay administration (see Chapter 1). Thus, the illegal drug industry was a problem that would not receive the most attention. The high priority of the guerrilla problem was reinforced by the fact that the military considered the guerrillas its chief enemies and was leery of the peace initiatives. Furthermore, there was no agreement about the dangers posed by paramilitary organizations related to the drug industry. Indeed, General Landazábal, minister of defense, argued for an economic strategy to fight the illegal PSAD instead of a military one (Tokatlian, 1990).

As noted above, the 1979 legalization debate had evolved into a tax amnesty issue, which was revived in the fourth quarter of 1982, after the Betancur administration was installed. A new tax amnesty was considered on the grounds that it would help the government confront a grave budget deficit, and that it was necessary to shrink the underground economy and its corrupting effects. Several tax amnesty proposals were suggested, designed mainly to allow for the legalization of hidden capital.

Producer associations were some of the strongest supporters of the tax amnesty. As shown in Chapter 1 by 1982 economic growth had slowed and Colombia's financial sector was facing a crisis generated by the bankruptcy of several institutions. In addition, this was the year when international interest rates skyrocketed and the Latin American debt crisis materialized. While Colombia fared relatively well, the commerce, manufacturing, and agriculture sectors did not and their producer associations were quite concerned. Not surprisingly, these associations viewed the illegal capital accumulated in the country as a possible source of funds. The National Industrialists Association (ANDI) proposed a specific amnesty and argued it was similar to the guerrilla's amnesty that was being debated (Orjuela, 1990: 220–221). However, ANDI's self-interest was clear: its proposal "consisted in authorizing the firms whose shares were traded in the stock exchange to issue a pre-determined number of special shares, to be bought with hidden capital, that would not be allowed to be traded for a pre-determined length of time" (Orjuela, 1990: 221; author's translation). This proposal was supported by *La República*, the newspaper supported by the mainstream of the Social Conservative party, but strongly opposed by *El Espectador*. Again, the debate lost steam and attention turned to other facets of the drug industry.

The reluctance of Colombia's executive branch to enforce the extradition treaty did not mean it was totally inactive against the illegal PSAD industry. The government, in collaboration with American authorities, located the "Tranquilandia" cocaine manufacturing complex and destroyed it on 10 March 1984: at the time this was the largest drug bust ever. International cocaine prices were then reaching their highest historic levels, and some of the drug barons were attempting to develop a political base, actions that were actively opposed by Justice Minister Rodrigo Lara Bonilla (see Chapter 4), even though he appeared not to have widespread support within the government. Then on 30 April 1984, Rodrigo Lara Bonilla was assassinated in apparent retaliation for his antidrug posture and the "Tranquilandia" operation. The government associated this crime with the Medellín "cartel." This assassination left President Betancur with no choice but to counterattack with all the means at his disposal, including extradition (Tokatlian, 1990: 318).

The president authorized five extraditions of jailed drug dealers requested by the United States and signed Carlos Lehder's (who was at large), established a state of siege, ordered all drug-related crimes to be judged by the Military Penal Justice system that was more averse to threats and bribes, and began a strong military campaign against the illegal drug industry. Hundreds of suspected drug traffickers were rounded up and jailed, and many had their farms and houses thoroughly searched and occupied; confiscation procedures began in some cases. Some authors argue that the quick reaction of the government to Lara Bonilla's assassination suggests it had information about the identity, whereabouts, and properties of illegal drug entrepreneurs (Orjuela, 1990: 234; Gugliotta and Leen, 1990: 286–287). The crackdown did not immediately lead to the capture of any industry leaders, but it forced them into hiding. Further, "Lara Bonilla's murder marked the moment when Colombia first identified the Medellín cartel as the enemy: savage, ruthless killers willing to challenge the integrity of the Colombian state" (Gugliotta and Leen, 1990: 286).

Three weeks after Lara Bonilla's death the aerial spraying of the marijuana crop was approved, with glyphosate replacing paraquat.[4] While there is agreement that this measure lowered the marijuana supply in the short run, various authors emphasize different long-term effects. Reuter (1992a) argues that the supply disruption led to a decline in U.S. consumption;[5] Tokatlian (1990: 321) claims the disruption was only transitory and simply led to a shift of marijuana plantings to the Cauca region and, more importantly, it did not destroy the violence network organized by drug traffickers. Independent of the marijuana spraying success, its economic effects on the overall illegal drug industry could not have been large since, as shown in Chapter 6, by 1983 the lion's share of the industry's revenues was generated in cocaine manufacturing and trafficking, not in marijuana.

The crackdown in the wake of Lara Bonilla's assassination significantly increased Colombia's armed forces participation in the "war on drugs." However, this was to a significant degree the result of the administration's need to respond quickly to what was seen as a clear threat to the establishment, and of the fact that the executive and judicial branches did not have contingency plans to deal with illegal PSAD industry problems.[6] One of the more undesirable effects of the increased military involvement in the antidrug fight was that it raised the level of violence and the risk of a violence spiral if drug traffickers sought to strengthen their own armed organizations.

Because the crackdown sent the drug leaders into hiding, many found safe refuge in Panama, from where they sought to establish a dialogue with the government. Some had made prior unsuccessful attempts to open a dialogue with the government to find a way for them to join the social mainstream.

In late May 1984 former President Alfonso López-Michelsen and the attorney general visited Panama separately on business, and a remarkable set of meetings took place between them and a group of high-level drug traffickers. The two Colombian public figures had legitimate business in Panama, but some authors (Gugliotta and Leen, 1990: 290) argue they were aware ahead of time of the drug traffickers' wishes to meet with them. In any case, in those meetings the drug industry leaders asked the two Colombian public figures to transmit a proposal to the government. They offered to destroy their organizations, end their business, and bring most of their capital to Colombia in exchange for their re-incorporation into the social mainstream and the impartial application of the Colombian laws to them. They also denied any involvement in the Lara Bonilla assassination (Orjuela, 1990: 235; Gugliotta and Leen, 1990: 290–298).

The Colombian government did not initially make the proposal public, and it only became known more than a month later when it was leaked, apparently through the U.S. embassy, which had apparently received a copy of the proposal.[7] This news elicited a strong denial from the Colombian government, in which it stated it had never negotiated with the drug traffickers, nor would it ever do so. This position of denial was broadly supported by the press and political parties, but some important political figures, including former President López-Michelsen and Doña Bertha vda. de Ospina Pérez, the widow of a former president and leader of a powerful faction of the conservative party, encouraged the negotiations (Orjuela, 1990: 237). Then, in the midst of the ensuing debate, on 23 July, the judge investigating Lara Bonilla's homicide was assassinated (Tokatlian, 1990: 330).

The crackdown after Lara Bonilla's assassination produced some significant short-term results that were not so positive in the long run. Only a few of the 398 individuals arrested after the assassination could be held beyond questioning. Among those who had to be let go was Fabio Ochoa, Sr., the father of the main members of the

Ochoa clan. And in the dragnet that followed, only two "extraditables" were caught (Gugliotta and Leen, 1990: 304–304). Unfortunately, the crackdown raised the level of violence and intimidation the drug industry was willing to exert, and after a few months public support for it waned.[8] The seizures of many properties did not stick either, because most of them were not titled to the suspected drug traffickers. The legal system protected property rights, and some of those in the judicial system having to decide on confiscations could be bribed anyway. The laws and the state's weakness made it clear that it was very difficult, if not impossible, to "go after the money," which some would consider the most effective antidrug policy. Perhaps more importantly, the cocaine supply was not disrupted. According to Gugliotta and Leen (1990, chap. 18), the wholesale kilogram cocaine price in Miami rose somewhat in the aftermath of the Lara Bonilla assassination to U.S. $25,000, but five months later had fallen below $14,000, the lowest level on record at the time.

The crackdown also induced the illegal PSAD industry to seek new means to defend its interests and strengthen its connections with the guerrilla organizations. As discussed in Chapter 4, there has existed a "narco-guerrilla connection" that has been unstable and short-lived because of the groups' fundamentally opposite goals. While there has been no "narco-guerrilla" conspiracy, the illegal PSAD industry and guerrilla groups have cooperated in some endeavors because their differences did not prevent attempts to form temporary alliances when the government hardened its posture. This alliance became evident in the eyes of many when a heavily armed M-19 guerrilla group took over the Palace of Justice on 6 November 1985.

The government refused to negotiate with the guerrillas and the military forces reacted strongly trying to take back the building, an action that led to a battle in which at least 95 people died, including 11 of 24 Supreme Court Justices, others who worked or happened to be at the building at the time, and apparently all the guerrillas (Gugliotta and Leen, 1990: 417). The Palace of Justice was burned down and many files dealing with extradition, other drug-related cases, human rights violations, and so on, were destroyed. Those who postulate the link between the drug industry and the guerrillas in this action do so on the bases that the Supreme Court Justices dealing with drug related cases had received very strong threats and on the burning of the drug case files. There are those who also argued that the strong military reaction that led to the burning of the building was an opportunity used by the military to destroy the files of human rights violation cases (Gugliotta and Leen, 1989, chap. 25).

The Palace of Justice incident weakened President Betancur because it was a setback to his efforts to strengthen grass roots democracy and to assimilate the guerrillas into the political system. It also highlighted the risks and failures of his negotiations with the guerrillas. Even though the president took full responsibility for the armed forces' handling of the takeover, public opinion doubted whether he had actually been able to control the military's actions. The incident also led to a further increase in the level of violence. The government responded by continuing the crops eradication campaign and extraditing a few drug traffickers. The drug industry escalated with increased threats and intimidation against the government and the legal political left (Tokatlian, 1990: 336).

At the time President Barco took over on 7 August 1986, internal and external forces had also contributed to increasing the level of violence. Within the three-week period before Barco's inauguration, the United States began operation "Blast Furnace" in Bolivia with the participation of the U.S. military; and in Colombia a journalist, a police captain, and a magistrate, all well-known for their antidrug stands, were assassinated (Tokatlian, 1990: 336).

The list of assassinations of those who opposed the illegal PSAD industry had begun to grow a few days before Barco's inauguration and continued thereafter; the following is a nonexhaustive list of the main victims of the drug traffickers during this period:

- 3 July, Luis F. Briceño, Avianca Airlines ticket manager;
- 23 July, Judge Tulio Manuel Castro, who was investigating Lara Bonilla's assassination and had indicted Pablo Escobar and Gonzalo Rodríguez-Gacha;
- 31 July, Hernando Baquero Borda, supreme court magistrate;
- 17 August, Luis Alfredo Macana, anti-narcotics police;
- 30 August, León Posada, Patriotic Union (U.P.) congressman;
- 31 August, Pedro Nel Jiménez, U.P. senator, as he was boarding a plane to attend Posada's funeral;
- 17 September, Raúl Echavarría, deputy director of *Occidente*, Cali's largest newspaper;
- 30 October, Gustavo Zuluaga, Medellín's superior tribunal magistrate;
- 17 November, Jaime Ramirez Gómez, former director of the antinarcotics police; and
- 17 December, Guillermo Cano, the *El Espectador* director.

Besides the increase in drug industry violence against those who openly opposed it, this period also saw a sharp increase in intra-industry violence (see Chapter 4) and paramilitary actions against peasants. The frequency of massacres, tortures, and other human rights violations was alarming.[9]

In spite of the increased violence, the apparent contradiction between Colombia's political and economic policies continued. As noted in Chapter 1, soon after President Barco was inaugurated, a new tax reform that provided more widespread tax amnesty than previous ones was enacted. This reform significantly facilitated foreign exchange laundering, and thus, favored the illegal PSAD industry.

The assassination of Guillermo Cano, a patriarch of Colombian journalism and the director of a newspaper that had maintained an outspoken and aggressive antidrug position for a decade, was a new catalytic factor for government action. That same day President Barco signed a decree increasing the powers of the police and the military in the antidrug campaign, and signed two days later another decree expanding the jurisdiction of the military justice system over civilians.

The government antidrug efforts faced, however, some legal setbacks. On 12 December the Supreme Court had declared invalid the law that had approved the extradition treaty, and on 5 March 1987 it declared unconstitutional the decree that had expanded the jurisdiction of the military justice system. These Supreme Court decisions seriously constrained the government's chosen policies, which were delivered an even worse blow on 25 June 1987, when the Supreme Court found the extradition treaty invalid because its elaboration and ratification had not followed the required legal procedures. Until that moment fourteen Colombians had been extradited to the United States (Tokatlian, 1990: 349).

Barco and Enrique Low, his justice minister, began a search for other ways to extradite, appealing to and reviving old treaties dating back to the 1880s. Simultaneously, the American government pressured the Colombian administration in that direction. President Barco also continued the chemical eradication begun during the Betancur administration, despite frequent warnings by the Natural Resource Institute (INDERENA) about the ecological costs of this policy and the protest of area residents (Tokatlian, 1990: 331–333). Further, Barco appeared quite willing to increase military participation in the antidrug campaign, but the military was hesitant to do so for the same reasons they objected during the Betancur administration.

A series of events during 1987 made evident the need for new ways to fight the drug traffickers. On 13 January Colombia's ambassador to Hungary, Enrique Parejo, who had followed Lara Bonilla as justice minister and continued the latter's tough antidrug campaign, survived an attempt on his life in which he was shot five times in Budapest (Gugliotta and Leen, 1990: 480–481). A few weeks later, on 3 February the Barco administration did have a success, as a combination of luck and the honesty of a police captain led to the capture of Carlos Lehder, who was extradited within a few hours (Gugliotta and Leen, 1990: 482–489). On 11 October 1987 Jaime Pardo Leal, the M-19 leader and its probable presidential candidate, was assassinated. On 21 November, another chance event led to the capture of Jorge Luis Ochoa, but by then he could not be extradited. The United States sent a six-member legal team from the departments of Justice and State to "observe the machinations at close range and to offer suggestions" (Gugliotta and Leen, 1990: 518). According to these authors, the American team found the Colombians to be obstructionists and they ended up doubting the honesty and willingness to cooperate of even Enrique Low, despite his frequent antidrug statements and record. Ochoa obtained the best legal advice money could buy, including the services of several former Supreme Court justices, and in a series of events that grossly illustrate the weakness of the Colombian legal system, he was set free on 30 December after a habeas corpus recourse was approved by a judge against the formal orders of the justice minister.[10]

The United States government reacted strongly and quite irrationally to this event, punishing people who happened to travel to Colombia or do business there: the inspection of Colombian flower exports at the Miami airport was delayed until the produce was lost, passengers returning from Colombia were purposely harassed, and so on.[11]

The drug-associated violence continued, and on 25 January 1988 Attorney General Carlos Mauro Hoyos was assassinated. By then, the obvious weaknesses of Colombia's legal system and the increased violence against public officials and political figures had begun to convince some military segments of the need for their more active participation in antidrug activities. There were also external pressures in that direction. Opinion polls taken during the U.S. presidential campaign showed that the American public considered drugs a greater threat to American society than communism, and some influential conservative American think tanks were recommending greater militarization of the war on drugs (Tokatlian, 1990: 338–339).

President Barco was increasingly pressured from within the country and abroad to do something. He made several military personnel changes and military antidrug actions increased, resulting in larger amounts of cocaine seized, refining laboratories destroyed, and increased arrests. However, increasing military involvement had to proceed with caution because of doubts about the trust that could be given to some armed forces personnel, who were suspected of having links with paramilitary groups heavily funded by drug traffickers, and some of whom possibly had direct links with the illegal PSAD industry. Bagley (1989–1990) argues that one of Barco's main concerns was cleaning up the national security establishment.

In spite of the government's increased efforts (or perhaps in reaction to them), during 1988 and 1989 there was an increase in violence associated with the illegal PSAD industry. Since the Betancur administration the government had been negotiating with several guerrilla groups, attempting to incorporate them into the political system. Significant political reforms were being implemented to strengthen grass roots democracy, weaken the clientelistic system, and increase the autonomy of local governments and their response to citizens' concerns and needs.

The government had succeeded in persuading some guerrilla groups to participate in the political process. Most people elected by these left-leaning groups had not participated actively in the guerrilla organizations, but supported their cause. These political newcomers became targets for the paramilitary groups. And in the two years mentioned many of them became victims of these groups. At this time there was also a substantial increase in conflicts within the illegal drug industry that led to another massacre (Tokatlian, 1990: 341). It is important to recognize that guerrilla organizations were continuing their practice of kidnapping and extortion, which became a source of some public support for the killings of left-wing politicians.

The presidential campaign for the 1990–1994 period was a bloody one. This was the first campaign in which the political left linked to the guerrilla movements had their own presidential candidate. However, those who dared represent the left coalition were putting their lives on the line by doing so. As noted above, U.P. leader Jaime Pardo Leal was killed late in 1987. Another U.P. possible presidential candidate, José Antequera, was gunned down in Bogotá's airport on 4 March 1989 while waiting to take a plane. Also shot in this incident was Ernesto Samper Pizano, a young Liberal politician with an excellent chance at a future presidency, who just happened to run into Antequera and was greeting him. Later that month Bernardo Jaramillo, U.P.'s presidential candidate, was killed, as was his successor, Carlos Pizarro, a couple of months later. From then on, one of the primary concerns for the Barco administration was to guarantee the life of whomever was going to represent the U.P. in the presidential election. This was the first presidential campaign in Colombia in which problems associated with the illegal PSAD industry became the main political issue and the industry's negative effect on the struggling Colombian democracy became clear.

On 1 May 1989 Freddy Rodríguez, the young son of Gonzalo Rodríguez-Gacha, was captured as he attempted to board a private plane in Medellín's airport carrying a few unregistered guns (Castillo, 1991: 262). Antioquia's governor Antonio Roldán made sure that the young Rodríguez would remain in jail. The governor was assassinated on 4 July.

Another important violent act in June was a 100 kg dynamite car bomb set off in Bogotá's downtown, aimed at General Miguel Maza Márquez, head of Colombia's secret police. General Maza, a leading antidrug figure, had recently discovered some leaks of highly confidential minutes of the Councils of Ministers and Security to drug organizations, which indicated they had infiltrated these top-level policy making centers (Castillo, 1991: 264).[12]

The increased level of violence associated with drug trafficking and the apparent lack of success that the government campaign was having despite impressive data about drug seizures and destroyed laboratories,[13] inclined President Barco to search for other ways to extradite. On the morning of 18 August 1989 the Council of Ministers decided to establish an extradition system as an administrative measure, not a judicial one (Tokatlian, 1990: 351). It appears that for President Barco extradition was still the main weapon against drug trafficking, perhaps because he could not see any alternatives. "Lacking other imaginative options, and prisoner of a repressive logic, President Virgilio Barco worked until the end of his period with an instrument that does not provide any realistic solution to the Colombian drug trafficking problem" (Tokatlian, 1990: 353; author's translation). Coincidentally that evening, Luis Carlos Galán, the leading presidential candidate and odds-on favorite to win the election, was assassinated.

The level of drug-related violence against the state had been increasing dramatically before the assassination of Galán to the point that Gugliotta and Leen (1990: 558) write: "Still, in the Colombian context, Galán's murder did not at first seem an extraordinary incident. The cartel had already committed three major homicides in August: Judges Maria Helena Díaz and Carlos Ernesto Valencia were murdered for refusing to revoke arrest warrants against cartel bosses Pablo Escobar and Gonzalo Rodríguez-Gacha. Antioquia police chief Colonel Franklin Quintero Vargas—who had seized ten tons of cartel cocaine in the Magdalena River Valley in July and August—was killed in Medellín the same day as Galán."

However, Galán's murder shocked Colombia and the government because it was qualitatively different from those previously committed by the drug groups. The drug industry's traditional targets had been people involved in the judiciary and law enforcement branches of the government, journalists who had opposed them, or left-leaning politicians who competed with the drug-supported right wing organizations in regions where the drug traffickers had invested. "In Galán's case, however, the drug bosses had made a preemptive strike against one of the most popular and respected men in Colombia. Galán was killed not for something he had done, but for something he might do" (Gugliotta and Leen, 1990: 559). Galán, like many politicians, had supported the extradition treaty; he also supported the dialogue and amnesty for guerrillas, and he was close to Rodrigo Lara Bonilla. Thus, the drug industry saw him as a threat and killed him before his almost certain election as president.

The reaction of the Barco administration was swift and strong, declaring an all-out war against the "narco-terrorists" that led to an unprecedented increase in militarization of the antidrug effort. The day after Galán's death President Barco made public the extradition decree signed the day before, and issued a series of new ones that "allowed the arbitrary confiscation of cartel properties, and for the first time made shadow ownership of these properties a crime" (Gugliotta and Leen, 1990: 559–560). With the new decrees in place the government concentrated all its efforts in capturing the drug traffickers, confiscating their assets, and destroying their producing capabilities and their networks. Large numbers of properties were immediately seized, hundreds of individuals arrested, and extradition resumed within days when some "extraditables" were captured.

The Colombian government requested help from the United States, which quickly complied. President George Bush publicly praised and supported the Barco administration, and immediately supplied U.S. $65 million worth of military aid to the Colombian government, and "these demonstrations of U.S. support were unquestionably of great symbolic importance to the Barco government. However, the key word is symbolic. For not only did the package fail to respond to Colombia's expressed tactical needs for conducting its war, but it was directed to the wrong sector. The package's heavy reliance on conventional military equipment for the Colombian armed forces—such as A-37 fighter planes, jeeps, and non-portable radios—was not suitable for an unconventional war against narco-terrorists. Indeed, the Colombian military is not responsible for domestic law enforcement and is not primarily responsible for the war on drugs" (Bagley 1989–1990: 164). This author also argues that American officials denied that this had been the result of a preference for the military over the police (which was believed to be more corrupt), and explains that "the package fell short of the Colombian requests simply because the Pentagon did not stock all the items in the sufficient quantity to deliver immediately and because other items could not be obtained from other federal agencies without prior authorization from Congress. The U.S. Justice Department was similarly constrained by resource limitations and legal restrictions" (Bagley, 1989–1990: 164–165).

The new crackdown was different from the previous ones because it appeared to have actually harmed the Medellín "cartel" and for the first time Colombian government actions began to resemble a frontal war (Gugliotta, 1992). However, the government's attack on the illegal PSAD industry was only partial, because it primarily targeted the Medellín "cartel" that was associated with anti-state violence. In particular, the government targeted Pablo Escobar, Gonzalo Rodríguez-Gacha, the Ochoas, and their organizations. The rest of the industry that was not directly targeted maintained a low profile, and appears to have done relatively well during and after the crackdown.

The Medellín group was forced into hiding. After Lara Bonilla's 1984 assassination, some of the group members went to Panama and others went to Spain where perhaps they hoped to remain and invest some of their capital (Gugliotta and Leen, 1990, chap. 19). They found, however, that Spanish institutions were not as vulnerable as Colombian ones, and one of the Ochoas and Gilberto Rodríguez Orejuela were detained. After a legal battle in which the Colombian and United States governments requested extraditions, they were extradited to Colombia.

Meanwhile, those who sought refuge in Panama had to deal with a government that, while perhaps willing to allow them to launder some of their assets, was not willing to allow them to remain for long or to operate freely within the country. The Colombian drug traffickers had learned they could operate better within Colombia where they could count on their networks. Thus, during the 1989 crackdown they decided to remain in the country and fight back rather than go to another country.

On 24 August the Medellín group issued a communiqué declaring "total and absolute war" against anyone who had opposed them, including government officials, the industrial establishment, judges, and union leaders. According to a summary report in *El Tiempo* (17 September, 1989), in the month after Galán's murder, the drug traffickers had set 36 fires and detonated 37 bombs, including a large one, which, on 2 September caused extensive damage to the *El Espectador* building in Bogotá in an obvious attempt to silence the most outspoken antidrug newspaper. About 75 people were injured, mainly those who happened to be in a passing bus. The drug traffickers warned the Medellín citizenry against reading the newspaper, which then had to be sold under police protection.

The terror campaign continued in spite of government pressure, and the drug organizations demonstrated they could freely attack individual targets, particularly in Medellín. On 12 September former Medellín Mayor Pablo Peláez was assassinated, and in the first week of October, Medellín's *El Espectador* representative, Miguel Soler, and its office manager, Martha Luz López, were also murdered (Castillo, 1991: 269).

On 26 September the administration peace initiatives with guerrilla organizations paid off, as the M-19 movement signed an agreement to surrender its weapons to an independent commission and return to civilian life. The government continued negotiating with other guerrilla groups, except the National Liberation Army (ELN) (The Economist Intelligence Unit, *Colombia Country Report*, #4, 1989). On 3 October President Barco appeared to have had another success when the Supreme Court ruled the new extradition procedures constitutional. However, it "ruled unconstitutional the decree by which Colombian security forces had arbitrarily confiscated more than a thousand drug trafficker properties" (Gugliotta and Leen, 1990: 574).

While the frequent bomb explosions injured and killed relatively few people, they had a damaging psychological effect on Colombia and generated widespread fear and a feeling of insecurity among the citizenry. Media surveys showed that public opinion supported strong government actions; however, as the war environment expanded and no "big fish" were caught, public support for the war on "narco-terrorism" began to diminish. A particularly serious blow to the government was the explosion that destroyed an Avianca plane that had just taken off from Bogotá for Cali on 27 November. This terrorist act killed 111 people. A week later, on 6 December, a massive truck bomb virtually destroyed the twelve-story headquarters of the National Security Forces (DAS) in Bogotá, killing 72 people and injuring hundreds.

The government needed some victories, preferably the death or capture of Gonzalo Rodríguez-Gacha and Pablo Escobar, who were widely believed to be the main promoters of the Medellín's "cartel" violence. On 14 December 1989 the government achieved one of these objectives when Gonzalo Rodríguez-Gacha died in a shoot-out with the army. As noted in Chapter 4, there are several versions of the events that led to this result. Regardless of how it was achieved, Rodríguez-Gacha's death was quite important because it was the first time the Colombian government had killed a top drug trafficker.

This event is likely to have been perceived by other top traffickers as a sign they were not invincible after all.

The international antidrug war hardened a week later when on 20 December the United States invaded Panama to illegally extradite Panamanian leader Manuel Antonio Noriega. At the same time, Colombian drug barons continued their fight and kidnapped the son of the president's chief of staff and several notables from Medellín. These people could be used as shields in case of encounters with the armed forces.[14] The violence continued and, as noted above, two U.P. presidential candidates were killed in succession in early 1990.

At the same time, drug traffickers were trying to establish a dialogue with the government, a move that had the support of the weary population. In January an ad-hoc commission of notables was formed to seek a solution to the war. The commission's members were former Presidents López, Turbay, and Pastrana; First Archbishop Mario Revollo; and Diego Montaña Cuellar, a U.P. representative. The Medellín drug traffickers contacted the commission and offered to cease the war and negotiate their integration with society. President Barco took a hard line and refused the offers. It is likely that Barco did not have any other option because of strong domestic and foreign pressures (Tokatlian, 1990).

Still, the heightened violence and insecurity generated strong public pressure on the government to "do something." President Barco seized this opportunity and initiated procedures to change the constitution in an effort to make the government more accountable to the people and to break the grip of the clientelistic system on the state. Simultaneously, the government began a process to open the economy to international competition in an attempt to revive economic growth (see Chapter 1).

The 1990 election was won by César Gaviria, a politician in his early forties with economics training. Gaviria had been finance and interior minister in the Barco administration, and had joined Galán's movement when he had become a serious presidential contender. Gaviria did not have a long record within the New Liberal party, but had excellent links with the main Liberal party. The 1990 election produced some surprising results, particularly the relatively high vote for Antonio Navarro, an M-19 member of the U.P. Gaviria received 48.1 percent of the vote, however; Alvaro Gómez, the right-wing conservative candidate, came in second with 23.7 percent and Navarro obtained 12.6 percent, edging Rodrigo Lloreda (11.9 percent) of the Social Conservative party.

A few days before Gaviria's inauguration the "extraditables" declared a truce, expecting Gaviria had to change government policies.

Indeed, Gaviria had clearly distinguished between the "war on drugs" to be fought internationally and the "war against narcoterrorism," which was the one that Colombia had to, and could, fight. The government continued to pressure drug groups and on 11 August, Gustavo Gaviria, the reputed deputy of Pablo Escobar, was killed in Medellín.

By the time Gaviria took office, the unprecedented process to convene a constitutional assembly had cleared all legal and political hurdles and he set 9 December as the assembly's election day. In the meantime the drug industry began to lobby possible representatives to the Constitutional Assembly to make sure the new constitution would ban extraditions. Gaviria's primary goals for the new constitution were to strengthen the judiciary system, to guarantee human and economic rights, and to decentralize power and decision-making to promote real democracy.

The election for the Constitutional Assembly produced a few more surprises. First, the turnout was very low: less than 30 percent of the electorate voted. Second, the Assembly had strong representation of the extreme political left and right. The Liberal Party fragmented into a large number of different lists of candidates and obtained a total of 25 seats that did not form a unified block. The Democratic Alliance (mainly the M-19) gained 19 seats, forming the largest single group. The right wing of the Conservative Party got 11 seats and the mainstream Social Conservative party only 5. Evangelical groups, native tribes, and the U.P. each gained two seats. Four independent Conservatives rounded out the list of 70 representatives. Two other leftist groups, the Workers Revolutionary Party and the Indian-based Quintín Lame movement each had a representative with voice but no vote (Dugas, 1993: 46–47).

On election day the army attacked FARC headquarters in a surprising and unprecedented move, killing about 70 guerrillas. This action led to a violent retaliation by FARC and the ELN. During the first week of 1991 there were 200 killings and 60 oil pipeline explosions (The Economist Intelligence Unit, *Colombia Country Report*, #1, 1991). Two other guerrilla groups, the Popular Liberation Army (EPL) and the new, smaller Workers Revolutionary Party, renounced violence in exchange for two and one seats in the Constitutional Assembly, respectively.

At the end of 1990, after sixteen months of war against narcoterrorism without a definite victory, the Gaviria administration began to look for ways to negotiate with drug traffickers. As a first step, an offer of reduced sentences in Colombia was made to those who turned themselves in voluntarily. Between mid-December and mid February the three Ochoa brothers turned themselves in, after it appeared quite certain that the new constitution would ban extraditions.

Despite these successes, violence against political figures continued. On 25 January 1991 former president Turbay's daughter Diana, a well-known journalist who had been kidnapped, died in a rescue attempt. On 30 April former Justice Minister Enrique Low was gunned down in Bogotá. The negotiations with drug traffickers continued as 84-year-old Father Rafael García Herreros (a famous priest who in the 1950s and 1960s had a nightly TV show through which he collected charity funds and built several housing developments for low income people) became the main liaison with Pablo Escobar. On June 20 Pablo Escobar surrendered and was to stand trial for the assassinations of Rodrigo Lara Bonilla and Luis Carlos Galán (The Economist Intelligence Unit, *Colombia Country Report*, #3, 1991). Escobar's surrender was negotiated: he was to be jailed in a special, comfortable prison built outside his hometown, Envigado, which was designed to guarantee his security and that of his jailed partners.

On 5 July the new constitution was approved. It banned extradition, weakened the president's power by allowing the impeachment of ministers (all presidential appointees) by Congress, attacked the foundations of clientelism by declaring representatives were to be elected nationally instead of in each department, established the election of mayors, entitled Colombians to important economic rights (health, education, and so on), and also strengthened the judiciary. The Constitutional Assembly also closed the existing Congress until a new one was elected.

The elections for Congress and governors took place on 27 October 1991, and as usual, the results were surprising. The Liberal party bounced back with 56 of the 100 senators, 87 of 160 representatives, and 17 of 27 governors. M-19 gained only 9 senate and 13 representative seats and one governorship. The new constitution opened the door for significant political change, but it appeared that most of the support for the left in the 1990 elections had come from a protest vote that carried little ideological commitment. The resurgence of the old Liberal party certainly raises serious doubts about how different the new congress will be from past ones.

At the beginning of 1992 the main members of the Medellín "cartel" were all in jail in Colombia and the war against narco-terrorism appeared won, inasmuch as drug trafficking did not seem to threaten the status quo. However, negotiations with the guerrillas did not seem to progress, the volume of cocaine exports had not declined, and the drug industry was diversifying into the heroin branch. Overall violence continued to affect Colombia at record levels, and the trials of jailed drug traffickers did not seem promising. On 2 January 1992, Andrés Gutiérrez, the confessed assassin of M-19 presidential candidate Bernardo Jaramillo and a witness in Escobar's trial, was assassinated. The total number of murders during 1991 reached another record at about 26,000 (The Economist Intelligence Unit, *Colombia Country Report*, #1, 1992).

During 1992 narco-terrorism declined, but the illegal drug business continued to flourish. The jailing of leaders of the Medellín group did not have an impact on the business, and indeed, it appeared that they continued to run their operations from inside their jail. Rumors that the jail was not typical, but rather a comfortable building in which the drug entrepreneurs had a life more akin to that of hotel guests than prisoners became stronger. By July 1992, there had been several incidents in which some suspected drug entrepreneurs were assassinated soon after visiting their jailed comrades, which led to speculations that the Medellín "cartel" leaders had conducted trials and sentenced to death some of their associates in their jail.

The new constitution, requiring that trials begin within 120 days of a prisoner's capture, opened the door for a possible release of Escobar since his trial had not begun. On 10 June President Gaviria declared a "state of emergency" to allow him to keep Escobar in jail. This move was seen by Escobar as a breach of the agreement under which he had surrendered, and the president ordered Escobar's move on 26 June to a military prison to prevent his escape. The president charged an armed group headed by the vice-minister of justice to enforce his order. When this group arrived at Escobar's prison, it was clear Escobar had prison guards under his control. He took the vice-minister and others hostage for a few hours and then escaped. Escobar's escape made a mockery of the negotiation policy of the government, highlighted once more the weakness of the Colombian state, and raised new questions about the viability of any government policy toward the drug industry.

Notes

1. For instance, in the late 1970s the Carter administration argued that human rights were a primary U.S. foreign policy goal; however, this policy criterion was applied against Argentina had refused to comply with a wheat embargo on the USSR, but was not applied to the Marcos regime in the Philippines.

2. This was also the case with studies by multilateral lending agencies that extensively analyzed the Colombian economy without making any reference to the illegal drug industry.

3. For instance, the pioneering work of Junguito and Caballero (1978) talks about "the other economy," contrasting it with the formal.

4. Glyphosate is a very strong defoliant sold in the United States under the brand name "Roundup."

5. Reuter argues that this has been the case on several occasions when there has been a significant PSAD supply disruption in the United States in the last two decades, and not only in the case of marijuana.

6. See Tokatlian's (1990: 321–323) detailed analysis of these developments.

7. Tokatlian (1990: 329) cites Eddy, Sabogal, and Walden (1988) and Kolton (1990), who argue that the United States military was concerned that the Colombian government had responded to the drug traffickers.

8. When "the impact of Rodrigo Lara's death had diminished somewhat, *Orientación Liberal*, a newspaper published by the Antioquia's Liberal Party directorate, proposed again the legalization of the drug traffickers' fortunes through a tax amnesty conditioned to the use of those monies in productive enterprises. This amnesty would be accompanied with penalties when it could be proved that the legalized monies were used in activities directly or indirectly related to the illegal drug industry" (Orjuela, 1990: 237). Of course, the proponents of the amnesty did not explain how the state was going to be strengthened to enforce its proposed clauses.

9. For a detailed analysis of what was occurring see, for example, *Americas Watch* (1990).

10. Journalist Fabio Castillo (1991: 70–82) relates this episode, highlighting several procedural deficiencies, and implies that several judges, prison, and other government officials helped Ochoa escape after receiving substantial bribes.

11. I happened to fly from Bogotá to Miami on 4 January. There was only one line for all passengers coming in three flights from Colombia, and every single piece of luggage was thoroughly searched. Going through customs that day took somewhat over three hours, causing many travellers to miss their connections. One can only wonder what the United States gained with this retaliatory behavior.

12. In early 1989, during a visit to Washington General Maza gave a lecture at the School of International Studies of Johns Hopkins University in which he confirmed these leaks.

13. These data from the Andean countries and the United States are frightfully reminiscent of the famous enemy body counts made by the American government during the Vietnam War.

14. According to Tokatlian (1990: 358), these kidnappings represented an attempt of the drug traffickers to couch their fight as a class struggle.

Part 3

THE IMPACT OF THE ILLEGAL DRUGS INDUSTRY AND GOVERNMENT POLICY ALTERNATIVES

... 8 ...
Impact and Consequences of Production and Traffic

The combined effect of the large economic size and illegal nature of the drug industry has had a complex and dramatic impact on Colombian society. Economic size and illegality frequently have effects that operate in opposite directions. For instance, the growth of a large export-oriented industry normally has many positive effects, although it also creates some problems if the industry's exports are subject to boom and bust cycles. In the case of PSAD, the effects of illegality can also be positive and negative. Illegality increases industry revenues and is likely to lower PSAD consumption, both positive effects, but it also has negative effects that arise from the increased violence, corruption, underground economic activity, tax avoidance, economic instability, money laundering, and so on, that an illegal industry spawns. Since Colombia does not appear to be vulnerable to a cocaine epidemic (see Chapter 9), the main benefit of illegality is the large illegal income, to be weighed against the host of negative effects which will be shown here to be greater than the industry's "positive" contributions.

The illegal PSAD industry is very important for Colombia. However, the nature and magnitude of the industry's impact are subject to a complex debate. First, many of the effects commonly attributed to the industry are caused by its illegality, which results from the policy decision to tackle consumption problems generated by some PSAD primarily by criminalizing the industry and trying to repress supply. Second, many industry effects are difficult to quantify; and third, once they are quantified, the data analysis presents serious identification problems because the industry grew in the midst of quickly changing social, political, and economic environments.

Further, the industry's size and illegality are also inextricably related since illegality is the main reason for the industry's high profits.

Alternative policies to criminalization are considered in Chapter 10. In this chapter, the effects of drug production and trafficking are considered under the assumption that the industry's illegality cannot be changed. From Colombia's point of view, this is a realistic assumption since legalization and decriminalization are not open alternatives in the foreseeable future (see Chapter 10).

The complex impact of the illegal PSAD industry on producer countries has frequently not been reflected in official data, so one of the first challenges faced by any researcher is to understand it. In Chapter 6 size estimates for the industry were surveyed, and its large size relative to the Colombian economy was confirmed. In the following sections, some industry impacts on Colombia's economy and society will be examined. This exercise does not pretend to be either exhaustive or a modified cost-benefit analysis, but only attempts to identify some of the primary effects of illegal PSAD industry growth and to survey and evaluate the evidence available about those effects.

This chapter starts with a dicussion of some methodological issues and rejects the applicability of traditional cost-benefit analysis in evaluating the industry's impact on Colombia. Continuing the discussion in Chapter 2, it explains the importance of the industry's catalytic effect that accelerated the delegitimation process taking place in the country. Next there is a survey of evidence of the industry's impact on the construction industry, and another for the rural sector, including the impact of the industry's investments and the development of coca production. The illegal PSAD industry's impact discussed in these two sections is perhaps the easiest to measure. Several macroeconomic impacts on the overall level of economic activity, the rate of GDP growth, and fiscal and monetary policy formulation, implementation, and effectiveness are discussed. I argue here that, contrary to what many might think, the illegal PSAD industry has most likely hurt Colombian development. A short summary concludes the chapter.

Methodological Issues Concerning the Illegal Drug Industry's Economic Impact on Colombia

An economist confronted with the task of determining whether the illegal PSAD industry is or has been beneficial to a country is tempted to use cost-benefit analysis. However, efforts to do so show very quickly that cost-benefit analysis techniques are not particularly useful and that they do not provide a good framework to answer many of the important questions related to this industry. Any cost-benefit analysis of Colombia's illegal PSAD industry would have to measure the opportunity cost of the factors of production used in the industry, the income it receives, and economic externalities (positive and negative) generated by illicit drug consumption, money laundering, and any other economic activities that grow as a result of PSAD industry growth. Since many of the negative economic externalities of drug consumption take place mostly outside Colombia, an economic cost-benefit estimate is likely to come out highly positive.[1]

Even if one could compensate for those variables, cost-benefit analyses fail on several grounds: first, cost-benefit analysis is applicable to projects that are marginal relative to the size of the economy, so that income- and wealth-distributions are not altered by them, which is not the case with the illegal drug industry. When a project has substantial income-and-wealth distribution impacts, there are important identifiable gainer and loser groups. In order to decide if a project's benefits exceed its costs, it is necessary to compare costs and benefits of different groups, which requires making value judgments about the social convenience of the implied distributive changes. These value judgments determine the evaluation results. Furthermore, the illegal drugs industry has also affected the power structure of the producer countries and has contributed to the overall growth of the underground economy and to the weakening of the state. An evaluation of all these changes requires further value judgments.

Second, since the industry breeds violence, it has important social costs to be estimated. To do so it would be necessary to estimate the value of life for different groups of people, a process that may result in socially unacceptable results. For instance, in the United States many deaths associated with the illegal PSAD industry are of young, poor, inner-city males. Had they lived, they would have been, on average, unemployed or welfare recipients for long periods of time and they would have spent a significant portion of their lives in jail at a high cost to taxpayers. The results of a cost-benefit analysis of their deaths could actually show "social savings" that would be counted as "economic benefits" to society. A similar result may arise from a cost-benefit analysis of the deaths of young Colombian sicarios.

Third, cost-benefit analysis is not geared toward evaluating the costs of macroeconomic changes and restrictions caused by an industry to the fiscal and monetary authorities of a country. Fourth, it is also not capable of considering the illegal PSAD industry's acceleration of delegitimation, which altered the power structure. Such an effect cannot be evaluated without making value judgments. Clearly, then, the analysis of the effects of the illegal PSAD industry should transcend the cost-benefit framework and should not be geared only toward estimating the industry's private or social economic profitability.

The Catalytic Effect

As argued in Chapter 2, the main effect of the illegal PSAD industry has been its catalytic role of accelerating the delegitimation process occurring in Colombia. The PSAD industry achieved this by influencing or creating several variables: the underground economy, growing violence, disregard for the legal system, judicial branch intimidation, corruption in state bureaucracies, the expectation of high short-term profits that promoted speculative investments, and the government's ability to implement social and economic measures such as land reform or anti-inflation policies. Each variable contributed to the gap between de jure and de facto socially accepted behaviors—accelerating regime delegitimation and weakening the state.

These issues have received plenty of attention in the journalistic, popular, and academic literature (Gugliotta and Leen, 1990; Gugliotta, 1992; Castillo, 1987 and 1991; Craig, 1983; Dombois, 1990; Kalmanovitz, 1990; Krauthausen and Sarmiento, 1991; Sarmiento, 1990a and 1990b; Thoumi, 1987). While the most eye-catching references mention increased violence and cruelty in the industry's actions against the State, the most important effect has been its influence on the behavior of the rest of the society that has fallen into what may be described as a "dishonesty trap," in which most Colombians show widespread disrespect for any laws and the rights of other citizens (Thoumi, 1987). This is a trap in the sense that nonmarginal social, political, and economic reforms are required to escape it.

Some authors have not recognized the catalytic effect as important, and have argued the illegal PSAD industry has mainly positive economic benefits and has not weakened the regime but only produced a clash within the capitalist upper class. Arango (1988) emphasizes the positive effects of the cocaine industry on Antioquia's economy. He argues that the capitalist development of that region led to a manufacturing crisis during the 1970s, a decline in the profit rate of manufacturing, and high unemployment, followed by a financial crisis. These developments "created an environment in which those who were frustrated by their economic losses found in drug trafficking a way to vindicate themselves and regain their capital" (p. 97, author's translation).

Other analysts may recognize the catalysis, but do not necessarily accept it as negative. Greater regime delegitimation and increased violence are considered "negative externalities" of the industry. However, since the process of delegitimation was already taking place, and the illegal drug industry only hastened it, those who believe history teaches that troubled societies must have a crisis and hit bottom before they recover from their ills would argue that the externalities are only negative in the short run, but positive in the long run because they accelerate crisis resolution. In this case, the overall impact could be either positive or negative, depending on the weight given to each social group's gains and losses, and on the rate of discount used (that is, on the importance of the present versus the future).

Yet such a conclusion is inherently flawed because, while the industry may force the government to belatedly take drastic steps to counter its power through greater democratization, it has also become one of the main obstacles to democratization. Indeed, the industry's capital resources and real estate investments in areas targeted for land reform, the traditional paternalistic attitudes of its entrepreneurs, their raw capitalism and disrespect for legality, and their propensity to appeal to violence are great obstacles to the development of a democratic capitalist system that responds to the need for political empowerment of most of the citizenry. The industry's ability to hinder progress is magnified by the fact that the growing violence, kidnappings, instability, and other effects have generated significant illegal capital flight from Colombia, resulting in a process in which capital whose origin is related to the illegal PSAD industry has substituted for older capital of different origins.[2]

Evidence of other debilitating influences of the illegal PSAD industry is readily available. As extensively analyzed by Krauthausen and Sarmiento (1991), the illegal drug industry needs to develop clandestine networks to obtain inputs for drug manufacturing, to protect stocks of products, laboratories, and shipments, to defend members against the judicial system, to launder money, and to protect accumulated wealth. The need for such networks, combined with the entrepreneurs' resources have resulted in a situation in which every individual and institution is vulnerable to their proposals. Besides, the drug industry's propensity to intimidate and use violence further enhances its capacity to enlist the personnel needed to achieve its goals.

This characteristic promoted the development of the sicario industry by generating a demand for individuals willing to use violence. The drug industry has not been the only user of sicarios, and at least some of the sicario organizations sprang from guerrilla training camps (see Chapter 4). However, the illegal drug industry's willingness to kill and use its vast resources promoted the growth of the sicario industry once established. Wirpsa (1989) reports that in 1989 there were some 2,000 contract killers in the country and that the drug traffickers had even established an "academy for killers." The long-term social implications of these developments are likely to be devastating, as attested to by those who have worked in and researched the sicario industry (Salazar, 1990; Gaviria, 1991).

The Impact on the Construction Industry

One of the most visible effects of the growth of the illegal PSAD industry has been in the construction industry, since real estate has been a good money laundering channel widely used by illegal PSAD entrepreneurs. The industry's growth and cycles have been reflected in the construction sector, particularly in cities where industry entrepreneurs have been concentrated.

Gómez (1985 and 1988) shows that Barranquilla, the city where marijuana traders were reportedly concentrated, experienced a construction boom and low unemployment levels during the late 1970s (when marijuana was booming), while Medellín, the center of the best known cocaine "cartel" had a construction boom during the early 1980s (when the cocaine industry was growing). Furthermore, as marijuana's importance faded, Barranquilla experienced a construction bust. Giraldo Isaza (1990) studies some trends of the country's construction sector and finds that in recent years, particularly from 1985 on, the relationship between mortgage finance volume and the amount of new construction (the area of new construction for which building permits were issued) breaks down. For instance, in 1987 the real value of the construction finance supplied by the official constant value mortgage system (UPAC) declined by about 20 percent, while the total licensed construction area increased by 14.6 percent. Giraldo attributes this inconsistency to the fact that illegal PSAD businessmen invest heavily in construction with their own financing. He also argues that the construction financed with illegal capital is likely to be underreported since a significant portion is probably done without permits.[3]

In Colombia there are few sources of nonhousing mortgage funds, so a substantial proportion of commercial and industrial construction is financed through the informal capital market, shorter term bank loans, or the owners' resources. Interestingly, until 1985 about 75 percent of the licensed construction area was zoned for housing, a share that declined to 67 percent in 1988, indicating a substantial relative growth in nonhousing construction. Giraldo Isaza argues that these changes in the composition of new construction are due to illegal drug industry real estate investments that according to his estimates are approximately U.S. $1 billion per year.

The Impact on Rural Areas

The Impact of Investment

PSAD industrialists have invested heavily in certain rural areas of Colombia, particularly in the Middle Magdalena Valley, the Urabá area in Antioquia, the neighboring Córdoba department, and the eastern piedmont and prairies. These regions are characterized as having seen significant guerrilla activity, having been recently settled, and frequently having weak and questionable property rights (Reyes, 1989). Sarmiento and Moreno (1990) studied these regions and found that, in areas where there had been significant guerrilla activity before illegal PSAD investments took place, the cattle and dairy industries improved because industry-financed paramilitary groups increased the safety of property in the region and the level of rustling declined. They also found there was an increase in land tenure concentration, even in areas targeted for land reform, indicating a violent land counterreform has taken place.[4]

The contradictory end result is technological progress with social decline. That is, wealthy drug entrepreneurs were able to increase the capital intensity of the production process, introduce new technologies, and increase productivity. Yet they simultaneously established paramilitary groups that use violence to discourage political participation among the peasants, and have concentrated land tenancy. Sarmiento and Moreno (1990) also found that rural wages have increased in those areas, but that may be due as much to the emigration of rural workers escaping the violence as to higher productivity. These authors further argue that the development of paramilitary groups and the accompanying changes pose a dilemma for the old landlords: if they pay the old security contributions (the "vaccine" against kidnappings) to the guerrillas as before, the paramilitary groups will burn their farms and even kill them. If they don't pay, they have to support the local paramilitary. And, higher wages and the landlords' lack of access to the kind of capital resources enjoyed by the illegal drug businessmen put them at a disadvantage to compete in the region. Thus, many of the old landlords sell out to the illegal PSAD businessmen, increasing land tenure concentration in those regions.

Paramilitary groups have frequently used random and indiscriminate violence to establish an environment of fear in which they can operate freely and impose their own law (Medina, 1990: 183). These groups would not have become that powerful without financial backing from the illegal PSAD industry with its experience and willingness to use violence. The relative abundance of funds for paramilitary groups allowed them to pay even for technical assistance provided by international mercenaries, mainly Israelis and Britons, who provided them with anti-guerrilla military training.[5]

The Impact on Coca Growing Regions

As discussed in Chapter 3, coca is grown mostly in isolated, newly settled regions. In spite of high coca crop returns, these regions have experienced the typical fluctuations associated with primary product price cycles and with "Dutch disease." Mora's (1989) study of the Caguán and Molano's (1987) of the Guaviare show that the development of the coca industry produced dramatic labor and other price increases in both regions, making it impossible to produce any goods or service that could otherwise have been imported to the region. These authors complain the profits generated by coca growing were not reinvested in the producing regions, where the only other economic activities that prospered were nonimportable services.

Interestingly, analysts do not recognize the "Dutch disease" nature of the regions' problems and frequently seem to have the causality relations backward. For instance, Molano (1987: 97–99) claims that because of the high costs of labor and other services it was impossible to produce anything besides coca, without fully understanding that the reason that labor and services costs were so high was precisely the high return to coca growing.

Mora (1989) and Molano (1987) also found that coca growing completely changed regional social and political structures. Many newly attracted migrants were ready and willing to use violence; the income jump changed consumption patterns drastically because, for the first time in their lives, the peasants had substantial sums to spend on items beyond those necessary for subsistence; and alcohol consumption and prostitution expanded, as did the demand for imported electrical appliances, luxury goods, and cars. The economic boom increased violence since the state's weak presence made it easy to kill and rob, and did not provide peaceful conflict resolution mechanisms. Political change occurred as left-leaning organizations lost their stronghold on the regions when residents became increasingly interested in money-making activities.

When coca prices fell in 1982 as a result of a government crackdown on cocaine producers, many peasants went bankrupt, particularly heavy borrowers who had been too confident of continuous high coca prices. In both growing regions, the peasants who survived the price decline tended to be the long-time residents who had not fully specialized in coca growing and who had not fallen prey to the consumption and credit binge. The price drop was an important contributor to further increases in violence to settle unpaid accounts and busted deals, and also led to an increase in land tenure concentration when many peasants had to sell in distress.

The guerrilla organizations filled the power vacuum left by the weak state presence in the coca growing regions, and tried to respond to the economic and social effects of the coca bust. They reestablished order and forced peasants to produce not only coca but also foodstuffs, limiting coca growing to a portion of the land controlled by each peasant. In part because of these government-like activities, some guerrilla groups became involved in the coca and cocaine industry.

The Macroeconomic Impact

In order to study the possible macroeconomic effects of the illegal PSAD industry, several important questions may be raised regarding whether the industry has contributed to Colombia's relatively positive economic performance discussed in Chapter 1; what the industry's impact has been on long-term GDP growth; how the industry's growth has affected the government's ability to formulate and implement fiscal and monetary policies; what impact the industry has had on other economic sectors; and whether the Colombian economy could survive today without the illegal drug industry. In considering these questions, there is a bias (particularly in the press) to answer them emphasizing the positive economic effects of the illegal drug industry. There are many journalists and some academics who argue that the illegal drug industry allowed Colombia to avoid the external debt crisis that plagued the rest of Latin America and the Caribbean.[6]

The Impact on Foreign Exchange Flows

The illegal PSAD industry has had a significant impact on the foreign exchange supply in Colombia's official and black markets. As discussed in Chapter 6, foreign exchange generated by illegal drug exports that comes back into the economy does so through various channels; some of it shows up in the official balance of payments, but a significant proportion does not. Furthermore, not all of the illegal foreign exchange that shows up in the official balance of payments is generated by illegal drug exports. Despite these inaccuracies, the illegal foreign exchange that does register in the official balance of payments is very important because it significantly affects the macroeconomic analyses of government and international agencies, and influences policy formulation and implementation.

Estimating the true impact of the illegal drug industry on the official balance of payments is quite difficult. Drug-earned foreign exchange can be reflected in the balance of payments in several ways, including through fictitious service exports or transfers, or financing import underinvoicing and export overinvoicing. However, the foreign exchange used for these purposes may come from other sources. Thus, there is a problem determining the origin of these flows.

The balance of payments has been the subject of research to determine the size of hard-to-explain flows. Illegal foreign exchange inflows that affect the official balance of payments have fluctuated, responding to current economic conditions in Colombia. Correa (1984) has shown that the difficult-to-explain flows of the balance of payments are statistically explained by changes in the real exchange rate and in the difference between the official and the black market exchange rates. Therefore, when the real value of the peso increased relative to the dollar, and when the black market exchange rate increased relative to the official one, these flows declined. Whatever the origin of these flows, then, they do respond to an economic logic.[7]

A particular episode worth mentioning occurred in 1982–1983, the period of highest international cocaine prices, and perhaps also the period when the illegal PSAD industry's revenues were at their peak. During these years the suspicious balance of payments inflows declined. It is worth remembering (see Chapter 1) that during this period of record-high international interest rates, Colombia's international reserves were falling sharply, the government budget deficit reached record levels, the official exchange rate was overvalued, and for the first time since December 1974 the black market exchange rate significantly exceeded the official one (Herrera, 1990: 69–70). Obviously, incentives to bring capital to Colombia and to sell illegally obtained foreign exchange to the Central Bank were quite weak. The 1982–1983 experience led Urrutia (1990b) to argue that since the capital that the illegal PSAD industry brings to the country increases when international reserves are also increasing, and vice-versa, these flows are pro-cyclical and complicate the macroeconomic management of the economy.

Urrutia implicitly assumes that without the drug industry, "hot" money flows in and out of the country that take advantage of varying short-term macroeconomic conditions in Colombia and the international economy would have been significantly lower. It is possible that Urrutia is right, but the experience of many Latin American countries from the mid-1970s on indicates that anytime a government allows the exchange and interest rates to misalign to the point that short-term international capital flows become highly profitable, those flows take place. Thus, while the availability of funds generated by the illegal drug industry may have accentuated the 1982–1983 recession, it is not possible to determine the magnitude of their contribution since capital flows would have occurred as long as they were profitable.

Sarmiento (1990a and 1990b), analyzing the same data, arrives at a different conclusion. He argues that the drug-generated capital flows led, instead of followed, the macroeconomic indicators. Sarmiento's point is that GDP growth and the level of worker remittances are highly correlated. Colombia's GDP growth stalled in the early 1980s but recovered in 1986 and 1987 when it reached a level above 5 percent, coinciding with a sharp increase in worker remittances. During these two years there was also a "mini" coffee boom caused by high international coffee prices. Most analysts (Ocampo, 1991) attribute the GDP growth recovery to the high coffee prices. But Sarmiento discounts the coffee boom effect and attributes high growth to the increase in repatriated drug capital reflected in the high worker remittances. Sarmiento supports his argument with two graphs that show GDP growth and worker remittances time series for 1980–1987. However, he does not superimpose the two series, shown in Table 1.2. A simple look at the two series since 1970 indicates that the high growth of the 1970s was achieved with much lower worker remittances than during the late 1980s. Furthermore, since 1985 the two series do not necessarily move together.

Indeed, the highest growth rate was achieved in 1986 when worker remittances were U.S. $393 million. During the following five years the GDP rate of growth was lower, while worker remittances were significantly higher. This discrepancy appears more marked in 1987, when worker remittances reached the all time record of $616 million and GDP growth declined. It should be noted that when the two series are superimposed, one can conclude that worker remittances are more likely to lag behind GDP growth than vice versa.

Thus, this comparison would support Urrutia's position against Sarmiento's.

The relationship between GDP growth rates, worker remittances, and other capital inflows, both legal and illegal, is quite complex and cannot be determined just by looking at a couple of time series. For instance, increases in difficult-to-explain balance of payments flows can simply be the result of shifts in the way illegal capital comes into the country. When the exchange rate makes it profitable, illegal flows that enter through contraband financing can be shifted to official balance of payments accounts, particularly if the Central Bank relaxes its purchase requirements. Furthermore, it is very difficult to argue that the country had a boom in one particular year because illegal drug entrepreneurs decided to increase the amount of foreign exchange they brought into the country. That would require one to explain why the entrepreneurs changed their minds, independent of the macroeconomic changes that took place in the country. No one has yet provided such an explanation. Since empirical evidence indicates that the balance of payments capital inflows are explained by changes in economic variables, it also supports the contention that illegal drug entrepreneurs respond to changes in economic conditions and thus, their capital inflows lag behind macroeconomic indicators rather than lead them.

The Impact on Aggregate Demand and Inflation

An issue related to the one just discussed is the impact of the illegal PSAD industry on aggregate demand and inflation. Urrutia (1990b: 117–118) has argued that since most of the industry's repatriated revenues come via contraband, the industry has had a small impact on aggregate demand and, therefore, does not stimulate GDP growth. "Contraband competes with domestic production and lowers the demand for domestically produced industrial products. Other foreign exchange transactions (induced by the illegal PSAD industry) do not generate aggregate demand either. This is the case with the foreign exchange that narco-traffickers use to purchase land in areas where there is violence between guerrillas and paramilitary: most likely, the land sellers take their capital out of Colombia through the black market. In this case, the inflow of black market dollars does not generate aggregate demand either" (Urrutia, 1990b: 118, author's translation). Sarmiento (1990a and 1990b) also concludes that most of the money used by traffickers to buy land finds its way out of the country as capital flight.

It is very likely that increases in aggregate demand generated by the illegal PSAD industry are not "very large," as Urrutia argues.

However, they are similar to those of other foreign sector loans. The point is that any primary export boom of the magnitude of the illegal PSAD industry in Colombia would have had a similar effect. A large shift in exports increases the foreign exchange supply, and would force either a large accumulation of international reserves or an increase in imports. If reserves are accumulated, this process has to be financed by lowering the government budget or expanding the money supply. In the first case government spending must fall, lowering aggregate demand, in the second, inflation will take place and have the same real effect. If international reserves are not accumulated, then legal imports must increase, generating an effect similar to that of contraband.

Therefore, since the effect of any primary product boom on aggregate demand is similar, the main differences between a legal and an illegal primary product export boom lie simply in the control the government has over some of the sectoral and tax collection effects. In the Colombian economy of the last forty years, coffee booms were controlled by the government through exchange controls and import licenses in an attempt to protect some sectors against a decline in demand. When there were booms, to minimize the disruptive effects of the boom on domestic production, the policy goal was to increase imports of products that did not compete with domestic industries and whose demand had been repressed by the foreign exchange control and license systems. However, the success of this policy approach depended on the government's ability to enforce the exchange control system and to control contraband. The growing gap between de jure and de facto behavior, and the growing legitimacy of contraband, made it increasingly difficult for the government to achieve this goal by the time the illegal PSAD industry developed.

A second issue has to do with the causes of capital flight. A key question here is simply to what extent capital flight by land sellers is caused by the illegal PSAD industry, by guerrilla extortion and kidnappings, or by tax laws and other government policies. This question cannot be answered with a high degree of certainty, and the true answer is likely to be a combination of those factors. Thus, it is rather difficult to attribute causality to the illegal PSAD industry, except that as the main catalyst of regime delegitimation, it increases the incentives for capital flight.

The nature of the industry generated other important effects on aggregate demand. The illegal PSAD industry has very few backward and forward linkages in Colombia. Indeed, the cost of the Colombian factors of production purchased by the industry is quite low and because of that, it has not contributed much to aggregate demand that way. Furthermore, some of the economic linkages are clearly undesirable, unproductive, or both. For instance, the industry has contributed to the growth of the private security industry that clearly signals declining quality of life, even though counted as a positive contribution to GDP.

The industry's impact on inflation is more difficult to determine. In this respect the main issue is whether the monetary base has increased because of the illegal drug boom. Urrutia's (1990b) argument that drug-originated "sinister window" inflows have been small implies that the industry's inflationary effect has also been minor, since the international reserve accumulation is not due to the industry. However, according to Sarmiento and the discussion of Chapter 6, it is likely that a large proportion of the capital inflows purchased by the Central Bank do originate with the illegal PSAD industry, in which case they have had an inflationary effect. Yet one must keep in mind that these flows are explainable by changes in the real exchange rate and in the difference between the black market and official exchange rates, and they are not related to illegal PSAD revenue estimates or cocaine prices. One should thus argue that most capital flows would have occurred anyway, and they could not be attributed to the availability of illegal PSAD foreign exchange. In other words, international capital flows are related to monetary and fiscal policies and not to the illegal PSAD industry.

Impact on Policy Formulation and Implementation

The growth of the illegal PSAD industry has made it more difficult to formulate and implement macroeconomic policies. One problem arises simply because as the underground economy grows, the quality of data used by the government to formulate policy declines.[8] For example, it has become increasingly difficult to determine the actual amount of goods and services exported and imported, and of capital flows in and out of the country. The level of measured unemployment tends to be overestimated as some of those who work in the underground economy are counted as unemployed. The increased use of dollars as currency as a result of the need to launder foreign exchange, regardless of the peso's soundness, makes monetary policy more complex. Another problem arises from the difficulty of taxing the informal economy, which penalizes legitimate economic activity and erodes the tax base. All these effects of a larger underground economy make it more difficult to formulate the right policies and to implement them.

Impact on Economic Growth

As noted above, several observers have argued that Colombia's relatively good growth performance during the 1980s was due to drug income, which allowed the country to avoid the external debt crisis and the GDP decline experienced by the rest of Latin America and the Caribbean. This view is however, highly naive. Colombia's post–World War II macroeconomic management has been stable and cautious, and there is no reason to argue that, without illegal PSAD-generated foreign exchange, Colombia would have experienced the debt crisis. Indeed, as shown in Table 1.1, GDP growth before the drug industry took off was significantly higher than during the drug industry period. This has led some Colombian economists to search for the causes of the GDP growth decline. As Ocampo (1991) notes, several factors have contributed to the growth decline, including the relative improvement of the mining sector and the relative decline of manufacturing that resulted in weaker backward linkages, and the completion of a national market by the early 1970s that meant new external economies from increased market integration were declining.

There are, however, many reasons that the growth of the illegal PSAD industry has also contributed to a decline in economic growth. First, the illegal nature of the industry and the inherent difficulty to invest industry profits led to investments which were not necessarily the most productive. Since one of the primary goals of illegal drug entrepreneurs is to launder their capital, their investments are influenced by the varying ability of investments to launder "dirty" capital, rather than yield the highest returns. As shown by Gunter (1991), "dirty" capital has replaced a significant amount of "clean" capital. This substitution has been encouraged by the heightened violence and uncertainty promoted by the illegal drug industry, it has changed the country's economic power structure, has chased away many of the old entrepreneurs, and may have an impact on efficiency and growth.

Second, many drug entrepreneurs are rough capitalists with values similar to those that prevailed in earlier times. They have the ability to succeed in the illegal PSAD industry, but their qualities do not necessarily make them good modern entrepreneurs. This does not mean there are no sophisticated entrepreneurs among them, but only that on average, they are likely to be less qualified to manage a modern business than the best managers the country has produced.

Third, the illegal PSAD industry's catalysis of regime delegitimation has produced a boom in many industries that contribute very little to higher real income, such as the booming security industry. The private sector in Colombia today provides a myriad of security-related services, including private guards and bodyguards, alarms, armored cars, bullet proof vests, kidnap negotiators, and so on. The demand for these services arises from the need to compensate for the negative effects of higher violence and lawlessness, and contributes little to measured growth. For instance, private guards and bodyguard services have very few backward linkages, and do not have the economies of scale that public security forces could have. Besides, the physical equipment used has a very high imported component. Indeed, this is a case of privatization of some of the state's most fundamental functions, which results in grave inefficiencies.

Fourth, the environment for direct foreign investment has greatly deteriorated. The weakening of the judicial system has made it increasingly difficult to resolve civil conflicts; the increased insecurity has increased the costs of operating in the country and has made it more difficult to manage the firms from within the country. Indeed, many foreign subsidiaries have their management outside Colombia. One should note, however, that the illegal drug industry is not the most important direct contributor to direct foreign investment disincentives. Indeed, foreign enterprises fear guerrilla-sponsored kidnappings and bombings more than illegal PSAD industry problems. The point is that the indirect effects of the catalytic role played by the illegal drug industry have been highly negative for foreign investment.

Fifth, the increased uncertainty about the future and the PSAD industry's high short-term profits have promoted a short-sighted perspective in the country. People expect quick high profits and tend to invest in fairly speculative, fast-turnover assets. These high expectations discourage investments in projects that take a longer time to mature, but that contribute to sustained growth.

Sixth, the fight against drug trafficking and its violence has required significant increases in police and military expenditures, which are fundamentally "consumption" costs and do not contribute to growth.[9]

Seventh, by promoting growth in the underground economy, the drug industry also contributes to a lower rate of GDP growth. Coincidentally, underground firms are limited in their expansion as they cannot become conspicuous. They find it difficult to market their products within formal channels and to export in significant quantities.

The negative impact of the illegal PSAD industry on economic growth is confirmed by Urrutia (1990b: 115), who additionally finds that the periods of increased antidrug activity in Colombia do not generate recessions, in spite of some short-term declines in capital inflows.

Summary and Conclusions

The growth of the illegal PSAD industry has had pervasive effects on the Colombian economy, the most important of which has been its catalytic effect that promoted greater disregard for the law and social norms. This effect cannot be judged as positive or negative without making strong value judgments about the changes it has brought to the social power structure and income distribution. However, the illegal drug industry has disrupted the development of several regions affected by a "Dutch disease" phenomenon; it has blocked government attempts to redistribute lands in target rural zones; it has made macroeconomic policy more complex and government policy more uncertain; it has forced a redistribution of government expenditures from promoting growth to security and arms; it has encouraged a "get rich quick" mentality; and it makes investment choices based on the need to launder and hide capital. These and other industry characteristics have contributed to a decline in the rate of GDP growth.

It is no wonder that most Colombian economists argue the negative effects clearly outweigh the positive ones, and do not consider the illegal PSAD industry beneficial to the country's economy. Clearly, if the illegal PSAD industry were to disappear, Colombia would run a risk of having a recession for a couple of years (Sarmiento, 1990a and 1990b). However, it is likely that even a mild recession might be avoided. Since the illegal drug industry is likely to be responsible for promoting substantial "clean" capital flight, its elimination could actually be compensated for by "clean" capital repatriations. Since income from capital investments that the illegal drug entrepreneurs are likely to have outside the country may be as large as current cocaine profits, the elimination of the industry would allow for an easier repatriation and assimilation of that income. In conclusion, there is no question that Colombia's economy could do better without the illegal drug industry than with it.

Notes

1. From the point of view of cost-benefit analysis the illegal PSAD industry is similar to any industry that generates exported pollution; that is, it transfers a large share of the social costs to other countries.

2. It should be remembered that the older capital was not necessarily legitimately accumulated.

3. For instance, Castillo (1991: 81) reports that in January 1988, after a bomb placed by the Cali cartel seriously damaged a ten-story building in Medellín that Pablo Escobar used as one of his main residences, it was found the site was registered in official city records as a vacant lot.

4. See also Collett, 1989.

5. The links of the paramilitary groups with these mercenaries are well-established. There have also been uncorroborated rumors about their links with Belgian and Basque (ETA) advisors. Krauthausen and Sarmiento (1991: 99–101) provide a good summary of the evidence of these relationships.

6. See, for example, *The Economist* (1988) and Collett (1988). Urrutia (1991) points out that as late as July 1990, *The Economist* still argued this way. This view has also been expressed by non-journalists like Mishan (1990: 448) and Lee (1988: 101). However, in private communications with me, Dr. Lee has confirmed he has changed his mind on this matter.

7. Since these flows were illegal in Colombia, Correa's findings also illustrate the widespread disrespect for the law in Colombia.

8. For instance, McGee and Feige (1989) argue that the growth of the underground economy in the United States during and after the Vietnam War resulted in overestimations of unemployment and inflation levels in the late 1970s, which induced policymakers to implement stronger policy measures than were necessary and that deepened the recession of the early 1980s.

9. Orjuela (1990: 251) also argues that the pressures to increase military expenditures forced a decrease in social expenditures of 17 percent in real terms between 1984 and 1989.

... 9 ...
The Demand for Psychoactive Drugs and Drug Addiction

Understanding the factors that affect PSAD demand is important because, first, successful policies cannot be formulated unless both demand and supply are understood. Second, it is useful to determine whether the increased output of illegal PSAD has contributed to an increase in PSAD use in Colombia, and whether the increased availability heightens society's vulnerability to illegal drug consumption in the future. Below I survey the economic and psychological theories that explain the demand for PSAD and addictive products. This discussion is also relevant to Chapter 10, which focuses on the effectiveness of government policies. Then I explore knowledge gaps that have created "black and gray boxes" of understanding. Evidence about drug addiction in Colombia, is followed by a section that evaluates the risks of a cocaine and other epidemics.

The Demand for Psychoactive Drugs and Addictive Goods

The demand for PSAD has some very puzzling characteristics that are difficult to model. PSAD consumption generates addiction among some users, but not others, and the patterns of addiction among those who do become addicts vary significantly. Consumers clearly enjoy PSAD but recognize that consumption, especially if they become addicts, can be harmful in the long run. Many PSAD consumers and addicts seem to want to end their use and addiction, but are incapable of doing so. Because of this, addiction leads to the creation of "antimarkets" (Winston, 1980), that is, to treatments in which addicts pay for not consuming and learning not to consume. Despite the growth of the medical addiction treatment industry, which has become very successful particularly in the United States, an evaluation of these treatments raises many questions since the number of people that "mature out" of their addiction is frequently not increased by the treatments (Zinberg, 1972; Clague, 1973; Winston, 1980; Fingarette, 1988).[1] And in most cases, consumers who stop using PSAD go back to using them after a period of time. Yet some former users simply will not touch them again, and become strong anti-PSAD advocates. Addicts to some drugs frequently consume in binges, that is, go through periods of extremely heavy consumption during which they seem to "lose control" of their actions, even resorting to violence and other means to satisfy their consumption needs. A few addicts reach a point where they behave destructively towards themselves and society; they resort to stealing, violence, and other crimes to obtain income to sustain their habits, and disregard their jobs and families.

Another important characteristic of market demand for PSAD is that it varies greatly through time, independent of price and income changes, and tends to experience peaks (considered by many as epidemics) and valleys. These wide variations are extremely important and must be understood if PSAD consumption is going to be kept within socially tolerable limits.

The characteristics of PSAD demand have been difficult to incorporate into economic theory models, although there have been recent advances that incorporate some of these elements. The simplest conventional economic analysis indicates that the amount of PSAD demanded by a consumer in a society at one particular point in time depends on the individual's preferences (i.e., utility function), on the PSAD price, and on the consumer's income. Economic analysis implicitly assumes that consumers are sovereign and capable of deciding in the marketplace what to buy with their income, and it does not make any assumptions about the convenience of a particular type of consumption; that is, it does not make value judgements about whether a good or service is "good" or "bad" for the consumer. Since PSAD consumption is associated with addiction, simple economic analysis concludes that the demand for these products tends to be price inelastic. Indeed, cigarette demand is a favorite example used in introductory economics textbooks to explain demand inelasticity.

Conventional economic theory assumes that consumer preferences and tastes (the utility function) are stable, and economists are fond of maintaining this assumption because they fear they would otherwise open a Pandora's box with every demand variation explained in ad hoc fashion through preference changes. This creates a conflict with popular views that PSAD consumption changes consumer preferences. Recent models of PSAD consumption developed by economists focus on addiction as the main characteristic of PSAD demand. In most cases, they assume the utility functions remain constant, and as is the norm in economics, do not attempt to deal with the causes and reasons that an individual consumer would have a preference for PSAD use.

Stigler and Becker (1977) developed a model in which the consumer has constant preferences and goods are used to produce "commodities" that yield satisfaction. In this model the consumer has a "production function" that converts goods into commodities. This theoretical framework is used to explain addiction: the addictive good is one whose consumption changes the way in which the consumer converts goods into commodities. The authors apply this model to explain the development of beneficial addiction and use classical music appreciation as an example. It is central to their argument that "the enjoyment of 'a unit' of music appreciation is *not* affected by experience—the utility function remains unchanged—but that *more* music appreciation is produced with the same inputs of time and goods as a consequence of learning by listening" (Winston, 1980: 300). This enhanced ability to convert the consumed good into the commodity that produces utility leads to increased amounts of consumption, that is, to addiction.

The Stigler-Becker model contributes to understanding addiction formation. However, this model's consumer decides without any regrets to become an addict and the model does not explain how or why people quit their addiction, and even less why people pay for help to do so. This model focuses on beneficial addiction and "simply avoids most of the economic implications of addiction" (Winston, 1980: 302).

Winston (1980) builds a model that reflects the fact that people "are often freighted with personal conflict as people find themselves 'of two minds', simultaneously wanting to consume something and to avoid it" (pp. 295–296). This model incorporates two characteristics of addictive commodities: "(1) a consumer's future choices are affected by current consumption of an addictive commodity (for worse or for better), and (2) controlling one's own consumption of an addictive commodity—regulating it or stopping it—is typically difficult involving personal conflict and inconsistent behavior" (p. 297). Winston extends the Stigler-Becker approach to harmful addiction so that "the consumption of addictive commodities reduces the human capital—skills and sensitivities—employed in the production of other commodities and not just, or even primarily, in the production of the addictive commodity itself" (p. 306). Winston modifies the assumption about constant consumer preferences, assuming that within a period of time the consumer flip-flops between two preference states: during a portion of time the consumer has one utility function, and during the rest of the time another, so the consumer is "of two minds."

The Winston model produces some plausible results and it explains several behavior patterns not explained by previous models. Winston (p. 314) lists the main implications of the model as: (1) "The addiction will typically begin and end—and maybe persist—sporadically, with consumption of the addictive commodity some of the time but not others; withdrawal from harmful addiction or sticking to beneficial consumption will often be difficult, it will be characterized by periodic conflict and temptation to backslide." Thus, age and experience have an influence on starting or stopping consumption. (2) "Harmfully addictive commodities will induce anti-markets and institutions to help consumers control their weakness of will as they try not to consume those commodities." (3) "Self-control can reduce consumer welfare; hedonistic inconsistency is better under some circumstances." (4) People play tricks on themselves to try to control addiction, that is, to force themselves to do things they ought to, and to keep from doing the things they ought to foreswear. (5) "Suppliers of addictive goods have incentives to systematically undermine consumers' efforts at self-control." (6) "Stable but non-constant preferences and awareness of one's place in time can also generate metapreferences" (preferences about one's preferences).

Barthold and Hochman (1988) criticize Winston's model for not explaining why or how people flip-flop from one preference state to the other and why there is addiction reversal. They argue there is a widespread consensus among psychologists about the fact that addicts are different from the majority of individuals, although they have not been able to pinpoint the factors that cause the differences. Still, their point is that the addicts' indifference curves might be convex at least for a range, which could lead to corner solutions or extreme seeking (compulsion). They argue that a minority of the population may have that characteristic, which combined with a Stigler-Becker time of capital accumulation (history), can lead to addiction. That is, compulsion can lead to addiction. The Barthold-Hochman model explains certain addict behavior patterns quite well. The model is also useful to understand the behavior of ex-alcoholics who tend to retain their extreme seeking characteristics in reverse. In the Barthold-Hochman model, lower prices play a role in increasing the addictive good demand, but prices are not good tools to reverse an addiction. "In sum, once a consumer moves to a corner, imbalance is best reversed through changes in tastes and nonprice constraints" (p. 101).

Michaels (1988) criticizes Barthold and Hochman's assumption that addict preferences are different from those of the majority of the population. He uses the consumption technology model of Lancaster (1966) and Becker (1965) and develops a parallel concept of addictive technologies. Michaels assumes a utility function in which the individual places a premium on maintenance of self-esteem, and generates verifiable patters of habituation, withdrawal, and the compulsive restarting of an abandoned habit, and argues that the frequent failure of medical treatment programs is the result of an unwarranted emphasis on deterring the addictive activity rather than on encouraging acceptable behavior.

The model assumes that consumer utility levels depend on self-esteem (S) and physiological pleasure (P). Goods consumed have one or both of those attributes, and the consumer uses them to produce S and P. The consumer converts these goods into their attributes using a "consumption technology." This allows the author to attribute the addiction to the characteristics of the individual's "consumption technology" instead of the utility function or preferences. While this difference might be of value to a theoretician, it is hard to see its policy importance.

The main characteristics of the Michaels model "include (1) the frequent restarting (or temptation to restart) of a once-broken addiction; (2) the commonly observed movement to close substitutes when an addictive good is in short supply; (3) the possibility of radical change in which a drug addict becomes, e.g., a religious fanatic; (4) a more complete description of the causes and consequences of painful withdrawal from an addiction; and (5) an explanation of the frequently-observed ineffectiveness of treatment programs that focus on the addictive good" (p. 75).

Becker and Murphy (1988) expand on the earlier Stigler-Becker model, and obtain some quite interesting results. They argue the consumer tries to maximize utility through his or her lifetime and assume the utility function is stable. They exploit two ideas: first, the utility produced by the consumption of many goods depends on past consumption levels; that is, the consumption of addictive goods is complementary through time. Second, accumulated past consumption produces "consumption capital" that depreciates through time at a rate that varies with the good and consumer in question. This model obtains results that show some apparently irrational behaviors of drug addicts are consistent with economic rationality, that is, with a consistent plan to maximize utility over time. For instance, Becker and Murphy shows that "other things the same, individuals who discount the future heavily are more likely to become addicted. The level of incomes, temporary stressful events that stimulate the demand for addictive goods, and the level and path of prices also affect the likelihood of becoming addicted" (p. 694). Furthermore, "permanent changes in prices of addictive goods may have a modest short-run effect on the consumption of addictive goods," but "the long-run demand for addictive goods tends to be more elastic than the demand for non-addictive goods," and "temporary changes in the price of an addictive good have smaller effects on current consumption than permanent changes" (p. 695). The key to these conclusions is that they question the belief in a long-term, low price elasticity of demand, and imply that in order to affect demand it is necessary to sustain a price increase and make it permanent. In other words, a campaign that raises the price of a PSAD only in the short run would not have a significant effect on long-term demand. This model also shows that rational behavior is consistent with consumption binges and "cold turkey" attempts as a way to get away from addiction.

As shown, economic models have made significant advances in explaining many of the behavior patterns associated with addiction. These models are still limited and perhaps disappointing. They do not pretend to provide a comprehensive answer to society's addiction troubles, but their contributions to policy formulation have increased with each new model, even though at times these appear to be contradictory. For instance, Becker and Murphy conclude that long-term price increases do have an important effect on demand, while Barthold and Hochman conclude the opposite. However, the contradictions can be solved if one looks at the assumptions of each model. Barthold and Hochman assume addicts are extreme seekers, while Becker and Murphy do not make any specific assumption about the characteristics of consumer preferences. Thus, it may be concluded that if there is a group of addicts that are extreme seekers, they are not likely to respond significantly to long-term PSAD price increases, while addicts that are not extreme seekers will respond more to those price increases.

Another important contribution of these models is that they formally address the complexity of addiction issues, and their limited policy contributions illustrates the overall lack of knowledge on the subject, as well as the limit of policy statements that can be made without jumping to value-laden recommendations that are likely to fail.

Perhaps a primary contribution of these models is that they show most addictive behavior can be consistent with economic rationality, and that there is no need to appeal to irrationality or mental illness to explain it. Thus, the results provided by economic models reinforce the view that a substantial part of the addictive problems are behavioral, that many addictions are not illnesses, and many addicts are not sick.[2]

Some limitations of these models arise from their failure to incorporate some relevant behavior patterns and social structures. In particular, the consumer models assume the amount of goods the consumer can buy during a lifetime is limited by income constraint. Thus, they cover only "good" addicts who do not appeal to illegal means for funds to support their addiction. Another problem arises from the fact that they look at consumers interchangeably as individuals or households, but do not look at the distribution of addiction costs and benefits within the household. Since some negative externalities of addictive behavior affect members of an addict's household, these models do not contribute policy recommendations in this regard. Also, the theoretical models say very little, if anything, about the large changes that characterize market demand for many addictive substances, since their main focus has been on explaining complex individual consumer behavioral patters as rational economic behavior, yet they do not deal with the social, psychological, and other causes of demand changes.

Since economics leaves us wanting, it is useful to look for stronger answers in psychology, where perhaps deeper insights into the causes of PSAD demand may be found. Here again, however, one fails to find definite answers as psychologists have a myriad of theories but have not developed a consensus about the causes of PSAD consumption. Still, it is useful to look at what they have to say about the demand for PSAD, particularly because many of the addiction surveys and data have been highly influenced by them.

Lettieri (1978) presents a short and useful survey of the theories of drug abuse that illustrates their great diversity. He also notes there are significant differences "of opinion as to distinctions between drug use, drug abuse, drug dependency, and drug addiction" (Lettieri, 1978: 31). Lettieri classifies theories in four categories: psychological theories, based on one's relation to oneself; social psychological theories, based on one's relation to others; sociological theories, based on the individual's relation to society; and naturistic theories, based on a person's relation to nature.

The causes of drug use, abuse, dependency, and addiction posited by these theories are many and varied. They may have to do with an individual's genes and personality; the characteristics of the mother, father, and family, and the relationship the person has with them; the individual's standing in the society; society's tolerance towards deviant behavior and drug use; the strength of natural drives to use PSAD, which may depend on each individual's genes; and many other factors. Some factors considered to be drug-use facilitators are: a person's lack of self-esteem, a weak sense of belonging to a group, weak relationships with the community, low quality of family relations, low social status, failed expectations of social and personal achievements, and social tolerance of deviant behavior. Conversely, some social institutions that act as protective factors are: strong extended and nuclear families, strong religious practices, strong traditions, individual self-esteem, and a strong sense of belonging to a larger entity such as a nation or the military.

Psychologists accept that the main goal of those who use PSAD is to alter their state of mind and their perception of reality, so theories try to posit the reasons that individuals want to do it. Since PSAD effects vary (drugs can be narcotic, stimulant, depressant, hallucinogenic, can have combined effects, and so on) the demand for different drugs is expected to be associated with different reasons that individuals want them. In other words, some factors are likely to result in increased demand for a particular drug but not another.

These works have a much stronger empirical content than those of economics. They have found that different variables are associated with different stages of PSAD use: initiation, continuation, cessation, and relapse. They have also found that the variables that influence the relationship between the use of one PSAD and other drugs (the tendency toward multi-drug use) also vary depending on the drugs in question.

Psychologists agree the use of PSAD is a universal phenomenon that extends even beyond the human race into the animal kingdom (Siegel, 1989).[3] This has led some analysts to argue that "the desire to alter consciousness periodically is an innate normal drive analogous to hunger or the sexual drive" (Lettieri, 1978: 44). Siegel (1989) supports this view, and shows in great detail that all societies have used PSAD, and that when confronted with PSAD epidemics, in the long run they have devised methods and regulations that allow PSAD consumption within socially tolerable levels. Thus, they have "tamed" the drugs. Societies achieve this in several ways: they ceremonialize the use of PSAD, control its use through social pressures, and appeal to other methods like social shunning and legal punishments. These social controls implicitly accept the fact that people will use PSAD, do not seek to completely eliminate their use, and aim only to control and limit it. When a society experiences substantial social changes, some of these controls may be lost or weakened, and the use of PSAD tends to increase beyond tolerable levels, a process that results in a search for new social ways to control their use.

It must be stressed that psychological works do *not* establish causality in a formal sense, but associations between addiction and some independent variables. For example, it is clear that not all individuals characterized by having a particular gene, a dysfunctional family, growing up in a bad neighborhood, having low self-esteem, and so on, become addicts. The fact that these theories do not establish causality is extremely important for policy purposes because it remains unclear whether PSAD addiction is a disease or a behavioral problem,[4] and which policies might have a significant effect on consumption levels.

Psychologists disagree about the ranking and interactions of the variables that influence drug use, but their theories do contribute to understanding the nature of demand for PSAD, and they allow for the formulation of a relatively simple model. The probabilities[5] that an individual tries drugs, becomes a regular user and then an addict, ceases to use a PSAD and then relapses, depend on (besides price and individual income) psychological and genetic make up, on the quality and quantity of inputs used in upbringing, on relations with the family and others in society, on the person's relative position in society, on the social control mechanisms in existence at the time, and on the characteristics of each individual drug. As expected with multi-causal phenomena, psychologists disagree on the relative causal importance of each factor and their interrelations, an issue that eventually should be settled empirically. Still, there is a consensus that the probabilities mentioned depend broadly on the listed variables.[6]

In spite of its lack of specificity, this simple model has important implications for the study of PSAD demand and government policies toward it. First, since the gene pool and distribution of individual personalities do not change significantly from one generation to the next, the explanations of major changes in a society's use of PSAD must be based on social changes. In other words, gene- and personality-based theories can explain why a particular individual is more vulnerable than others to drug use and abuse, but they cannot explain why the consumption of a particular drug becomes widespread in a country at a particular time, and why this consumption subsides. To explain these demand changes one should then search for changes in the society's facilitator and protective factors. Second, the social characteristics of each group within a society determine its degree of vulnerability and the chances of its members becoming addicts. Thus, the model predicts the concentration of drug addiction in social groups with characteristics that increase their vulnerability.

The psychological model also implies, first, that policies designed to raise the price of PSAD are unlikely to have a major impact on widespread drug use unless accompanied by other measures to confront the causes of PSAD addiction. Such changes in consumption that take place over time are primarily related to societal factors, not price changes, so a drug epidemic cannot be attacked by simply raising prices and the risk and consumption costs of a drug, since doing so will not do away with the underlying PSAD demand causes. Second, any strategy to control PSAD addiction should identify the most vulnerable social groups and the variables that determine their vulnerability. Once identified, the group should be targeted with policies that have an impact on relevant social variables. Third, the most effective drug control policies should be derived from the understanding of the factors that determine drug use and abuse. Criminalization of PSAD use and trade is not necessarily the most cost-effective policy to lower drug use, and indeed, these policies can be used by the government to avoid the need to cope with the social causes of PSAD consumption increases. It is easier to pass judgment on drug users and traffickers than to correct the source of the problem. This does not imply that criminalization and law enforcement have no impact on PSAD consumption; it only says that such a policy is unlikely to be the best way to control that consumption.

Since these policy implications are vague, it is necessary to know much more to design an effective policy. Indeed, the identification of the variables that make a group vulnerable, and the way they interact with each other, is an extremely complex task about which little is known. Recent experiences with "Therapeutic Community" approaches to drug treatment, based on creating community support groups to increase the sense of self-esteem and belonging, have proven substantially more successful than traditional medical treatments (Mullen and Arbiter, 1992). These experiences indicate that positive results can be achieved despite a lack of knowledge about the interaction among facilitating and blocking addiction factors.

Some economists have recently borrowed the psychological framework, and have tested some of these theories. Sickles and Taubman (1991) find that in the United States the probability of use or addiction to marijuana and cocaine is affected by race, religious affiliation, and other socio-demographic variables that support the general psychological model.

The "Black and Gray Boxes"

One problem with evaluating the demand for PSAD and to formulate reasonable policies lies in the substantial lack of knowledge about the subject. There is great ignorance about the level of legal and illegal PSAD consumption and addiction in the United States, Colombia, and the rest of the world, and about many important demand-related relationships. The available data are weak, highly uncertain, and even speculative and inconsistent.[7] Therefore, our knowledge about demand is full of gaps ("black boxes") and partial data that may be interpreted in various ways, resulting in "gray boxes." It is useful to consider some of those.

Consider first price elasticity of demand. A good estimate of price elasticity is extremely important to determine the impact of price changes on drug consumption. The theoretical economic models discussed above posit that price elasticity can vary depending on whether consumers are extreme seekers, and on the time frame, such that demand price elasticity is expected to be higher in the long run than in the short run.

Becker, Grossman, and Murphy (1991) summarize the evidence about short-run and long-run price elasticity for alcohol and tobacco and cautiously confirm the predictions of the Becker-Murphy model. Miron and Zwiebel (1991) support this finding. They carefully evaluate the impact of Prohibition on alcohol consumption in the United States, and find that "alcohol consumption fell sharply at the beginning of Prohibition, to approximately 30 percent of its pre-Prohibition level. During the next several years, however, alcohol consumption increased sharply, to about 60 to 70 percent of its pre-Prohibition level. The level of consumption remained virtually the same immediately after Prohibition as during the later part of Prohibition, although consumption increased to approximately its pre-Prohibition level during the subsequent decade" (p. 242).

It must be noted that market price elasticities measure the total response of the quantity demanded to price changes, but do not indicate if the number of users changes, or the amount consumed by each one changes. Thus, even if one gets a good elasticity measure, it is not a good measure of demand response for some purposes.

Recent evidence about cocaine consumption changes in the United States is quite contradictory. During the 1980s the price of cocaine dropped dramatically. Simultaneously, consumption by casual middle- and upper-class users declined sharply, but consumption by lower-class users increased sharply (Falco, 1992; Reuter, 1992b). This paradox indicates there are many nonprice variables that determine demand, and that one cannot easily predict what would actually happen if a substantial change in policy would lower cocaine prices. Kleiman (1992) argues there is no evidence that a dramatic fall in cocaine price associated with a decriminalization policy would not increase consumption sharply. Nadelmann (1992) argues that on the contrary, the demand for PSAD is already concentrated in the vulnerable groups in inner-city ghettos, while middle- and upper-class users are reacting to better information about the effects and declining social tolerance of cocaine consumption, and thus, a decriminalization or liberalization policy would not lead to a significantly higher number of users. This conclusion is supported by other interesting arguments. For instance, Mishan (1990) points out that in a liberalized, but controlled, market the number of pushers and their efforts to gain new addicts would decline sharply. The amount of free samples given to junior high students to hook them would decline, and the number of users might actually decline. In spite of these research efforts, the fact is that one cannot make a good forecast about quantity demanded in response to a change in policy.

Risks of addiction vary substantially among PSAD. Most non-economists implicitly define addiction as a situation in which the individual consumer "loses" the ability to decide what to consume, and becomes a compulsive user. The incidence of this type of behavior varies substantially among drugs, but in all cases most users do not become addicted.[8] Indeed, many recreational users of even the most feared drugs can do so for a long time without significant social costs, in a way similar to that of many social alcohol drinkers. Many who become compulsive users begin consuming small quantities and increase consumption in stages. However, most users do not go through this process, that is, they remain at low levels of consumption.

The effects of PSAD consumption on consumers' bodies vary significantly. The short-run effects of alcohol can be devastating when they lead to drunk driving, sexual abuse, and violence. On the other hand, marijuana use does not lead to violence, and cocaine use might actually enhance work performance. However, there are wide knowledge gaps about long-term effects of use and addiction to PSAD. For instance, it has taken over twenty years for the U.S. government to determine that cigarette smoking and second-hand smoke are important causes of cancer. Even now, there are those who argue that the studies on which the government based these conclusions are flawed. One of the most dramatic effects of illegal cocaine use has been the effect of crack cocaine on pregnant women and their unborn. Pictures of crack babies have been presented as one of the strongest pieces of evidence to prove the evil nature of cocaine addiction. There is no doubt that crack babies are innocent victims, and that the social costs caused by their mothers' addiction are great. Nevertheless, recent data show that the long-term effects on crack babies are not necessarily high (Reuter, 1992b). It is thus not surprising that various authors arrive at contradictory conclusions about the social costs of cocaine liberalization.[9]

Contradictory conclusions aside, there is consensus about the differences in PSAD affects on casual or social users and on addicts. Indeed, the negative private and social costs of casual use of most PSAD do not appear to be major. This suggests that drug policies should differentiate between heavy and light users. However, the process by which a casual or light user becomes an addict is not well understood. Consumption of various PSAD have different effects, and produce various types of "highs" and "lows." Some PSAD have legitimate medicinal uses, and others don't.[10] The effects of some are subtle, and those of others are quite obvious. Some drugs produce one effect, others a combination, i.e., a euphoric "high" followed by a depressing "low." The wide range of PSAD effects raises questions about whether drugs are good substitutes for each other (Reuter, 1992a).

Statistical evidence about substitutability and complementarity is weak. This poses many policy problems because important questions may not be answered including, among others, whether cutting the supply of one PSAD would lead to an increased demand for another; whether lowering the price of cocaine would lead to a decline in the use of crack and lower overall social costs; and whether an increase in the use of a drug would lead to increases in the use of others. For instance, is the decline in marijuana use among U.S. high school seniors during the last ten years related to their sharp increase in alcohol consumption? The fact is that here we have another "black box."

There are also great knowledge gaps about the effects of drug addiction treatments. Medical drug addiction treatment is advocated frequently as a solution to drug addiction problems, but evaluations of various programs fail to find systematic evidence that rigorous treatments produce better results than self-help programs, and environmental factors predict success better than the type of treatment (Fingarette, 1988).[11] Bohanon (1991) develops a simple economic explanation for it: "This paper offers a simple cost-benefit argument explaining how treatment can interfere with certain natural processes conducive to permanently abandoning an addiction. The paper argues that a stable remission from addiction depends on the historic costs of the addiction relative to the historic benefits as perceived by the user. Because treatment intrinsically mitigates the cost of addiction but does not directly influence the benefits of addiction, treatment can make returning to addiction more likely" (Bohanon, 1991: 116).

Experiments with relatively long non-medical treatments that focus on helping addicts live in a community, and increasing their self-esteem and communal ties, have been relatively successful (Mullen and Arbiter, 1992). These programs do not treat addiction as an illness, but as a behavioral problem that can be solved by increasing the individual's self-esteem, personal responsibility, and stake in the community.

The medical profession, however, considers PSAD addiction a disease. Defining addictions as illnesses has important policy implications because it conditions the social attitude toward drug addicts and the policies that are eventually implemented. There is no doubt that the medical profession has an interest in broadening the coverage of what is defined as a disease. There are groups that adjust their interpretation of the evidence to retain the "disease" terminology to increase their own social role, status, and income. "We now read that 'of course alcoholism is an illness that consists of not just one but many diseases, having different forms and causes.' We also hear—in pronouncements addressed to more knowledgeable audiences—that alcoholism is a disease with biological, psychological, social, cultural, economic, and even spiritual dimensions, all of them important. This is startling amplification of the meaning of 'disease,' to the point where it can refer to *any* human problem" (Fingarette, 1988: 17–18). Indeed, there has been a tendency in the United States during the last few decades to define as a disease any condition that makes a person not feel well. By this broad definition, life itself would be an illness since everybody has to face times when he or she does not feel well.

Aside from what the medical profession says, addiction is not a disease in the traditional sense. Genetic causes once thought relevant are now considered highly questionable;[12] if addiction is left untreated, it does not progress in the way in which a normal illness does; and in the case of many PSAD, using them under different settings produces vastly different results in the same person.[13] Independent of treatment, a percentage of drug addicts stop using on their own at a particular time in their lives; that is, they "mature out" of the drug.

The debate about whether addiction is an illness or a behavioral problem is also important from the point of view of individual responsibility. If an illness, it is much easier to view drug users as victims who have no choice but to become addicts. If a behavioral problem, one can explain that various social ills increase the temptation to become a drug user, without necessarily condoning such behavior. Regardless of the moral issues involved, how addiction is defined affects the policy agenda, as well as the allocation of resources for treatment prevention, education, and repression. Unfortunately, there are interest groups that benefit with each definition, and this biases their position. The "caring" establishment is a group that benefits from PSAD illegality and from making individuals irresponsible for their actions, and they are likely to contribute to addiction inasmuch as they lower the costs of addiction.[14]

Another "gray box" is evident in the relationship between drug consumption and criminal or violent behaviors. There is no doubt that in the United States many criminals use drugs. A substantial proportion of those arrested are drug users (Nadelmann, 1988b and 1989b; Reuter, 1992b). Similarly, a large proportion are arrested on drug charges, mainly dealing. And a large proportion of crimes against property are committed by either users or dealers of illegal drugs (Mishan, 1990). These data may be impressive but they do raise causality questions. The main issue is to what extent crime is generated by PSAD consumption and to what extent by illegality. If one accepts there are not many individuals committing crimes against property to buy legal PSAD, and that most of the crimes that are committed are "systemic" (i.e., due to illegality), then the causality goes from illegality to crime, not the other way around. The only possible counterargument is one that claims PSAD drugs *must* be illegal for moral reasons, so there is no separation between illegality and drugs as causes of crime.

Benson and Rasmussen (1991), in an econometric study of South Florida, researched the relationship between illegal drug addiction and increases in property crime. Their findings show another element that adds to the complexity of the relationship: the increase in property crime is explained indirectly by the illegal nature of the drug market that required the diversion of scarce police resources and lowered the risks of property theft.[15]

The violence associated with PSAD consumption can be classified in three categories: "psychopharmacological," which results from direct drug affects on human behavior and takes place while the user is under the influence; "economic compulsive," which arises from the continuous need the addict has to obtain resources to consume; and "systemic," which is caused by the systems in which drugs are regulated, produced, traded, and consumed. Most drug-associated violence is systemic. Interestingly, the effect of various drugs on violent behavior differs significantly and one drug that contributes most to psychopharmacological violence is alcohol, which is a main cause of family violence, child abuse, and other violent crimes. On the other hand, some illegal drugs like marijuana tend to have the opposite effect.

Psychoactive Drug Addiction in Colombia

The theories of addiction and the model discussed above predict a high level of PSAD use in Colombia, since the country's development strengthened many facilitating factors while weakening the protective ones. The country's social inequality and institutions that excluded large segments of the population from political empowerment, growing regime delegitimation, rapid urbanization and large migrations, the high level of violence, dramatic changes in the role of women in society, and the weakening of the Catholic Church's influence are all factors that increased tolerance for deviant behavior, weakened the nuclear and extended family, weakened social solidarity and cohesion ties, and lowered government law enforcement capabilities. These are, in turn, all factors that contribute to raising the probability that an individual will try and use PSAD. The population age structure, heavily youth-skewed, is a further factor expected to contribute to high PSAD use.

Not surprisingly, as discussed in Chapter 3, there is a long history of PSAD use in Colombia. PSAD use has been socially accepted and frequently encouraged by government policies since, for a long time, taxes on PSAD consumption provided one of the main sources of government revenue.[16] However, while there are multiple references to social problems caused by PSAD consumption, particularly alcoholic beverages, studies about addiction are few and very recent.

Alcohol consumption was traditionally seen as a problem mainly of the lower classes, whose males are perceived as having had a tradition of spending their wages first on chicha, and later on beer, in detriment to their families. Illegal PSAD consumption until the early 1970s was relatively confined to marginal social groups and a few eccentrics. Therefore, the illegal PSAD consumption was not perceived as a threat to the establishment and it was not considered a problem. For instance, Caro de Casas (1988) argues that in the 1960s marijuana consumption increased, but its growth was associated mainly with the development of the local hippie and *nadaista* movements, and no data were found about that phenomenon. By the early 1970s the consumption of PSAD (mainly marijuana) had risen along with concerns about it—to the point that in June 1972 the First National Symposium on Substance Dependency took place, where the first empirical study on the subject was presented (Prieto, 1988). This study was based on a sample taken in Medellín, and found that 31.5 percent of its residents were heavy users of cigarettes, 8.1 percent of alcohol, 5 percent of marijuana, 2.7 percent of tranquilizers, and 1.9 percent of narcotics, LSD, solvents, mushrooms, and other drugs. However, the data did not permit determining what percentage of the residents were multiple drug users. Apparently, the concern about the growing use of PSAD led to other studies that confirmed the heavy PSAD use (Prieto, 1988: 69).

During the 1980s the use of PSAD increased, particularly of bazuco. It was apparently not easy at first for the government and society to accept that there was a problem (Pérez, 1988). However, by 1986 there were reports about 435 locations in which bazuco was sold in Medellín, and 513 in Bogotá; drugs also began to be combined and consumed in different forms and addiction to multiple illegal PSAD began to be clearly identified, particularly among bazuco users (Pérez, 1988). While there were clear signs of a growing illegal drug abuse problem, it was not possible to establish at the time the extent of the phenomenon.

One policy response to the growing PSAD addiction was to tighten applicable laws, and in January 1986 a new statute on illegal PSAD was enacted (Law 30 of 1986). The main features of this law are: it banned production and marketing of many substances; regulated the trade in chemical precursors and some plant seeds; established drug education programs in the schools; required higher education institutions to establish free chemical dependency centers; regulated the sale of alcohol and cigarettes; and defined many illegal PSAD business crimes and established harsher penalties, both pecuniary and jail sentences.

Greater PSAD addiction also induced some government branches to establish programs to control it. These have developed at the municipal level in most of the largest cities. The main approach followed by these is "integral" and focuses on the most vulnerable groups in society. While social workers' opinions suggest these programs are relatively successful, there are no evaluations of their overall impact on drug addiction levels, partly because they are relatively new.

There have been a few recent surveys that provide an indication of the magnitude and profile of drug abuse in Colombia. Torres de Galvis and Murrelle (1987) used a 1,400-person sample of the four largest cities stratified by age, sex, marital status, education level, and social class in a study that provides a good profile of PSAD addiction. Unfortunately, this study provides a great amount of data but very little interpretation. Perhaps the most remarkable result of the study is that it shows the widespread prevalence and extreme importance of alcoholism and alcohol abuse, which is unquestionably the main drug addiction problem in Colombia. Alcohol consumption is widespread and socially acceptable; however, the large numbers of frequent users in relatively large quantities is remarkable. Applying a modified Michigan test (MAST), which is accepted as an international standard, this study found that 13.8 percent of the men and 2.2 percent of the women ages 12–64 were alcoholics, and that another 12.1 and 2.4 percent (respectively) were at high risk of becoming alcoholics. For the population at large, these figures were 8 percent and 7.3 percent. However, in several developed countries, people in these two categories are classified as alcoholics. Accordingly, about one-fourth of the adult male population in the four largest cities may be classified as alcoholic! This percentage is particularly high in the 20 to 49 age groups, in which about 34 percent of the males are in that category.

The use of other legal PSAD is also widespread in the country. Cigarettes are regularly consumed by about 30 percent of the people interviewed, and tranquilizers by about 6 percent. The consumption pattern of tranquilizers differs from that of other PSAD in two ways: it continuously increases with age and it is the only PSAD for which the proportion of women that consume it is higher than that of men. Indeed, sex is one of the main determinants of the probability to become an addict in Colombia and drug addiction is preponderantly a male problem.

Among illegal PSAD, marijuana was the one most commonly used. It was used by about 1.1 percent of the population, and there were 6.3 men for each female user. Bazuco was consumed by 0.6 percent of the population and by three men for each woman. Cocaine was used only by 0.3 percent, and it had the same ratio of three men to one woman.

The survey also indicates that PSAD consumption varies by region, age, social class, and sex. Bazuco consumption is higher in Cali and Medellín, and among lower-class individuals; marijuana and cocaine tend to be upper-class drugs. Cocaine use in the Caribbean coast port of Barranquilla is more widespread than in the rest of the country. Alcoholism is a problem in all social classes, although it is greater for male slum dwellers and for the residents of the central mountainous region. Another main determinant of the level of addiction for all PSAD was family structure: belonging to a complete nuclear family significantly lowered the probability of all types of drug addiction.

The survey also considered the prevalence of severe clinical depression and suicide attempts, and found both to be significantly related to unemployment. A strong relationship was also found between bazuco and marijuana consumption and suicide attempts. Another, perhaps obviously, strong link was found between alcoholism and automobile accidents during the year prior to the interview.

It is interesting to note that the consumption of other illegal PSAD (such as LSD and mushrooms) that had been used in the 1970s appeared to have declined considerably, and were not seen as important enough to be included in the Torres de Galvis and Murrelle survey. Similarly noticeable was the exclusion of glue sniffing and other inhalants, since there are abundant reports of their use among certain groups of the population, particularly street urchins.[17]

While Torres de Galvis and Murrelle do not go far in interpreting their results, they do appear to be consistent with the model posited above based on the psychological theories of drug addiction. In particular, the importance of the nuclear family supports the notion of strong social ties and sense of belonging; and the cocaine consumption concentration in the upper class is expected since cocaine is a stimulant and not used to escape reality, which is one effect of the lower-class-consumed bazuco. The higher prevalence of tranquilizer consumption among women is consistent with the traditional subservient position of women in society and pressure for them to tolerate the inequities and abuses imposed by social norms. Similarly, the particularly high consumption of alcohol and bazuco among the lower-class males is in part a reflection of their machismo and their feelings of inadequacy. The decline of the use of LSD and other hallucinogens is related to the fall in popularity of the hippie and nadaist cultures in Colombia.

A more recent, less detailed study of drug addiction in Bogotá (Alcaldía Mayor de Bogotá, D. E., 1989) confirms the main findings of the Torres de Galvis and Murrelle survey. This study was used to establish an integral addiction prevention program that emphasizes the importance of self-esteem and social relations of the individuals.

Risks of Drug Addiction Epidemics and Conclusion

Based on the few available surveys, and on interviews with some key Colombian experts,[18] it is clear that Colombia has an alcohol epidemic. However, the high level of alcohol consumption is socially accepted. A group of health officials consider alcohol abuse as the main health problem of the country, but it is not a main social policy issue, perhaps because the high level of violence and the country's political and economic problems loom in the eyes of most individuals as greater problems that take precedence in government policy priorities. The experts interviewed concur that alcohol is a drug that complements some of the traits of Colombian society. It is a social mediator whose use has been ritualized to express friendship and promote social interaction.

Cigarette smoking is also seen as a health problem. The use of tobacco has been widespread, but it appears to be declining among the younger generation. It is likely that its decline is linked to increased environmental concerns among the young. Cigarette smoking is also quite high among women, although not as high as among men. However, it is believed that cigarette smoking among women had been increasing until very recently since it became a symbol of their liberation.

Health officials see the use of both alcohol and tobacco as big health problems, and are pressuring the government to adopt some of the restrictions on advertising and labeling that exist in the United States. It should also be noted that in the last thirty years there has been a profound change in the demand for tobacco in Colombia—away from the dark Colombian tobacco and toward the light Virginia varieties—so that imported cigarettes as a proportion of the total consumed has increased drastically. During this period American cigarettes became one of the most important and the most conspicuous contraband import, a fact used by some left-leaning authors as evidence that the United States government applies a double moral standard in dealing with PSAD and that its antinarcotics policies are basically a form of protectionism (Del Olmo, 1988). Given the widespread cigarette consumption, there is no doubt the Winston-Salem "cartel" poses a greater threat to the health of Colombians than the Medellín and Cali ones.

Among the illegal PSAD consumed, bazuco is seen as the main problem. Of all PSAD, bazuco is the one that is more frequently associated with polyaddiction.[19] Bazuco is seen as a problem because it is highly addictive, and because it is linked with violence, criminality, and problems at work and at home. Bazuco consumption is a social clandestine activity in the slums, and is closely associated with violence and the sicario industry. However, bazuco consumption is not widespread and it is concentrated in clearly identified social groups —mainly young, very poor urban dwellers and perhaps some rich young people associated with the illegal PSAD trade.

Health officials and researchers interviewed concur that cocaine is consumed, but it is not an epidemiological problem. They claim that cocaine is consumed in Colombia for reasons very different from those in the United States. They argue that cocaine is a very appropriate drug for the United States because it is a stimulant that makes consumers feel empowered, and allows them to work more, very suitable characteristics in a highly competitive, fast-paced society that values individual assertiveness and individuality. In Colombia cocaine is consumed more as a social drug in conjunction with alcohol. Frequently, the main purpose of cocaine is to mitigate some of the undesired effects of alcohol, and to allow the user to continue consuming alcohol, or to make it easier to drive a car. No doubt both of these uses can be very dangerous, but there is still a consensus among the health officials interviewed that the nature of cocaine consumption in Colombia, and the characteristics of that society, make it unlikely that a cocaine epidemic will develop in the future. The price of cocaine in Colombia is relatively low. During the fall of 1991 Bogotá's health officials estimated the retail price of 70 percent pure cocaine at about U.S. $3 per gram. Since it is unlikely that this price will fall significantly, the demand for cocaine is not expected to rise in the future as a result of price declines.

Although these opinions are impressionistic, the relatively low risk of the development of a cocaine epidemic is also supported by a recent study by Estupiñán and Torres de Galvis (1990), based on very detailed interviews with 7,165 urban residents in the 15 to 59 year age bracket. These authors built a risk index for each person interviewed and for each kind of PSAD. The results indicate that about 8.5 percent of the population face a "high risk" of becoming marijuana users, 4.3 percent of becoming bazuco users, and 2.7 percent of becoming cocaine users.

Another point to be made is that in spite of the obvious importance of the addiction to some PSAD, particularly alcohol, PSAD addiction is not one of the main policy issues in Colombia. The country faces many other problems that are perceived as more pressing and important than PSAD addiction, and cocaine addiction is not presently seen as posing a grave problem or as having the potential to become one in the foreseeable future.

The available data strongly support the conviction of Colombian health officials that the main PSAD addiction problems are alcohol and cigarette consumption, where there is more room to achieve significant health improvements, and where the mechanisms to achieve them are not likely to contribute to the high level of violence prevailing in the country.

Notes

1. For instance, the 97 percent failure rate in the treatment of American heroin addicts led to dire predictions about the impact of the return of Vietnam

War veterans since their addiction rate was quite high; however, 90 percent of the Vietnam-veteran addicts stopped when they returned (Zinberg, 1972).

2. See for example Fingarette's (1988) essay on alcohol addiction.

3. Interestingly, Siegel (1989) shows that animal societies also develop controls to the use of PSAD, and that some of the social characteristics that make a human vulnerable to becoming a drug addict, also make some animals vulnerable. For instance, when cocaine was offered to a rat colony, the lower status rats at the bottom of the social structure, who presumably have lower self-esteem, were significantly more likely to become addicted.

4. Indeed, in the case of alcoholism, Fingarette (1988: 4) points out: "yet this much is unambiguous and incontrovertible: the public has been kept unaware of a mass of scientific evidence accumulated over the past couple of decades, evidence familiar to researchers in the field, which radically challenges each major belief generally associated in the public mind with the phrase, 'alcoholism is a disease.'"

5. The use of probabilities supports the idea that there is an association among variables and not a definite causality.

6. Although empirical research has questioned some of them, such as genetic contribution to alcoholism.

7. For instance, looking at addiction references for the United States, one finds that Bagley (1988) states there are 20 to 25 million marijuana smokers; Van Wert (1988) argues that more than 25 million Americans buy and use illegal drugs; while Siegel (1989: 298) says that the United States "supplies 27 percent of the needs of the 64 million marijuana users." To put these figures into perspective, given the age structure of the American population (Bogue, 1985), the 20 million figure implies that one in six Americans in the 13 to 50 year bracket is a marijuana user, while the 64 million figure implies that one in two is a user.

8. In the case of "crack," believed to be among the most addictive drugs, Kleiman and Saiger (1990) report that studies in New York City estimate that one in six users becomes a compulsive user.

9. Kleiman and Saiger (1990), and Jacobs (1990) believe they are negative enough to make decriminalization unadvisable, while Nadelmann (1988b, 1989b) believes that they are not high enough to support that conclusion.

10. At least within Western medical tradition.

11. Fingarette's (1988) work is focused on alcoholism, but Clague (1973) finds the same treatment ineffectiveness in the case of heroin addiction.

12. For instance, Fingarette's (1988) detailed study of alcoholism shows there is no evidence that it has genetic causes. In the United States 17 percent of the children of alcoholics grow up to become alcoholics, while that percentage is only 5 percent for the total population. However, since there is no gene yet identified as "causing" alcoholism, the statistical difference may still be explained by social settings and other factors. Fingarette (1988) points out that this same evidence may be interpreted as showing that 83 percent of the children of alcoholics *do not* become alcoholics.

13. "The point is that it is precisely settings, circumstances, and motivations that are the crucial influences on how alcoholics choose to drink" (Fingarette, 1988: 16). Double-blind tests also show that "what the alcoholics *believed* was in the beverage did make a difference—in fact, all the difference" (p. 17).

14. "Drug-addicts, too, effectively enjoy compassion-endowed rights to prey on the tax-paying public. . . . The 'caring' fraternity would, of course, regard it as bad form to point out that the kind of victim whose cause they ardently commend to the public has in fact no one but himself to blame; that it is he who chooses to expose himself to well-known risks. Rather than acknowledge his culpability, they prefer to believe that he is a hapless victim of circumstances over which he has little control" (Mishan, 1990: 450).

15. "The increased effort to control drug markets has been accompanied by increasing property crime. The fact is that law enforcement resources are scarce, and many resources now being devoted to enforcing drug laws have been shifted away from enforcing laws pertaining to other crimes. This has reduced deterrence for property crime and, as a result, such crime has increased" (Benson and Rasmussen, 1991: 106).

16. During the postwar period "sin taxes" and "sin production" have been a main source of departmental revenues, since the departmental governments have had hard liquor–production monopolies and run lotteries. The financial dependency of departmental governments on "sinful" activities is consistent with the popular Colombian dictum that "who sins and prays, ties," that is, a bad deed can be compensated by a good one.

17. It is curious to note that the Colombian lexicon has adapted the anglicism *esnifiar*.

18. To clarify the drug abuse picture, and to try to determine the risks of drug addiction epidemics, interviews were conducted in September 1991 with Dr. Fernando Yepes, the coordinator of the 1990 health sector study elaborated by the Health Ministry, and with Dr. Carlos A. Carvajal, the General Coordinator of the Integral Prevention Unit of the Municipality of Bogotá, and three members of his staff: Ms. María Elsa Pulido, Ms. María Cecilia Castro, and Mr. Alvaro Rodríguez.

19. Pérez (1988: 99) shows that among drug addicts treated in La Casa, the Universidad de Los Andes drug rehabilitation program, 80.5 percent of the polyaddicts consume bazuco.

... 10 ...
Drug Policy Alternatives for Colombia

Two opposite rationales can be used to formulate PSAD policies: a moralistic and a pragmatic one. Under the moralistic rationale, policies are derived from a religious or philosophical structure which attempts to persuade people to adopt social behavior consistent with it. This approach is common even to people who may have opposing views, for example libertarians who advocate total freedom of the PSAD market, and religious fundamentalists who argue for criminalization of drug-taking on moral or religious grounds. Current drug policies that ban and criminalize most PSAD production and consumption have been highly influenced by religiously based moral arguments.

The pragmatic rationale seeks policies that keep social and economic costs of drug use and abuse at socially tolerable levels but without attempting to make social behavior consistent with any religious or philosophical norms. This approach requires one to understand the causes of consumption, productive structure and market of PSAD, and the capacity of the involved governments to formulate, implement and sustain each policy. Those who follow this approach do not have an a priori preference for a particular policy; they recommend those which, in their view, minimize social costs.

In practice, policies are also affected by other factors that are not explicitly recognized in policy formulation debates. The knowledge gaps and fears of the effects of many drugs combine to encourage repressive policies. Also, each policy has and generates a constituency that benefits from it and has an interest in having the policy formulated and sustained. Policy constituencies tend to become entrenched when policies have been in effect for several years; this can be one of the main obstacles to policy change.

The effectiveness of moral-based policies is constrained by economic forces: consumers who enjoy the product, and entrepreneurs who want to maximize profits. The degree of success of moral-based policies depends also on the existence of a wide normative consensus in the society about imposing social and moral constraints on individuals, and/or on a strong, authoritarian government that believes in those constraints and is willing to impose policies on society that sacrifice individual freedoms. In other words, moral-based policies can work in very authoritarian states, or very normatively cohesive societies.

The approach taken here is pragmatic. Thus to evaluate market and nonmarket policies it is necessary to understand the demand, supply, and market of PSAD, the nature and strength of social constraints to production and consumption, and government law-enforcement capabilities. Since cocaine constitutes the main illegal PSAD associated with Colombia, most of the specific references made in the rest of this chapter deal with that substance.

Policy Implications of the PSAD Market

Implications of Theoretical Economic Models

Economic models of addiction do not contribute much to policy recommendations, but they make important points. First, addiction per se is neither good nor bad; nor is it a problem that merits government intervention. Addictive behavior creates social problems when it generates large external negative effects. In this sense addiction problems should be treated in ways similar to pollution in which "market failure" justifies the possibility of government intervention. However, proving that optimal government intervention would increase social welfare does not guarantee a particular government will intervene in that fashion, since "government failure" may be as frequent as "market failure." Economic policy formulation and implementation is still an art, and for a nonmarket solution to be superior it is necessary to have an institutional framework that would make it so. Thus, an important conclusion from economics is simply that one should be cautious about government intervention.

Second, addiction models tested for some legal PSAD consumption show that when addicts are not extreme seekers the long-term price elasticity of demand can be relatively high, and thus, in order to have a significant effect on consumption reduction, a price increase should be sustained for a long time. In other words, short term increases in price do not change consumption much, but long term increases do.

Third, price increases do not significantly affect the consumption of addicts who are extreme seekers. This indicates that to lower long term consumption among all social groups, policies that increase prices are not enough.

Implications of Psychological Theories

Psychological models identify variables that can play a role in increasing an individual's propensity to abuse PSAD. These models posit relationships among variables, which may be used as policy guidelines. However, as with any inductively derived hypothesis, causal verification of these posited relationships is frequently difficult since so many factors have a bearing on human behavior in addition to those being perceived as affecting addiction probabilities. Although the wide diversity among psychological theories illustrates the complexity of the addiction phenomenon, they provide a few policy guidelines:

First, PSAD addiction has existed in all societies, and cannot be totally eliminated.[1] All societies devise ways to cope with PSAD addiction problems and thereby lower the negative effects of addiction to socially tolerable levels. Thus, "zero tolerance" policies cannot succeed. Thus policies should distinguish between casual or social users and addicts.

Second, PSAD addiction changes are strongly dependent on changes in social structures and institutions such as the family, church, schools, neighborhoods, and so on, that provide social controls to PSAD use and abuse. When some of the addiction constraining social factors weaken, societies experience addiction epidemics. One interesting implication of this relationship is that when there is a drug epidemic, the success of government policies depends on the support of the very nongovernment organizations that have somehow become weakened, thereby allowing the epidemic.

Third, epidemics subside when their social costs appear in the eyes of society to be serious enough to generate a strong social reaction that lowers the degree of tolerance for PSAD use and in which the society searches for ways to allow PSAD under controlled conditions that minimize social costs. This reaction comes not only from government policies but very importantly from the family, church, schools, peer groups, and so on.

Fourth, there is a need for policy flexibility and trial-and-error experimentation. Since the causality of addiction is not well determined, policies should be changeable when they do not work, especially in consideration of the fact that policies applicable to one social setting may not work in another.

Fifth, since addiction is associated with slow changes in social variables, successful policies must have a long-term horizon.

Psychological theories are valuable because they emphasize the search for the causes of PSAD addiction (a matter that the economists' "utility function" hides or ignores), and they point out the social reforms needed to eliminate addiction problems. However, they are not very helpful to many policymakers since the institutional changes they suggest are long run, politically difficult to manipulate, and uncertain in their results. The time horizon that the political system in the United States and other countries imposes on politicians is too short to seek those solutions, most of which can be controversial; and since some of the relations that they posit are likely to be proven false, there is a possibility of discouragement as policies fail. Thus, politicians tend to pay lip service to these theories but do not heed their advice. Indeed, in most cases institutional change takes place only after the social costs of maintaining the existing institutions are perceived as critically high. In this sense, the psychological theories of addiction suggest that before institutional changes to lower the costs of PSAD addiction are tried, it is necessary to have a crisis of significant magnitude.

Policy Implications of the Industry's Structure

The illegal PSAD industry's structure has some important policy implications. First, the industry is transnational. The illegal PSAD international market is integrated to the point that production in Bolivia, Peru, Colombia, and other countries is strongly influenced by what occurs in the United States and European consumer markets. Thus, any economic analysis of the industry must evaluate policies in all countries involved, not just in Colombia. Profits at every stage are high relative to factor costs, so the incentives to cooperate across countries and legal jurisdictions are quite high. Hence the international character of the market creates a problem for law enforcement as it requires coordination across national, regional, and bureaucratic jurisdictions. The goals and interests of the various governments and institutions involved differ, and turf and other bureaucratic fights tend to interfere with policy design, implementation, and changes.[2] These bureaucratic differences and squabbles make nonmarket policies hard to coordinate and implement.

Second, illegality is an obstacle to integration of various productive stages under one organization. Business groups have difficulty imparting orders to be followed beyond the closest associates and controlling prices of inputs (coca) and output in the consumer markets. Because of this, a policy aimed at jailing or extraditing a lead trafficker is likely to have at best a minor short-term impact on the industry, but it will not have any significant long-term impact on output. Similarly, negotiations with the industry leaders would fail because they do not have sufficient control over the industry to enforce a negotiated agreement. Furthermore, for a repressive policy to discourage new entrants to the business, it needs to be sustained for a longer time than what is likely to be socially and politically tolerable, especially in democracies.[3]

Third, because of illegality there is need for the industry to continuously seek new marketing routes, input sources, production locations, protection networks, and so forth. Thus, illegality encourages industry flexibility and adaptability.

Fourth, illegal PSAD consumption is a victimless crime in the sense that the consumer consciously decides to use the product. In these cases it is rare for consumers to turn in the sellers, adding difficulty to law enforcement of prohibition laws.

Fifth, most actors in the industry are the disenfranchised, ethnic minorities, and other marginal social groups. In Bolivia, coca is produced by peasants organized in unions that frequently see the government as their enemy. In Peru, the "Shining Path" is heavily involved in coca production. In Colombia, coca is produced in areas with very weak government presence and strong guerrilla influence. In the United States the black underclass and other minority members (including Colombian born) are significantly overrepresented in the industry. Most of these individuals do not have strong loyalties to the mainstream society and are not going to be swayed by arguments about the damage of their actions to society.[4]

Sixth, price estimates at various stages in the industry show that the lion's share of the value added is accrued in the United States. Indeed, a recent estimate by the DEA, cited by Falco (1992: 8) shows that around 1991, the coca required to produce one kilogram of cocaine cost U.S. $750 at the farm. The export price of that kilogram of cocaine was $2,000. The price increased to $15,000 at the wholesale level in Miami, and $23,000 when sold by the kilogram in Detroit, to $47,000 when sold by the ounce, and $135,000 by the gram. The implications of this price structure are quite clear: increasing the costs at the source have only marginal impact on retail prices in the United States. A doubling of coca costs due to increased eradication and other policy control measures would do nothing to change street cocaine prices. Seizing and destroying even half the cocaine exported from Colombia before it got to Miami would have only a marginal impact on street supply costs.

Implications of the Ability of the Governments Involved to Formulate and Implement Policies

Considering the extensive analysis of Colombian institutions elaborated in Chapter 2, it is clear that they are particularly ill-prepared to enforce administrative nonmarket policies. And, as argued in Chapter 5, this weakness was precisely one of the main reasons that the illegal PSAD industry developed in Colombia. The large underground economy, regime delegitimation and the weakening of the state, the high rent-seeking propensity of most Colombians, increasing illegality and corruption, and the political clientelist system, are all factors that increase the difficulty of the Colombian government to implement its own policies.

The government faces a complex set of challenges besides coping with the illegal PSAD industry: incorporating into the social mainstream the active guerrilla movement, while protecting citizens from extortion and the oil industry from guerrilla factions' bombing the pipelines; implementing political reforms to improve the level of democracy according to the new constitution; improving social services, education, health, urban infrastructure, and other development projects; trying to lower the high inflation rate; keeping the government budget deficit low, and so forth. All these goals use political, economic and bureaucratic resources and weaken the government's ability to deal with the illegal PSAD industry. It is therefore not surprising that Colombia's appeal to policies based on repression and punishment has not had an impact on cocaine supply, nor has it prevented the recent development of the opium and heroin industries.

The United States government is also limited in its efforts to succeed through the punishment of drug dealers and users. U.S. repressive policies are limited by an extensive civil rights legislation that prevents the government from using certain means to obtain criminal evidence, and from using illegally obtained evidence in legal trials.[5] These policies are also constrained by a governmental delegitimation crisis similar to Colombia's, but of smaller dimensions. During the last three decades the government has lost legitimacy among several groups. Its ability to enforce policies in some areas of the country, mainly in some inner-city neighborhoods, has been weakened. This is not the place to analyze the U.S. government. But to design effective polices it is necessary to acknowledge that social realities deny the government its ability to implement certain policies.

A further constraint on U.S. policies arises because many of the measures required to successfully implement repressive policies contradict fundamental U.S. civil rights ideals. For example, as noted above, most of the cocaine industry profits and money laundering take place in the United States. However, confiscating illegal profits would require a degree of "big-brother" U.S.-style government interference with individual rights repugnant to most citizens.[6]

An Evaluation of Past Colombian Drug Policies

As discussed in Chapter 7, the Colombian government has followed criminalization and repression policies for coca, cocaine, opium, heroin, and other PSAD, but the production and use of alcohol and tobacco products is legal with some restrictions.

However, policies have disregarded the economics of PSAD and the weakness of the Colombian state; they have failed because they have been extremely ill-suited to the characteristics of the government and the nature of the illegal PSAD industry. Supply repression policies require a strong governmental capability to implement administrative and regulatory controls, which is a function of the size of bounty (rents) created by the policies, regime legitimacy, and social controls and cohesion provided by schools, family, churches, and community. In all these aspects the Colombian government has been at a disadvantage to implement any nonmarket policies.

The policy failure is highlighted by the sharp increase in cocaine production in the Andes and consumption in the United States during the 1980s, and by the violence associated with the industry that has reached epidemic proportions in Colombia and U.S. inner cities.[7] Indeed, during the 1980s "war on drugs," new products were developed and the illegal PSAD industry flourished, becoming more diversified and sophisticated. Violence and the number of people jailed on drug charges has increased drastically in both Colombia and the United States, along with the social costs associated with drug addiction and criminalization policies. And no clear solution appears on the horizon (Nadelmann, 1988b and 1989b; Reuter, 1992b; Falco, 1992; Kleiman, 1992).

The supply suppression policies followed have an implicit contradiction for Colombia. They sought to maximize the difference between producer and consumer prices. The goal was to make coca prices as low as possible and production unattractive, and to make cocaine prices in the consumer markets as high as possible to stifle consumption. Given the nature of the value added in the industry, these goals are achieved by increasing the risk of the production and marketing process between coca growing and retail markets. In practice, this increased the violence associated with those processes, resulting in high social costs for Colombia. Various Colombian governments have tried to minimize those costs by tolerating some drug activity and discriminating between the "war on drugs" and the "war on narcoterrorism." No matter what the government does, this strategy inflicts very high costs on Colombia.

The extradition of drug traffickers to the United States became the cornerstone of Colombia's antidrug policy, but the characteristics of the industry meant that this policy could produce many pyrrhic victories but have no real affect on the supply of illegal PSAD. The total number of extradited Colombians was relatively small (under 50), but the increasingly violent reaction to this policy was totally out of proportion to the benefits it produced.[8]

Other policies have faltered because the government could not implement or sustain them for long periods of time. For instance, expropriation of many assets associated with drug industry leaders was tried after the assassinations of Rodrigo Lara and Luis Carlos Galán; while the seizures provided some good press and were covered extensively by the media, they were only temporary because the judicial system could not find a legal basis for many seizures because properties were titled to other individuals, or simply because of the power and bribes of the accused PSAD traffickers.

Many other policies were and are actually aiding some illegal PSAD operations. Frequent tax amnesties, the current opening of the economy (including capital markets) to international competition, the frequent relaxation in the requirements to sell foreign exchange to the Central Bank, and so on, were at odds with the main goals of the antidrug policies.

Policies followed by the U.S. and Colombian governments are not inspired by any economic or psychological analyses or theories of addiction. These policies have been value-laden and are consistent only with a highly moralistic interpretation of the PSAD demand. Inconsistency with the economic models led to a policy disregard for market forces, and to a low probability of impacting short-run demand and supply of illegal PSAD unless repression is raised to a very high level. Given the disregard of psychological theories, those policies have a low probability of lowering long-term demand. Thus, the "drug problem" does not go away. However, these policies (with a moralistic base) are useful to the social establishment because they allow politicians to shirk the responsibility of facing a problem whose solution appears to be costly, difficult, or unachievable within the politicians' time horizon. Therefore, political incentives to tackle the "drug problem" at its core are not great.

The failure of U.S. policies is also clear. Commenting on this and the growth of the illegal PSAD industry since Reagan declared the "war on drugs" in February 1982, Bagley (1988b: 190) was moved to state: "Illicit drugs of all types were more readily available and cheaper in the United States in January 1989 than they had been at the outset of the Reagan Presidency in 1981. Drug use and abuse in U.S. society had increased dramatically over the 1980s, and the U.S. drug market remained the biggest and most lucrative in the world. Drug-related crimes and violence had reached epidemic proportions in many U.S. cities, greatly exacerbated by the introduction and rapid spread of a highly addictive form of cocaine known as 'crack.'" Since then, things have only gotten worse while the U.S. government has continued the "war on drugs" without achieving a socially acceptable solution.

Incarceration data confirms that perspective. Between 1985 and 1989 the number of persons incarcerated increased 45 percent, and those on probation and on parole over 31 percent. In 1989 the United States had 1,076,670 people jailed, and 2,977,276 on probation and parole (Mullen and Arbiter, 1992: 186). These two groups account for over 1.6 percent of the total population. "The incarcerated population became richer in drug users over that time; in 1988 nearly one third of those sent to state prison were convicted of drug offenses, compared to only 23 percent in 1986" (Reuter, 1992b: 38–39). It is now well known that there are more young black males in jail than in college, and that drug-related violence is the main cause of death within that group. Still, the drug supply does not fall.

One of the main problems that any policy change has is the difference in the distribution of costs and benefits among policies. The current policy mix produces a distribution of costs and benefits that is very biased against Colombia and U.S. inner cities. Despite large drug incomes (and perhaps because of it), Colombia's economy has suffered substantially with the development of the industry (see Chapter 8). Colombia's social fabric has undoubtedly suffered even more, and a significant proportion of the assassinations and other crimes in Colombia are related to drug trafficking. In the United States, increased violence in inner-city ghettos is also related to increased drug use and traffic. The benefits of the current policy are perceived to be mainly accruing to the American middle- and upper-middle classes for whom the probability of addiction declines with PSAD illegality. There are however, other beneficiaries: drug traffickers and those who work in the repression industries.

Policy changes to decriminalize the industry and eliminate the huge rents obtained in the illicit drug traffic would eliminate a major source of violence in Colombia and in U.S. inner cities, but would increase perceived risks for the U.S. middle- and upper-middle classes. One of the primary obstacles to a change towards a policy mix that decriminalizes the use of some PSAD is the fear the middle class in the United States has of confronting some of their most pressing and hidden problems, and having to deal with the "dirty linen" of U.S. culture in public. Given the structure of the electorate and the low minority voting participation in the United States, it is highly unlikely that a decriminalization policy will be implemented.[9] Other changes like a government expenditure shift away from supply control to a demand-oriented policy based on prevention, treatment, research and education, would contribute a lot to a long-run solution of the demand problem, but would likely be opposed by those in the repression industry who benefit from the current policy mix.[10]

There are additional reasons for the current policy failure. The many knowledge gaps about PSAD effects, which make it difficult to design optimum policies, and the fact that illegal drug production and distribution have been treated as an intolerable "evil," contribute to this failure. Imperfect knowledge about PSAD demand, the industry structure, and governments' ability to enforce criminal laws have not been primary factors in policy design. Policies frequently result from the need to provide short term politically satisfactory responses to specific events, and to deal with a problem that touches a very raw nerve in many people. This has been particularly the case in the United States.[11]

Another weakness of these policies is that once they are in place, they develop their own momentum and constituencies that make them difficult to change (Reuter, 1985). For instance, the failure of repression policies leads to stronger repressive measures because their failure is not perceived by their constituencies as the result of their inadequacy, but of lack of political resolve or resources.

Colombia, like most countries, has accepted supply repression of the PSAD industry as the best way to deal with problems arising from PSAD consumption, except for alcohol, tobacco, and some minor PSAD such as caffeine. The legality of these latter PSAD has not provided a strong argument for decriminalizing marijuana, cocaine, and other PSAD, nor have many proposed that alcohol and tobacco be criminalized. Official policies implicitly accept that there are significant qualitative differences between legal and illegal PSAD that justify the different treatment. Simultaneously, policies do not discriminate between users and addicts, implicitly assuming that there are no qualitative differences between them. While Colombia's policies coincide with those of the United States and other countries, they are not "imposed" by external forces, since in Colombia there are strong groups that also support the repressive approach to drug control.

As discussed in Chapter 7, there was a debate in the late 1970s about marijuana legalization in Colombia. More recently, several American authors and important personalities have questioned the appropriateness of criminalization policies, and a mostly academic debate has ensued. The debate about PSAD decriminalization is an emotional one in both the United States and Colombia; people's positions tend to be highly influenced by moral values and preconceptions about drugs, polarizing the debate and making it difficult to have a purely rational discussion about the social costs of various policy alternatives (Kleiman and Saiger, 1990). In spite of some "dialogue among the deaf" traits of this debate, there have been important advances toward building a consensus, if the two extremes are excluded.

At one extreme are those who take a libertarian position based on the assumption that every individual is sovereign and autonomous, so the state does not have the right to impose consumption choice restrictions on anyone.[12] Libertarians recognize that individuals are not islands in society, and that even when a negative addiction or compulsive behavior appears to hurt directly only the addict, such behavior can generate negative externalities. However, to cope with these problems they would look for alternatives different from government intervention, which they would justify only in extreme cases.[13]

At the other extreme are those who would argue that PSAD production and consumption must be eliminated on moral grounds. This position has had a strong hand in shaping U.S. policies and has led to the emphasis on supply control efforts and incarceration of dealers and users.[14]

Fortunately, a middle ground has been growing in which ideology plays a weaker role and empirical evidence and pragmatic politics influence policy recommendations. This middle ground is based on the widespread realization that current policies have not worked and must be changed, independent of whether illegal drugs are decriminalized. Both, nonextreme legalizers and criminalizers, agree about a significant number of policy changes that could substantially improve the current situation. The middle ground holds that intelligent, honest, and well-meaning individuals can have different opinions about social phenomena because of their different ideologies and perceptions, and due to weak or complex data and significant knowledge gaps.

More importantly, the polarization of policy choices between two extremes is simplistic because there are innumerable and very different policy alternatives that fall under each category (Kleiman and Saiger, 1990, Nadelmann, 1992). For instance, criminalization may describe the immediate execution of a PSAD dealer caught in the act, or a sentence to a few months probation. Legalization may include a totally free market, or a highly controlled one.

The emphasis on legality and illegality as the main policy defining factor may also be misleading. There is no doubt that whether a drug is legal is important, but there are other policy characteristics that can be as important, or even more important to achieve a particular policy goal. For instance, if the goal is to lower PSAD long-term demand, psychological theories suggest that it is necessary to strengthen the social factors that constrain PSAD use and weaken those that promote it. In this case, the main question is not whether the PSAD is legal, but what the government is doing to solve the difficult social problems that led to the growth of PSAD use.

Recent works (Kleiman and Saiger, 1990; Kleiman, 1992; Reuter, 1992b; Nadelmann, 1992; Falco, 1992) have built the basis for a middle-ground consensus that shies away from a confrontation between the two extreme policies, and concentrates on seeking ways to change the current policy mix to minimize costs and improve results. These authors make a strong case to focus on the costs and benefits of various drug policy alternatives for marijuana, heroin, and cocaine. They illustrate the wide range of policy alternatives open to a government that wants to minimize the social costs of drug addiction. They emphasize that some of the costs and benefits are hard and even impossible to quantify, and that the final result depends on the weights given to various costs and benefit dimensions. Their approach also requires the government to define the costs and benefits of any policy in detail, and to reveal the weights assigned to various types of costs and benefits, a degree of transparency in government that is highly unlikely to be achieved. The main point is, however, that while the various authors may disagree about the relative costs of various policy alternatives, they agree about the need to change the policy focus.[15]

One common characteristic of these works is their tendency to include only U.S. costs and benefits, implicitly tendering a zero value to any consideration of Colombian costs and benefits. While this is standard practice in social science studies, it recognizes the importance of countries as the last entity in whose name humans can legitimately discriminate (and kill in the case of war) in the West, and it also confirms the lack of policy autonomy of the Colombian state.

Colombian Government Alternatives

The failure of past policies and the high costs borne by Colombian and American societies make it imperative to investigate alternatives. From the Colombian perspective, it is necessary to raise many questions about current policies such as whether current PSAD production and trafficking-criminalization policies are the best way to cope with PSAD consumption problems; whether extradition of drug traffickers has been the most effective Colombian policy; and whether the increased militarization of the "war on drugs" or the "war on narcoterrorism" has produced positive results at a tolerable cost. Does Colombia have alternative policies that will lower social costs? If so, what are they? Since Colombian policies have been consistent with those of the United States, U.S. policies can also be questioned on similar grounds.

From the Colombian point of view the policy choice is not simply between "criminalization and repression" and "legalization and decriminalization" because the country does not have the autonomy to make a choice between policies of that type, even if it wanted to. In other words, the Colombian government cannot contemplate a more market-oriented policy approach toward the PSAD industry unless the U.S. government goes along.

However, the Colombian government does have some room to influence the policy outcome. Of primary importance to the Colombian and other governments that confront increases in illegal PSAD production and consumption is to differentiate between short- and long-term policies. The current policies have emphasized short-term issues and disregarded long-term solutions. To succeed, governments must pay more attention to long-term policies.

Looking at short-term policies, Colombia has few policy choices. One possible policy goal is to promote the displacement of the illegal PSAD industry to somewhere else. To achieve this the government would have to increase the risk of doing business in Colombia. This can be done in two ways: wage a bigger war with its inherent higher violence; and strengthen the government's own capacity to enforce its antitrafficking laws and prevent money laundering, bribes, and corruption. The first of these paths is quite undesirable and the second is unrealistic, at least in the short and medium run. Furthermore, even if the first path were successful, there is no guarantee that Colombians would get out of the illegal drug business, only that they would physically move their activities out of the country.

A different policy alternative is to negotiate with the drug traffickers. However, as illustrated by Pablo Escobar's escape from his own prison, the government at best might be able to negotiate successfully with some drug traffickers, but not with all of them. Thus, this policy would not lead to the end of the illegal drug industry in Colombia.

Independent of new policies, the government has to cope with the effects of the past. The Colombian government cannot avoid confronting the fact that drug traffickers have committed many crimes. What to do about this is a political issue that does not have a clear answer. Any amnesty similar to those granted to guerrilla groups would generate strong opposition from those who have fought drug trafficking, have been its victims, or feel that negotiations would be immoral. An amnesty without incarceration of drug traffickers could also lead to the international isolation of the government. At the same time, the ability that drug groups have to terrorize society could make amnesty appealing.

Independent of what short-term policies the government follows, its main challenge is to simultaneously follow other policies that contribute to an elimination of the drug problem in the long run. The government must therefore try other strategies. First, it should involve nongovernment institutions in the antidrug fight. In the current policy framework the government is fully responsible for antidrug policies. However, any long term solution implies strengthening other Colombian social institutions that have become weakened through time. It must be accepted that the current institutional crisis is not just the government's problem, but everyone's. The Catholic Church, other churches, political parties, government teachers' union,[16] business clubs (Lions, Rotary, etc.), neighborhood organizations and other social groups are candidates to be involved in Colombian institutional reconstruction and antidrug policies. It must be clear that this policy goal is very ambitious: its goal is to build strong social cohesion and social controls that would discourage antisocial behavior—which includes illegal drug production, marketing, and consumption. This policy requires an assimilation into the Colombian mainstream of large parts of the population, to build strong communities, and to make people feel that they have a stake in the establishment. In many ways it is inseparable from a nation building project, but it reflects the systemic crisis faced by the country.

Second, international cooperation between Colombian and U.S., and other non-government organizations should be promoted as a way to strengthen the capabilities of Colombian organizations and the consensus for a need of Colombian, U.S., and international policy shift towards prevention, treatment, research, and education. This policy's goal is also very ambitious. It also entails strengthening community organizations and assimilating into the mainstream of the consuming countries their underclasses who do not have much at stake in the system.

One of the most frustrating conclusions of this book is that there are indeed very few policy suggestions for Colombia. One should unfortunately recognize the sad fact that the Colombian government alone cannot cope with the problems that arise from the growth of the illegal PSAD industry. Acting alone, at best it can buy some time in the midst of internal violence. Unfortunately, as argued in Chapter 2, the process of delegitimation has evolved to the point where the government has lost the capacity to implement many policies and has become extremely vulnerable to the illegal PSAD industry. Thus, in the short run, the government does not have meaningful policy alternatives open to it. Indeed, Colombia is in a situation in which the current generation is paying for the sins of the past, without significant autonomous alternatives. The long-run solution to the "drug problem" requires a significant international and U.S. policy change based on accepting the implications of the economic structure of the drug industry, psychology of drug consumption, and the weaknesses of the Colombian, U.S., and other governments. The goal of these changes should be mainly to lower illegal drug consumption in the long run, and to develop social controls to minimize the social costs of PSAD use. Using the United Nations Drug Control Programme framework, what is needed is to follow "Alternative Development" strategies for Colombian peasants, drug manufacturers and traffickers, and consumers both in Colombia and the main markets of Colombian drug products, along the lines suggested above. This is a tall order indeed, and one that Colombia cannot achieve alone. If policies to achieve these goals are not formulated and implemented, there is no long-term solution to the illegal drug problem.

Notes

1. Anthropologist Billie Jean Isbell has commented to me that only the traditional Eskimo society did not consume PSAD, principally because they did not have any products to use. However, they had a time during the winter during which they could psyche themselves and "run amok."

2. For instance, the internal conflicts among the United States government agencies involved in drug policy formulation and implementation are well documented. Bagley (1988a) shows that U.S. policies have lacked coordination and leadership, and that the responsibility for the country's drug policy remains diffuse and overlapping among government branches.

3. Recall that in the past the "all out wars" against "narcoterrorists" in Colombia lost public support after a few months.

4. The same is the case in other illegal PSAD industries. For example, opium and heroin are produced in Pakistan in the Northwest Territories in areas controlled by autonomous tribes with very little (if any) loyalty to Pakistan (Buddenberg, 1992).

5. The U.S. Congress chose to disallow illegally obtained evidence to be presented in court rather than allowing such evidence and then punishing law enforcement officials who broke evidence-gathering laws to obtain it. Consequently, the congress chose to protect the criminals' civil rights over finding the truth.

6. The United States has recently tightened its money laundering policies so as to require that any transaction in which more than U.S. $10,000 in cash changes hands be reported to the Internal Revenue Service. This has led to sporadic fines against businesses who do not comply, and to seizures of a few assets. However, the seizures' volume is pitifully small when compared with the illegal drug industry's profits of over $100 billion a year. Unfortunately, in January 1994 the U.S. Supreme Court declared unconstitutional provisions of the law that made it illegal to divide large cash deposits into smaller ones under $10,000. This decision was based on the grounds that reporting cash deposits of over $10,000 created risk and jeopardized the depositor's right to privacy.

7. The drug related violence in Colombia has been documented in this volume. For references to the U.S. problem see Nadelmann (1988b and 1989b).

8. To add insult to injury, three extradited drug traffickers were returned to Colombia by the United States because the evidence used to build the legal case against them in the United States had been obtained illegally and it could not be used in court!

9. Colombians do not vote in the United States even though, paraphrasing the Boston Tea Party, "policy impact without representation is tyranny." One sad corollary of the current policy mix is that it implicitly accepts that the value of a human life differs depending on whether the person is born in the U.S. inner city ghettos, Colombia, or the U.S. middle class.

10. Reuter (1992b: 21) estimates that in the United States, 75 percent of the total 1990 drug control budget of $28 billion was spent in enforcement activities.

11. Musto perhaps the best known PSAD historian in the United States, analyzes PSAD policy formulation in that country and shows that it has followed cycles determined by the changing perception of mainstream society about the magnitude of the problem. This perception has been based mostly on fear and moral arguments.

12. The most coherent exponent of this view in the United States is Szasz (1974, 1992).

13. "Regarding the family as the irreducible social cell from which all forms of society are constructed, this freedom to choose is generally conceived by the libertarian as being conferred on the family itself whose individual members arrive at family decisions in their own way, though influenced always by legislation, by prevailing custom, and by morality. . . . To be sure, even in well ordered societies abuses within the family will occur. The libertarian is not so unworldly as to overlook the possibility of iniquity or irresponsibility among parents. But the remedies he envisages are of the kind that empower direct state intervention only in particular and limited

ways, and only where there is already evidence of mistreatment or neglect. The mere risk of abuses occurring in no way justifies abridgments of personal freedom or surrender to the state of powers to regulate or monitor family behavior" (Mishan, 1990: 455).

14. The moralistic position led Reagan to refer to drug abuse as an "evil scourge" in his 1981 presidential inauguration address, and to declare a "war on drugs." U.S. government officials during the 1980s were among the most articulate proponents of this view, particularly "drug czar" William Bennett.

15. For instance, Kleiman and Saiger (1990) and Kleiman (1992) conclude that the costs of marijuana legalization are likely to be small, but those of cocaine and heroin are likely to be very high. In the case of cocaine they are high because of a feared increase in crack consumption, not in the use of less-potent forms of cocaine. Nadelmann (1992) is more willing to consider a wider liberalization scope.

16. During the first half of this century public schoolteachers were people with strong pedagogic vocations who took great pride in their job. Substantial expansion of the education sector accompanied by an insidious clientelism turned teaching into just another union-protected job. The government must confront the public schoolteachers with their responsibility to contribute to form the value system and internal controls (consciences) of the pupils.

Glossary

• • •

aggregate demand (also known as *aggregate expenditure*): The sum total of nominal expenditures on goods and services in the economy. That is, consumption, investment, and government expenditures together with exports, less imports.

backward linkage: The relationship between an industry or firm and the suppliers of its inputs. A change in the output of the firm will be transmitted backwards to the supplier of its inputs by a change in demand for inputs.

cadastral: Relating to the *cadastre*, an official register of the size, boundaries, value, ownership, and other details of real estate, used in apportioning taxes.

cartel: Formal agreement between firms in an oligopolistic market to cooperate with regard to agreed procedures on such variables as price and output. The result is diminished competition and cooperation over objectives as, for example, joint profit maximization or avoidance of new entry. In general, side-payments must be made between cartel members in order to induce adherence to these objectives.

corner solution: In an optimization problem, a situation in which one or more of the choice variables has a zero value at the optimum. In a consumption model, the individual could choose to spend all his income on one good, and consume zero of the rest.

cost-benefit analysis: A conceptual framework for the evaluation of investment projects. It differs from straightforward financial appraisal in that it considers all gains (benefits) and losses (costs) regardless of

---

Most definitions presented in this glossary are taken from David W. Pearce, 1992, *The MIT Dictionary of Modern Economics*, 4th ed., MIT Press, Cambridge, Mass.

to whom they accrue (although usually confined to the inhabitants of one nation).

crawling peg (creeping peg): A method of controlling exchange rates, this is a general term applying to any proposal with the characteristic that par values—the official exchange rate as declared by the International Monetary Fund (IMF)—can be adjusted over time. In the case of Colombia, the goal was to avoid the large periodic devaluations caused by domestic inflation being higher than the international inflation rate.

duopoly: A market structure where there are only two firms.

Dutch disease: A term used to denote some hard-to-avoid macroeconomic effects of primary product booms, such as currency revaluation, difficulty in producing locally any other internationally or regionally traded goods, and the disproportionate growth of the services sector.

economic rent: A payment to a factor of production in excess of what is necessary to keep it to its present employment.

economic welfare: That part of human welfare which results from the consumption of goods and services.

economies of scale: Reductions in the average cost of production in the long run, resulting from an expanded level of output.

elasticity: A measure of the percentage change in one variable in respect of a percentage change in another variable. Measures of elasticity tend to be carried out for very small changes in the variable causing the response.

external reserve(s): This normally refers to a country's holdings of internationally acceptable means of payments for the purpose of covering short- to medium-term deficits on its external balance of payments, and the related purpose of exerting control over the movement of the exchange rate of its currency. Such reserves are held principally in gold or in one or the other of the major currencies widely used in international trade and settlements.

footloose industries: Industries that are not bound to particular locations by specific requirements and thus can effectively set up anywhere.

Gini coefficient: A measure of the inequality of a distribution, usually applied to the income distribution. It can be calculated as:

$$G = 1 + 1/n - 2/n^2 y \{y_1 + 2y_2 + 3y_3 + \ldots + ny_m\}$$

where $y_1 \ldots y_m$ represent individual incomes in decreasing order of size, y is the mean income, and n the number of individuals. The Gini coefficient has a maximum value of unity (absolute inequality) and a minimum value of zero (absolute equality).

monetary base: A term often used interchangeably with *high-powered money* to denote those assets, largely public sector monetary and short-term liabilities, which in the traditional theory of credit creation are held to determine the total supply of money through a credit (or money) multiplier.

oligopoly: A market structure within which firms are aware of the mutual interdependence of sales, production, investment, and advertising plans. Hence, manipulation by any firm of variables under its control is likely to evoke retaliation from competing firms. These structures are commonly attributed to markets in which the number of sellers is few.

price elasticity of demand (elasticity of demand): The responsiveness of the quantity demanded of a good to its own price. To avoid the measure of elasticity being sensitive to the units in which quantities and prices are measured, the elasticity of demand is expressed as the percentage change in demand that occurs in response to a percentage change in price.

production function: The relationship between the output of a good and the inputs (factors of production) required to make that good.

rent seeking: The use of real resources in an attempt to appropriate a surplus in the form of rent.

secular decline: The slow decline a variable shows over the long term. The decline is not necessarily continuous because it possible to have increases and decreases; however, the statistical trend is negative and small.

utility: Widely construed in economics to be synonymous with "welfare," economic welfare, satisfaction, and occasionally, happiness.

utility function: A function stating that an individual's utility is dependent upon the goods he consumes and their amounts.

Bibliography

• • •

Acosta, Olga L. 1986. Estructura Financiera de las Sociedades: Ejercicio de Aplicación de las Cuentas Financieras. *Ensayos Sobre Política Económica* 10(December):133–181.
Aguilar, Luis I. 1990. "Tendencias en la Distribución del Ingreso." In *40 Años de Desarrollo: su Impacto Social*, edited by Miguel Urrutia, 65–79. Bogotá: Biblioteca Banco Popular.
Alcaldía Mayor de Bogotá, D. E. 1989. *Bogotá y el Consumo de Substancias Psicoactivas: un Estudio, una Solución.* Bogotá: Imprenta Distrital.
Alvarez, Elena. 1992. "Coca Production in Peru." In *Drug Policy in the Americas*, edited by Peter H. Smith. Boulder: Westview Press.
Americas Watch. 1990. *The "Drug War" in Colombia: The Neglected Tragedy of Political Violence.* Human Rights Watch.
———. 1992. *Political Murder and Reform in Colombia.* Human Rights Watch.
Anonymous. 1988. The Drug Economy. *Economist.* April 2.
———. 1989. *Un Narco se Confiesa y Acusa.* Bogotá: Editorial Colombia Nuestra.
Arango, Mario. 1988. *Impacto del Narcotráfico en Antioquia.* 3rd ed. Medellín: J. M. Arango.
Arango, Mario, and Jorge Child. 1987. *Narcotráfico: Imperio de la Cocaína.* Mexico: Editorial Diana.
Arbeláez, María A. 1990. "Los Indicadores de Bienestar que se Deterioran." In *40 Años de Desarrollo: su Impacto Social*, edited by Miguel Urrutia, 173–207. Bogotá: Biblioteca Banco Popular.
Asencio, Diego. 1979. "E.U. Paga Cuantioso Precio en Salud a Causa de la Marihuana." In *Marihuana: Legalización o Represión*, edited by Asociación Nacional de Instituciones Financieras (ANIF), 9–14. Bogotá: Biblioteca ANIF de Economía.
Asociación Nacional de Instituciones Financieras (ANIF). 1979. *Marihuana: Legalización o Represión.* Bogotá: Biblioteca ANIF de Economía.
Ayres, Clarence E. 1978. *The Theory of Economic Progress: A Study of the Fundamentals of Economic Development and Cultural Change.* 3rd ed. New Issues Press, Western Michigan University.
Bagley, Bruce M. 1979. "Political Power, Public Policy and the State in Colombia: Case Studies of the Urban and Agrarian Reforms During the National Front: 1958–1974." Unpublished Ph.D. Dissertation, University of California Los Angeles.
———. 1988a. The New Hundred Years War? US National Security and the War on Drugs in Latin America. *Journal of Interamerican Studies and World Affairs* 30(Spring):161–182.

———. 1988b. US Foreign Policy and the War on Drugs: Analysis of a Policy Failure. *Journal of Interamerican Studies and World Affairs* 30(Summer/Fall).
———. 1988c. Colombian Drug Wars. *Foreign Affairs* 67(Fall):70–92.
———. 1989–1990. Dateline Drug Wars: Colombia: The Wrong Strategy. *Foreign Policy* 77(Winter):154–171.
Bank for International Settlements. 1989. *57th Annual Report.* Basel, June.
Barthold, Thomas A., and Harold M. Hochman. 1988. Addiction as Extreme-Seeking. *Economic Inquiry* 26(January):89–106.
Barzel, Yoram. 1989. *Economic Analysis of Property Rights.* Cambridge: Cambridge University Press.
Becker, Gary S. 1965. A Theory of the Allocation of Time. *Economic Journal* September: 493–517.
Becker, Gary S., Michael Grossman, and Kevin M. Murphy. 1991. Rational Addiction and the Effect of Price on Consumption. *American Economic Review* 81(May):237–241.
Becker, Gary S., and Kevin M. Murphy. 1988. A Theory of Rational Addiction. *Journal of Political Economy* 96(August):675–700.
Benson, Bruce L., and David W. Rasmussen. 1991. Relationship Between Illicit Drug Enforcement Policy and Property Crimes. *Contemporary Policy Issues* 9(October):106–115.
Berry, R. Albert. 1971. "Some Implications of Elitist Rule for Economic Development in Colombia." In *Government and Economic Development*, edited by Gustav Ranis. New Haven: Yale University Press.
———. 1992. "Agriculture During the Eighties' Recession in Colombia: Potential Versus Achievement." In *The Colombian Economy: Issues of Trade and Development*, edited by Alvin Cohen and Frank R. Gunter, 185–215. Boulder: Westview Press.
Berry, R. Albert, Ronald G. Hellman, and Mauricio Solaún, eds. 1980. *Politics of Compromise: Coalition Government in Colombia.* New Brunswick: Transaction Books.
Berry, R. Albert, and Francisco E. Thoumi. 1977. Import Substitution and Beyond: Colombia. *World Development* 5(January-February):89–109.
———. 1986. Crecimiento y Políticas Económicas en Colombia. *Cuadernos de Economía* VII(First Semester):9. Universidad Nacional de Colombia.
———. 1988. "Post-War and Post–National Front Economic Development of Colombia." In *Democracy in Latin America: Colombia and Venezuela*, edited by Donald L. Herman, 63–85. New York: Praeger Publishers.
Bird, Richard M. 1984. *Intergovernmental Finance in Colombia.* Boston: Harvard University Law School.
Blomström, Magnus, and Patricio Meller. 1991. "Issues for Development: Lessons from Scandinavian–Latin American Comparisons." In *Diverging Paths: Comparing a Century of Scandinavian and Latin American Economic Development*, edited by Magnus Blomström and Patricio Meller. Baltimore: Johns Hopkins University Press.
Bogue, Donald J. 1985. *The Population of the United States: Historical Trends and Future Projections.* New York: Macmillan Free Press.
Bohanon, Cecil E. 1991. An Economic Explanation for the Ineffectiveness of Addiction Treatment. *Contemporary Policy Issues* 9(October):116–119.
Botero, Rodrigo. 1981. El Modelo Colombiano de Desarrollo 1958–1980. *Colección Estudios CIEPLAN* 5(July):189–198.

Brotherson, Festus, Jr. 1989. Foreign Policy of Guyana, 1970–1985: Forbes Burnham's Search for Legitimacy. *Journal of Interamerican Studies and World Affairs* 31 (Fall): 9–35.

Buddenberg, Doris. 1992. "Illicit Drug Issues in Pakistan." Geneva, Switzerland: United Nations Institute for Social Development, Mimeo.

Bula, Mayra. 1988. "Antecedentes en las Culturas Nativas." In *Historia de la Drogadicción en Colombia*, compiled by A. Pérez G., 9–28. Bogotá: Tercer Mundo—Ediciones Uniandes.

Caballero, Carlos A. 1988. La Economía de la Cocaína: Algunos Estimativos para 1988. *Coyuntura Económica* 18(September):179–184.

Calvo, Guillermo A. 1991. "Comment." In *The Macroeconomics of Populism in Latin America*, edited by Rudiger Dornbusch and Sebastian Edwards, 390–91. Chicago: University of Chicago Press.

Camacho Guizado, Alvaro. 1988. *Droga y Sociedad en Colombia: el Poder y el Estigma*. Bogotá: CIDSE Universidad del Valle—Fondo Editorial CEREC.

Caro de Casas, Constanza. 1988. "Los Años Sesentas." In *Historia de la Drogadicción en Colombia*, edited by Augusto Pérez G., 43–50. Bogotá: Tercer Mundo—Ediciones Uniandes.

Castillo, Fabio. 1987. *Los Jinetes de la Cocaína*. Bogotá: Editorial Documentos Periodísticos.

———. 1991. *La Coca Nostra*. Bogotá: Editorial Documentos Periodísticos.

Clague, Christopher. 1973. Legal Strategies for Dealing with Heroin Addiction. *American Economic Review* 63(May): 263–269.

Clavijo, Sergio. 1990. Productividad Laboral, Multifactorial y la Tasa de Cambio Real en Colombia. *Ensayos Sobre Política Económica* 17(June): 73–97.

———. 1992. "Overcoming a Financial Crisis During the Transition of a Repressed System to a Market Based One: Colombia 1970–89." In *The Colombian Economy: Issues of Trade and Development*, edited by Alvin Cohen and Frank R. Gunter, 93–118. Boulder: Westview Press.

Collett, Merrill. 1988. Colombia's Sophisticated Drug Traffickers Trigger Economic Boom, Political Violence. *Latinamerica Press* 29(September):3.

———. 1989. Collision Course in Colombia: Traffickers Threaten Land Reform. *The Christian Science Monitor*. 24 January:3.

Comisión de Estudios Sobre la Violencia. 1989. *Colomba: Violencia y Democracia*. Bogotá: Universidad Nacional de Colombia—COLCIENCIAS.

Conroy, Michael. 1976. "Urbanization, Internal Migration and Spatial Policy in Colombia." World Bank, June.

Corporación para el Fomento de las Investigaciones Económicas, ed. 1972. *Controversia sobre el Plan de Desarrollo*. Bogotá: Oveja Negra.

Correa, Patricia. 1984. Determinantes de la Cuenta de Servicios de la Balanza Cambiaria. *Ensayos Sobre Política Económica* 6(December).

Craig, Richard B. 1981. Colombian Narcotics and United States-Colombian Relations. *Journal of Interamerican Studies and World Affairs* 23(3):243–270.

———. 1983. Domestic Implications of Illicit Colombian Drug Production and Trafficking. *Journal of Interamerican Studies and World Affairs* 25(August):325–350.

Cubides, Fernando. 1989. "Estado y Poder Local (Organización Comunitaria y Política en el Medio y Bajo Caguán)." In *Colonización, Coca y Guerrilla*, edited by Jaime E. Jaramillo, Leonidas Mora, and Fernando Cubides, 159–191. 3rd ed. Alianza Editorial Colombiana.

Cuellar, Fidel H. 1991. "Incidencia del Cultivo de Coca en la Economía Colombiana y Comparación con los Casos de Perú y Bolivia." Instituto Interamericano de Cooperación para la Agricultura (IICA). Bogotá, mimeo.
Currie, Lauchlin. 1965. *Ensayos sobre Planeación.* 2nd ed. Bogotá: Ediciones Tercer Mundo.
———. 1966. *Accelerating Development: The Necessity and the Means.* New York: McGraw Hill, Inc.
Del Olmo, Rosa. 1988. *La Cara Oculta de la Droga.* Bogotá: Editorial Temis.
———. 1992. *¿Prohibir o Domesticar? Políticas de Drogas en América Latina.* Caracas: Editorial Nueva Sociedad.
Departamento Administrativo Nacional de Estadística (DANE). 1989. *Colombia Estadística 1989.* Vol. 1. Bogotá.
Departamento Nacional de Planeación. 1975. *Para Cerrar la Brecha: Plan de Desarrollo Social, Económico y Regional 1975–1978.* Bogotá.
———. 1980. *Plan de Integración Nacional 1979–1982.* Vols. I and II. Bogotá.
———. 1983. *Cambio con Equidad: Plan Nacional de Desarrollo 1983–1986.* Bogotá.
———. 1990. Programa de Modernización de la Economía Colombiana. *Revista de Planeación y Desarrollo* 22 (January-June).
De Soto, Hernando. 1986. *El Otro Sendero: La Revolución Informal.* Lima: Editorial El Barranco.
Dewatripont, Mathias, and Gerard Roland. 1992. Virtues of Gradualism in the Transition to a Market Economy. *Economic Journal* 102 (March): 291–300.
Díaz-Alejandro, Carlos F. 1976. *Foreign Trade Regimes and Economic Development: Colombia.* New York: National Bureau of Economic Research.
Díaz-Díaz, Fernando. 1978–1979. "Estado, Iglesia y Desamortización." In *Manual de Historia de Colombia,* Vol 2. Instituto Colombiano de Cultura.
Díaz-Uribe, Eduardo. 1986. *El Clientelismo en Colombia: Un Estudio Exploratorio.* Bogotá: El Ancora Editores.
Dix, Robert. 1980. Consociational Democracy: the Case of Colombia. *Comparative Politics* 12 (April):303–321.
———. 1986. *The Politics of Colombia.* New York: Praeger.
Dombois, Rainer. 1990. "¿Por qué Florece la Economía de la Cocaína Justamente en Colombia?" In *Economía y Política del Narcotráfico,* edited by Juan Tokatlian and Bruce Bagley, 109–116. Bogotá: Ediciones Uniandes.
Dornbusch, Rudiger, and Sebastian Edwards. 1991. "The Macroeconomics of Populism." In *The Macroeconomics of Populism in Latin America,* edited by Rudiger Dornbusch and Sebastian Edwards. Chicago: University of Chicago Press.
Dugas, John. 1993. "El Desarrollo de la Asamblea Nacional Constituyente." In *La Constitución de 1991: ¿Un Pacto Político Viable?* edited by John Dugas. Universidad de Los Andes, Departmento de Ciencia Política.
Echavarría, Hernán. 1983. *El Escándalo de los Fondos Grancolombiano y Bolivariano en el Gobierno del Dr. Turbay Ayala.* Medellín: H. Echavarría O.
Economic Commission for Latin America and the Caribbean. 1990. *Statistical Yearbook for Latin America and the Caribbean 1989.* Chile: United Nations.
Economist Intelligence Unit. Various years. *Colombia Country Report* various issues.
Eddy, Paul, with Hugo Sabogal and Sara Walden. 1988. *The Cocaine Wars.* W. W. Norton.

Escobar, Jaime. 1990. "40 Años de Desarrollo Económico en Colombia, 1950–1990." In *40 Años de Desarrollo: su Impacto Social*, edited by Miguel Urrutia, 17–43. Bogotá: Biblioteca Banco Popular.

Escobar, Juan G. and Olga L. Gaitán. 1990. "La Política Criminal: Sus Planteamientos, Normas, Prácticas y Críticas. Perspectiva Socio-Jurídica." In *Narcotráfico en Colombia: Dimensiones Políticas, Económicas, Jurídicas e Internacionales*, edited by Carlos G. Arrieta, et al., 99–197. Bogotá: Tercer Mundo Editores—Ediciones Uniandes.

Estupiñán, Diana E., and Yolanda Torres de Galvis. 1990. *Encuesta Nacional sobre Conocimientos Actitudes y Prácticas en Salud: 1986–1989. Sustancias Sicoactivas: Escala de Riesgo*. Bogotá: Ministerio de Salud and Instituto Nacional de Salud.

Fajardo, Darío M. 1986. *Haciendas, Campesinos y Políticas Agrarias en Colombia, 1920–1980*. Bogotá: Empresa Editorial Universidad Nacional de Colombia.

Falco, Mathea. 1992. Foreign Drugs, Foreign Wars. *Daedalus* 121(3):1–14.

Fals-Borda, Orlando. 1965. "Violence and the Break-up of Tradition in Colombia." In *Obstacles to Change in Latin America*, edited by Claudio Véliz. Oxford University Press.

Farné, Stefano. 1990. "Calidad de la Vivienda, Nutrición e Indices de Calidad de la Vida." In *40 Años de Desarrollo: su Impacto Social*, edited by Miguel Urrutia, 45–63. Bogotá: Biblioteca Banco Popular.

Federación Nacional de Comerciantes (FENALCO). 1987. "El Contrabando de Importación 1980–1987." Presented in the 42nd National Commerce Congress, Pasto, October.

FEDESARROLLO. 1983. El Plan de Desarrollo 1982–1986: Desarrollo con Equidad. *Coyuntura Económica* 13(March).

FEDESARROLLO and Instituto SER de Investigación. 1990. Indicadores Sociales. *Coyuntura Social* 2(May).

Fingarette, Herbert. 1988. Alcoholism: The Mythical Disease. *The Public Interest* 91(Spring):3–22.

Flores, Gonzalo, and José Blanes. 1984. *¿Hacia Dónde Va el Chapare?* Cochabamba, Bolivia: CERES.

Flórez, Luis B. and César González M. 1983. *Industria, Regiones y Urbanización en Colombia*. Bogotá: La Oveja Negra.

Frank, Thomas M. 1988. Legitimacy in the International System. *American Journal of International Law* 82(October): 705–759.

Freemantle, Brian. 1986. *The Fix*. New York: Tom Doherty Associates, Inc.

Galvis, Ligia. 1986. *Filosofía de la Constitución de Colombia de 1886*. Bogotá: Lucía de Esguerra.

García-García, Jorge. 1981. "The Effects of Exchange Rates and Commercial Policy on Agricultural Incentives: 1953–1978." Research report 24(June). Washington, D.C.: International Food Policy Research Institute.

———. 1988. "Coffee Boom, Government Expenditure, and Agricultural Prices: The Colombian Experience." Research report 68(August). Washington, D.C.: International Food Policy Research Institute.

———. 1991. "Macroeconomic Crisis, Macroeconomic Policies and Long Run Growth: the Colombian Experience 1950–1986." Washington, D. C., March, Mimeo.

García-García, Jorge, and Lea Guterman. 1988. Medición del Déficit del Sector Público Colombiano y su Financiación: 1950–1986. *Ensayos Sobre Política Económica* 14(December):115–133.

García-Sayán, Diego, ed. 1989. *Coca, Cocaína y Narcotráfico: Laberinto en los Andes*. Lima, Peru: Comisión Andina de Juristas.
Gaviria, Víctor. 1991. *El Pelaíto que no Duró Nada*. Bogotá: Planeta Colombiana Editorial.
Gillis, Malcolm and Charles McLure. 1978. Taxation and Income Distribution: The Colombian Tax Reform of 1974. *Journal of Development Economics* 5.
Giraldo Isaza, Fabio. 1990. Narcotráfico y Construcción. *Economía Colombiana* 226–227(February-March):38–49.
Gómez, Hernando J. 1985. "Colombian Illegal Economy: Size, Evolution and Economic Impact." Brookings Institution, Mimeo.
———. 1988. La Economía Ilegal en Colombia: Tamaño, Evolución e Impacto Económico. *Coyuntura Económica* 18(September):93–113.
———. 1990. El Tamaño del Narcotráfico y su Impacto Económico. *Economía Colombiana* 226–227(February-March):8–17.
Grupo de Estudios del Departamento de Investigaciones Económicas del Banco de la República. 1982. Controles Monetarios y Distorciones Estadísticas. *Ensayos Sobre Política Económica* 1(March): 149–170.
Gugliotta, Guy. 1992. "The Colombian Cartels and How to Stop Them." In *Drug Policy in the Americas*, edited by Peter H. Smith, 111–128. Boulder: Westview Press.
Gugliotta, Guy, and Jeff Leen. 1990. *Kings of Cocaine: An Astonishing True Story of Murder, Money and International Corruption*. New York: Simon and Schuster.
Guissarri, Adrián. 1989. *La Argentina Informal: Realidad de la Vida Económica*. Buenos Aires: Emecé Editores.
Gunter, Frank R. 1991. Colombian Capital Flight. *Journal of Interamerican Studies and World Affairs* 35(Spring).
Guzmán, Germán, Orlando Fals-Borda, and Eduardo Umaña-Luna. 1962. *La Violencia en Colombia: Estudio de un Proceso Social*. 2nd ed. Bogotá: Ediciones Tercer Mundo.
Harrison, Lawrence E. 1985. *Underdevelopment Is a State of Mind: The Latin American Case*. Cambridge, Mass.: The Center for International Affairs, Harvard University and University Press of America.
Hartlyn, Jonathan. 1985. Producer Associations, the Political Regime, and Policy Processes in Contemporary Colombia. *Latin American Research Review* 20(3):111–138.
———. 1988. *The Politics of Coalition Rule in Colombia*. Cambridge: Cambridge University Press.
Healy, Kevin. 1991. Political Ascent of Bolivia's Peasant Coca Leaf Producers. *Journal of Interamerican Studies and World Affairs* 35(1):87–121.
Herrán, María Teresa. 1987. *¿La Sociedad de la Mentira?* 2nd ed. Bogotá, Colombia: Fondo Editorial CEREC-Editorial la Oveja Negra.
Herrera, Santiago. 1990. Eficiencia y Determinantes del Funcionamineto del Mercado Paralelo de Divisas en Colombia. *Ensayos Sobre Política Económica* 17(June):39–72.
Hirschman, Albert O. 1963. *Journeys Toward Progress*. New York: Twentieth Century Fund, Inc.
Hommes, Rudolf. 1992. "Challenges to the Private Sector in the 1990s: Colombian Economic Policies and Perspectives." In *The Colombian Economy: Issues of Trade and Development*, edited by Alvin Cohen and Frank R. Gunter, 87–92. Boulder: Westview Press.

Horowitz, Irving Louis. 1992. Revolution, Longevity and Legitimacy in Communist States. *Studies in Comparative International Development* 27 (Spring):65–73.
Ibañez, Dionisio. 1974. Algunos Aspectos de la Reforma Tributaria. *Coyuntura Económica* 4(December):132–148.
Inter-American Development Bank. 1982. *Economic and Social Progress in Latin America: The External Sector, 1982 Report.* Washington, D.C.
Jacobs, James B. 1990. Imagining Drug Liberalization. *The Public Interest* 101(Fall):28–42.
Jaramillo, Jaime E. 1989. "Historia y Dimensiones Socioculturales del Proceso Colonizador." In *Colonización, Coca y Guerrilla*, edited by Jaime E. Jaramillo, Leonidas Mora, and Fernando Cubides, 15–101. 3rd ed. Bogotá: Alianza Editorial Colombiana.
Jaramillo, Juan Carlos. 1982. El Proceso de Liberación del Mercado Financiero en Colombia. *Ensayos Sobre Política Económica* 1(March):7–19.
Jaramillo, Juan C. and Armando Montenegro. 1982. Cuenta Especial de Cambios: Descripción y Análisis de su Evolución Reciente. *Revista del Banco de la República* 55(January):651 and 55(February):652.
Jaramillo, William, Rodrigo Marín, and Roberto Arenas. 1982. *Informe de la Comisión Senatorial sobre los Fondos de Inversión.* Bogotá: n.p.
Junguito, Roberto. 1979. "Financiación de la Industria Manufacturera en los Años Ochenta: Aspectos Crediticios y Tributarios." In *El Sector Financiero en los Años Ochenta*, edited by Carlos Caballero Argaez, 399–420. Bogotá: Asociación Bancaria de Colombia.
Junguito, Roberto and Carlos Caballero. 1978. La Otra Economía. *Coyuntura Económica* 8(December):103–139.
———. 1982. "Illegal Trade Transactions and the Underground Economy of Colombia." In *The Underground Economy in the United States and Abroad*, edited by Vito Tanzi, 285–313. Lexington, Mass.: Lexington Books.
Justiniano, José G. 1992. "The Power of Coca Producers." In *Drug Policy in the Americas*, edited by Peter H. Smith, 99–104. Boulder: Westview Press.
Kalmanovitz, Salomón. 1988. *Economía y Nación: una Breve Historia de Colombia.* Bogotá, Siglo XXI Editores.
———. 1989. *La Encrucijada de la Sinrazón y otros Ensayos.* Bogotá: Tercer Mundo Editores.
———. 1990. La Economía del Narcotráfico en Colombia. *Economía Colombiana* 226–227(February-March):18–28.
Kaplan, John. 1988. Taking Drugs Seriously. *The Public Interest* 92(Summer):32–50.
Kleiman, Mark A. R. 1992. Neither Prohibition Nor Legalization: Grudging Toleration in Drug Control Policy. *Daedalus*, 121:3:53–83.
Kleiman, Mark A. R., and Aaron J. Saiger. 1990. Drug Legalization: The Importance of Asking the Right Question. *Hofstra Law Review* 18(Spring):527–566.
Kolton, Randy J. 1990. Combating the Colombian Drug Cartels. *Military Review* March.
Krauthausen, Ciro, and Luis F. Sarmiento. 1991. *Cocaína & Co.: Un Mercado Ilegal por Dentro.* Bogotá: Tercer Mundo Editores.
Lancaster, Kelvin J. 1966. A New Approach to Consumer Theory. *Journal of Political Economy* 74(April):132–157.
Lara, Patricia. 1986. *Siembra Vientos y Recogerás Tempestades.* Bogotá: Planeta Colombiana Editorial.

Leal, Francisco. 1984. *Estado y Política en Colombia*. Bogotá: Siglo Veintiuno Editores.
———. 1989. El Sistema Político del Clientelismo. *Análisis Político* 8(September-December):8–32.
———. 1990. "Estructura y Coyuntura de la Crisis Política." In *Al Filo del Caos: Crisis Política en la Colombia de los Años 80*, edited by Francisco Leal and León Zamosc, 27–56. Bogotá: Tercer Mundo Editores.
Leal, Francisco, and Andrés Dávila. 1990. *Clientelismo: el Sistema Político y su Expresión Regional*. Bogotá: Tercer Mundo Editores.
Leal, Francisco, and León Zamosc, eds. 1990. *Al Filo del Caos: Crisis Política en la Colombia de los Años 80*. Bogotá: Tercer Mundo Editores.
Lee, Rensselaer W., III. 1988. Dimensions of the South American Cocaine Industry. *Journal of Interamerican Studies and World Affairs* 30(Summer/Fall): 87–103.
———. 1989. *The White Labyrinth: Cocaine & Political Power*. New Brunswick, N.J.: Transaction Publishers.
Lettieri, Dan J. 1978. "Theories of Drug Abuse." In *Drugs and Suicide: When Other Coping Strategies Fail*, edited by Dan J. Lettieri. Newbury Park, Calif.: Sage Publications.
Londoño, Juan L. 1990. "Income Distribution During the Structural Transformation." Unpublished Ph.D. Dissertation, Harvard University.
———. 1992. "Had Kuznets Visited Colombia" In *The Colombian Economy: Issues of Trade and Development*, edited by Alvin Cohen and Frank R. Gunter. Boulder: Westview Press.
López Toro, Alvaro. 1970. *Migración y Cambio Social en Antioquia Durante el Siglo Diez y Nueve*. Bogotá: Centro de Estudios sobre Desarrollo Económico, Universidad de Los Andes.
Losada, Rodrigo, 1991. Estudios Explicativos sobre la Violencia Contemporánea en Medellín. *Coyuntura Social* 5(December):157–167. Instituto SER de Investigación and FEDESARROLLO.
Losada, Rodrigo, and Eduardo Vélez. 1988. "Muertes Violentas en Colombia, 1979–1986." Informe de Investigación, Instituto SER de Investigación. April.
———. 1989. Tendencias de Muertes Violentas en Colombia. *Coyuntura Social* 1(December). Bogotá: FEDESARROLLO and Instituto SER de Investigación.
MacDonald, Scott B. 1988. *Dancing on a Volcano: The Latin American Drug Trade*. New York: Praeger Publishers.
———. 1989. *Mountain High, White Avalanche: Cocaine and Power in the Andean States and Panama*. New York: Praeger.
Machicado, Flavio. 1992. "Coca Production in Bolivia." In *Drug Policy in the Americas*, edited by Peter H. Smith, 88–98. Boulder: Westview Press.
Maingot, Anthony P. 1988. Laundering Drug Profits: Miami and Caribbean Tax Havens. *Journal of Interamerican Studies and World Affairs* 30(Summer/Fall):167–188.
Mamalakis, Markos J. 1969. The Theory of Sectoral Clashes. *Latin American Research Review* 4(Fall):9–16.
———. 1971. The Theory of Sectoral Clashes and Coalitions Revisited. *Latin American Research Review* 4(Fall):89–126.
Martz, John D. 1992. "Contemporary Colombian Politics: The Struggle over Democratization." In *The Colombian Economy: Issues of Trade and Development*, edited by Alvin Cohen and Frank R. Gunter, 21–46. Boulder: Westview Press.

McGee, Robert T., and Edgar L. Feige. 1989. "Policy Illusion, Macroeconomic Instability, and the Unrecorded Economy." In *The Underground Economies: Tax Evasion and Information Distortion*, edited by Edgar L. Feige, 81–109. Cambridge University Press.

McGreevey, William P. 1980. "Population Policy Under the National Front." In *Politics of Compromise: Coalition Government in Colombia*, edited by R. Albert Berry, Ronald H. Hellman, and Mauricio Solaún, 413–432. New Brunswick, N. J.: Transaction Books.

McKinnon, Ronald. 1973. *Money and Capital in Economic Development*. Washington, D.C.: Brookings Institution.

Medina G., Carlos. 1990. *Autodefensas Paramilitares y Narcotráfico en Colombia*. Bogotá: Editorial Documentos Periodísticos.

Meisel, Adolfo. 1988. Consideraciones Acerca de la Presencia de Sobre (Sub) Facturación en las Estadísticas de Comercio Exterior de Colombia. *Ensayos Sobre Política Económica* 14(December):135–142.

———. 1990. Una Nota sobre: ¿Qué Tanta Subfacturación Hay en las Cifras de Importación de Colombia? *Ensayos Sobre Política Económica* 17(June): 99–106.

Melo, Jorge O. 1990. "Los Paramilitares y su Impacto sobre la Política." In *Al Filo del Caos: Crisis Política en la Colombia de los Años 80*, edited by Francisco Leal and León Zamosc. Bogotá: Tercer Mundo Editores.

Michaels, Robert J. 1988. Addiction, Compulsion, and the Technology of Consumption. *Economic Inquiry* 26(January):75–88.

Miron, Jeffrey A., and Jeffrey Zwiebel. 1991. Alcohol Consumption During Prohibition. *American Economic Review* 81(May):242–247.

Mishan, E. J. 1990. Narcotics: The Problem and the Solution. *The Political Quarterly* 61(October-December):441–462.

Molano, Alfredo. 1987. *Selva Adentro: Una Historia Oral de la Colonización del Guaviare*. Bogotá: El Ancora Editores.

Montenegro, Armando. 1983. La Crisis del Sector Financiero Colombiano. *Ensayos Sobre Política Económica* 4(December):51–89.

Mora, Leonidas. 1989. "Las Condiciones Económicas del Medio y Bajo Caguán." In *Colonización, Coca y Guerrilla*, edited by Jaime E. Jaramillo, Leonidas Mora, and Fernando Cubides, 103–157. 3rd ed. Bogotá: Alianza Editorial Colombiana.

Mora de Tovar, Gilma. 1988. *Aguardiente y Conflictos Sociales en la Nueva Granada Siglo XVIII*. Bogotá: Universidad Nacional de Colombia.

Morales, Edmundo. 1989. *Cocaine: White Gold Rush in Peru*. Tucson: The University of Arizona Press.

Morawetz, David. 1981. *Why the Emperor's New Clothes Are Not Made in Colombia*. New York: Oxford University Press.

Mosquera Chaux, Víctor. 1989. "Las Relaciones entre Colombia y los Estados Unidos y el Narcotráfico Internacional de Drogas." Presented at a Symposium on Colombia-U.S. Relations, School of Advanced International Studies, Johns Hopkins University, Washington, D.C., March 6, Processed.

Mullen, Rod, and Naya Arbiter. 1992. "Against the Odds: Therapeutic Community Approaches to Underclass Drug Abuse." In *Drug Policy in the Americas*, edited by Peter H. Smith, 128–201. Boulder: Westview Press.

Musgrave, Richard A., and Malcom Gillis. 1971. *Fiscal Reform for Colombia: Final Report and Staff Papers of the Colombian Commission on Tax Reform*. Cambridge: Harvard Law School, International Tax Program.

Nadelmann, Ethan A. 1985. International Drug Trafficking and U.S. Foreign Policy. *The Washington Quarterly* 8(Fall):87–104.
———. 1986a. Unlaundering Dirty Money Abroad: U.S. Foreign Policy and Financial Secrecy Jurisdictions. *Inter-American Law Review* 18(1):33–81.
———. 1986b. Latinoamérica: Economía Política del Comercio de Cocaína. *Texto y Contexto* 9(September-December):27–49.
———. 1987–1988. The DEA in Latin America: Dealing with Institutionalized Corruption. *Journal of Interamerican Studies and World Affairs* 29(Winter):1–39.
———. 1988a. U.S. Drug Policy: A Bad Export. *Foreign Policy*, 70(Spring):83–108.
———. 1988b. The Case for Legalization. *The Public Interest* 92(Summer):3–31.
———. 1989a. Víctimas Involuntarias: Consecuencias de las Políticas de Prohibición de Drogas. *Debate Agrario* 7:127–164.
———. 1989b. Drug Prohibition in the United States: Costs, Consequences, and Alternatives. *Science* 245(September 1):939–946.
———. 1991a. "Beyond Drug Prohibition: Evaluating the Alternatives." In *Searching for Alternatives: Drug-Control Policy in the United States*, edited by Melvyn B. Krauss, and Edward P. Lazear. Stanford: Hoover Institution Press.
———. 1991b. America's Drug Problem: Alternative Perspectives, Alternative Futures. *Bulletin of the American Academy of Arts and Sciences* XLV(December):24–40.
———. 1992. Thinking Seriously About Alternatives to Drug Prohibition. *Daedalus* 121(Summer):85–132.
Naylor, R. Thomas. 1987. *Hot Money and the Politics of Debt*. New York: Linden Press/Simon and Schuster.
Nelson, Richard R., T. Paul Schultz, and Robert L. Slighton. 1971. *Structural Change in a Developing Economy: Colombia's Problems and Prospects*. Princeton: Princeton University Press.
Ocampo, José A. 1984. *Colombia y la Economía Mundial 1830–1910*. Bogotá: Siglo Veintiuno Editores.
———. 1991. "The Transition from Primary Exports to Industrial Development in Colombia." In *Diverging Paths: Comparing a Century of Scandinavian and Latin American Economic Development*, edited by Magnus Blomstrom and Patricio Meller, 213–243. Inter-American Development Bank.
———. 1992. "Prospects for Medium-Term Growth in Colombia." In *The Colombian Economy: Issues of Trade and Development*, edited by Alvin Cohen and Frank R. Gunter, 301–423. Boulder: Westview Press.
Ocampo, José A., and Guillermo Perry. 1983. La Reforma Fiscal 1982–1983. *Coyuntura Económica* 13, 1 (March).
Orjuela, Luis J. 1990. "Narcotráfico y Política en la Década de los Ochenta: Entre la Represión y el Diálogo." In *Narcotráfico en Colombia: Dimensiones Políticas, Económicas, Jurídicas e Internacionales*, edited by Carlos G. Arrieta, et al., 199–276. Bogotá: Tercer Mundo Editores-Ediciones Uniandes.
Orozco, Jorge Eliécer. 1987. *Lehder . . . el Hombre*. Bogotá: Plaza and Janes.
Ortega, Francisco J. 1982. Notas Sobre la Reciente Evolución Económica e Institucional del Sector Financiero. *Ensayos Sobre Política Económica* 1(March):21–43.
Palacio, Germán, ed. 1990. *La Irrupción del Paraestado*. Instituto Latinoamericano de Servicios Legales Alternativos.

Pérez G., Augusto. 1988. "Los Años Ochentas." In *Historia de la Drogadicción en Colombia*, edited by Augusto Pérez G., 71–109. Bogotá: Tercer Mundo—Ediciones Uniandes.

Pérez G., Augusto, et al. 1988. "A la Búsqueda de Elementos para Explicar el Consumo de SPA." In *Historia de la Drogadicción en Colombia*, edited by Augusto Pérez G., 111–116. Bogotá: Tercer Mundo-Ediciones Uniandes.

Perry, Guillermo, and Mauricio Cárdenas. 1986. *Diez Años de Reformas Tributarias en Colombia*. Bogotá: Universidad Nacional de Colombia and FEDESARROLLO.

Prieto, Enrique. 1988. "Los Años Setentas." In *Historia de la Drogadicción en Colombia*, edited by Augusto Pérez G., 51–70. Bogotá: Tercer Mundo—Ediciones Uniandes.

Rafuse, Robert W. 1991. Fiscal Disparities in Chicagoland. *Intergovernmental Perspective* 17 (Summer): 14–19.

Restrepo, Juan C. 1985. Reflexiones Sobre la Rentabilidad Empresarial en Colombia. *Ensayos Sobre Política Económica* 7(June):11–25.

Restrepo, Juan C., Juan G. Serna, and Manuel G. Rosas. 1983. Inflación, Financiamiento y Capitalización Empresarial. *Ensayos Sobre Política Económica* 4(December):153–198.

Reuter, Peter. 1984. The (Continued) Vitality of Mythical Numbers. *The Public Interest* 75(Spring):135–147.

———. 1985. Eternal Hope: America's Quest for Narcotics Control. *The Public Interest* 79(Spring):79–95.

———. 1988. Can the Borders Be Sealed? *The Public Interest* 92(Summer): 51–65.

———. 1992a. "After the Borders are Sealed: Can Domestic Sources Substitute for Imported Drugs?" In *Drug Policy in the Americas*, edited by Peter H. Smith, 163–177. Boulder: Westview Press.

———. 1992b. Hawks Ascendant: The Punitive Trend of American Drug Policy. *Daedalus* 121(Summer):15–52.

Revéiz, Edgar and María J. Pérez. 1986. "Colombia: Moderate Economic Growth, Political Stability, and Social Welfare." In *Latin American Political Economy: Financial Crisis and Political Change*, edited by Jonathan Hartlyn and Samuel A. Morley. Boulder: Westview Press.

Reyes, Alejandro P. 1989. "Geografía de los Conflictos Sociales y de la Violencia en Colombia." Presented at the symposium on "Political Crisis in Colombia: Violence, Mobilization, and the Restoration of Legitimacy." Center for Iberian and Latin American Studies, University of California San Diego, La Jolla, December, Mimeo.

———. 1990. "La Violencia y la Expansión Territorial del Narcotráfico." In *Economía y Política del Narcotráfico*, edited by Juan Tokatlian and Bruce Bagley, 117–140. Bogotá: Ediciones Uniandes.

Rincón, Fabio. c1990. *Leyenda y Verdad de El Mejicano*. Aquí y Ahora Editores.

Rubio, María I. 1988. "Siglo xx: 1900–1960." In *Historia de la Drogadicción en Colombia*, edited by A. Pérez G. Bogotá: Tercer Mundo, Ediciones Uniandes.

Rueda, María C. 1990a. "La Transición Demográfica." In *40 Años de Desarrollo: su Impacto Social*, edited by Miguel Urrutia, 81–91. Bogotá: Biblioteca Banco Popular.

———. 1990b. "La Revolución Femenina." In *40 Años de Desarrollo: su Impacto Social*, edited by Miguel Urrutia. Bogotá: Biblioteca Banco Popular.

———. 1990c. "La Educación de una Sociedad." In *40 Años de Desarrollo: su Impacto Social*, edited by Miguel Urrutia. Bogotá: Biblioteca Banco Popular.
Ruiz Hernández, Hernando. 1979. "Implicaciones Sociales y Económicas de la Producción de la Marihuana en Colombia." In *Marihuana: Legalización o Represión*, edited by Asociación Nacional de Instituciones Financieras (ANIF), 107–228. Bogotá: Biblioteca ANIF de Economía.
Sah, Raj. 1986. "A General Equilibrium Model of Societal Beliefs and Behavior About Honesty." Department of Economics, Yale University, Mimeo.
Salazar, Alonso J. 1990. *No Nacimos Pa' Semilla*. Bogotá: CINEP.
Sarmiento, Eduardo. 1982. *Inflación, Producción y Comercio Internacional*. Bogotá: Procultura S.A. and FEDESARROLLO.
———. 1985. Las Fallas del Mercado Financiero. *Revista de la CEPAL* 27 (December).
———. 1990a. "Economía del Narcotráfico." In *Narcotráfico en Colombia: Dimensiones Políticas, Económicas, Jurídicas e Internacionales*, edited by Carlos G. Arrieta, et al., 43–98. Bogotá: Tercer Mundo Editores—Ediciones Uniandes.
———. 1990b. Economía del Narcotráfico. *Desarrollo y Sociedad* 26(September): 11–40.
Sarmiento, Libardo, and Carlos Moreno. 1990. Narcotráfico y Sector Agropecuario en Colombia. *Economía Colombiana* 226–227(February-March): 29–37.
Segovia, Rodolfo. 1989. "Colombia: Perception vs. Reality." Occasional Paper Series (No. 3). Bethlehem, Penn.: The Martindale Center for the Study of Private Enterprise, Lehigh University.
Selowsky, Marcelo. 1969. El Efecto del Desempleo y el Creciminento sobre la Rentabilidad de la Inversión Educacional: una Aplicación a Colombia. *Revista de Planeación y Desarrollo* 1(July).
Shaw, E.S. 1973. *Financial Deepening in Economic Development*. Oxford: Oxford University Press.
Sickles, Robin, and Paul Taubman. 1991. Who Uses Illegal Drugs? *American Economic Review* 81(May):248–251.
Siegel, Ronald K. 1989. *Intoxication: Life in Pursuit of Artificial Paradise*. New York: E.P. Dutton.
Stigler, George J. and Gary S. Becker. 1977. Da Gustibus Non Est Disputandum. *American Economic Review* 67(2): 76–90.
Szasz, Thomas. 1974. *Ceremonial Chemistry: The Ritual Persecution of Drug Addicts and Pushers*. Landover Hills, Md.: Anchor Books.
———. 1992. The Fatal Temptation: Drug Prohibition and the Fear of Autonomy. *Daedalus* 121(Summer):161–164.
Tenjo, Jaime. 1990. Opportunities, Aspirations, and Urban Unemployment of Youth: The Case of Colombia. *Economic Development and Cultural Change* 38(July):733–761.
Thoumi, Francisco E. 1981. Human Rights Policy: Basic Human Needs and Economic Implications for LDC's. *Journal of Interamerican Studies and World Affairs* 23(May):177–201.
———. 1983. La Estructura del Crecimiento Regional y Urbano en Colombia (1960–1975). *Desarrollo y Sociedad* 10(January).
———. 1987. Some Implications of the Growth of the Underground Economy in Colombia. *Journal of Interamerican Studies and World Affairs* 29(Summer):35–53.

---. 1989. "Colombian Laws and Institutions, Money Dirtying, Money Laundering, and Narco-Businessmen's Behavior." Presented at the Fifteenth International Congress of the Latin American Studies Association, Miami, Fla., November.

---. 1990. "The Basis of Property Rights and Predatory Behavior in Colombia." Presented at the meetings of the Association for Evolutionary Economics, Washington, D.C., Dec. 27–30.

---. 1992. "The Economic Impact of Narcotics in Colombia." In *Drug Policy in the Americas*, edited by Peter H. Smith, 57–71. Boulder: Westview Press.

Todaro, Michael P. 1969. A Model of Labor Migration and Urban Unemployment in Less Developed Countries. *American Economic Review* 59 (March):138–148.

Tokatlian, Juan G. 1988. National Security and Drugs: Their Impact on Colombian-US Relations. *Journal of Interamerican Studies and World Affairs* 30(Spring):133–160.

---. 1990. "La Política Exterior de Colombia Hacia Estados Unidos, 1978–1990: El Asunto de las Drogas y su Lugar en las Relaciones entre Bogotá y Washington." In *Narcotráfico en Colombia: Dimensiones Políticas, Económicas, Jurídicas e Internacionales*, edited by Carlos G. Arrieta, et al., 277–374. Bogotá: Tercer Mundo Editores—Ediciones Uniandes.

Torres, Camilo R. 1963. "La Violencia y los Cambios Socio-Culturales en las Areas Rurales Colombianas." Presented at the First National Sociology Congress, Bogotá. Reprinted in *Once Ensayos Sobre la Violencia*. 1985. Bogotá: CEREC-Centro Gaitán.

---. 1969. *Revolutionary Writings*. New York: Herder and Herder.

Torres de Galvis, Yolanda, and Lenn Murrelle. 1987. *Estudio Nacional sobre Alcoholismo y Consumo de Sustancias que Producen Dependencia: Colombia 1987*. Medellín: School of Public Health, Universidad de Antioquia.

Torres de Galvis, Yolanda, and Elvia Velásquez de Pavón. 1990. "Estudio de Casos y Controles sobre Factores de Riesgo Psicosociales para Violencia Juvenil." Medellín: Facultad Nacional de Salud Pública, Universidad de Antioquia. Processed.

Twinam, Ann. 1980. From Jew to Basque: Ethnic Myths and Antioqueño Entrepreneurship. *Journal of Interamerican Studies and World Affairs* 22 (February):81–107.

United States Department of State, Bureau of International Narcotics Matters. 1990. *International Narcotics Control Strategy Report*. March.

---. 1991. *International Narcotics Control Strategy Report*. March.

---. 1992. *International Narcotics Control Strategy Report*. March.

United States General Accounting Office. 1988. *Drug Control in Colombia*. Washington, D.C.

Urrutia, Miguel. 1983. *Gremios, Política Económica y Democracia*. Bogotá: Fondo Cultural Cafetero.

---. 1985. *Winners and Losers in Colombia's Economic Growth in the 1970s*. New York: Oxford University Press.

---. 1990a. "De una Sociedad Rural a un País Urbano." In *40 Años de Desarrollo: Su Impacto Social*, edited by Miguel Urrutia. Bogotá: Biblioteca Banco Popular.

---. 1990b. Análisis Costo-Beneficio del Tráfico de Drogas para la Economía Colombiana. *Coyuntura Económica* 20(October):115–126.

———. 1991. "On the Absence of Economic Populism in Colombia." In *The Macroeconomics of Populism in Latin America*, edited by Rudiger Dornbusch and Sebastian Edwards, 369–387. Chicago: University of Chicago Press.
Urrutia, Miguel, and Adriana Pontón. 1992. "Entrada de Capitales, Diferenciales de Interés, y Narcotráfico." Bogotá. Mimeo.
Valderrama, Fanny M. 1988. Metodología de Cálculo, Análisis y Aplicaciones de las Series del Producto Interno Bruto Trimestral. *Revista de Planeación y Desarrollo* 20(January):121–172.
Van Wert, J. W. 1988. The U.S. State Department's Narcotics Control Policy in the Americas. *Journal of Interamerican Studies and World Affairs* 30(Summer/Fall):1–18.
Vega C., Renán and Eduardo Rodriguez R. 1990. *Economía y Violencia: el Antidemocrático Desarrollo Capitalista de Colombia en los Años Cincuenta*. Fondo de Publicaciones Universidad Distrital.
Véliz, Claudio. 1980. *The Centralist Tradition in Latin America*. Princeton University Press.
Vernez, Georges. 1973. "Bogotá's Pirate Settlements: an Opportunity for Metropolitan Development." Unpublished Doctoral Dissertation, University of California, Berkeley.
Villar, Leonardo. 1991. "Las Restricciones al Crecimiento Económico: un Modelo Sencillo de Tres Brechas." In *Apertura y Crecimiento: El Reto de los Noventa*, edited by E. Lora. Bogotá: Tercer Mundo—FEDESARROLLO.
Vivas, Jaime R. 1983. Evolución de los Principales Indicadores del Sector Salud en Colombia en la Década del 70. *Coyuntura Económica* 13(June).
Warren, Robert P. and Jennifer Marks. 1980. Foreign-Born Emigration from the United States: 1960 to 1970. *Demography* 17(February):71–84.
Whynes, David K. 1992. "The Colombian Cocaine Trade and the 'War on Drugs'." In *The Colombian Economy: Issues of Trade and Development*, edited by Alvin Cohen and Frank Gunter. Boulder: Westview Press.
Wiesner, Eduardo. 1982. "El Origen Político del Desequilibrio." In *Déficit Fiscal*, Contraloría General de la República and FESCOL.
———. 1985. Latin American Debt: Lessons and Pending Issues. *American Economic Review* 75(May):191–195.
Wilde, Alexander W. 1978. "Conversations Among Gentlemen: Oligarchical Democracy in Colombia." In *The Breakdown of Democratic Regimes*, edited by Juan J. Linz and Alfred Stepan, 28–81. Baltimore: Johns Hopkins University Press.
Williams, Eric. 1970. *From Columbus to Castro: The History of the Caribbean 1492–1969*. André Deutsch Limited.
Winston, Gordon C. 1980. Addiction and Backsliding: A Theory of Compulsive Consumption. *Journal of Economic Behavior and Organization* 1(December):295–324.
Wirpsa, Leslie. 1989. Colombian Mafia Hurt by Testimony of Key Deserter. *The Miami Herald*, 12 June: 4A.
World Bank. 1990a. *World Development Report 1990*. Washington, D.C.
———. 1990b. *Colombia: Industrial Competition and Performance*. Washington, D.C.
———. 1990c. *Colombia: Policies for Efficient Growth in the 1990s*. Report No. 8346-CO. Washington, D.C.
Zinberg, N. E. 1972. Heroin Use in Vietnam and the United States: A Contrast and a Critique. *Archives of General Psychiatry* March: 486–488.

Index

Agrarian Reform Law, 38
Aid, multilateral, 39
Alcohol, x, 84, 124, 155, 240, 266, 267, 268, 269, 272n4, 272n6, 272n12
Alliance for Progress, 38
ANDI. *See* National Industrialists Association
Antequera, José, 220
Antimarkets, 251–252, 254
la Apuntada, 145
Argentina, 95
Assassination, 10, 56, 57, 76, 77–78, 101, 125, 128, 144, 157, 165n18, 215, 217, 219, 221, 223, 224, 227
Authoritarianism, 79, 81, 105, 116n8
Autonomy: governmental, 92–93, 105; landlord, 81; local government, 220; regional, 7, 47, 57

Balance of payments, 2, 8, 10, 18, 45, 54, 64n50, 165n17, 184, 189, 190, 191, 194, 201n10, 203, 242
Bank of International Settlements, 191
Bankruptcy, 53, 54, 108, 118n28, 174, 213, 241
Baquero Borda, Hernando, 217
Barco, Virgilio, 2, 6, 7, 13n5, 56, 57, 58, 75, 108, 163n3, 211, 212, 217, 218, 220, 221, 222, 225
Bateman, Jaime, 13n4
Bazuco, x, 149n11, 179, 196, 267, 268, 269, 270, 273n19
Behavior: addictive, 256–257; consumer, 97–98; predatory, 68, 82, 85, 102, 103, 104, 109; producer, 97–98; rent-seeking, 7, 8, 47, 59, 68, 82, 86–91, 102, 103, 104, 109, 174; risk-minimizing, 133, 140, 144, 171; socially accepted, 2, 68, 79, 83, 99, 100, 172, 236
Betancur, Belisario, 6, 13n5, 52, 53, 56, 105, 128, 209, 212, 214, 216–217, 220
Birth rates, 20

Bolivia, 168, 170, 171, 172, 175; coca growing, 130, 135, 140, 147, 167, 202n20; cocaine production, 147, 180; drug consumption in, xi, 181; share in U.S. markets, 175
Brazil: coca growth, 130; cocaine market in, 148; drug exports, 201n7
Budget: allocation of resources in, 108; composition, 32; control of, 33; deficits, 32, 38, 41, 55, 63n38, 213, 242; planning, 40
Bureaucracy, 40; accountability, 106; corruption in, 168
Bush, George, 222

Cali cartel, 9, 142, 145, 146, 147, 150n26, 157, 160–161
Cano, Guillermo, 157, 217, 218
Capital: consumption, 255; dirty, 152, 161, 198, 204; drug, 109; equipment, 80; fixed, 50; flight, 10, 54, 119n48, 173, 183, 184, 191, 193, 194, 198, 201n10, 237, 245, 249; formation, 90, 91; gains, 43, 99, 100, 161; hidden, 100, 102, 161, 204; human, 86, 253; illegal, 60, 213; inflows, 10, 54, 183–185, 194, 244, 246; international, 58; laundering, 5, 10, 51, 56, 99, 101, 102, 110, 119n48, 159, 161, 162, 173, 176, 194, 218, 223, 237, 238, 246, 247, 249, 290n6; legalization of, 7, 8, 209; long-term, 18; markets, 36, 37, 44, 45, 49, 56, 63n33, 63n35, 63n42, 96, 99, 104, 105, 108, 117n18, 138, 174, 203, 282; resources, 237
Capitalism, 174; contradictions in, 68; democratic, 5, 105, 109, 237; evolution of, 81; raw, 5, 237, 247; rent-seeking, 8
Cartels, 7, 9, 135, 142, 143, 145, 146, 147, 150n26, 222, 223, 224, 227, 228, 238
Carter, Jimmy, 127, 210, 228
Castro, Tulio Manuel, 217

Catholic Church: concept of society, 79; and conservative party, 87; land ownership, 84; monopoly on education, 22–23; opposition to drugs, 123; property expropriation, 84, 117$n23$; property ownership, 117$n23$; view of society, 83
Central Bank, 31, 37, 44, 48, 49, 51, 59, 101, 119$n45$, 161, 190, 197, 201$n12$, 207, 242, 246
Chicha, 123, 124, 125, 266
Chile: cocaine production, 130; violence in, 73
Civismo en Marcha, 158
Class: analysis, 68; consciousness, 68, 69, 116$n4$; emerging, 208; identity, 5; political, 33; struggle, 4, 68, 69
Clientelism, 7, 8, 32–33, 40, 48, 59, 69, 71, 81, 86–91, 103, 104, 106, 108, 158, 168, 225
Coca, 123; derivatives, x; growing, 138, 140, 147; harvesting, 130; paste, 131, 132, 140, 169, 183; prices, 146; production, 130–133; usage, 124
Cocaine, 2, 9, 268, 270, 271; crack, 262, 263, 272$n8$, 283, 291$n16$; exports, 36, 45, 58, 133, 144, 186tab, 187, 188; industry growth, 130–133, 180–183, 186tab; industry structure, 138–147; laboratories, 131; manufacturing, 131–132, 138; marketing, 132; prices, 146; production, 125, 171, 179; profits, 138; revenues from, 45; transport, 131
Coffee: booms, 36, 49, 174, 243, 245; dependence on, 18; prices, 18, 26, 27, 36, 37, 45, 57, 243
Coffee Growers Federation, 36
Colombia: advantages to drug industry, 104, 131–132, 167–176; capitalism in, 174; clientelism in, 7, 8, 32–33, 40, 48, 59, 69, 71, 81, 86–91, 103, 104, 106, 108, 168, 225; cocaine industry advantages, 131–132; cocaine processing, 169; conservative party, 6, 12$n2$, 41, 72, 87; drug use in, 10, 266–269; economic growth, xiii, 2, 8, 18–19, 26, 60; economic integration in, 18; economic policy in, 4; export assembly free zones, 100; geopolitical location as factor in drug industry, 167–171, 174; gross domestic product, 2, 3, 4, 8, 18, 19, 25–31; income levels, 1; institutional crisis in, 78–94; liberal party, 6, 12$n2$, 72, 87; political economy, 5; political system, 6; postwar development, 1, 3, 18–19; power structure, 32–33; underground economy in, 98–102

Colombian Coal, 89
Colombian Farmers Society, 209
Colombian Petroleum Company, 89
Colombian Revolutionary Armed Forces, 53
Colón Free Zone (Panama), 100, 177$n3$, 177$n6$
Colonialism, 8, 21, 79, 80, 84, 124
Communications, 30, 36, 47, 69, 78, 82, 116$n8$
Community Action Committees, 140
Competition, 70; in domestic markets, 57; in drug production, 9; international, 19, 69, 282; market, 92, 93, 108, 148; for resources, 51; threats against, 134
Conflict: civil, 91, 106, 248; class, 4; group, 102; of interest, 90; resolution, 2, 96, 134, 140, 141, 172, 240; social, 4, 67, 83; value, 82–83
Constitution, 7, 19, 57, 83, 105, 108, 156, 225, 227
Consumption: capital, 255; conspicuous, 162, 208, 240; costs, 248. See also Drug consumption
Contraband, 51, 100, 101, 161, 168, 169, 173, 184, 190, 191, 192, 193, 198, 201$n11$, 204, 244, 245; competition, 69; export, 98; import, 98; institutionalization of, 173
Contracts: enforcing, 92, 102; government, 109
Corruption, 2, 5, 92, 139, 141, 152, 168, 169, 170, 171, 177$n5$
Credit: access to, 117$n18$; collateralizing, 54; consumer, 45; development, 44, 118$n28$; export, 40; external, 44, 63$n32$; long-term, 37, 44, 51, 99, 100; official, 43; policies, 37; private sector, 50
Currency: appreciation, 45; devaluation, 37, 38, 39, 40, 43, 54, 55; revaluation, 44, 63$n32$, 169

Debt: crises, 1, 2, 3, 19, 70, 89, 241, 247; to equity ratio, 50; external, 2, 3, 8, 48, 35tab, 54, 55, 63$n38$, 70; international, 89; management, 46; maturity structure, 50–51; policy, 8; service ratios, 46
Delegitimation, 2, 10, 71; acceleration of, 236; advancement of, ix; regime, 3, 10, 85, 102, 104, 172, 173, 175, 205, 236, 237, 247
Democracy: capitalist, 5, 105, 109; grass roots, 220; oligarchical, 118$n27$; participatory, 60
Democratic Alliance party, 226

Development: agricultural, 39; credit, 44, 118n28; of drug industry, 9; economic, 1, 3, 17; failures, 70; infrastructure, 36, 58; paramilitary groups, 10; planning, 38, 47; rural, 25, 43, 203; social, 1, 3, 4–5

Díaz, Maria Helena, 221

"Dishonesty trap," 103, 236

Drug addiction, 78, 251–271; economic theories, x, 251–257; epidemic risk, 269–271; and family structure, 268, 269, 290n13; models of, 253–260, 276–278; policy implications, 10; in producer countries, x; psychological factors, x, 257–260, 277–278; resources for prevention, 110; reversal, 254; risk of, 262; therapeutic communities in, 260

Drug consumption, xi, 10, 205, 251–271; ceremonial, 148n1; in Colombia, 266–269; by drug traffickers, 155, 164n7; economic theories, x, 251–257; in Europe, xi, 148, 167, 177n10, 183, 201n7; gender in, 269; political costs of, xi; psychological theories, x, 257–260, 277–278; revenue from, 124; seen as American problem, 205; social cost of, xi, 124, 150n21, 235, 263; in United States, xi; utility function, 252–253, 255

Drug industry, illegal: advantageous location in Colombia, 104, 165n18; and aggregate demand, 244–246; assimilation into mainstream, 1, 109, 156–163, 215; capital inflow in, 183–185; catalytic effect, 236–238; characteristics of traffickers in, 154–156; competition in, 9; and construction industry, 238–239; criminality in, x, 109, 139, 153–154, 164n5; decriminalization proposals, 109–110, 209, 262, 283–284; development of, 9; economic impact of, 10, 102–111, 151, 233–249; economic integration, 160–162; economies of scale, 142; effect on coca growing regions, 240–241; foreign exchange effects of, 241–244; growth of, 3, 5, 10; history of, 123–148; income from, 185–199; and inflation, 244–246; institutional relationships, 156; joint ventures in, 144, 145; leftist analysis, 3–4; legalization proposals, 109–110, 209, 210, 213, 229n8, 262, 285; macroeconomic impact, 241–249; need for international cooperation to eradicate, 110; as obstacle to capitalist democracy, 109; overview, 123–148; political base, 141; as raw capitalism, 5; relations with guerilla organizations, 159–160; risk in, 9, 135, 136, 137, 140, 141, 142, 148n4, 171; role in institutional crisis, 71; rural impact, 239–241; size of, 179–200; social costs of, 5; strategies of, 151–163; structure of, 133–147, 278–279; trust in, 136; and underground economy, 51, 104; value-added characteristics, 134, 135, 137, 171, 182; and violence, 7, 136, 137, 140. *See also specific drugs*

Drug policy, 151, 203–228; alternatives, 275–289; ambivalence in, 203–207; choices in, 109–110; extradition, 9, 156, 207, 211, 212, 213, 214, 218, 221, 223, 224, 282; inconsistent, 203–207; militarization of, 110; past, 281–286; property confiscation, 222; repressive, 110; supply suppression, ix

Drug(s): ceremonial uses, 123; control efforts, ix, x; demand for, 10, 251–262; distribution, 133, 135, 145, 146, 148, 175, 183, 201n7; export, 2, 47, 51; laboratories, 140, 142; manufacturing, 2, 138, 213; marketing, 9, 10, 132, 133, 135, 138, 183; processing, 130–132, 169, 171; production, xi, 9, 10, 125–133, 169, 174; risk in, 144; trade, xi; transport, 9, 133, 135, 138, 142, 143, 144, 145, 150n16, 150n19, 169; use by native cultures, 123; and violence, x, 1; wars, 146

"Dutch disease," 118n25, 169, 240, 249

Echavarría, Raúl, 217

ECLAC. *See* United Nations, Economic Commission for Latin America and the Caribbean

Economic: change, 67; conventional analysis, 17–60; development, 1, 3, 17; diversification, 90; growth, xiii, 2, 3, 8, 22, 26, 60; illegality, 94–98; impact of drug industry, 10, 233–249, 247–249; inequality, 8, 107; institutions, ix, 70, 78; integration, 18, 156, 160–162; norms, 102; policy, 4, 18, 31–59; privilege, 7, 8, 13n5, 79, 84; reform, ix; rights, 226; stability, 31–59; theories of addiction, x, 251–257

Economy: closed, 3, 31, 57; external factors, 17; global, 31; inequality, 8; informal, 68, 94–102; institutionalist perspective, 68–116; liberalization, 105; local, 10; modernization of, 57; opening of, 2; political, ix, 5, 69; regional, 1, 10; rural, 20; structural change in, 58; underground, ix, 1, 2, 5, 8, 47, 51, 60,

161, 168, 175, 207, 208, 235, 236, 246, 248; urban, 3, 20
Ecuador: coca growth, 130; contraband in, 173, 192; devaluations in, 52; social evolution in, 78
Education, 1, 184, 198; access to, 3, 23; church monopoly in, 22; drug, 267; enrollments, 22; expenditures, 18, 24, 39, 107; levels of, 22, 78, 86; and migration, 20; private, 22–23; state responsibility for, 22; tertiary, 22, 23, 112
Elections, 2; clientelism in, 88; local, 53; mayoral, 53
Employment: cost of living adjustments, 55; government, 87, 88; non-agricultural, 25; rural, 25; security, 69; state, 69
Escobar, Pablo, 128, 141, 146, 154, 158, 163$n1$, 165$n17$, 217, 221, 223, 224, 226, 227, 228, 250$n3$, 287–288
Ethic of inequality, 82, 91
Europe, drug markets in, xi, 148, 167, 177$n10$, 183, 201$n7$
Exchange: black market rates, 59, 192, 198, 242; controls, 26, 36–37, 40, 57–58, 173, 245; crawling peg rate, 18, 26, 39, 40, 54, 101; fixed rate, 18, 26, 36–37, 39; fluctuating rates, 36–37; foreign, 26, 27, 32, 35tab, 36–37, 40, 45, 46, 49, 51, 53, 63$n32$, 69, 101, 119$n45$, 161, 169, 170, 173, 183, 184, 189, 190, 191, 193, 205, 207, 241–244; impact of drug industry on, 241–244; laundering, 51; multiple rates, 36–37; official rates, 192, 242; rate appreciation, 46; rate differentials, 189, 190; real rate, 55, 189
Export(s), 45; contraband, 98, 173; credit, 40; earnings from, 26; expansion, 27, 41; goods and services, 31; illegal, 47, 51, 101, 169; increasing, 44; minor, 39, 40, 41; non-traditional, 18, 46; overinvoicing, 51, 161, 183, 192, 194, 242; per capita, 18; primary, 85, 245; promotion, 26, 36, 39, 54, 203; revenues, 51; service, 161, 183; subsidies, 26, 40; tax, 49
Extradition, 9, 144, 156, 207, 211, 212, 213, 214, 218, 221, 222, 223, 224, 282

FARC. *See* Colombian Revolutionary Armed Forces
FEDESARROLLO, 74, 91
FENALCO. *See* National Federation of Retailers
Finance Corporation of Valle, 209

Galán, Luis Carlos, 157, 164$n3$, 176, 221, 222, 223, 227, 282
García Herreros, Rafael, 227
Gaviria, César, 7, 57, 58, 108, 109, 225, 226, 228
Gaviria, Gustavo, 226
Gender: and drug trafficking, 155; and migration, 20–21; participation in labor force, 23; and violence, 73; and wages, 21, 23
Gómez, Alvaro, 225
Government: ability to implement policy, 280–281; accountability, 106, 108; autonomy, 92–93, 105, 220; budget deficits, 32, 38, 41, 55, 63$n38$, 213, 242; civilian, 2; contracts, 109; decentralization of, 7, 57; employment, 87, 88; enforcement of laws, 96, 97; expenditures, 36; inefficiency, 2; intervention, 69, 92, 105, 107; local, 57; participation in illegal activities, 101; preferential treatment by, 13$n5$; social expenditures, 43. *See also* State
Gross domestic product: and clientelism, 104; composition of, 25–31; consistency in, 19; decline in, 2, 3, 4, 247; drug industry impact on, 241–249; government services in, 89; growth, 8, 25–31, 46–47, 58, 61$n13$, 69, 243; and international trade, 65$n57$; sectoral composition, 18, 28tab; underground economy in, 51–52
Guerrilla groups, 2, 13$n4$, 56, 77, 140, 164$n10$, 168, 172, 175, 203, 205, 212, 216, 220, 248; assimilation of, 56, 212; dialogue with, 53; kidnapping in, 75; liberal party support of, 72; peace agreement with, 72; relations with drug industry, 159–160; rural activity, 239
Gutiérrez, Andrés, 228

Hacienda system, 80, 81, 117$n19$
Hawkins-Gilman amendment, 212
Health care, 1, 107; access to, 3, 23
Herbicides, 126, 127, 128, 129, 180, 210, 214
Heroin, x, 124, 179, 183, 227
Housing: availability, 3; construction programs, 52, 53; deficits, 3; financing for, 18, 99, 108; quality, 21–22; underinvestment in, 118$n35$; urban, 41; without down payment, 52
Hyperinflation, 32

Identity: class, 5; national, 8

IFI. *See* Industrial Finance Institute
Illegality, 94–98; benefits of, 233–234; costs of, 96; effect on market structure, 133, 134, 138; and market segmentation, 134, 138; risks of, 97–98; value-added characteristics, 135, 171; and violence, 134
Illiteracy, 3, 22, 23, 86
Import(s), 46; contraband, 98, 161, 173; goods and services, 51; illegal, 101, 118$n36$; licensing, 37, 96, 173, 194, 245; non-refundable, 201$n13$; prohibited, 37; restrictions on, 54, 55; shortages, 45; subsidies, 48; underinvoicing, 51, 101, 161, 183, 192, 194, 242
Income: agricultural, 24, 25; concentration of, ix, 5, 105, 109; distribution, 1, 3, 19, 23, 25, 39, 43, 59, 82, 83, 84, 105, 112–114, 164$n8$; from drug industry, 185–199; expectations, 82; growth, 1, 3, 27; hiding, 97, 98; illegal, 60, 61$n14$, 95, 97; illusion, 113, 114; inequalities, 19, 23, 25, 43, 76, 82, 83–86, 112–114; interest, 49; labor, 184, 197; legitimacy, 83–86; middle-class, 113, 114; national, 2; non-labor, 24; per capita, 26, 61$n14$, 113; real, 24, 248; reporting, 98, 119$n37$; stagnation in, 3; tax, 49, 53, 62$n30$, 119$n43$, 194; transfers, 108; under-reporting, 62$n29$, 99; values, 48; wage, 25
INCORA. *See* Land Reform Institute
Individualism, 5, 68, 82, 108
Industrial Finance Institute, 39
Industrialization, import-substitution, 33, 37, 69, 70, 90
Inflation, 3, 8, 32, 37–38, 41, 43, 44, 45, 46, 47, 48, 50–51, 52, 55, 58, 62$n18$, 62$n20$, 63$n42$, 119$n46$, 203, 208, 244–246
Infrastructure, 38, 140; development, 36, 55, 58; expenditures, 18, 107; financing of, 36; growth, 1
Inhalants, 269
Institutions: building of, 40; change in, 4, 71; colonial, 79; corruption in, 5; crises in, 8, 67, 78–94; deterioration of, 105; development of, 49, 80; economic, ix, 70, 78; legitimacy of, ix, 152; political, ix, 78; pre-capitalist, 21; resistance to change, 78; social, 70; traditional, 83; weakness of, 171
Instituto SER de Investigación, 74, 91
Inter-American Development Bank, 46
Interest rates, 37, 41 48, 49, 50, 51, 54, 56, 59, 93, 118$n28$
International Coffee Agreement, 57, 173

International Monetary Fund, 40, 55, 201$n10$
Investment, 10, 63$n32$; abroad, 54, 201$n10$; alternatives, 50; capital equipment, 45; direct, 248; discouragement of, 27; dollar, 54; domestic, 56; drug, 77, 109; in export industry, 85; financing, 44; in fixed capital, 50; forced, 56; foreign, 58, 248; mining, 30; nonproductive, 247; policies, 39; private, 48, 197; public, 47, 48, 90; real estate, 160, 164$n13$, 237; rural, 239; soccer league, 162, 165$n18$; speculative, 104; underreporting, 119$n37$
Isolation: geographical, 27; national, 17–18; regional, 5, 33, 82, 138, 140, 174

Japan, cocaine market in, 148
Jaramillo, Bernardo, 220, 228
Judicial system, 106; crisis in, 91–92; intimidation in, 236; paralysis in, 2; weakness of, 248
Justice: administration of, 91–92; social, 52

Kidnapping, 74, 75, 85, 143–144, 150$n25$, 160, 164$n10$, 220, 225, 248

Labor: control of, 80; educational levels of, 24; family, 137, 138; force, 20, 21, 24, 78; forced, 80; income, 184, 197; legislation, 69, 96, 109; markets, 25, 68, 105, 109; relations, 21, 78, 81; remittances, 173, 183, 184, 190, 191, 194, 243, 244; remuneration, 112, 117$n18$; rural, 68, 83; shortages, 80; strikes, 44; supply, 52, 80; unions, 33, 89
Land, 80; concentration, 25, 139; disposition, 84; peasant struggle for, 3, 38, 75; public, 84, 85; redistribution, 249; reform, 2, 18, 38, 237, 239; tenancy, 21, 25; tenure, 239
Land Reform Institute, 39
Lara Bonilla, Rodrigo, 101, 128, 157, 213–214, 215, 217, 222, 223, 227, 229$n8$, 282
Laws: compliance with, 94–98, 102, 103, 119$n37$, 119$n38$, 172; disregard for, 97, 152–153, 161, 162, 172, 236, 249, 250$n7$; enforcement of, 96; legitimate breaking of, 103; perceptions of, 152–153; tax, 48, 51
Legitimacy: of contraband, 101; defining, 67; erosion of, 67; of income, 83–86; of legal system, 91, 152; loss of, ix; state, 177$n5$, of value system, 82; weakening of, 5

Lehder, Carlos, 141, 143, 146, 150n16, 154, 155, 158, 164n7, 164n11, 219
Liberalization: economic, 105; financial, 50; market, 19, 36, 44, 49, 50, 58, 63n33, 63n35, 69, 108, 118n28, 174; trade, 7, 57
Life expectancy, 1, 20
Lleras Camargo, Alberto, 38, 62n26
Lleras Restrepo, Carlos, 20, 30, 39, 40, 41, 43, 62n25, 105
Lloreda, Rodrigo, 225
López, Martha Luz, 224
López Michelsen, Alfonso, 25, 45, 46, 51, 62n28, 174, 207, 208, 209, 215, 225
Low, Enrique, 218, 219, 227

Macana, Luis Alfredo, 217
Manufacturing: drug, 2; growth, 27; productivity, 59; recession in, 52
Marijuana, x, 2, 9, 204, 268, 269; decline in profitability, 129–130; demand for, 126; eradication campaign, 127–129, 210, 214; exports, 45, 58, 125–130, 137, 187; industry growth, 125–130, 180–183; industry structure, 137–138; production, 125, 126, 127, 128, 179; revenues from, 45; role in underground economy, 208; Santa Marta Gold, 126
Market(s): anonymous price setting in, 106; biased, 93; black, 35tab, 45, 51, 59, 69, 101, 119n45, 173, 184, 189, 190, 192, 193, 198, 241, 242; capital, 36, 37, 44, 45, 49, 56, 63n33, 63n35, 63n42, 96, 99, 104, 105, 108, 117n18, 138, 174, 203, 282; capitalist, 81; competition, 57, 92, 93, 108, 133, 148; contraband, 100–101; distorted, 105; domestic, 40, 57, 58, 65n57, 69, 167; drug, 10; external, 40; flawed, 102; formal, 68; free, 93; informal, 68, 138, 238; integration, 1, 27, 107, 247; international, 48, 49; labor, 25, 68, 105, 109; liberalization, 19, 36, 44, 45, 49, 50, 58, 63n33, 63n35, 69, 108, 118n28, 174, 203; manipulation of, 91, 106; money, 49; mortgage, 108; national, 1, 18, 78; official, 241, 242; open, 48; prices, 93; protection, 40; regional, 27; regulation, 92; segmentation, 37, 58, 68, 69, 134, 137, 138, 174; system, 92–94
Mauro Hoyos, Carlos, 219
Maza Márquez, Miguel, 221, 229n12
Medellín cartel, 7, 9, 142, 143, 145, 146, 147, 149n13, 150n26, 154, 155, 157, 158, 160, 164n11, 164n13, 214, 223, 224, 227, 228, 238
Methaqualone, 127, 171, 179, 183, 196

Mexico, 168, 169; drug consumption in, xi; homicide rates, 117n12; marijuana production, 126; use of herbicides, 210
Migration, 177n7; control, 177n7; illegal, 174; patterns, 20, 21; rural-rural, 20; rural-urban, 20, 21, 41, 239; to United States, 174–175, 184, 185, 190; urban-rural, 139
Military: coup, 72; dictatorship, 12n2; expenditures, 248, 250n9; links with drug industry, 158; role in drug control, 9, 210, 214, 215, 216, 217, 218, 219; and violence, 2
M-19 guerrillas, 13n4, 56, 143–144, 150n25, 159, 160, 216, 224, 225, 227
Modernization, 86; evolution of, 81
Molina, Gilberto "Emerald King," 153
Monetary Board, 40
Money. See Capital
Montaña Cuellar, Diego, 225
Morphine, 124
Mortality rates, 19, 20
Movimeinto Latino Nacional Party, 141
Muerte a Secuestradores, 144
Musgrave, Richard, 43

Narco-terrorism, 6, 7, 56, 157, 222, 224, 226, 228, 289n3
National Coffee Fund, 89
National Federation of Retailers, 98, 191, 209
National Front, 8, 38, 41, 87, 88, 103, 118n28
National Industrialists Association, 213
National Integration Plan, 47
Nationalism, 40
National Liberation Army, 224
National Narcotics Intelligence Consumers Commission, 128, 180
National Planning Department, 31, 38, 40, 63n38
National Security Statute, 210
Navarro, Antonio, 225
New Liberal party, 225
NNICC. See National Narcotics Intelligence Consumers Commission
Noriega, Maneul Antonio, 225
Norman's Cay (Bahamas), 143, 150n16, 155
Norms: economic, 102; gap in, 83; legal, 84; social, 102; trespassing, 84
Nutrition, 1, 22, 43

Ochoa family, 143–144, 146, 150n25, 215, 219, 223, 227, 229n10
"Operation Blast Furnace," 217

"Operation Fulminant," 210
"Operation Stopgap," 210
Opium, 130, 179, 183
Opposition, 83; fragmentation of, 5

Panama, 100, 168, 170, 177n3, 215, 223, 225
Paramilitary groups, 56, 109, 144, 164n13, 211, 213, 217, 250n5; formation of, 10, 159–160; rural activity, 240
Paraquat, 126, 127, 210
Pardo Leal, Jaime, 219, 220
Parejo, Enrique, 218
Pastrana, Misrael, 41, 62n25, 174, 204, 225
Paternalism, 79–82, 86, 88, 93, 105, 109, 158, 237
Peace Corps, 126, 149n5, 149n13
Peláez, Pablo, 224
Peru, 169, 171, 172, 175; coca growing, 130, 135, 140, 147, 167, 202n20; cocaine production, 147, 180; drug consumption in, xi, 181; laws in, 95; share in U.S. markets, 175; Shining Path in, 175, 279; social evolution in, 78
Pinochet, Augusto, 130
Pizarro, Carlos, 220
Plantero system, 139–140
Policy: adaptation, 18; agenda, 102–111; alternatives, 10, 275–289; ambivalence in, 203–207; changes, 10, 26, 60, 105; continuity, 19, 58, 87; credit, 37; debt, 8; drug control, x, 6, 9, 151, 203–228; economic, 4, 18, 31–59; experimental, 203, 277; failure, 11; formulation, 31, 246; implementation, 17, 246; inconsistent, 6, 203–207; industrial, 104, 105; investment, 39; long-term, 9, 32, 278; macroeconomic, 1; management, 1; market-oriented, 47; monetary, 47, 241; past, 281–286; population, 20; protectionist, 100; reactive, 31; reform, 8; repressive, 11; short-term, 206, 279; social, 31; trade, 70; traditional, 36–39; variables, 92; wage, 25
Political: change, 19; clientelism, 7, 8, 32–33, 40, 48, 59, 69, 71, 81, 86–91, 103, 106, 158, 168, 225; costs of drugs, xi; decentralization, 47; economy, ix, 5, 69; inequality, 86; institutions, ix, 78; integration of drug industry, 156, 157–159; participation, 53; parties, 6, 12n2, 41, 72, 225; power, 87, 92, 156; reform, ix, 19, 220; systems, 30–59
Ponzi finance schemes, 50
Poppy cultivation, 2
Popular Liberation Army, 226

Population: control policy, 20; growth, 18, 19–25, 60n1, 60n2, 80
Populism, 32, 33, 40, 108, 119n47, 158
Posada, León, 217
Poverty, 24, 25, 43, 56, 61n11, 76
Power: abuses, 92, 110; concentration of, 49, 92, 117n19; distribution of, 92; elites, 4; inequalities, 81; monopoly, 88; political, 87, 92; structures, 32–33, 78; transfers of, 2; vacuums, 140
Price(s): anonymous setting, 106; coffee, 18, 26, 27, 36, 37, 45, 55, 56, 57, 243; consumer, 41; controls, 105; discrimination, 93; effect on drug demand, 252, 254–255, 256; elasticity, 252, 261; fluctuations, 36; incentives, 81; index, 41; manipulation of, 50, 91; market, 93; primary product, 26–27; retail, 196; rigidities, 94; staple goods, 38; stock, 50; wholesale, 34tab, 41, 135, 150n17, 150n27, 169, 196
Privatization, 89, 91, 248; security, 102
Production: agricultural, 25; cocaine, 125; domestic, 53, 244; drug, xi, 10; efficiency, 105; factors of, 80, 104, 170, 171, 177n5; marijuana, 125, 126; organization of, 80; short-term, 174; speculation, 85, 174, 175
PROEXPO, 39, 40
Profit: conglomerate, 64n44; and demand, 119n48; domestic, 201n5; maximizing, 96; paper, 49; private sector, 13n5; risk taking in, 9; short-term, 85, 248; underreporting, 119n37

Quintero Vargas, Franklin, 221
Quintín Lame movement, 226

Ramirez, Gómez, 217
Reagan, Ronald, 176n3, 212, 283, 291n14
Real estate, 160, 164n13, 205, 237, 238; financing for, 99; and hidden capital, 100, 102, 160, 161
Recession, 24, 26, 27, 36, 51, 52, 192
Reform: agrarian, 38, 39, 41, 56; constitutional, 40, 57, 87; economic, ix; failed, 2; financial, 50; implementation, 106; land, 2, 18, 38, 237, 239; policy, 8; political, ix, 19, 220; redistributive, 203; social, ix; tax, 2, 18, 41, 43, 44, 47, 53, 56, 58, 98, 203, 218
Regime delegitimation, 3, 10, 67, 85, 102, 104, 116n2, 172, 173, 175, 205, 236, 237, 247
Relationships: dependency, 81, 158; in drug industry, 144, 145; marketing, 201n7; paternalistic, 86

Rent-seeking, 7, 8, 47, 59, 68, 82, 86–91, 102, 103, 104, 105, 109, 174
Resources, 41; allocation of, 44, 45, 58, 108, 208; capital, 237; competition for, 51; constraints, 52; law enforcement, 97; mining, 47; transfer of, 96
Revollo, Mario, 225
Rights: economic, 226; human, 3, 110, 117$n11$, 217, 226, 228; land, 139; property, 5, 77, 80, 82, 83–86, 90, 92, 103, 104, 105, 137, 204, 216, 239; protection of, 103, 104
Rivera, Verónica, 154, 155
Rodríguez, Freddy, 221
Rodríguez-Gacha, Gonzalo, 146, 152, 153, 158, 163$n3$, 164$n11$, 217, 221, 223, 224
Rodríguez Orejuela, Gilberto, 223
Rojas Pinilla, Gustavo, 41, 62$n25$, 72, 204
Roldán, Antonio, 221
Rural: development, 43, 203; food security, 22; impact of drug industry, 239–241; investment, 239; labor, 68, 83; paternalism, 86; society, 33; violence, 18, 21, 73; wages, 239

Samper Pizano, Ernesto, 220
"San Andresitos," 161. *See also* Contraband
Sandinistas, 159
Sector, agricultural, 18, 30; infrastructure building in, 38; labor force in, 21; large-scale, 24; output, 27; performance of, 24; sharecropping in, 21
Sector, energy, 47
Sector, financial, 53
Sector, formal: benefits of, 96; costs of business in, 96; growth in, 53
Sector, industrial, 18; financial structure, 50; labor force in, 21
Sector, informal, 68, 94–102, 118$n34$
Sector, manufacturing, 27, 30, 52; growth in, 36; productivity, 59; tariff protection in, 37
Sector, mining, 27, 30, 47; growth in, 30, 31; illegality in, 139; investment in, 30; productivity, 59
Sector, private, 1; credit in, 48, 50; drug income in, 10; financing, 53; investment, 48; profits in, 13$n5$; protection of property in, 104
Sector, public: deficits, 34tab; expenditures in, 25; in gross domestic product, 89, 91; growth in, 89, 104; investment, 48; privatization in, 91, 248; revenues, 39, 52; role in education, 22–23
Sector, service, 30; labor force in, 21

Security: employment, 69; food, 22; private, 85, 102, 246; provision of, 3; services, 248
Sharecropping, 21
Shining Path, 175, 279
Sicarios, 10, 76, 160, 237, 238, 270
Sinister window, 51, 64$n50$, 101, 208, 209, 246
Slavery, 80, 117$n17$
Smuggling, 101, 118$n36$, 135, 142, 143, 145, 168, 173. *See also* Contraband
Soccer league investment, 162, 165$n18$
Social: change, 71, 82, 83, 85, 103; cohesion, 8, 67, 107; conflict, 4, 67, 71, 79, 83; costs of drugs, xi; decomposition, 104; development, 1, 3, 4–5; equality, 94; evolution, 78; expenditures, 7, 18, 43, 47, 57; hierarchy, 79; institutions, 70; justice, 52; mobility, 112; norms, 68, 71, 102; policy, 31; privileges, 79; programs, 18; recognition, 156, 157; reform, ix; structures, 4, 79; unrest, 19; values, 71
Social Conservative Party, 225, 226
Soler, Miguel, 224
Soviet Union, drug consumption in, xi
Spain, 223
Special Exchange Account, 34tab, 48, 49, 52, 53
Standard of living, 3, 4, 59, 139, 177$n7$
State, 1; accountability, 7, 57; corruption, 5, 169; distrust of, 82; economic role, 30, 31; elitism in, 86; employment, 69; enforcement of laws, 101, 106; expenditures, 6; growth of, 89; inability to perform, 4, 8, 59, 68, 172, 204; legitimacy, 177$n5$; role in education, 22; weakness in, ix, 2, 10, 71, 88, 99, 102, 110, 156, 172, 175, 241
Subsidies, 105, 194; export, 26, 40; foreign exchange, 49; import, 48

Tambs, Lewis, 159
Tariffs, 41, 54, 57, 70, 100, 118$n28$, 118$n36$, 173, 194; increased, 37; protection, 37
Tax(es), 36; amnesties, 43, 48, 53, 56, 98, 99, 161, 209, 213, 229$n8$, 282; avoidance, 44–45, 98, 204; capital gains, 99, 100, 161; collection, 5, 44, 48, 99, 245; direct, 48, 49; evasion, 43, 48, 99, 119$n42$; export, 49; havens, 118$n33$; income, 44–45, 49, 53, 62$n30$, 96, 119$n42$, 119$n44$, 194; increasing, 43; inflation, 44; laws, 48, 51; net worth, 99, 100, 161; progressive, 43, 99; reform, 2, 18, 41, 43, 44, 47, 53, 56, 58, 98, 203,

218; sales, 98; sin, 273*n16;* surcharges, 55; value-added, 55, 96, 194; wealth, 49
Technology, 71, 169, 170; agricultural, 24; effect on society, 116*n8;* encouragement of, 58
Tobacco, x, 84, 124, 267, 268, 270
Torres, Father Camilo, 12*n4*
Tourism, 173, 183, 184, 193, 197, 198
Trade: barriers, 57, 100, 105, 108; external, 18; foreign, 105; instability, 34*tab;* internal, 82; international, 7, 57, 65*n57;* liberalization, 7, 57; policies, 70; surplus, 48; terms of, 45
Tranquilizers, 268, 269
Transnational corporations, 48, 119*n37,* 183–184
Transportation, 30, 31, 36, 58, 63*n37,* 68, 169, 174
Turbay, Julio César, 47, 51, 63*n38,* 64*n54,* 127, 209, 210, 211, 212, 225, 227

Underground economy, ix, 1, 71, 94–102, 168, 175, 207, 208, 235, 236, 246, 248; development of, 51; and drug industry, 104; and government policies, 98–102; and gross domestic product, 51–52; growth of, 2, 5, 8, 47, 60; and illegal capital, 161
Unemployment, 2, 3, 168, 169, 170, 177*n7,* 236, 238, 246, 269; of college graduates, 52, 112; and drug industry, 139; urban, 39, 52, 56
United Nations: Declaration on Population, 60*n3;* Drug Control Programme, 289; Economic Commission for Latin America and the Caribbean, 38
United States: Central Intelligence Agency, 180; cocaine markets in, 142, 144, 167, 184, 201*n7;* Colombian migration to, 174–175, 184, 185, 190; deligitimation in, 206; Department of Justice, 223; Department of State, 128, 129, 146, 149*n11,* 195, 202*n20;* drug consumption in, xi, 206; drug distribution in, 145, 148, 168, 175; drug policy, ix, 283, 289*n2;* foreign policies, 205; gross domestic product, 26; Hawkins-Gilman amendment, 212; income reporting, 119*n39;* influence on drug policy, 6, 9,

204, 206, 207, 210, 211, 212, 222; interest rates in, 59; marijuana demand in, 126, 208, 272*n7;* supply disruptions to, 214
UPAC system, 41–42, 43
Urbanization, 3, 18, 20, 21, 33, 68, 78, 86, 87, 203

Valencia, Carlos Ernesto, 221
Valencia, Guillermo, 39
Value(s), 71; conflicts in, 82–83; system, 82
Vance, Cyrus, 211
Venezuela: coca growth, 130; contraband in, 173, 190, 192; debt crisis, 190; devaluations in, 52, 54; marijuana production, 129; service ratios, 46
Violence, 88, 172, 203, 216–225, 236; alternatives to, 141; anti-establishment, 157, 216–225; assassinations, 10; as barrier to entry in drug industry, 173; causes, 75–78; in conflict resolution, 141, 172, 173, 241; and criminality, 72–75; drug role in, 1, 265–266; and gender, 73; geographical distribution, 73–74; goals of, 76; and illegality, 134, 265–266; increased, ix, 3, 4, 9, 19, 56, 57; institutional factors, 71, 77; intra-industry, 146, 217; legitimatizing, 6; levels, xiii, 1, 2, 8, 68, 72–75; links to drugs, x; and the military, 2; peasant reaction to, 68; persistant, 2; prevention, 139; and property rights, 77; purposes of, 134; rural, 18, 21, 38, 73; state, 75; types, 75–78; underestimation of costs, 73

Wages: declines, 4, 55; differentials, 21, 23; increase in, 24, 38; in-kind payments, 21, 117*n18;* levels, 25; minimum, 96; policy, 25; and productivity, 93; rural, 239
Women: and drug consumption, 269, 270; educational levels, 23; and government employment, 23; literacy rates, 23; participation in labor force, 23; political roles, 23. *See also* Gender
Workers Revolutionary Party, 226
World Bank, 64*n55,* 201*n10*

Zuluaga, Gustavo, 217

About the Book and the Author

• • •

The rapid improvement in Colombia's aggregate economic development since the late 1940s has seen an improved standard of living for some, but a declining quality of life for most. Thoumi's analysis of this paradox shows that economic growth without increased political participation, leading to a delegitimation of the regime, provided fertile ground for the development of the country's illegal drugs industry.

Following his carefully reasoned analysis of the Colombian political economy, Thoumi discusses the structure of the illegal drugs industry, the characteristics of its entrepreneurs, it size and impact on the economy, government policies and the forces that have shaped them, and the nature of the demand for illegal drugs in Colombia and elsewhere. He closes with a consideration of the policy alternatives—if any—open to the Colombian government.

Francisco E. Thoumi is a director of the Center for International Studies at the Universidad de Los Andes, Bogotá, Colombia.

 **The United Nations Research Institute for Social Development (UNRISD)** is an autonomous agency that engages in multidisciplinary research on the social dimensions of contemporary problems affecting development. Its work is guided by the conviction that, for effective development policies to be formulated, an understanding of the social and political context is crucial. The institute attempts to provide governments, development agencies, grassroots organizations, and scholars with a better understanding of how development policies and processes of economic, social, and environmental change affect different social groups. Working through an extensive network of national research centers, UNRISD aims to promote original research and strengthen research capacity in developing countries.

Current research themes focus on the social dimensions of economic restructuring, environmental deterioration and conservation, ethnic conflict, the illicit narcotic drugs trade and drug-control policies, political violence, the mass voluntary return of refugees, and the reconstruction of war-torn societies, as well as ways of integrating gender issues into development planning.

A list of publications can be obtained by writing to the Reference Centre, UNRISD, Palais des Nations, CH-1211 Geneva 10, Switzerland.

 **The United Nations University (UNU)** is an international academic organization that provides a framework for bringing together the world's leading scholars to tackle pressing global problems of human survival, development, and welfare. It is an autonomous body of the United Nations, with academic freedom guaranteed under its charter to allow free collaboration with scholars worldwide. The University operates through a global network of its own research and training centers and programs and in association with individuals and other institutions throughout the world.

Currently, the University works in five program areas, each related to an area of major global concern: universal human values and global responsibilities, the world economy and development, global life support systems, advances in science and technology, and population dynamics and human welfare.